European Reformism, Nazism and Traditionalism

Osamu Yanagisawa

European Reformism, Nazism and Traditionalism

Economic Thought in Imperial Japan, 1930-1945

PL ACADEMIC RESEARCH

Bibliographic Information published by the Deutsche Nationalbibliothek
The Deutsche Nationalbibliothek lists this publication in the Deutsche Nationalbibliografie; detailed bibliographic data is available in the internet at http://dnb.d-nb.de.

Library of Congress Cataloging-in-Publication Data
Yanagisawa, Osamu, 1938-
[Senzen, senji Nihon no keizai shiso to nachizumu. English]
European reformism, Nazism and traditionalism : economic thought in imperial Japan, 1930-1945 / Osamu Yanagisawa.
pages cm
"First published 2008 by Iwanami Shoten, Publishers, Tokyo"–Title page verso.
Includes bibliographical references.
ISBN 978-3-631-65754-6 – ISBN 978-3-653-05222-0 (ebook) 1. Economics–Japan—History–20th century. 2. Japan–Economic policy–1918-1945.
3. Germany–Economic policy–1933-1945. 4. National socialism–Economic aspects. I. Title.
HB126.J3Y35513 2015
330.0952'09043–dc23
2014039806

SENZEN, SENJI NIHON NO KEIZAI SHISO TO NACHIZUMU
by Osamu Yanagisawa

First published 2008 by Iwanami Shoten, Publishers, Tokyo.
This English edition published 2015 by Peter Lang GmbH, Frankfurt am Main by arrangement with the proprietor c/o Iwanami Shoten, Publishers, Tokyo.

ISBN 978-3-631-65754-6 (Print)
E-ISBN 978-3-653-05222-0 (E-Book)
DOI 10.3726/978-3-653-05222-0

PL Academic Research is an Imprint of Peter Lang GmbH.

Peter Lang – Frankfurt am Main · Bern · Bruxelles · New York · Oxford · Warszawa · Wien

This publication has been peer reviewed.

www.peterlang.com

Acknowledgments

European Reformism, Nazism and Traditionalism. Economic Thought in Imperial Japan, 1930-1945 is the English version of my *Senzen-senji Nihon no keizai shiso to Nachizumu*, published in Japanese by Iwanami Shoten, Tokyo in 2008. Though based on this Japanese original, the present volume differs in some respects. First, the final chapter (Chapter VIII) of the original concerning economic ethics has been omitted, being of limited interest to non-Japanese readers. Second, the original first and second chapters have been reversed to make the context more easily understood for the readers of this English version. Third, the content throughout has been thoroughly revised with considerable additions as well as some elimination of material of interest only to Japanese readers. Despite these revisions, however, there is no change in the essential context of the original book.

In making this English version, I have received important support from many colleagues and friends. I thank Professor emer. Eckart Schremmer (Heidelberg), Professor emer. Jürgen Schneider (Bamberg), Professor emer. Rainer Gömmel (Regensburg), Professor Markus A. Denzel (Leipzig), Professor Hugh Rockoff (Rutger University), Professor Karl Hardach (Düsseldorf), Dr. Michael Rauck (former Assistant Professor at Okayama University) and Japanese colleagues, who supported my studies and encouraged me to make the translated version of my Japanese work.

I am grateful also to Professor Heinz D. Kurz (Graz), Professor Kiichiro Yagi (Setsunan University) and another participants at the annual meeting of the Dogmenhistorischer Ausschuss (DHA) of the Verein für Socialpolitik, held in Berlin in 2008, where I had the opportunity to speak about the influence of the economic thought of German National Socialism upon the Japanese. The discussions there were instructive and important for me in making this English version. The papers of this meeting were published as Heinz D. Kurz (Hsg.), Studien zur Entwicklung der ökonomischen Theorie XXVII (Schriften des Vereins für Socialpolitik, Bd. 115/XXVII), Berlin 2012.

The translation and editing of this volume were helped greatly by Dr. Gaynor Sekimori (former Assistant Professor at Tokyo University), and supported financially by a Grant in Aid of the Japan Society for the Promotion of Science, JSPS

KAKENHI Grant Numbers 226002 (mainly) and 25380433 (partly). Dr Sekimori also prepared the References for this English version. I thank Dr. Sekimori, and also JSPS, for their support.

This book is part of my ongoing interest in socio-economic developments in Japan and Europe, especially Germany, and the relationships between them. These comparative studies derive from my academic activities in Germany in 1973/74, when I was supported by a fellowship from the Alexander von Humboldt Foundation. I therefore thank also the Humboldt Foundation and the late Professor Hermann Kellenbenz, who accepted me and encouraged my scholarly work.

Contents

Introduction

This study is a first attempt to analyse the development of economic thought dominant in Japan in the critical period between the Great Depression and World War II in relation to European and American ideas about the transformation of capitalism from a liberal to a controlled economy. It pays particular attention to how the contemporary Japanese perceived their economic system, both in terms of a new stage of capitalism and its function in an age of total war, and how they received and modified ideas from Europe and the United States. This work also contributes to the study of the development of economic thought in Europe and the United States and their spread to the Far East by investigating western discussions about the reform of capitalism and their impact on the Japanese system. In this sense, it is a unique attempt to look at the history of European and American economic thought at a time of changing capitalism through developments in Japan.

The period, mired in the Great Depression and continuing serious recessions, was also heavily overshadowed by the rise of militarism and nationalism, as exemplified by the May 15 Incident of 1932 and the February 26 Incident of 1936,[1] and a parallel shift towards totalitarianism. Military incursions and wars, from the Manchurian Incident (1931) to the Second Sino-Japanese War (1937-) and the Pacific War (1941-45), ushered in a wartime economy and a system of national mobilization.[2] Nevertheless, it is not appropriate to define this turbulent period as a "Dark Valley"[3] marked by an abnormal degree of political and social repression, or as a transitional period of chaos, sandwiched between the 1920s

---

1 On May 15, 1932, the Prime Minister, Inukai Tsuyoshi, was assassinated by a group of young naval officers, whose light punishments led indirectly to the attempted coup d'état by the military in February 1936, following which the Okada Cabinet resigned, paving the way for increased military influence in the government. For further details, see Shillony 1973, Honjō 1982, Gow 2004.

2 For an outline of the socio-economic development of Japan in prewar and wartime Japan, see Nakamura 1998. For the war economy, see Schumpeter ed. 1940, Cohen 1949 (reprint 2000), Hara 1998, 2013, Pauer ed. 1999. Yamazaki 2011.

3 Jap. *kurai tanima*. This was an expression used by contemporaries after the war. See Ōkōchi 1979.

and the postwar period. Neither is it enough simply to focus on the wars Japan was involved in during the 1930s and 1940s and define the period only in terms of military conflict, a time of total war and national mobilization, as several scholars have asserted.[4] It is clear from studies of modern economic history that the period from the end of the 1920s through to the Second World War cannot be discussed separately from global trends towards a transformation of the capitalist economy that had been long in gestation, or apart from how these trends affected Japanese capitalism, so tightly associated with conditions world-wide, and brought it to the brink of crisis.[5]

The period of global change and crisis forced the Japanese policy makers and intellectuals of the time to assess their country's social and economic problems in the wider context of the development of capitalism in western countries. They were interested in the breakdown of the liberal economic system and the rise of state intervention in Europe and North America, and in plans to modify capitalism. They subsequently related this understanding of the world to forming their own ideas and planning policy.[6]

Japanese intellectuals were interested in English theories, such as Alfred Marschall's idea of "economic chivalry", those of J. M. Keynes in his *The End of Laissez- Faire* (1926) and the reformism of G. D. H. Cole and R. H. Tawney, as well as American ideas like Taylorism[7] and Gerard Swope's plan for industrial organization that influenced the National Industrial Recovery Act of 1933, one of the first pieces of legislation in President Roosevelt's New Deal. But they took a particular interest in the German situation, which they perceived to be very similar to their own, and its underlying ideas. The ideas of Walther Rathenau, a prominent German politician and industrialist, about reforming capitalism attracted the attention of reform-minded Japanese. The debates over structural changes in capitalism among German economists of the Historical School were observed closely

4 For example, Yamanouchi, Koschmann and Narita eds (1995, 1998).

5 For the structural changes in, and the crisis of, capitalism in prewar and wartime Japan, see Nakamura 1971 (part 2) and Hoston 1986.

6 Bai Gao accurately points out: "Economic ideas played an extremely important role in formulating the state policy in the managed economy. When the laissez-faire doctrine was discredited by the Great Depression, the Japanese searched for new solutions from various sources, especially Western countries. These elements from various sources together constituted a coherent logic for the managed economy." (Gao 1997, p. 99.).

7 For the influence of Taylorism on the rationalization movement in Japan at that time, see Tsutsui 1998.

by social scientists in the Far East. In particular, the concept of "Late Capitalism" introduced by Werner Sombart was widely accepted by Japanese intellectuals.

Contemporary Japanese regarded German National Socialism and its economic system to be distinctive phenomena that had arisen in the process of the transformation and modification of laissez-faire capitalism. The Nazi economic system was to have a great impact on Japan's policy formation, both in terms of a new stage of the economy and of preparation for total war.[8] The contemporary influence of German National Socialism and its theory of total war (*Wehrwirtschaft*) in Japan can be seen particularly in the policy of the New Order (*shintaisei*) for labour and the economy that was hotly debated throughout the second Konoe Fumimaro Cabinet (1940-41) and which provided the preconditions necessary for waging the Pacific War.[9] For Japanese leaders of the time, who had rejected the liberal means of mobilization in England, France and the United States, German National Socialism seemed to be the best model, since it had succeeded in establishing a war economy based on capitalism under totalitarianism. The connection between the Japanese and German New Orders has been remarked upon in many historical studies, but their inherent relationship has not been properly explored. This study therefore proposes to go into the subject as deeply as possible, clarifying how Japanese policy makers and thinkers incorporated Nazi ideas into their own concept of the New Order, and discussing the complementary fusion of both Nazi elements and distinctive Japanese features such as the emperor system (Tennoism) and its ideology.[10]

This study pays attention to the analyses about German National Socialism made by Japanese social scientists at the time.[11] They regarded the *Neuordnung*

8 See Ando 1963, Fletcher 1982, Garon 1987, Gordon 1991, Gao 1997, Kerde 1999, Lehmbruch 2001.

9 The "new economic order" of the Konoe cabinet and the important role played by leading bureaucrats and intellectuals are discussed in Fletcher 1982, Nakamura 1998, p. 3, Gordon 1991, p. 11, Gao 1997, p. 113.

10 Historians have discussed the affinities of totalitarianism between German National Socialism and Japanese emperor system, in which the similarities and differences between the Fascisms of two countries are made clear (see for example Maruyama 1969.) But the transfer of Nazism from Germany to Japan, its modified acceptance by the Japanese, and the process through which the totalitarian regime of the emperor system was moulded, have not received much attention (for exceptions to this, see Gordon 1991, Mimura 2011). The English term "Tennoism", referring to the system of imperial rule, is rather dated, but it can still be found.

11 For intellectuals in prewar and wartime Japan, see the interesting studies made by Andrew E. Barshay and Harry Harootunian. Barshay 1988 examines the political

of Nazi Germany as a modern phenomenon, in its criticism and totalitarian reform of *laissez-faire* capitalism. While many critical scholars questioned the political system of totalitarianism and the irrational and abnormal elements of Nazi thought (*Weltanschauung*), such as racism and anti-semitism, they also paid keen attention to the modern side of the structural reforms carried out in Nazi Germany. Comparing the social and economic progress of Japan and Germany, they linked their perception of Nazi Germany with an analysis of Japan's backwardness and its quasi-feudal traditionalism, which implied a criticism of Japan's existing emperor system. Such intellectual activity was bound to create sharp tensions with the authorities, who thought to preserve and utilize such traditional elements in society and the economy. Such critical thought and research were banned under the banner of the "Thought War", as the country moved toward a system of total war. Conservative intellectuals, on the other hand, who regarded the traditional inheritance, bound up with the emperor system, as indispensiable for the development of the country, were able to influence the government.

Studies by social scientists of the German system under Hitler attracted the attention of political leaders who would go on to utilise the Nazi New Order to build a mobilisation system for total war in Japan. Japanese of the time understood German National Socialism as a totalitarian regime for a time of crisis, comprehending it through how it resembled or differed from the liberal systems of Great Britain, France and the United States. By so doing, they recognised resemblances between Germany and Japan in terms of national development and so regarded German-type totalitarianism as suitable for the Japanese situation. At the same time, however, they discovered important differences in both policy and the economy between the two. There was no equivalent in Japan of the type of dictatorial power held by Hitler's NSDAP in Germany, and this proved to be a grave defect in attempts to form and enforce a totalitarian system in Japan. But Japanese leaders found a decisive substitute in the emperor system, and prevailing popular ideology lent valuable support to the formation of totalitarianism. This study analyses that elements of National Socialism were accepted and amalgamated into a Japanese style of totalitarianism under the emperor system, recognising both affinities and differences in developments in the two countries.

---

discourse and activities of two important intellectuals: Nanbara Shigeru (1889-1974), a professor at the Tokyo Imperial University, and Hasegawa Nyozekan (1875-1969), a prominent journalist of the time. Barshay 2004 studies two Marxian social scientists, Yamada Moritarō (1897-1980) and Uno Kōzō (1897-1977), who were also active after World War II. Harootunian 2000 examines the ideas of intellectuals in the fields of history and philosophy.

It is hoped that this analysis will contribute to the comparative study of international fascisms.[12]

Since the end of World War II, Japanese scholars have discussed changes and continuities in the political and economic system of the country between the prewar and postwar periods, insisting on a discontinuity between the two: that the quasi-feudal factors in the economy and the totalitarian emperor system had been abolished as a result of postwar reforms during the Allied (particularly American) Occupation and Japan had been transformed into a democratic country. Recent studies note, however, that many policy ideas of the prewar and wartime periods, and the economic institutions based on them, were carried over into the postwar period. It has also become increasingly clear that many elements of traditionalist and Japanist ideas were inherited by postwar society, despite the postwar reform efforts to eliminate them. It seems today that not only do such modern ideologies as globalization and a revised doctrine of *laissez-faire* coexist with a tendency towards a realignment of ideas about the emperor system and traditionalism, but they also often merge with one another. For example, the use of traditional era names (*nengō*) based on imperial reign names remains compulsory within the bureaucracy, pupils and teachers are obliged, during school ceremonies, to sing the national anthem (*Kimigayo*) that has strong ideological connections with the emperor system, particularly its wartime manifestation, and there is a growing patriotic (or nationalist) movement based on traditionalism and the emperor system among conservative politicians, economists, journalists and historians, who, supported by right-wing extremists, claim Japan's legitimacy vis-à-vis the Pacific War, in defiance of the critical interpretation of prewar and wartime militarism and totalitarianism in Japan.

I hope that this study will help shed light on aspects of both the continuities and discontinuities between prewar/wartime and postwar Japan.

12 Historians have argued about applying the word "fascism" to Japan. See Gao 1997, p. 68.

Chapter One: Capitalism and the Transformation of the Corporation

From around the turn of the twentieth century, capitalist economies in Europe and the United States underwent many changes, and these were accompanied by a transformation of capitalistic enterprises. Nineteenth-century capitalism was represented mainly by privately- or family-owned firms, where generally management and the ownership of capital were in the hands of one individual. After around 1900, however, limited liability corporations, especially joint-stock companies, grew gradually more prevalent, and by the end of World War I, their unique role, as well as the problems they posed, started attracting a great deal of attention. Issues that attracted particular concern included the circulation of share certificates, the dispersal of shareholders, and, especially, the relationship between investors and management and between the general meeting of shareholders and the board of directors.

Joint-stock companies facilitated the association and mobilization of capital, and so promoted the development of large-scale capitalistic enterprises, whose expansive business activities and pursuit of profit had a significant influence on economic life. They attracted attention due to the social and public role of their corporate activities, but they also drew criticism over problems arising from profit-centred activities such as speculative share dealing, price manipulation by cartels, and the high dividends and unearned income received by shareholders. In response, a school of thought emerged in Europe that sought to restrain the capitalistic, profit-maximizing principle in corporations and to focus on the social and public aspects of corporate activity and on improving corporate management.

In November 1924, John Maynard Keynes (1883-1946) gave the Sidney Ball Lecture at the University of Oxford in which he spoke of managed capitalism and the rejection of the laissez-faire economy, and he reiterated his contention at the University of Berlin in June 1926. An essay based on these lectures entitled *The End of Laissez-faire*, published in both English and German, appeared the same year.[13] Two years later, the German professor Eugen Schmalenbach (1873-1955) gave the main paper at the meeting of the Association of German Scholars

13 Keynes 1926.

of Business Economics (Tagung des Verbandes der Betriebswirtschaftler an deutschen Hochschulen), held in Vienna on May 31, 1928, on the topic of "Business economics on the threshold of the new economic order"("Die Betriebswirtschaftslehre an der Schwelle der neuen Wirtschaftsverfassung"). He predicted that future economic historians would probably call the nineteenth century "the century of the liberal (free) economy", falling between two eras of a "bound" economy, and argued that rising fixed costs would eventually transform the economy into a state-controlled cartel.[14]

As Keynes and Schmalenbach pointed out, the development of capitalism from the turn of the century through World War I (and on to World War II) can be characterised as the decay of "laissez-faire" and the transformation of the economy from liberal to "bound". As the self-regulating mechanism of capitalism declined, organization and control in economic life were increasing, with the economy being regulated more and more by the state through nationalised or public enterprises (such as railways, the post, banks, insurance and electricity) and through diverse government policies (such as the regulation of foreign trade, prices and wages). But together with state economic control, the influence of large capitalistic enterprises and their organizations was also growing in the economic life: the effectiveness of large-scale production and transportation forced the centralization of powers of economic control into the hands of large corporations, trusts and related organizations. In 1938, the Swedish economist Bertil Ohlin (1899-1979) wrote that "the chief characteristic of change in the organization of society in the last half-century has been the growth of central organization and control. Trusts and cartels have increased in number and importance. Some of them have been created entirely on private initiative, others have been fostered by public measures. Looser industrial and branch associations also attract growing interest and acquire a rising influence. Furthermore, municipal and government enterprise now covers a much wider field, and government supervision also reaches many kinds of private economic activity".[15]

The rapid growth of enterprises and their combinations that eliminated a competitive, liberal economy had been spurred on by the formation of the joint stock company, which made it easy to associate and mobilise individual capital. As Rudolf Hilferding (1877-1941) had pointed out before World War I, capitalist development can only be comprehended in terms of the ascendancy of the

14 Schmalenbach 1928.
15 Ohlin 1938, p. 66.

corporation.[16] Companies became the principal factor in economic organization in the United States as well. In the 1932 preface to *The Modern Corporation and Private Property*, Adolf A. Berle, Jr. (1895-1971) wrote: "It was apparent to any thoughtful observer that the American corporation had ceased to be a private business device and had become an institution… the financial machinery was developing so rapidly as to indicate that we were in the throes of a revolution in our institution of property, at least as applied to industrial economic uses". Berle came to the conclusion that "American industrial property, through the corporate device, was being thrown into a collective hopper wherein the industrial owner was steadily being lost in the creation of a series of huge industrial oligarchies". He pointed out that "It is obvious that the corporate system not only tends to be the flower of our industrial organization, but that the public is in a mood to impose on it a steadily growing degree of responsibility for our economic welfare".[17]

Such ideas attracted those who were critical of the unearned income of shareholders and the emphasis that companies placed on profits, and who were acutely conscious of the real division between those who owned the capital and those who actually managed the business. Seeking to modify and transform capitalism through rational management and taking into consideration the public and social role of corporate activity, they placed their hopes on a rational and autonomous corporate management, manned by trained and professional administrators, that was able to counter the demands of investors for high returns. These views attracted particular attention in Japan in the 1930s, when the country was moving towards an increasingly controlled economy in preparation for total war, and issues such as the expansion of production and the mobilisation of the economy had become matters of urgency. Of particular concern, both to the bureaucrats on the Cabinet Planning Board (Kikakuin)[18] and interested intellectuals was the question of separating capital and management. However, as their ideas involved restricting dividend payments and placing limitations on the rights of shareholders, policy makers faced strong opposition from business

16 Hilferding 1910, chapter 7.
17 Berle and Means 1932, Introduction.
18 The Cabinet Planning Board was set up in May 1937 under the Hayashi Cabinet. It combined the (Cabinet) Resources Bureau (Shigenkyoku, 1927) and the (Cabinet) Planning Agency (Kikakuchō, 1935). Under the direct control of the Cabinet it had twenty members and fifteen assistants, as well as permanent advisers seconded from other government bureaus. The Board was responsible for regulating the supply and demand of commodities and drawing up a materials mobilization plan.

circles, and they were forced to backpedal to a large extent. After World War II, however, the separation of capital and management was the central pillar of "corporate democratisation", with the result that it became a basic feature of the postwar Japanese corporate system.

In this chapter, I will examine the significance of the concept of the separation of capital and management in Japan by tracing its development from the standpoint of intellectual history, elaborating how the idea evolved under the considerable influence of European economic thought. In the process I will demonstrate that the concept was associated with a far wider array of issues than just the economic New Order (*keizai shintaisei*) and the total war system (*sōryokusen taisei*), or what the institutional forms of the corporate system or proper corporate governance should be. Rather, it was closely connected with economic ideas that criticised the primacy of profits and aimed to transform the capitalist society of the day into a functionalist society run by experts.

Discourse on the Separation of Capital and Management

The ownership of capital and corporate activity in capitalistic enterprises, especially the relationship between shareholders and the company directors, became a serious political issue around 1940. With the war in China dragging on, there was an urgent need for economic reform in order to set up a wartime economic system. Under these conditions, the construction of a "new order" for the economy was keenly debated. Nakamura Takafusa and Hara Akira plot the course of development of this economic New Order in three stages:[19]

(1) In the summer of 1940, the Prime Minister, Konoe Fumimaro, announced a "new political order".[20] A vigorous discussion then ensued, lasting into the summer of the following year, about an economic new order. This topic had in fact been taken up at least a year earlier, most notably in *Nihon keizai no saihensei* (Reorganising the Japanese Economy, 1939) by the economist and journalist Ryū Shintarō (1900-1967),[21] in which the separation of capital and management had been one of the most important issues under discussion. Ryū, on the editorial staff of the Asahi newspaper and a member of the Shōwa Research Association (Shōwa kenkyūkai) from

19 Nakamura and Hara 1973.

20 For Konoe's announcement of August 28, 1940, see De Bary ed. 2008, pp. 620-621. For a contemporary report and reaction, see *The Oriental Economist*, September 1940, pp. 525-527.

21 Ryū 1939. See also Fletcher 1982, Gao 1997, p. 115.

1938, maintained that corporate management should take precedence over the pursuit of profits, and asserted that it was imperative to shift corporate objectives from profits to productivity. This idea was accepted within the Shōwa Research Association,[22] and passed on to the Cabinet Planning Board.

(2) Reform bureaucrats on the Planning Board, such as Minobe Yōji (1900-1953), Sakomizu Hisatsune (1902-1977) and Mōri Hideoto (1902-1947), were closely involved in drafting the economic New Order.[23] They placed great importance on the prioritizing of production over profits and on separating corporate ownership from corporate management, and made this the core of their ideas for reform. However, when the Outline for the economic New Order was made public in September 1940, it was denounced by business leaders, who attacked the reform bureaucrats promoting "red ideas" antagonistic to capitalism.

(3) In December 1940, the cabinet finally agreed on an Outline for the Establishment of a New Economic Order. The opposition had succeeded in modifying the wording to a vague "organic unity of capital, management and labour", but the document still recognized that that there should be a clear division between capital and management in a company, and emphasized the importance of managers, and their creativity and responsibility, in relation to the owners of capital.

In the increasingly tense situation that followed the outbreak of the Pacific War in December 1941, a new Munitions Corporation Law (*gunju kaishahō*) was enacted in October 1943 to stress the national importance of the munitions industry and to set up a system of responsibility for production. The law aimed to increase production by upholding the autonomy of management over capital and by demanding that managers (both executives and employees) be professionally aware. The issues of the "separation of capital and management" and the establishment of an autonomous and corporative management body had thus resurfaced in a new guise. Okazaki Tetsuji has pointed out that the Munitions

22 The Shōwa Research Association was an organization set up in 1936 by Gotō Ryūnosuke with the baking of Konoe Fumimaro as a think-tank for bureaucrats, academics, businessmen and the military, to come up with innovative ideas for political reform. It drafted a proposal for the reorganization of Japanese economy for Konoe. See Fletcher 1979, 1982.

23 For more about the role of these three figures in contemporary policy, see Kerde 1999, particularly pp. 28-32. For reform bureaucrats, see Mimura 2011.

Corporations Law restricted the roles and rights of shareholders in joint-stock companies while strengthening the position of management, and calls it "an epoch-making piece of legislation in that it restricted shareholder rights as defined by commercial law." He emphasizes that, like the corporate democratisation plan that was drafted after the war by the Japan Association of Corporate Executives (Keizai dōyūkai), the Munitions Corporations Law focused on management.[24] This postwar plan was drafted by Ōtsuka Banjō (1896-1950), a former banker and director of Nittetsu during the war, and studies suggest that he had already come up with the idea of separating capital and management around 1940 while working at Riken (the Institute of Physical and Chemical Research) under Ōkōchi Masatoshi. This would suggest that the ideas that led to the postwar reforms had already been formed at that time.[25]

It has been thought that issues like separating management and capital and management autonomy were discussed mainly in relation to the wartime economy at a time of total war. Asai Yoshio, however, has shown that these questions were already being addressed by Ueda Teijirō (1879-1940), a business economics expert and professor at the Tokyo University of Commerce (later Hitotsubashi University), in pioneering works from the second decade of the twentieth century, long before the implementation of the wartime economy, and that they were examined further in the 1930s by economists such as Masuchi Yōjirō (1896-1945) of the same university. Asai speculates that Ryū Shintarō might have incorporated arguments of up-and-coming scholars of business management like Masuchi into his own ideas on the eve of the formation of the economic New Order.[26]

The understanding of the corporation held by economists such as Suzuki Yoshinori and Haruyama Hideo lend support to Asai's view.[27] They make it clear that discussions held in the prewar period about the separation of management and capital in corporations were strongly influenced by current ideas about corporations in North America and Europe, which implies that the issue was not

24 Okazaki and Okuno eds. 1993, chapter 4, pp. 116ff. and 126ff., Okazaki 1991, Nagashima 1986, chapter 7, paragraph 2. In English, see Okazaki 1997, p. 300, Tsutsui 1998, chapter 4.

25 Okazaki, Sugayama, Nishizawa and Yonekura 1996, chapter 1, p. 2 (Sugayama). Regarding "A Draft for Corporate Democratisation" and Ōtsuka Banjō, see Hirschmeier et al 1975, pp. 278-279, Nishizawa 1996, pp. 104-105 and Suzuki 2005, for further on Keizai Dōyūkai.

26 Asai 2001, see pp. 129ff. See also Mimura 2011, p. 153.

27 Haruyama 1981-1982. See part 1, pp. 170ff., Suzuki 1983, chapter 3, paragraph 1.

unique to wartime Japan, but had already been discussed in USA and Europe prior to World War II.

The debate on the separation of management and capital did not stop at issues like the corporate system or laws regulating joint-stock companies; it also had an ideological edge, the transformation of capitalism itself, and as such it was to be associated with the economic New Order and draw the ire of business leaders as being communist. The argument continued after the war in relation to the modification of capitalism, when the democratisation of the economy was being considered as a basic postwar reform. Let us therefore now reexamine the separation of management and capital in relation to the transformation of the capitalist economy and associated economic ideas, in the light of trends in, and points raised by, previous scholarship. This we will do by studying in detail how the idea developed in Japan under the influence of European economic theories.

The role of managers and criticism of profit maximisation

The ideas of Ueda Teijirō

When the economic New Order was under deliberation, economists vigorously debated the need to separate management from capital and to free management from shareholder interests as far as possible to enable it to concentrate on productive corporate management. In 1943, Ueda Tatsunosuke (1892-1956) of the Tokyo University of Commerce drew attention to points of similarity in the Outline with the function of the "enterprise man" (manager) advocated by the recently deceased Ueda Teijirō, observing that Ueda's views were reflected in points such as the "organic unity of capital, management and labour" and the recognition of autonomous management through managerial responsibility and creativity, and in its guiding principles, public profit (*kōeki*) and work responsibility (*shokubun hōkō*). His conclusion, nevertheless, was that "the Outline has not come any closer to resolving questions that the professor raised twenty years ago about the separation of capital and management. It allocates independent positions to management, labour and capital, assigning each its own role and having the three working together in cohesion. In this sense we have to acknowledge the prophetic nature of the professor's ideas about the function of the manager."[28]

Ueda Teijirō's ideas about the importance of the manager in the functioning of the enterprise and about the separation of capital and management can already

---

28 Ueda Tatsunosuke 1942b, p. 40.

be found in an early form in his *Kabushiki-gaisha keizairon* (Economic theory of the corporation), first published in 1913 and then in a revised and enlarged edition in 1921. Ueda argued that the joint-stock company was characterised by the conversion of invested capital into securities and movable property in the form of stocks and shares, by the "separation" of "management and capital" and by limited liability, and that it had given rise a "propertied class" on the one hand, and a "powerful class" that "manages the property" on the other. He paid particular attention to the role played by directors and executives in corporate management and to the fact that company executives shouldered the "duties of managers" vis-à-vis the powerless general shareholders' meeting. Executives were no longer entrepreneurs in the old mould; the entrepreneur's duties and functions had been taken over by the corporate organisation and were divided within the organisation: the duty of shareholders as investors was to shoulder business risks, while the duty of executives was to manage and guide business operations. In the terminology of the German economist Gustav Schmoller_(1838-1917), the executive was a "working entrepreneur" (*arbeitender Unternehmer*) and the ordinary shareholder a "non-working entrepreneur" (*nicht arbeitender Unternehmer*), while in Britain a division was made between a "captain of industry" (who ran the business) and a "financier" (who took care of the financial side).[29]

Ueda's views on the corporation had been shaped through discussions with his colleagues at the Tokyo Higher Commercial School (predecessor of the Tokyo University of Commerce), Fukuda Tokuzō (1874-1930) and Seki Hajime (1873-1935), a future mayor of Osaka, and his ideas about the economic theory of the corporation are acknowledged to comprise "the pioneering discussion about capital and management" in Japan.[30]

Ueda, however, did not discuss only the separation of management from capital and the managerial role of executives as part of his theory about the corporation, his main focus actually being on the social problems caused by corporations, which he associated with inherent problems within the capitalist economy.[31] He regarded the existence of "unearned income", that is, income not generated by labour, as one of the defects of capitalism, and pointed out that the prevalence

29 Ueda 1913, see pp. 90ff. (1st edition), pp. 99ff. (6th revised and enlarged edition, 1921), pp. 85ff., p. 374, p. 429 (*Kabushiki gaisharon,* part 1, 1944). See also Ueda 1928, pp. 28ff, 116ff. Nishizawa 1995, Nishizawa 2002 (in English). For the Schmoller terminology, Ueda used as a source Gustav Schmoller's *Grundriss der allgemeinen Volkswirtschaft*, vol. 2, §, 231, S. 495.

30 Haruyama 1981-1982, vol. 1, pp. 173ff., Nishizawa 1995, pp. 155 ff.

31 Ueda 1928, chapter 4, Ueda 1944a, part 2, chapter 5, Nishizawa 1995, p. 156.

of joint-stock companies increased unearned income through stock speculation and dividends not arising from business activities, while "inheritance" further aggravated the problem of unearned income. However he also recognised that the diffusion of joint-stock companies had given rise to both "captains of industry," who took charge of corporate management as company executives, and to an "employee class" (*Privatbeamten*: lit. "private clerks", "white-collar workers"), in other words, to a system of senior salaried employees, comprising a new middle class, distinguished from manual workers (*Privatbeamten* were later called "private *Angestellte*", comprising salaried workers such as engineers, subsection chiefs, and clerical workers such as accountants and sales staff). He looked to this new class of worker as perhaps being able to remedy the "defects" of "today's profit seeking" capitalism. He wrote: "It goes without saying that where these people come from and what training and knowledge they bring will greatly influence the development of the nation's industries and character. Therefore, we must study the *Privatbeamten*."[32]

This view was consolidated further in his book, *Shakai kaizō to kigyō* (Social reform and the corporation, 1926), in which he predicted a future where those who were competent and gifted would assume important roles, and "brain work" would be valued. He had high expectations of creative activities by corporate managers, saying: "The corporate system bestows on the modern economic system the division of corporate function. In the past, when there was no form of enterprise other than the private firm, the entrepreneur was the provider of capital as well as the manager of the enterprise. In joint-stock corporations, however, shareholders provide the capital, and the running of the business is entrusted to the executives. In the future, corporations will no longer have individual shareholders, for public bodies will be the sole shareholders, and executives will manage the corporations, not as representatives of the shareholders, but of the public bodies."[33]

Ueda Teijirō's concept of the corporation is thus closely connected with ideas about the transformation of capitalist society. Ueda applied the idea of the separation of capital and management not only to the role of the executives ("captains of industry") who managed and led the business, but also to that of the company employees, the *Privatbeamten*, who supported them. He held high hopes that this talented new social class would actively participate in efforts to amend the defects of capitalism, such as the unlimited pursuit of profit.

32 Ueda 1944a, part 2, chapter 5, p. 371.

33 Ueda 1926, pp. 24 ff.

Nishizawa Tamotsu, a scholar of the history of economic thought, stresses the importance of the connection between the manager and the transformation of society in Ueda's ideas. He points out that in the process of forming his own ideas about economics and economic thought, Ueda gained a critical understanding of European economics and economic thought, particularly through an extensive study of British economic thought with a particular interest in the economic chivalry of Alfred Marshall (1842-1924) and the guild socialism of R.H. Tawney (1880-1962).[34]

Economic Chivalry and Guild Socialism

Ueda drew attention to the "new ethics" that company executives would create and the new trends that *Privatbeamten* would generate. He focused on the sense of satisfaction they would derive from their work as well as society's appreciation of their achievements, and found here much in common with Alfred Marshall's ideas about economic chivalry.

Alfred Marshall was Professor of Political Economy at the University of Cambridge between 1885 and 1908 and published his influential *Principles of Economics* in 1890. He first spoke of economic chivalry at a lecture in London entitled "Social possibilities of economic chivalry" that was then published in the *Economic Journal* (March 1907). The idea became a crucial part of Marshall's economic thought, and was incorporated into the concluding part of the revised edition of his *magnum opus*, *Principles of Economics* (1927).[35] His economic chivalry theory divides entrepreneurs into two categories: those who actively seek creative and constructive work, and those who pursue nothing but profit-generating activities by fair means or foul. He regarded the former type highly, for to them the pursuit of profit was proof of their successful business activities rather than of their own gain.

Economic chivalry was a set of economic ethics that included creative work by entrepreneurs, effort to surmount obstacles, constant exertion and steady work, and contributions to society. Not only did Marshall demand this code of ethics of entrepreneurs, but he also hoped that the code would become part of the

34 Nishizawa 1995.

35 Marshall 1907, Marshall 1907 (5th ed.), p. 719, Marshall 1927 (8th ed.), p. 719. See also Groenewegen 1998, Cook 2008. Marshall's economic theories and views were examined in prewar Japan not only by Ueda but also by his university colleagues, such as Fukuda Tokuzō, and by Otsuka Kinnosuke, who translated *Principles of Economics* into Japanese in 1919 and 1925-26. See also Nishizawa 2001.

social norm, and that economic chivalry and social norms would inspire each another. Marshall's economic chivalry had a great influence on Ueda Teijirō, who regarded highly such characteristics of the "captain of industry" as social responsibility, trust, a "motivation to be creatively active" and a "motivation to contribute socially".

Ueda acknowledged that his concept of the corporation, as well as that of the separation of capital and management, were strongly connected with the "functional society" advocated by the British economic historian, R.H. Tawney. Ueda said of Tawney's work, *The Acquisitive Society* (first edition, 1921): "Since World War I, many new ideas about the reconstruction of society have been published, but no other book has spoken to me as strongly as this one. It was as if the book expressed, in both conception and conclusions, both what I have already said and what I am going to say, only in a foreign language."[36]

In *The Acquisitive Society*, Tawney attached the greatest importance to "function" in social activities.[37] A function, he said, is an activity that embodies the ideal of social purpose. It is not performed for personal gain but because a person recognizes that he is responsible to a higher authority for its discharge. Modern society, though, is founded, not on functions but on rights, and this has meant that the acquisition of wealth and the enjoyment of property are not contingent on the performance of services. He called societies in which individuals are directed to the attainment of some personal purpose "acquisitive societies" because "their whole tendency and interest and preoccupation is to promote the acquisition of wealth," not upon the "discharge of social obligations". A "functional society", on the other hand, is one aimed at "making the acquisition of wealth contingent upon the discharge of social obligations", that seeks to "proportion remuneration

36 Ueda 1926, p. 225. This appeared in Ueda's *Shakai kaizō to kigyō*, which also included discourses about English socialism, such as Alfred Marshall's critical comments on the cooperative and collective organization of industry (Marshall 1919, 4th ed. 1924, Appendix P) and the criticism of guild socialism by Hartley Withers (Withers 1920) and by Sydney and Beatrice Webb (1920, 1921).

37 For Tawney's thought, see Terrill 1973, Dennis and Halsey eds 1988. Together with G. Unwin, A. P. Wadsworth, M. James and others, Tawney was to create a new trend in the study of economic history in the UK, one which focused on the middle and lower classes who shouldered the greater part of economic activity. Tawney exerted a great influence over contemporary scholarship in Japan in this respect and this new trend was greatly influential in prewar Japan, for example in shaping Ōtsuka Hisao's research on European economic history. For Tawney's place in the world of British economic historians, see Koot 1987.

to service" and deny it to those who perform no service, and values "not what men possess but what they can make or create or achieve."[38]

Tawney deplored the destructiveness inherent in property rights that had no function, the divorce of gain from service, the weakening links between the pursuit of profit and productive activity, conflicts between the profit principle in business and the scientific management of industry, and the separation of business and management. He saw as problematic the relationship between shareholders and the business, and thought that management had to be formulated as "a profession" invested with specific objectives, and further transformed into an organised trade assigned with the task of carrying out its functions. Business should be run, not for the benefit of property owners, but for the benefit of the public, and it should be carried out directly by managers under public supervision. This vision was, however, to be realised, not by the total renunciation of ownership, but by its curtailment. One way of achieving this goal was to make the status of the owners of capital similar to that of corporate bond holders, who neither received any payment other than regular interest on their investment, nor possessed any rights of control. Industry could be liberated by professionalization and organisation, the "extinction of the Capitalist", and the abolition of property rights that were without function. To achieve this, workers must have the professional expertise to carry out creative work, labour unions have to co-operate, and activities must be based on brain power as well as physical labour.

Ueda Teijirō evaluated Tawney's views highly. He introduced Tawney's criticism of the acquisitive society to Japanese scholars, setting out in detail views about the pursuit of profit and the concept of the functional society. He interpreted Tawney's interest in guild socialism, an English economic and socialist doctrine of the early twentieth century, which advocated that industry not be owned by the state but managed by workers' guilds,[39] as an outcome of his dissatisfaction with old-fashioned Fabian Society collectivism. He did not seek to create an ideal society "in haste" by class struggle, but looked for the "germs of change in present society." Though Ueda agreed with many of Tawney's ideas, he distanced himself from guild socialism, critical of Tawney's concept about realising a functional society through labour unions and guilds of white-collar workers, regarding it as too optimistic. Nevertheless, it was highly significant that an

38 Tawney 1921, 1922, pp. 8-29. As the corporation evolved in the first half of the nineteenth century in Britain, corporation law was enacted in conjunction with the development of the workers' cooperative movement, as by extension did also ideas about social reform. On this point, see Okada 1987.

39 For guild socialism, see Cole 1921, Carpenter 1973.

eminent scholar like Ueda Teijirō studied guild socialism and introduced it in his own work. He paid particular attention to Tawney's denouncement of the unrestrained pursuit of profit by capitalist corporations and of property rights without function resulting from the separation of capital and management in corporations, as well as to his advocacy of a functional society in which the workers should assume control. There can be no doubt that it was due to Ueda that Tawney's economic thought left its mark on Japanese thought regarding the separation of capital and management. And of course Ueda's own ideas about corporate economics did the same. Throughout the 1920s and 1930s and down to his death in 1940, Ueda played a significant role through his influence on colleagues and students at the Tokyo University of Commerce, whose president he was between 1936 and 1940, through his activities in the Society for the Study of Social Policy (*Shakai seisaku gakkai*) and through the wide-ranging work he was involved in outside academia related to the problems of small and medium industries and rural industries.[40] It was no accident that Ryū Shintarō, who argued for the structural reorganization of the Japanese economy to be based on the separation of capital and management, with leadership to come from a production-oriented management rather than shareholders, was also a graduate of the Tokyo University of Commerce.

The supercorporation

Mukai Shikamatsu and Kojima Seiichi

The debate about corporations and the economic thought concerning them advanced significantly from around the mid 1920s. Of particular importance was the work of Mukai Shikamatsu (1888-1979), then a professor at Keio Gijuku University in Tokyo, and his ideas about the autonomous enterprise (which he termed "supercorporation") and corporate independence. Haruyama Hideo, who has analysed Mukai's ideas about the corporation in great detail, writes that "even though it contained many logical leaps and erroneous factual assumptions, Mukai's theory should be highly evaluated as a pioneer in the new field of corporate management. When Ueda Teijirō presented his ideas about the separation of capital and management, the discussion was still at a rudimentary stage. It was Mukai who developed and shaped those ideas into a coherent theory. He

---

40 Ueda was the chairman of a committee within the Japan Society for the Promotion of Science investigating the problems of small- and medium-sized industries, which began in 1938. He published a book in English about these industries (Uyeda 1938).

recognised the significance of stock dispersion, advocated the new idea that a company should be controlled by its management, and pointed out the conflict that existed between large shareholders and management. In this he demonstrated a thorough understanding of the key features of corporate management, and this contributed greatly to its later development."[41]

Mukai developed his ideas of turning a company into a social and autonomous entity based on his concept of the corporation as expounded in his *Keiei keizaigaku sōron* (Introduction to business economics, 1929).[42] He further explored the question in *Tosei keizai genri* (Principles of the controlled economy), the first volume of the series "Collected works on the controlled economy in Japan" (*Nihon tosei keizai zenshū*), where his ideas about corporate independence were closely linked to state control of the national economy, in other words, to the controlled economy (see Chapter 2).

Mukai's concept of restructuring joint-stock corporations (what he called supercorporations), was severely criticised by the up-and-coming critic Kojima Seiichi (1895-1966). He agreed with Mukai that shares in joint-stock companies tended to disperse, hired executives were likely to gain control, and executives and shareholders tended to differ in their ideas about the direction of management. Kojima, however, expressed doubts about the feasibility of turning the corporation into an independent body. First, he maintained that stock dispersion lowered the threshold for certain shareholders to gain control. "[Stock dispersion] makes it easier for powerful Zaibatsu to seize control of companies, thus expanding their sphere of dominance." Second, he asserted that hired executives were not "free, independent agents" as Mukai supposed, but "mere henchmen of the head of the powerful Zaibatsu", and it was unthinkable that they could voluntarily go against the interests of the Zaibatsu in order to carry out a management plan that would benefit the public. He also pointed out that, with executive pay both directly and indirectly connected with company profits, it was inevitable that executives should devote themselves to increasing those profits.[43]

Indeed, Mukai's theory of the autonomous corporation had serious weaknesses. The debate between Mukai and Kojima on corporate management was the first of many such debates about the relationship between shareholders and

---

41 Haruyama 1981-1982, part 1, pp. 195 ff.

42 Mukai 1929. See Tsutsui 1998, p. 128.

43 Kojima 1930, vol. 1, chapter 4. Haruyama 1981-1982, part 1, pp. 192 ff. Nakanishi Torao (1896-1975) also examined the separation of ownership and management around the same time as Kojima. See Nakanishi 1932, especially p. 70. For further details and analysis of the problems arising from this book, see Haruyama *ibid.*

management. It is particularly noteworthy that Mukai did not advocate his ideas about the corporation, corporate autonomy and the "supercorporation" merely in terms of corporation theory and management, but also presented them as related to the corporation's role in the national economy and in terms of its social and public function. At issue here was the search for a new model of corporate management at a time when the laissez-faire capitalist economy had hit an impasse. His new ideas about corporate management were closely linked with the need to overcome problems in the national economy as a whole and create a new economic system. Mukai conceived a system of state control of the national economy as the stage following the laissez-faire capitalist economy, and so linked forward thinking about corporate management with the controlled economy. In this way, the separation of capital and management formed one part of the debate about the transformation of the capitalist economy and the shift from a laissez-faire economy to an organized or controlled one.

Mukai was also active outside academia. As a member of the Committee for the Controlled Economy (*Tōsei iinkai*) in the Temporary Industrial Rationalization Bureau (*Rinji sangyō gōrikyoku*) established by the Hamaguchi cabinet in 1930 within the Ministry of Commerce and Industry, he was involved in drafting the Important Industries Control Law of 1931, and he was also appointed a specialist member of the Cabinet Research Bureau (*Naikaku chōsakyoku*), established in May 1935. He was a key figure too in policy formation for state control of the national economy, and was the most prominent advocate of the controlled economy. Because he took part in the economic restructuring that led to a state-controlled national economy, his ideas about the separation of capital and management were able to exert considerable influence on his contemporaries.

Walther Rathenau and the "Corporation without shareholders"

Mukai's views on the autonomous enterprise and the "supercorporation" were greatly influenced by Walther Rathenau (1867-1922) and John Maynard Keynes, and especially by Rathenau's notions of "autonome Wirtschaft" ("autonomous economics") and a "new economic system." The economist Nakanishi Torao said of Rathenau that "As far as I know, it was Walther Rathenau, a prominent German entrepreneur as well as a scholar of economic thought, who at the beginning of the early 1920s first advocated the separation of ownership and management in large corporations, a course of action he examined in his book *Von kommenden Dingen*."[44]

---

44 Nakanishi 1968.

Walther Rathenau was the son of the founder of the electrical combine Allgemeine Elektrizitäts-Gesellschaft (AEG), and joined its board in 1899, eventually succeeding his father. At that time he contributed significantly to the growth of industrial organization within German industry. He played a leading role in putting Germany's economy on a wartime footing during World War I and after the war served as Minister of Reconstruction (1921) and Foreign Minister (1922). He was assassinated in June 1922.[45] Despite his busy public life, Rathenau gave innumerable lectures and wrote extensively. Mukai was especially interested in his *Von kommenden Dingen* (In Days To Come, 1917) and *Die neue Wirtschaft* (The New Economy, 1918).

Rathenau conceived and advocated a new form of capitalism motivated not by the desire for profit but by a sense of social responsibility, so as to resolve the serious problems confronting capitalist societies, such as the alienation of human freedoms, as well as to provide an alternative to socialism, then attracting growing support. Focusing on the evolution of the joint-stock company, he observed that securitisation and the circulation of stocks and shares had already depersonalised ownership and that property rights had become fragmented and widely dispersed. Under these conditions, the enterprise eventually assumes an independent life, with its operations in the hands of a body of leaders similar to state bureaucrats. Eventually it would accumulate enough profits to buy back the shares from their owners and assume sole ownership for itself. The objectification of enterprise and the abolition of private ownership (the company without shareholders) results in the transformation of the enterprise into an institution, like a foundation or a state organ. Rathenau called this type of organization "autonomous" (*autonome*).

Rathenau discussed his theory of the autonomous enterprise in *Von kommenden Dingen*. To bring it about, share capital must gradually be returned to the shareholders, and some of the proprietary rights be allocated to its staff and workers. An autonomous enterprise is run on the basis of recognized responsibility, rather than on greedily pursuing profit. However, since private initiative remains, this new type of organization stands midway between private enterprise and a government scheme. Productivity is increased by eliminating all forms of waste, by making labour more efficient, and by rationalizing production. Surplus profits are set aside to finance improvements and to expand the enterprise, and to give workers a share of the return on their labour.[46]

---

45 For details of Rathenau's life, see Pogge von Strandmann ed. (1985), "Biographical sketch", pp. 1-26.

46 Rathenau 1917 (1925), especially p. 150ff. For Rathenau's ideas, see Solzbacher 1933, Laux 1998. In English, see Pogge von Strandmann 1985, Michalka 2010.

Rathenau's *Von kommenden Dingen* won a broad readership in Germany, and following its publication in 1917 went through 62 editions as a single volume, selling 24,000 copies in the first three months. Included in his *Collected Works*, by 1929 it ran to its 83rd edition. His *Die neue Wirtschaft* (The New Economy), published in 1918, also became a bestseller, selling 30,000 copies in its first month and running to a 54th edition before being included in the *Collected Works*.[47] *The New Economy* outlined his view about the new economic order that should be put into place after World War I. Based on the premise that the economy "was not a private concern, but the concern of the community (*Gemeinschaft*)", the book discussed how to organise the postwar national economy and transform it into a cooperative economy (*Gemeinwirtschaft*).[48] Here his idea of the functional transformation of the corporation merged with his ideas about the formation of an organic and cooperative national economy based on autonomous bodies founded on initiative and duty. Industry would be organized through two groups, both supervised by the state. The first Rathenau called a "professional union" (*Berufsverband*), made up of enterprises of the same kind (in manufacturing, trade, etc,) and the second he termed an "industrial union" (*Gewerbeverband*), a grouping of industries most closely connected with each in the above groups (the cotton textile industry, the iron industry, etc.). The former would take the form of a corporation with each enterprise being a member, and it would act like a syndicate. Rathenau's thought thus did not differ greatly from Mukai Shikamatsu's idea of the autonomous corporation (the supercorporation) which had become inseparable from the view of a controlled national economy.

In his book *Autonomous Economics* (Autonome Wirtschaft), published in 1919 immediately after the end of World War I, Rathenau once again took up the ideas of a company without shareholders and the collective economy. The concepts of "autonomous economics" and the "new economy", being based on the autonomous corporation, were here closely linked with his fierce criticism of socialism and social democracy, as a means to counter the Marxist doctrine of socialisation and nationalisation.[49] Rathenau's "autonomous economics" emphasized the solidarity and cooperation among specialist managers (board members), staff, technical experts and labourers in the running of the business. In the face of class conflict, he argued for managerial collectivism and social unity

47 Rathenau 1918 (1929).

48 For "Deutsche Gemeinwirtschaft", see "German Collective Economy", Bowen 1971, chapter 5.

49 Rathenau 1919.

based on harmony among classes with the viewpoint of maintaining the capitalist system.

Rathenau's thought attracted not only Mukai Shikamatsu but also Nakajima Kumakichi (1873-1960) of the Furukawa Zaibatsu who, as an adviser to the Temporary Industrial Rationalization Bureau and later a Minister of Commerce and Industry, exerted a great deal of influence on industrial organisation. During a visit to Berlin between February and April 1922, he met "Dr. Rathenau, the German industrialist, economic philosopher and great statesman, whose untimely death was a great loss" and "had the opportunity to hear his opinions about state socialism".[50] Nakajima said that he had learned from Ratheanu that an economic organization should not be treated as private property but as collective property, and that the state should supervise its management and take part in the distribution of the profits from its operations. Concerning rationalization, he reported that Rathenau spoke of the necessity of corporate reorganization through centralizing and unifying the various bodies within the enterprise, and of effective management aimed at common objectives by means of an independent and central executive body. Recognising that Rathenau's idea of a rational industrial organization was based on trust corporations that concentrated and connected related branches and that those trusts were associated by a central independent organ, Nakajima interpreted Rathenau's economic system as a state based on the "trust" system and recognised that "it suggested a future course for state social policy".[51]

---

50 Nakajima wrote that he visited Germany and stayed in Berlin for two months in 1922. He was a member of a group of business leaders visiting the United States and the United Kingdom, leaving Japan in October 1921. Their official visit ended in London in January 1922 and Nakajima went immediately to Germany. In Berlin he concluded the contract for the enterprise planned between Siemens and Furukawa (Fuji denki). He makes no mention in this work about visiting Rathenau. Incidentally, while in London he attended open lectures at Toynbee Hall and the YMCA and with his colleagues visited leaders of the Labour Party, such as Sydney Webb (Nakajima 1951, chapter 13).

51 Nakajima 1931, pp. 21-22. While Nakajima pointed out that there was an international trend towards government intervention in the economy, he also perceived that the government should approve to some extent monopolies within the economic system. He referred regarding this to the Report of the Liberal Industrial Inquiry of the Liberal Party, published in 1928 under the title *Britain's Industrial Future.* He quoted from the Japanese digested translation of this report. "In modern conditions a tendency towards some degree of monopoly in an increasing number of industries is, in our opinion, inevitable and even, quite often, desirable in the interests of efficiency.

The 1932 edition of the *Keizaigaku Jiten* (Dictionary of economics) describes Rathenau's thought as "promoting gradual social reconstruction through industrial control based on socialistic, solidary principles", and explained it as the idea of "the centralisation of industry through the conscious collaboration" of labour and capital and of "a new state that has achieved industrial rationalisation and has been endowed with a new set of ethics founded on the stability of work and status in life." It is apparent that Rathenau's economic thought was widely known among the Japanese intellectuals of the time.[52]

Rathenau's views about the functional transformation of the corporation, specifically "the company without shareholders" and "the autonomous corporation", drew the attention of Japanese scholars of commercial (corporate) law. They understood it as the theory of "enterprise-in-itself".[53] One of these scholars, Ōsumi Ken'ichirō (1904-1998) of the Kyoto Imperial University, explained in a 1932 essay based on the views of the lawyer Fritz Haussmann, that Rathenau asked shareholders (both investors and speculators) to respect the enterprise-in-itself and protect it for the public interest, and he went on to develop this corporate essence further and link it to the collective economy. Ōsumi noted that Haussmann coined the term "enterprise-in-itself" (*Unternehmen an sich*) to refer to this idea of Rathenau's, and it became the basic concept that united Rathenau's ideas of the collective economy and his corporate theory.[54]

Rathenau's thought also attracted great attention in the United Kingdom. *Von kommenden Dingen* was translated into English as *In Days to Come* and

---

It is, therefore, no longer useful to treat trusts, cartels, combinations, holding companies, and trade associations as inexpedient abnormalities in the economic system to be prevented, checked, and harried. The progression from purely private individualistic enterprises to the Public Concern is one of endless gradations and intermediate stages. We believe that there is still room at one of these intermediate stages for large-scale enterprises of a semi-monopolistic character which are run for private profit and controlled by individuals. We must find a place for such enterprises within our national economic system and create an environment for them in which they can function to the public advantage." (*Britain's Industrial Future*, pp. 93-94). Nakajima 1931, pp. 32-33. J.M. Keynes was a member of the executive committee of Liberal Industrial Inquiry.

52 *Keizaigaku Jiten* 1932. Entry by Fujita Keizō.

53 For the theory of "enterprise-in-itself" see Lüpold and Schnyder 2009. Here it is described as a "transpersonal, quasi-organic entity with interests and a life of its own" (p. 24). The term was translated into Japanese as *kigyō jitai*. See also Laux 1998.

54 Ōsumi 1932. Ōsumi mainly relied on Rathenau's *Vom Aktienwesen. Eine geschäftliche Betrachtung*. See also Ōsumi 1953, part 3, chapter 2.

published in London in 1921.[55] There are similarities in the wording of this work and *Self-Government in Industry* (1917) by G. D. H. Cole (1889-1959), who had developed and popularized the theory of Guild Socialism as a means to reform industry cooperatively.[56] However, though they appeared at the same time, English Guild Socialism and Rathenau's collective economy were very different in outlook. Nevertheless, they overlapped one another in that they both sought to reform capitalism.

Rathenau's ideas also had an impact in the United States, and his influence is clear in *The Modern Corporation and Private Property* (1932) by Adolf Berle and Gardiner_Means. At the beginning of the book, the authors referred both to T. Veblen's *Absentee Ownership and Business Enterprise in Recent Times: the Case of America*[57] and to Rathenau's *The New Economy*, and examined Rathenau's views closely in the concluding chapter, "The New Concept of the Corporation". "Most fundamental to the new picture of economic life must be a new concept of business enterprise as concentrated in the corporate organization. In some measure a concept is already emerging. Over a decade ago, Walther Rathenau wrote concerning the German counterpart to our great corporation."[58] They then included a long quotation from *In Days to Come*, which concluded with the forecast that "The depersonalisation of ownership, the objectification of enterprise, the detachment of property from the possessor, leads to a point where the enterprise becomes transformed into an institution which resembles the state in character."[59]

By this, Berle and Means wanted to demonstrate that the corporation was in the process of being separated from shareholders, its lawful owners, and being managed by small power-wielding groups, that is, boards of directors. At the end of the chapter, they discussed, with this point in mind, the increasing economic power of corporations, the concentration of authority in the hands of a few individuals, and the problems that consequently arise. They then offered a "wholly

55 Translated by Eden and Cedar Paul (see Rathenau 1917 for bibliographic details). See also Bowen (1971 [1947]) p. 172, n. 16.

56 Bowen (1971 [1947]), p. 179, n. 33. Bowen remarks that Rathenau "was not in the habit of acknowledging intellectual indebtedness to others" and notes that "a number of passages in Rathenau's later writings read … remarkably like paraphrases of certain pages in G. D. H. Cole's *Self-Government in Industry*." See also Solzbacher 1933, pp. 125 ff.

57 Veblen 1923.

58 Berle and Means 1968 [1932], p. 309.

59 Rathenau 1917, 1921, pp. 120, 121. Quoted in Berle and Means 1968 [1932], p. 309.

new concept of corporate activity". "Neither the claims of ownership nor those of control can stand against the paramount interests of the community," they wrote. This means that corporate leaders should, for example, provide fair wages, give their employees security, render reasonable service to the public, and stabilize their business. They concluded that the '"control" of the great corporations should develop into a purely neutral technocracy, balancing a variety of claims by various groups in the community and assigning to each a portion of the income stream on the basis of public policy rather than private cupidity."[60] The influence of Rathenau here is undeniable. *The Modern Corporation and Private Property* had a considerable impact on Japanese thinking, which meant that the Japanese readers were indirectly influenced by Rathenau's economic thought.

Keynes' public corporation

Economists like Mukai Shikamatsu and Kojima Seiichi_also paid great attention to John Maynard Keynes and his work, *The End of Laissez-faire* (1926). Here Keynes criticised *laissez-faire* and predicted its end, but at the same time he noted the changes occurring within corporations. He was particularly interested in the trend for "joint stock institutions… to approximate to the status of public corporations", in "the tendency of big enterprise to socialise itself", and in the fact that "owners of the capital, i.e. its shareholders, are almost entirely disassociated from the management". In his 1932 essay, Ōsumi Ken'ichirō stated that "the significance of 'enterprise-in-itself' as the fundamental consideration of the corporation has been fostered by a British economist, Keynes" and quoted a relevant passage from the German translation of Keynes' *The End of Laissez-faire*.[61] Keynesian theories about the separation of the ownership of capital and management and about the public corporation exerted a considerable influence over Japanese intellectuals of the time.

In *The End of Laissez-faire*, Keynes critically reviewed the intellectual history of ideas about individualism, laissez-faire and the harmony between private

60 Berle and Means 1968 [1932], p. 312.

61 Ōsumi 1932, pp. 581-2. (From the German translation *Das Ende des Laissez-Faire, Ideen zur Verbindung von Privat- und Gemeinwirtschaft*, pp. 32-33, corresponding to *The End of Laissez-faire*, pp. 42-43). Before the publication of his *General Theory of Employment, Interest and Money* (1936), Keynes was known in Japan as the author of *Indian Currency and Finance* (1913), *Economic Consequences of the Peace* (1919), *A Tract on Money Reform* (1923) and *A Treatise on Money* (1930). *A Tract on Money Reform* was translated into Japanese in 1924. For Keynes' economic theories in prewar and wartime Japan, see Hadley 1989, Ikeo 1997.

advantage and public good, pointing out that they were based on unreal assumptions while stressing the importance of analysing actual facts. He maintained that capitalism, if managed wisely, could be made more effective for attaining economic objectives than any alternative system, but laissez-faire was no longer appropriate, and the "captains of industry" on whom Marshall's economic chivalry had looked to improve society could not be expected to play a leading role. "Yet [the industrialist] in his turn is becoming a tarnished idol," commented Keynes.

Keynes used Jeremy Bentham's terminology "Agenda" and "Non-Agenda" to discriminate what the State should or should not do,[62] and stated that it was the "task of politics to devise forms of government within a democracy capable of accomplishing the 'Agenda'". He advocated semi-autonomous bodies as "the ideal size for the unit of control and organization." Keynes commented on "the trend of joint-stock institutions, when they have reached a certain age and size, to approximate the status of public corporations rather than that of individualistic private enterprise", noting that a point arrives in their growth "at which the owners of the capital ... are almost entirely dissociated from the management", with the result that the emphasis of management shifts from maximising profits for the shareholders to maintaining "the general stability and reputation of the institution". He also contended however that this process might "promote conservatism and a waning of enterprise", but in order to counter socialism and State Socialism that opposed private profit, it was necessary for enterprises to be semi-socialised or semi-autonomous.[63]

Keynes's views on the separation of the ownership of capital from management did not simply belong to his theories about the corporation and corporate organization, but were also a part of his criticism of the laissez-faire economy. What was distinctive about his ideas, linked as they were with a recognition of the socialisation of the enterprise, was the concept of the public corporation as a semi-autonomous organisation within a democratic framework. One example of this was the National Grid, set up by the Central Electricity Board in the UK, which operated as a privately-owned, state-operated system. The Central Electricity Board was established by an Act of 1926 "to concentrate production of electric power in a number of efficient stations and to erect high tension transmission lines to interconnect these stations and link the existing regional

62 Bentham, 1798(Bowring 1843, 1962)

63 Keynes 1931, pp. 272 and 287. For Keynes's views, see Thirlwall ed. 1978, especially the article by Cairncross, Fitzgibbons 1988. In German, see Geiger 1959.

systems into a National Grid. The Board did not own the generating stations nor did it have any control over distribution".[64]

Werner Sombart: the decline of the capitalistic spirit and the bureaucratisation of management

When formulating his theory of the semi-autonomous, public enterprise, Keynes pointed out the trend for corporate management to focus on the stability of the institution rather than on maximising profits for shareholders, a trend that might in some cases lead to a waning of the enterprise. This was a problem associated with the bureaucratisation of large corporations. In Germany too, Werner Sombart (1863-1941) focused on the bureaucratisation and "spiritual reification" (*Vergeistung*, "despiritualising") of management, defining this process as a phenomenon that appears in the final stage of capitalism (*Spätkapitalismus*, "Late Capitalism").[65] Sombart's "Late Capitalism" had a great influence on his contemporaries, including Mukai Shikamatsu.

Sombart defined the changes in the capitalist economy in terms of the decline of the capitalistic spirit (*kapitalistischer Geist*). He understood the capitalistic spirit to be characterised by the strained conditions existing between rationalism and irrationalism, speculation and calculation, a civic spirit and a rapacious spirit, and reflecting and venturing. The strained condition, however, has become reduced as rational considerations have increased in economic life and the rationalising spirit has become solidly entrenched in the enterprise. Sombart asserted that the increased availability of information and forecasts, as well as business activities carried out by rational organizations, have undermined entrepreneurial characteristics such as business instinct and sensitiveness. As a result, the enterprise has taken on the features of a bureaucratic organization: its managers have assumed the status of government officials, and the pursuit of profit and the entrepreneurial spirit that is not afraid to take risks have given way to the pursuit of safety and stability. He observed that the inclination for daring and recklessness and the desire for adventure and conquest diminish when the

64 Aldcroft 1970, p. 193.

65 Sombart thought the process of spiritual reification was a result of capitalism. "Rationalization goes hand in hand with reification in which individual animal spirits ('soul') are replaced by abstract concepts." As it evolved, capitalism was transformed "from a community of lively individuals tied to each other by personal relationships into a system of artfully designed interdependent work performances which are executed by functionaries in human shape" (Sombart, 1927, p. 895). See Michaelides and Milios 2009, p. 499, Lebovics 1969, Appel 1992, Lenger 1994.

owners of large enterprises live off their income from interest and accumulated profits (what Sombart calls "financial obesity"), as a direct result of concentration, price-cartels, joint-stock business, and so on.[66]

Sombart's discussion about the bureaucratisation and spiritual reification of corporations and Rathenau's theory of the autonomous corporation are two sides of the same coin. Mukai Shikamatsu understood Sombart's approach to be the transformation of the capitalistic enterprise into a joint-stock company and the weakening of its profit-seeking character, and on this premise developed his thesis of the supercorporation, which was akin to Rathenau's autonomous corporation. Now the "spirit" of the new executive became an issue: how could the specialist manager in charge of a supercorporation discern his social role within the trend towards bureaucratisation and spiritual reification in corporations?

As a premise to this question, there was another issue: to what degree could the managers (executives) act independently of the owners of the capital (shareholders)? Kojima Seiichi grasped the situation accurately when he noted that though directors played an increasingly important role in corporations, in general they still acted according to the will of the shareholders. Therefore they were not free from the profit- seeking principle but rather were always bound by it. But despite this reality, there was a new development that necessitated restraints on the rampant profit-seeking activities of corporations and subjecting them to rational management: the need to move towards a wartime economy.

German Corporation Theory under National Socialism

In the late 1930s the need became pressing on Japan to establish what might be called a national defence (or "war-preparedness") economy to cope with the exigencies of the on-going Sino-Japanese War and to prepare for total war. To create such a system, it was crucial to restructure the existing one, and so the question of a new economic order became very important. As the article by Nakamura Takafusa and Hara Akira quoted above showed, the most hotly debated point was the separation of capital and management.[67] Furthermore, as we have also seen, this subject was debated, not simply as a temporary policy issue related to the setting up of a wartime economic system, but also as a topic concerning the renovation and modification of capitalism.

---

66 Sombart 1932, pp. 8-9. Also Sombart 1927. As is well known, Sombart's concept of the capitalistic spirit differed fundamentally from that of Max Weber. See Ōtsuka 1982, part 2.

67 Nakamura and Hara 1973.

As we have seen above, the issue of the separation of capital and management did not suddenly emerge in the late 1930s; it had already been actively discussed, with Japanese economic thought overlapping the European to a certain degree and the former being deeply influenced by the latter. The separation of capital and management, a point of contention for the economic New Order in Japan, has to be understood in this context. The economic New Order was being debated at a time when fascist influence, particularly that of the Nazi ideology of Germany, was clear. If "[Japan's] New Order (*shintaisei*)" was "an imitation of the Nazi New Order (*Neuordnung*)",[68] it is even more important to examine how it was associated with the National Socialism and Nazi economic thought.

Anti-capitalism was one of the most notable features of Nazi economic thought. Presented as a criticism of laissez-faire capitalism and its emphasis on unlimited profit-making, anti-capitalism played an important role in the expansion of the Nazi movement. It was most strongly expressed as a provision in the 25 Point Programme of 1920 to abolish unearned income and break debt slavery.[69] Criticism was mainly targeted at financial, or usury, capital (especially Jewish financial capital) as well as at speculative investment in the stock market and share-derived earnings. Also attacked were shareholders who took no part in management but focused their interest only on the high dividends and stock prices that gave them their unearned income. This criticism came to be associated with broader issues concerning the corporation itself, and the separation of company ownership and management.

The National Socialists in Germany stressed labour and industriousness, creative and productive economic activity, individual initiative and responsibility, and so valued the actual workings of business and the role played by management over the ownership of shares. Those in charge of management, like directors and industrialists, were given positions of leadership and workers were asked to cooperate with them as their subordinates ("followers"). The weight given to the role of management in business was closely related to the leadership principle (*Führerprinzip*), a characteristic feature of Nazi ideology. Democratic decisions by majority rule were abolished, since the right to make decisions was considered the responsibility of the leader. The leadership principle was

68 Andō 1963, p. 255.

69 For the 25 Point Programme, see Lee 1996, p. 28, Barkai 1977, pp. 27 ff., Barkai 1990 [English translation], pp. 23ff. Point 11 of the Programme of the NSDAP (*Nationalsozialische Deutsche Arbeiterpartei*) stipulated the abolition of income unearned by labor or effort (*Abschaffung des arbeits- und mühelosen Einkommens*) and breaking the bondage of interest (slavery) (*Brechung der Zinsknechtschaft*).

introduced into the economic sphere in legislation such as the Labour Organization Law (Gesetz zur Ordnung der nationalen Arbeit) of 1934 (see Chapter 6). It was therefore unsurprising that the National Socialists initially criticised corporations for having anonymous shareholders with no responsibility. Having seized power, however, they modified their stance and set out to amend corporate law taking the continued existence of joint stock institutions as a given. The fundamentals of their amendments were the leadership principle and responsible management (*verantwortliche Führung*).

The Capital Investment Law (*Kapitalanlagengesetz*) was enacted in March 1934 and the Dividend Limitation Law (*Anleihenstockgesetz*) the following December. The purpose of the former was to restrict capital returns: when a return on capital exceeded the amount paid the previous year, any gains above the predetermined percentage (6%) of capital had to be reinvested in public bonds of an equal value. A law concerning the reorganisation of joint-stock companies (*Kapitalgesellschaft*) was enacted in May 1934, promoting the "personal" company such as a general or limited partnership, and a limited liability company. Then in 1937 the Stock Corporation Law (*Aktiengesetz*) came into effect. It greatly changed the existing structure of corporations, most notably expanding the rights of directors and restricting those of shareholders' meetings. The board of directors ceased to be a mere representative body that executed business following decisions made at shareholders' meetings. Instead, directors assumed the authority and responsibility to manage business themselves. Subsection 1 of Paragraph 70 obliged directors to take responsibility for directing (*leiten*) the company for the good of the management (*Betrieb*) and employees (*Gefolgschaft*), as well as the common interest (*gemeiner Nutzen*) of the people (*Volk*) and the country (*Reich*).[70]

The views held by those who drafted Nazi Germany's corporation law and the reviewing process of that law were introduced to Japan in great detail by scholars of commercial law, such as Ōsumi Ken'ichirō, Yagi Hiroshi (1907-1981) and Ōmori Tadao (1908-1972). They judged that the basic object of the amendment "was to modify the traditional concept of corporations as being part of the liberal economy and reform it according to the design of a controlled economy based upon National Socialism". They also noted that "according to the leadership principle, the powers of the meeting of shareholders, who were considered to be irresponsible and incompetent, were decreased in favour of the authority of

70 Ōsumi, Yagi and Ōmori eds. 1956 [1937], p. 182. See Schlegelberger et al eds. 1937, especially p. 305ff., Vagts 1966, p. 40.

responsible and competent directors".[71] This was in accordance with the Labour Organization Law (*Gesetz zur Ordnung der nationalen Arbeit*) of 1934 that stipulated "the entrepreneur as the leader, and his staff and workers as his followers, should work together to realise their common business objectives and devote themselves to the pursuit of the common interest of the people and the country".

Those scholars also referred to German views which argued that the board of directors had already assumed a leadership role under the democratic legislation brought in before the Nazis seized power, and that the evils of the corporate system were partly due to the fact that the law had ignored this reality.[72] Actually, the 1937 Stock Corporation Law had Weimar origins in regards corporate structural change (*Strukturwandlung*), within which the concept of "enterprise -in-itself" (*Unternehmen an sich*) deriving from Rathenau was apparent.[73] The Nazi revision of the corporation law can be understood as having been carried out under such circumstances and as a development of such prior discourse. The 1937 Corporation Law was to be handed down, almost intact, to West Germany after World War II.[74] In 1965, it underwent a complete revision; it eliminated Subdivision 70 entirely, but there was no real change between the old and new laws regarding the rights and responsibilities of the directors.[75]

It was true that the strengthening and broadening of the power that the board of directors had over the general meeting of shareholders was linked with the functional changes within enterprises and the emphasis on the importance of management and with the concept of "enterprise-in-itself". In this sense, it cannot be denied that there were many points in common with Rathenau's views.[76] However, Rathenau had envisioned not only corporate modification, but also the disappearance of shareholders and the emergence of a "joint stock company without shareholders". The 1937 Corporation Law in fact presupposed the continued existence of shareholders and shareholders' meetings, and did nothing more than restrict their power; the shareholders' meeting was still allowed to execute its rights regarding the affairs of the corporation and to vote to dismiss directors.

The Nazi Corporation Law came into being against a background of corporate evolution and the increasing importance of the Board of Directors. It grew

---

71 Osumi, Yagi and Omori eds. 1956 [1937] p. 42. See Okushima 1996, Masai 1996. For a contemporary view, see Mann 1937.

72 Ibid. p. 29.

73 Ibid. p. 11, Masai 1996.

74 Ōsumi, Yagi and Ōmori eds. 1956 [1937], p. 638ff. See also Vagts 1966.

75 Verdinger and Kawamoto, eds. 1969, pp. 28ff. See also Vagts 1966.

76 Ono 1996.

out of discourse current during the Weimar Republic and the modernity of some of its elements is reflected in the fact that it was inherited by West Germany after World War II. But it should be also noted that it was at the same time backed by Nazi ideology. Thus Section 70 placed an emphasis on "leadership by the board of directors", and although the word *Führer* is missing, it was clearly linked to the basic principle of Nazism, the leadership principle, and its stated object, that "the common interest comes before self-interest" (*Gemeinnutz geht vor Eigennutz*), was a fundamental Nazi postulate.

After World War II, Ōsumi Ken'ichirō dismissed this connection as "a political embellishment",[77] but before the war Ōsumi himself had associated it with "the controlled economy based on National Socialism". As is well known, the anti-capitalistic provisions in the 25 Point Programme to abolish unearned income and break debt slavery were not realised. To gloss over this failure, the Nazis emphasised all the more the curtailment of the power of shareholders and their general meetings (since speculation on the stock market and unearned income like dividends were targets of criticism) and the transference of their power to directors, to be in charge of management. These objectives they then associated with Nazi ideology. The connection might have been an "embellishment", but the embellishment served a political (and ideological) end, and furthermore, it is important to note that even experts in commercial law could not see it for what it was at the time. The measures above, together with the 1934 legislation placing restrictions on capital returns, should be understood as the means the Nazis adopted to counter the laissez-faire profit principle of capitalism.

Reform bureaucrats and the separation of capital and management

The separation of ownership and management was the greatest discussion point in the discourse about the economic New Order. The studies of Nakamura and Hara and the research on Mōri Hideoto by Itō Takashi[78] give a general outline of how the reform bureaucrats involved in its planning interpreted the separation of capital and management. Mōri, who advocated a controlled economy, considered that under "a new national economy liberated from capitalism" the entrepreneur would be a "corporate technocrat" (*kigyō gijutsuka*) rather than a

77 Ōsumi, Yagi and Ōmori eds. 1956 [1937], p. 638. See also Tsutsui 1998, pp. 103-104.
78 Itō 1987. See also Okushima 1996, Masai 1996. For an analysis of Mōri as an ideologue of fascism, see Mimura 2011, pp. 126-137.

capitalist.[79] Mōri also made the separation of capital and management a premise, and placed more weight on management. What were the opinions of other bureaucrats?

Along with Mōri Hideoto, Minobe Yōji was an important figure among the reform bureaucrats. Minobe described his own thoughts about the question of the separation of capital and management in an essay entitled "The significance and structure of the New Economic Order" (*Keizai shintaisei no igi to kōzō*).[80] His argument can be described in six points:

(1) "The Outline for setting up an economic New Order defines an enterprise as an organic combination of three factors - capital, management and labour. This is undeniable."

(2) "The enterprise is a combination of capital and labour, which is operated by management. This management is appointed or dismissed by the holders of capital stock... The management assumes full responsibility to the holders of capital stock for the profitable operation of that capital stock.

(3) "Under the new economic structure, however, an enterprise forms a component part of [the] national economy under a coordinated State plan. Furthermore, being a component of an economic organization,[81] machinery for co-operative management, the enterprise must be managed in conformity with its own position under the new economic structure. It must also assume responsibility in public service to the State through the directors of the economic organization to which it belongs."

(4) "The management of an enterprise, therefore, assumes dual responsibility. As the holder of responsibility for public service, the management of an enterprise is called upon to direct the enterprise under its care."

(5) "With regard to the dual responsibility which the management of an enterprise must shoulder, it is inconceivable that there should be any limit to

---

79 Itō 1987, pp. 139ff.

80 Minobe 1942. Minobe 1941, pp. 186-187 (in English). See also Berger 1988, pp. 329ff and Mimura 2011, pp. 164-167, 169.

81 According to Minobe 1941, under "the projected new economic structure... all industries will be divided into their component industrial departments in which economic organizations (*keizai dantai*) will be set up with those engaged in the same line of industry or dealing with the same goods as members. These economic organizations will be led by directors.. [They] will play their designated parts in the operation of the co-ordinated activities in bringing the total national resources into full play, by fully realizing their responsibilities in public service and giving full rein to their abilities as their own initiative." (p. 186).

the responsibility which it assumes to the State. Therefore, it is but natural a limit should be set on the responsibility which the management assumes toward the holders of capital stock in the form of restrictions on dividends. In other words, a definite limit has been set to the responsibility which the management of an enterprise holds toward holders of capital stock in the form of dividend restrictions."

(6) "At the same time, the leaders of the economic associations (later established as *tōseikai*) can interfere in the appointment or dismissal of the management of an enterprise which belongs to the organization, thereby establishing their leadership over the management of member enterprises."

Minobe's argument on the separation of capital and management is clear. First, using the capitalist economy as his foundation, he acknowledges the principle of "economic activity" by a private enterprise, and, as the central theme of his argument, pays special attention to the significance of the enterprise, management and managers. He does not reject capitalism (he was not arguing for anti-capitalism), but proposes a modification of capitalism that corresponds with the structural transformation of the corporation. At the same time, under a coordinated state plan, the enterprise is a component part of the national economy and its economic organization, and it assumes responsibility for "public welfare". Finally, Minobe asserts that while the management of an enterprise has unlimited responsibility for public welfare, it has only limited responsibility towards shareholders.[82]

An important element in the plan devised by the reform bureaucrats to separate capital from management was controlling dividends to shareholders. Legislation allowing the state to impose controls on the distribution of profits was passed in April 1939, promulgated and enforced under Section 11 of the National Mobilisation Law (*Kokka sōdoin-hō*) of March 1938. This ordinance had been introduced to increase the mobilization of resources for war, but in practice it was used to prevent any increase in dividends.[83] It was replaced in October 1940 under the second Konoe Cabinet by the Company Accounts Control Ordinance

82 For legislation restricting capital returns, see Hasegawa 1937, 1942. For a more recent study, see Shibata 1992.

83 This was the Company Profits, Dividends and Funds Accommodation Ordinance (*Kaisha rieki haitō oyobi shikin yūzū-rei*) of April 1, 1939. See Hoshi and Kashyap 2004, pp. 55-57. Its effectiveness is demonstrated by the fact that between April 1939 and October 1940 only fifty of the 130 requests to raise dividends were approved (Okazaki et al eds 1999, p. 111). See also Mimura 2011, p. 142.

(*Kaisha keiri tōsei-rei*). It too was designed to tighten control over dividends but it differed from the previous ordinance, which had been based on the concept of paid-up capital (*haraikomi shihon*), thus acknowledging the maintenance of high returns on capital as a kind of vested interest. The new ordinance was based rather on the concept of equity capital, and set eight percent of the equity capital as the highest rate for dividends.

State control of dividends was exercised first and foremost as part of a set of policies relating to the wartime economy, and it had a number of objectives, such as constraining excess profits during wartime, mitigating the suffering of consumer industries (called the "sacrificed industries", *sangyō gisei*[84]), and offsetting deficit-covering bonds by retaining profits within the company. The bureaucrats on the Cabinet Planning Board, however, regarded control on returns as part of the separation of capital and management, one of the main pillars of the economic New Order, rather than simply as an issue concerning the wartime economy. The general public though understood it to be a more fundamental control on profits, an example of state intervention in the very profit principle that was the essence of capitalism, and the first step of a plan to convert "profit" into "interest". This was one of the reasons that the business community considered the separation of capital and management, discussed as part of the new economic system, to be "communist" and antagonistic to capitalism. In fact, as we have seen, there were some scholars at the time who saw the new economic order as bringing about controls over profits and finances.

Conclusion

The economic New Order advocated by Minobe and other Japanese economists had much in common with the principles of Nazi Germany's New Order (*Neuordnung*), which included an acceptance of the capitalistic profit principle, priority given to management, the leadership of the entrepreneur (manager) who was responsible for the welfare of the public and state, the "enterprise community" (Ger. *Betriebsgemeinschaft*[85]), and restrictions on returns to shareholders. There

---

84 See Teranishi 2005, p. 175. Teranishi 1994 notes that "food products and textiles were the so-called 'sacrificed industries'. A contemporary description of "sacrificed industries" appears in Asahi 1939.

85 A collective enterprise or community of the interests of both the entrepreneur and workers; the unity of employer (or chief manager, the "leader") and employees (followers) as integral parts of the enterprise. Also translated as "shop" or "factory" communities. See Nathan 1944, Gardon 1987, p. 212.

is no doubt that Nazi policy ideas influenced the Japanese reform bureaucrats to some degree. As we have seen, though, the debate on the separation of capital and management in Japan was already more than a quarter of a century old, from Ueda Teijirō to Mukai Shikamatsu and Ryū Shintarō. The plans discussed by the reform bureaucrats were based on this earlier debate, and any direct influence from Nazi ideas – if indeed there was any such influence – could only have been a mere reinforcement of pre-existing ideas. The views of Ueda, Mukai and others were strongly associated with the economic thought prevalent in Europe at the time, particularly the ideas of economists such as Tawney, Rathenau and Keynes. Thus, the reform bureaucrats' ideas about the economic New Order were not influenced just by the Nazi New Order (*Neuordnung*) but also, even if indirectly, by the broader, global development of ideas from the 1920s.

The separation of capital and management had a certain bearing on the relationship between shareholders and the executives and board of directors of large corporations, as well as on its legal bases, commercial and corporation law. Taking into consideration the social influence wielded by large corporations and the evils that were caused by that influence, this issue also called into question problematic nature of the relationship between the capitalistic pursuit of profit and an ideal style of rational management. In short, it posed a fundamental question that went beyond the confines of corporation law and the corporate system to have a bearing on the capitalist system itself. It is therefore unsurprising that the separation of capital and management was linked with ideas such as the elimination of non-functional owners of capital, the functional society, autonomous corporations without shareholders, the supercorporation, semi-autonomous public corporation, and a neutral technocracy. Such ideas were part of the debate about reconstructing capitalism in order to counter the surge of Marxism and socialism, and so at root were of a defensive character, seeking to preserve the existing system. They thus possessed the potential to emerge, in a time of crisis for the capitalist system, as powerful theories for modifying capitalism in common among all capitalist countries.

In Germany, the revision of the corporation law by the Nazi government in 1937 diminished the power of the shareholders general meeting in a corporation, and strengthened the authority of the board of directors. In Japan also corporation law underwent revision in 1938, though here it tightened the penal regulations for the violation of duties by directors and expanded the authority of the shareholders' meeting. Matsumoto Jōji (1877-1954), a professor at the Tokyo Imperial University and a counsellor in the Cabinet Legislation Bureau (Hōseikyoku) who was involved in the revision said: "Recently it has become popular to do things based on some new ideology or another, but laws and regulations like civil and commercial law are not supposed to take their cue from these new ideologies in order to go forward."[86] In 1938 too, Ōtsuka Hisao published *Kabushiki gaisha hasseishi ron* (The history of the joint-stock company in Europe), in which he argued, by analyzing the development of the East India Company, that the historical transformation of the corporation from "an autocratic model" to "a modern democratic type" in England could be achieved by giving the shareholders' meeting a "democratic structure".[87] As Ishii Teruhisa (1906-1973), a specialist in commercial and labour law, has pointed out, Japan's 1938 Corporation Law seemed, albeit belatedly, to strengthen "the structure of an institution originating in the principles of capitalistic democracy" by expanding the power of the shareholders' general meeting.[88]

The reality was not quite so straightforward, however. The economic dominance of conglomerate (Zaibatsu) capital was deemed problematic at the time. Under these circumstances, the expansion of the authority of the general shareholders' meeting posed the danger of further fortifying Zaibatsu dominance by increasing the control of majority shareholders.

On the other hand, many of the conditions that affected corporations were changing. As Mitsufuji Tadashi (1907-1992), a professor at the Ōkura Higher Commercial School (now Tokyo Keizai University) and a specialist in corporation law (and a professor at Seijō University in Tokyo from 1957 and its president 1978-1981), pointed out, the character of corporation law began to change in essence through the basic principles contained in the 1940 Outline for the new economic order. The first was the emphasis on corporate ethics. Outwardly, this refers to the importance given to the public aspect of the corporation, which meant giving priority to the public interest and performing duties fully (but it did not mean denying the pursuit of profit), providing reasonable profits and eliminating monopolies. The corporate ethic was further clarified through the emphasis placed on autonomous management based on the manager's creativity and responsibility. The second was that the functions of economic organizations (*keizai dantai*) were defined as public in nature and their leadership was to be in the hands of management led by semi-bureaucratic officials. Of particular concern was the right of a chairman of a control association (*tōseikai*)[89]

---

86 Matsumoto 1940, pp. 8ff. See also Okushima 1996.

87 Ōtsuka 1969 [1938], part. 2, chapter 4, paragraph 2.

88 Ishii 1952, 1959 (*kaitei sansatsu*), p. 154, Okushima 1996, pp. 21ff., Masai 1996, pp. 169 ff.

89 "Public entities that represented a particular industry or material." Mimura 2011, p. 152.

to dismiss board members. The control association of an industry was to be led and controlled by the chairman, who had the right to dismiss the executives of a member firm of the association under certain conditions. Thus the rights of decision-making by the chairman were strengthened. The third was the semi-governmental corporations (*eidan*).[90]

Mitsufuji concluded by saying: "I have come to realise that the corporate system and corporate law, by undergoing change, are facing a new stage of development. This has occurred as a result of evolution, which was neither mechanical nor accidental but fundamental and inevitable."[91] The Munitions Industry Law, on which Okazaki Tetsuji focused, could also be included in this argument, though he examined the Law solely as an institution, and made no mention of the economic thought and social ideology behind it.[92] It was through the long-term development of such debates within Japan and abroad that the preconditions were formed for the democratization of corporations in the postwar reforms and the 1950 revision of the commercial law that strengthened the control of the board of directors over the general shareholders' meeting.

---

90 For *eidan*, see Johnson 1978, p. 74.

91 Mitsufuji 1941.

92 For views of contemporary social scientists regarding the Munitions Industry Law and the *eidan*, see Sugimura 1943, Masuchi 1944. Ōkōchi Masatoshi of Riken (Institute of Physical and Chemical Research) staunchly advocated the separation of capital and management as a means to promote the expansion of production and place more emphasis on the public interest. See Ōkochi 1941, pp. 1-29. For a study of Ōkōchi, see Saitō 1987. Previous studies have noted that Ōtsuka Banjō was a director at Riken, headed by Ōkōchi Masatoshi, when he formulated a plan for "the democratisation of corporation", which became part of postwar reforms. See the relevant passage above and footnote 25.

Chapter Two: The Crisis of Capitalism and the Controlled Economy

In prewar and wartime Japan, there was no economic term used more widely, and one which engendered greater debate, than "controlled economy" (*tōsei keizai*).[93] The issue of state control over economic activity began to be discussed widely in the 1930s, and reached a climax with the move to a wartime economy as the war against China (1937) expanded into the Pacific War (1941). By then, state regulation of the economy affected not only the activities of enterprises, but also deeply impacted on the daily lives of people as consumers, and "controlled economy" had become a virtual synonym for "wartime economy", so much so that it was often spoken of in the compound form, "wartime controlled economy" (*senji tōsei keizai*).

Certainly, the most obvious form into which a controlled economy may develop is a wartime economy, that is, the economy of total war, with its demand for wholesale state intervention in, and control of, the economic system. However, in Japan the issue of state control of the economic process cannot be confined solely to the wartime economy itself, for it had been widely discussed before that time. The intensification of social and economic problems arising out of the growth of capitalism, and in particular, the increasingly urgent situation brought about by the domestic financial crisis of 1927 and the world depression of 1929 made state economic control seem necessary in order to combat, and ameliorate, the hardships being suffered. Taking place against the background of the state's response to the depression, the debate about the controlled economy was also a policy issue, as the state introduced measures that called upon business circles to regulate themselves through a system of cartels and trade associations.

Social scientists too had by that time become very interested in the nature and future prospects of the capitalist economy, in view of the fact that it had given rise to a depression of unprecedented severity and to long-term recession. The

93 The term *tosei keizai* has been translated variously in English-language studies: "managed economy" (Gao 1994, 1997), "regulated economy", "organized economy". The preferred translation of "controlled economy" used here has been employed by Pauer ed. (1999) and others. In Japan at the time, *tosei* (controlled) was preferred to *keikaku* (planned) because of the socialist connotations of the latter.

debate about state economic control thus went beyond the sphere of a temporary policy to deal with the social ramifications of the depression – unemployment and poverty – and was more broadly linked to questions about structural changes to the capitalistic economy, such as the concentration of capital and the formation of monopolies which had transformed the market economy. The debate was also associated with a criticism and reconsideration of the laissez-faire economy, and it engendered ideas about revising and restructuring capitalism through state intervention and the creation of a new economic fabric and order.

Between 1937 and 1941, economic regulation acquired many aspects of a wartime controlled economy. For example, in September 1937, soon after the outbreak of war with China the previous July, three wartime control laws were pushed through: the Temporary Funds Adjustment Law (*Rinji shikin chōseihō*), to control industrial investment, the Temporary Export-Import Commodities Measures Law (*Yūshutsunyūhin tō rinji sōchihō*), to control imports and exports as well as the production, sale and consumption of articles for foreign trade, and the enabling act that allowed the 1918 Munitions Industry Mobilization Law (*Gunjū kōgyō dōinhō*) to be invoked.[94] But even here, economic regulation was not simply a reaction to the economic circumstances of war and the necessity to mobilize resources; rather, it was closely related to the debate about restructuring the capitalist system in the context of transforming capitalism itself, and to how such a transformation was perceived. Thus we need to look at the debate about the controlled economy as it was connected with a new stage of capitalism. We will examine how the debate evolved during the period leading up to the implementation of the war economy, looking both at its character and the influence on it of European economic ideas and theories, particularly those of Germany and Austria.

Central figures in the debate were generally not Marxian economists, the dominant influence in university economics department by the late 1920s, but more often the leading economists and scholars who opposed them. Discussion about the controlled economy had emerged during the final stages of the debate on Japanese capitalism by Marxian economists that had begun in the 1920s, carried on largely by university professors and scholars of the social and economic theory of socialism. It gained in intensity after Marxist input was silenced around 1937, when Marxian participants in the debate were arrested or forced

94 For a detailed listing of the economic controls put in place between August 1937 and December 1941, see Nakamura 1971.

to resign from their academic positions.[95] Then, as the country moved towards war, it took the centre stage of Japanese economics. Since it incorporated issues such as revising and restructuring capitalism, it was influenced to some extent by theories about capitalism and its stages, and this provided a cover under which certain Marxian economists were able to continue to participate in it.

In this sense, Sugihara_Shirō (1920-2009), a specialist in the history of economic thought, has described the period 1935-1945 as being "especially significant in terms of the history of the social sciences in Japan". He says that it is correct overall to identify the trend among the intelligentsia of the time as "apostasy,[96] jumping on the bandwagon, and retreat", but the situation for the social sciences at that juncture was complicated. Sugihara suggests that restrictions on freedom of research and expression actually had the opposite effect of encouraging a wider diversity of viewpoint. "Outcomes of research in the social sciences at this time" were, he says, "more prolific and richer than might be expected".[97] These "research outcomes" refer to the fields of Marxian economics and Western and Japanese economic history, as well as to the history of economic ideas. Sugihara has pointed out that he was first convinced of the implication of these "outcomes" by "following, comprehensively and from many different points of view, the trail of the social sciences in the period 1935-45".[98] However, as I will argue in this chapter, debate about the controlled economy occupied the mainstream of economics and economic history at that time, and was closely tied to "apostasy, jumping on the bandwagon, and retreat" in the field of economics, and so in this sense, it is difficult to see the debate as a "research outcome" of the social sciences, at least on the surface, and this has resulted in a tendency to exclude it from research into the history of academic trends and ideas. Nevertheless, looking below the surface, it is apparent that the debate about the controlled economy points to a particular perception of economics, which, because it was directly connected with the specific circumstances of a particular period, is important for understanding, "comprehensively and from many different points of view", the social sciences of the period.

Many eminent Japanese economic historians, including Nakamura Takafusa, Hara Akira, Nagashima Osamu, Miyajima Hideaki and Shirakizawa Asahiko,

---

95 See Morris-Suzuki 1992, p. 62.

96 *Tenkō*, a radical ideological conversion. Originally it was employed to describe defection from the Communist Party. See Steinhoff 1991.

97 Sugihara 1985, pp. 91-92, Sugihara 1992, p. 85.

98 Sugihara 1992, p. 107.

have studied trends in the debate about the controlled economy.[99] A feature of their research has been their focus on, and analysis of, discussions among bureaucrats, politicians, financiers, the army and intellectuals, and how the debate was portrayed in magazines and other forms of journalism. Shirakizawa's research, for example, is particularly valuable because it allows us to understand views about the controlled economy in the 1930s as a whole, as well as shifts within them. He distinguishes the subject of the debate that arose in the first part of the 1930s from that of the wartime controlled economy, stating that "we cannot explain the Japanese social situation of the 1930s without considering the idea of the controlled economy",[100] and categorizes views about it at that time into three streams: modified capitalist, post-capitalist, and pre-socialist.[101] The 1973 study by Nakamura and Hara pays particular attention to the 1939 proposal by Ryū Shintarō, who proposed in his *Nihon keizai no saihensei* (Reorganizing the Japanese Economy) that there should be greater government control under an economic New Order,[102] while the research of Nagashima and Miyajima focuses on arguments between business leaders and bureaucrats. I have incorporated their results into this study, though my own interest lies more in the history of ideas: considering perceptions from the social sciences about the controlled economy and, in particular, the views of economists and those closely involved in the debate.

Previous studies have made clear that what led to the debate about the controlled economy in the early 1930s was the economic recession that began with the Great Depression, and, particularly, the passing of the Important Industries Control Law (*Juyō sangyō tōseihō*) in 1931. The purpose of this law, as Miyajima Hideaki points out, was, in contrast to former policies of industrial rationalization, to promote the formation of cartels in each industry in an effort to achieve economic stability and escape the recession. At the same time, it allowed the state to intervene in order to prevent any harmful influences that might arise out of cartelization.[103] From the very beginning, discussion

99 Nakamura and Hara 1973, Nagashima 1986, Miyajima 1993, 2004, Shirakizawa 1999. Also important is the intellectual climate of Japan in the 1930s and the war years, for which there is a large amount of research: for example, Shisō no kagaku kenkyūkai ed. 1959-62, Chō and Sumiya 1971, Ishida 1984. Also relevant are Yamanouchi 1999 and the special issue of *Shisō* in 1997. In English, see Mitchell 1976, Fletcher 1982, Hoston 1986, Gordon 1991, Gao 1997, Barshay 1988, 2004.

100 Shirakizawa 1999, Introduction, p. 4.

101 *Ibid*. chapter 7.

102 Ryū 1939.

103 Miyajima 1984, Miyajima 1988, Miyajima 1993, Miyajima 2004. See also Matsuo 1935, p. 105 et seq.

about the controlled economy was not simply about dealing successfully with the Depression and escaping from the recession, but was simultaneously related to tackling problems arising from the formation of monopolies, as a new stage of capitalism.

Shirakizawa Asahiko attaches great importance to the significance of the debate on the controlled economy in the early part of the period. He does not view it simply as a policy to overcome the Depression, but draws attention to the wider question of the impasse of capitalism and the awareness of the structural defects instrumental in giving rise to that impasse.[104] These were issues then being addressed by western nations too, and so Shirakizawa links trends in 1930s Japan with a worldwide, simultaneous and widespread move from "freedom" (*jiyū*) to "control" (*tōsei*).[105]

The understanding of capitalism as it appeared in the debate was closely linked to the perception of the world and the conditions of the times held by those involved. Pre-war economists and those interested in economic questions had a fairly detailed grasp of global conditions, by way of western economic theories and thought. Miyajima points out the influence that German cartel theory had on bureaucrats in the Ministry of Commerce and Industry, and Shirakizawa mentions that discussion surrounding the first Soviet Five-Year Plan (1928-32) and the 1931 World Social Economic Congress held in Amsterdam was the trigger for the debate on the controlled economy.[106] However, the influence of western economic ideas and theories on the debate was far greater than Miyajima and Shirakizawa have indicated.[107] Austrian and German economic thought was particularly decisive here: discussion about the transformation of capitalism by German-language economists especially influenced the Japanese. We will now examine this point in more detail.

---

104 Shirakizawa 1999, p. 187. Shirakizawa's arguments are a development of similar studies on the characteristics of the debate on the controlled economy by Nakamura Takafusa (Nakamura 1989) and Itō Takashi (Itō 1989). Shirakizawa however defines "controlled economy" in a very narrow fashion: "Instead of a laissez-faire economy based on free competition, [the controlled economy] was a new economic policy and economic behaviour which attempted to control price fluctuations and free the economy from depression by artificially calculating the equilibrium between supply and demand" (Shirakizawa 1999, p. 3 et seq.).

105 Shirakizawa 1999, p. 3 et seq.

106 Studies other than those concerning Japanese economic history also point out the importance of the influence on prewar Japan of western ideas about economic policy. See, for example, Takeda 1993, pp. 134, 140, Okazaki 1991, pp. 378 et seq., et al.

107 See Yamanouchi 1999, p. 83, note 30.

Two models in the discussion of the controlled economy

The term "controlled economy" (*tōsei keizai*) first began to appear widely in Japan around 1930-31.[108] In 1930, Kojima Seiichi (1895-1977) published *Kigyō tōseiron* (On Corporate Control), in which he explored a number of issues involving the word *tōsei* ("control", "regulation", "management"), such as "industrial control" (*sangyō no tōsei*), "socialized control" (*shakaikateki tōsei*), "planned economy-type control" (*keikaku keizaiteki tōsei*) and "corporate control" (*kigyō tōsei*). In May 1932 the journal *Keizai Ōrai* (Economic Review) put out a special issue on the subject of the "planned economy" (*keikaku keizai*), to which leading economists like Hijikata Seibi (also referred to as Shigeyoshi; 1890-1975), Mukai Shikamatsu, Suehiro Izutarō (1888-1951), Okura Kinmochi (1882-1968), Kajima Morinosuke (1896-1975), Yamakawa Hitoshi (1880-1958), Kojima Seiichi and others contributed articles. Kojima's *Nihon keikaku keizairon* (On the Japanese Planned Economy) appeared the same year.

It was after the Important Industries Control Law was passed in 1931, however, that "controlled economy" became a household word, though at the time it was used in conjunction with the term "planned economy". It was also used in association with expressions like "organized market economy" (*shijō keizai no soshikika*) and "the organized economy" (*soshiki keizai*). Other terms, such as "bound economy", i.e. gebundene Wirtschaft (*kōsoku keizai*), "cooperative economy" i.e. Gemeinwirtschaft (*kyōdō keizai*) and "economic intervention" (*kanshō keizai*), also appeared in this period.

The beginnings of the debate on the controlled economy seems to have coincided with the publication in 1932 and 1933 of *Nihon shihonshugi hattatsushi kōza* (Lectures on the History of the Growth of Capitalism in Japan) and it got into its stride when *Nihon tōsei keizai zenshū* (Collected Works on the Controlled Economy in Japan) came out in ten volumes in 1933 and 1934. The latter was a collection of research papers by leading scholars, including Marxian economists, such as Mukai Shikamatsu, Ryū Shintarō, Kawai Yoshinari (1886-1970), Itō Hanya (1894-1974), Takahashi Kamekichi (1894-1977), Arisawa Hiromi (1896-1988), Hijikata Seibi, Kojima Seiichi, Inomata Tsunao (1889-1942) and Sakisaka Itsurō (1897-1985), who stated their respective stances in the various

108 The term "planned economy" (*keikaku keizai*) appears as a separate item in the *Dictionary of Economics* edited by the Institute of Economics, Osaka University of Commerce and published 1930-36. However "controlled economy" (*tōsei keizai*) does not appear.

volumes for which they were responsible.[109] This publication was the key to an increasingly vigorous debate.

We can distinguish two models in the way the controlled economy was discussed at that time. According to the first, the specific purpose of the controlled economy was to bring the Depression under control and prepare for a war economy. Discussion was restricted to these purposes: how to effect "control", concrete policy measures, and the special theories underlying them. In other words, "control" was treated in the main in a technical and functional way, which implied that state economic control contained the seeds of its own demise: once the war ended, it would disappear, as the conditions that had led to its adoption were eliminated. The wartime controlled economy was a case in point, though it would not necessarily be a short-lived policy if preparations for total war by the state are included. This model sees the controlled economy as an interim stage in an economic system for national defence.

The second model was more general, concerned with capitalism and the changes occurring in it, and was linked with ideas about a new system to rectify and overcome the various problems that capitalism had given rise to. The controlled economy was seen as a stage succeeding the liberal economy. State regulation of economic activities was regarded not as a temporary measure but as a permanent economic system that would continue even after the depression was over and the war concluded.

The first model is exemplified by a work called *Senji tōsei keizairon* (On the wartime controlled economy) published in 1933 by Mori Takeo (1889-1981), an army major and a teacher in the Military Paymasters' School. Mori analysed European policies during World War I in terms of the control of production, labour, consumption, distribution, trade, prices, finances, credit and so on, in order to study the relationship between total war and the controlled economy. In his understanding, "control" was limited first to the elimination of unnecessary expenditure in management based on the laissez-faire economy, and second to the rationalization of the national economy and the comprehensive deployment of resources. He opposed any "permanent change" to the guiding principles of the peacetime economy. This model can also be seen in the work of the Marxian economist Arisawa Hiromi of the Tokyo Imperial University, who played an important role in the Showa Research Association,[110] and

---

109 See References (*Nihon tōsei keizai zenshū*, 1933-34) for details of the individual volumes and their authors.

110 For Arisawa, see Gao 1994, 1997.

who was also active in the research section of the Army Finance Bureau (the so-called Akimaru Unit).[111] Arisawa made a special study of national mobilization and economics during World War I, and in *Sangyō dōin keikaku* (Planning industrial mobilization, a volume in the above-mentioned "Collected Works on the Japanese Controlled Economy"), he acknowledged the possibility of a controlled economy, though only in a time of war or preparation for war. However he adopted a medium-term viewpoint in *Sensō to keizai* (War and the economy), published in 1937, in view of contemporary global economies of national defence.

An example of the second model is Mukai Shikamatsu's general remarks about the controlled economy in *Tōsei keizai genri* (Principles of the controlled economy), published as the first volume of the "Collected Works on the Japanese Controlled Economy". Other studies according to this model include *Sangyō tōseiron* (On industrial control), a 1937 work by Akamatsu Kaname (1896-1974) of the Nagoya Higher Commercial School, the *Tōsei keizai no riron* (Theory of the controlled economy, 1938) by Hon'iden Yoshio (1892-1978) of Tokyo Imperial University and *Bōeki tōsei no kenkyū* (A study of trade control, 1935) by Taniguchi Yoshihiko (1891-1956) of Kyoto Imperial University.[112] Also falling into this category is the study by Arisawa Hiromi of cartels and industrial associations in Japan and their regulation by the state, in relation to the present stage of capitalism, in *Nihon kōgyō tōseiron* (On industrial control in Japan, 1937), a subject he had been interested in since analysing the process of capital accumulation and concentration in various countries in his *Karuteru, torasto, kontsuerun* (Cartels, Trusts, Konzerns, 1931). Further, Inomata Tsunao, a lecturer of economics at Waseda University, developed the criticisms of the controlled economy by Mukai Shikamatsu and others from a Marxist standpoint in his *Tōsei keizai hihan* (Criticism of the controlled economy), as did the Marxian scholar Sakisaka Itsurō, a professor at the Kyushu Imperial University, in his *Tōsei keizairon sōkan* (General view of the debate over the controlled economy),

---

111 Other influential economists also associated with this unit included Takemura Tadao, Miyakawa Minoru (1896-1985) of Rikkyō University, Nawa Tōichi (1906-78) of the Osaka University of Commerce, and Nakayama Ichirō (1898-1980) of the Tokyo University of Commerce. See the June 1940 article about the Akimaru Unit in *Shōwa shakai keizai shiryō shūsei*, vol. 10, 1985, the Introduction to *Nakayama Ichirō zenshū*, and Akimaru 1988, p. 20 et seq. See also Wakimura, 1997. In English, see Hein 2004.

112 Taniguchi was purged from the university after World War II because his publications were considered to be support militarism.

both of which were published in 1934 in "Collected Works on the Japanese Controlled Economy".[113] Since their arguments were confined to a criticism of ideas to reform capitalism, they can be said to belong to the second model. Takemura Tadao (1905-87) of Keio Gijuku University (from which he was forced to resign after World War II), the author of *Tōsei keizai to keiki hendō* (The controlled economy and economic fluctuations, 1938), also placed the greatest importance on changes in the economic structure of capitalism, and regarded the controlled economy to be the stage following on from liberal capitalism and monopolistic capitalism.

In the early period of the debate, Marxian economists like Arisawa, Inomata and Sakisaka just managed to be able to contribute critical arguments to its development, but they were soon completely suppressed by the state. As a result, later debate on the subject came to be closely connected with the wartime economy, and, as was apparent in the 1940 publications of Hon'iden and Taniguchi, *Shintaiseika no keizai* (Economics under the New Order) and *Shintaisei no riron* (Theory of the New Order) respectively, it was linked to the ideology of the New Order.[114] The ideas discussed in these works, such as a "new stage of a controlled economy" and a "national cooperative economy" where the public good took priority over the individual interest, and the historical necessity of the new economic order in the context of the new world order, attracted enormous popular interest. This is clear from the fact that Hon'iden's work had reached its sixteenth printing within months of its publication, and Taniguchi's was reprinted 150 times within only forty days of its first publication. These works severely criticized the priority that capitalists placed on the pursuit of profits, and declared that the controlled economy, in seeking a "new economic order", was capable of bringing structural reform to the capitalist economy. In 1939, Ryū Shintarō

---

113 Inomata Tsunao had founded Japan's original Communist Party. He lost his position at Waseda University following his arrest in the first Communist Party Incident in June 1923, when police arrested more than a hundred left-wing sympathizers under the Radical Social Movements Control Law (1922). For a short biography, see Beckmann and Ōkubo 1969, p. 366. See also Kasza 1993, p. 48. Sakisaka Itsurō was dismissed from his position at Kyūshū Imperial University in 1928, following the March 15 Incident. He then became a journalist and political activist, and was reinstated at Kyūshū University in 1945 and became its president the following year. See Marshall 1992, p. 205, Barshay 2004, p. 88.

114 The New Order movement refers to proposals for a raft of political, economic, and other reforms in the years 1940 and 1941, and is particularly associated with Konoe Fumimaro and reform bureaucrats who were influenced by the views of the Showa Research Association. See Berger 1983.

published *Nihon keizai no saihensei* (Reorganizing the Japanese economy), which also went through twenty-four printings in four months.[115]

This second model of the discussion, taking place against the war with China, developed into new areas in conjunction with ideas about reforming existing capitalistic economics and constructing a New Order. As it developed, it was coloured by concepts associated with the overthrow of the old world order: a new East Asian order (*Tō-a shintaisei*), a new world order, and a cooperative and totalitarian state based on the emperor system and its ideology. Examples of such thinking are two Kyoto Imperial University scholars, Ishikawa Kōji (1892-1976), who wrote *Shintaisei no shidō genri* (Guiding principles of the New Order) in 1940, and Sakuta Sōichi (1878-1973), who wrote *Keizai no michi* (The way of the economy) in 1941. Ishikawa talked of an emperor-centric national community and Sakuta proposed "restoring" the way of *musubi* ("creation") as the principle of economic life.[116]

We will now look more closely at the thought of Mukai Shikamatsu and Hon'iden Yoshio, two men who stood at the heart of the second model of the debate.

The Perception of Capitalism

(1) The view of capitalism behind the Important Industries Control Law

The Important Industries Control Law enacted in 1931 both promoted cartelization among industries at a policy level, and made it possible for the government

---

115 For Ryū's ideas on the controlled economy, see Nakamura and Hara 1973. For Ryū's connection with the Shōwa Research Association, see Shōwa dōjinkai ed. 1968, Sakai 1992. In English, see Fletcher 1975. Taniguchi Yoshihiko and Ōkōchi Kazuo (1905-84) were also associated with this group. Ōkōchi was a professor in the Faculty of Economics at the Tokyo Imperial University, and its president 1963-1968. For Ōkōchi's stance on the controlled economy, see especially Takabatake 1959-62, p. 217 et seq. For a comparison of the ideas on economic reform between Ryū and Shibata Kei (1902-86) of Kyoto University, see Yagi 1999, chapter 8. Shibata was initially purged after World War II, but after reinstatement was a professor at Yamaguchi University, Aoyama Gakuin University, and Kyūshū Sangyō University.

116 Sakuta wrote that *musubi* was an "ancient" concept referring to the "act of becoming" or "creation" and signifying the "spirit of generation". Sakuta 1941, pp. 289, 290. According to the *Encyclopedia of Shinto* (Kokugakuin daigaku), *musubi* is the "workings that cause heaven, earth, and all things to come into being." The so-called "creator" deities were believed to "possess the ability to inspire and motivate a person's spirit in situations where it is weakened and approaching defeat."

to order the revocation or modification of cartel agreements that were not in the public interest. This legislation, which had been prepared by the Control Committee of the Temporary Industrial Rationalization Bureau (*Rinji sangyō gōrikyoku)* set up by the Ministry of Commerce and Industry in 1930,[117] was an important first step towards state intervention in capitalistic profit-making activities. It represented a stimulative measure, promoting voluntary industrial cartelization to combat the economic slump that had taken place against the backdrop of world depression, and targeting overproduction and excessive competition in particular. Underlying it, though, was a clear perception of how the capitalistic economy was developing.

Matsuoka Kinpei (1876-1960), a baron and a doctor of law who was a former director of the East Asia Economic Research Centre, 1911-1921, a Mitsubishi executive, and a senior adviser to the Temporary Industrial Rationalization Bureau, was the chairman of the Control Committee responsible for preparing the bill.[118] He held that organizing the market economy through associations such as cartels was not simply a short-term policy but was in line with the way the capitalistic economy was developing. Under a *laissez-faire* system, each firm could act as it wished, resulting in industrial progress and expansion. But the capitalistic economy also promoted organization, since corporate activities were necessarily restricted by the operation of market economics that were beyond the control of individual firms. Though socialism says that production chaos is an essential flaw of capitalism, it is only a temporary phenomenon, one born out of the operation of extreme *laissez-faire* in the past. At the present time, says Matsuoka, capitalism is gradually moving from noninterventionist to normative, from the individual to the group, from a *laissez-faire* economy to economic

117 The Bureau was the main government organ promoting "rationalization", coordinating with business leaders with a long-held similar interest. The Japan Industrial Club had sent a group of business leaders to the United States and Europe from October 1921 to May 1922, in part to study the state of "rationalization" there. Leading figures from economic circles held responsible positions in the Bureau; members of its Advisory Council included Nakajima Kumakichi of the Japan Industrial Club, Ōkōchi Masatoshi, Matsuoka Kinpei, Isaka Takashi (1870-1949) of the Yokohama Fire Insurance Company, and Makita Tamaki (1871-1943), president of Mitsui Coal Mining. See Sasaki 1998, p. 168. For scientific management and the state, see Tsutsui 1998, p. 72, chapter 2. The Control Committee was one of the most important standing committees of the Bureau, and one of its main functions was legislation concerning the combination of enterprises and associations. *Sangyō gōrika*, vol. 1 (December 1930), pp. 22 ff. For the Bureau itself, see Tsūshō sangyōshō ed. 1961.

118 *Sangyō gōrika,* 3 (June 1931), pp. 7-44. In English, see Tsutsui 1998, p. 64.

dirigisme. "As scholars such as Werner Sombart and Eugen Schmalenbach in Germany, and John Maynard Keynes in England have made clear, it is inevitable and unavoidable that we are propelled forward socially by the great power of the times that transcends the individual. We can distinctly perceive in the economic policies of modern states how things are moving according to this law of evolution", he wrote.[119]

Matsuoka did not regard cartels and trusts simply as discrete phenomena but understood them as corresponding to a new stage in the development of capitalism, as it headed towards an organized market economy and globalization. Through organization, capitalism reaches a higher developmental stage ("a new age marked by the organized economy"). At that point, the state may allow regulatory agreements among firms, but must at the same time supervise them. Matsuoka drew particular attention to the German cartel law (*Kartellrecht*) of 1923 as an example of this. The German legislation both recognized cartels, and provided supervision and control over them to prevent abuse. Matsuoka also accepted the theories of German scholars acknowledging that cartels contributed to mutual collaboration among firms and industrial rationalization, and also had a regulatory role.[120] This is the positive significance that he saw in the Important Industries Control Law.

(2) The controlled economy as a modification of capitalism

The committee of the Temporary Industrial Rationalization Bureau that prepared the Important Industries Control Law included, besides Matsuoka and its secretary Kishi Nobusuke (1896-1987), then a bureaucrat with the Ministry of Commerce and Industry,[121] two scholars: Mukai Shikamatsu, then a professor

119 Ibid. pp. 12-13.

120 Matsuoka argued about German views on cartel law based on the works of scholars such as Robert Liefmann (1874-1941), Siegfried Tschierschky (1872-1937), Richard Passow (1880-1949), Herbert von Beckerath (1886-1966) and Oswald Lehnich (1895-1939). For their works, see References.

121 Kishi Nobusuke was secretary to the Minister of Commerce and Industry when he was sent to Europe in 1930 to study the development of rationalization, especially in Germany (*Sangyō gōrika*, vol. 4 [January 1932], Sasaki 1998). He had previously (1926) been sent to the United States, and also travelled in Britain and Germany. He was interested at that time in the Taylor and Fordist movements for scientific management, and also in the promotion of trusts and cartels in Germany to improve industrial efficiency. He became Vice-Minister of Commerce and Industry in 1940 and Minister in 1941. He was imprisoned until 1948 as a Class A war crimes suspect

at Keio Gijuku University and a specialist in economics and management, and Tanaka Kōtarō (1890-1974) of the Tokyo Imperial University, a specialist in commercial law and later in international law (in 1946 he became the Minister of Education and in 1950 the Chief Justice of the Supreme Court). Also contributing to drawing up the legislation, were leading figures from the world of government and finance, like the "economic bureaucrat" Yoshino Shinji (1888-1971), the Minister of Commerce and Industry in the First Konoe Cabinet, 1937, and adviser to Manchukuo and, in 1955, the Minister of Transport; Watanabe Tetsuzō (1885-1980), a professor in the Economics Faculty of Tokyo Imperial University until 1927, and then director of the Japan Chamber of Commerce and Industry; Takashima Seiichi (1885-1960) of the Japan Economic Federation (Nihon keizai renmeikai), and Zen Keinosuke (1887-1951), formerly a bureaucrat and then managing director of the Japan Industrial Club (Nihon kōgyō kurabu). In 1935 Mukai was added to the staff of the Cabinet Research Bureau (*Naikaku chōsakyoku*), joining the reformist entrepreneur Ōkōchi Masatoshi (1878-1952), head of the Institute of Physical and Chemical Research (Rikagaku kenkyūjo: Riken). Also on the staff were reformist bureaucrats like Uchida Genbei (1899 -1982) of the Cabinet Planning Board (Kikakuin), Wada Hiroo (1903-67), a reformist bureaucrat in the Department of Agriculture, the Cabinet Planning Board, and a member of the Shōwa Research Foundation,[122] and Hashii Makoto (1902-77) and well-known economic analyists like Yamazaki Yasuzumi (1894-1966) and Takahashi Kamekichi, who studied industrial issues.[123]

Mukai was not only a prominent academician in the field of managerial economy, but was also at the core of policy-making and involved with control legislation well before the breakout of full-scale war in China. In 1937 he left Keio Gijuku University and joined the board of the Nagoya Chamber of Commerce and Industry. Then in 1941 he became managing director of the Central Society

---

though he was never indicted. He served as Prime Minister 1957-1960. Sasaki 1998, p. 166. In English, see Johnson 1982, p. 103.

122 Wada Hiroo, Minister of Agriculture and Forestry and Vice-Chairman of the Japan Socialist Party after the war, was arrested in 1941 in the Cabinet Planning Board (Kikakuin) Incident. The Board had advocated a radical New Economic Order; it was aborted in 1940 because of opposition from business leaders and seventeen members of the Board were arrested as subversives the following year. Wagner 1991 regards this as a struggle between "conservative" and "'innovate', economic-oriented bureaucrats" (p. 225).

123 Itō 1974. For Takahashi Kamekichi, see also Hoston 1984.

of Commercial Associations (*Shōgyō kumiai chūōkai*)[124] and was also connected with the policy section of the Imperial Rule Assistance Association (*Taisei yokusankai*), a national organization formed in October 1940 by the Prime Minister, Konoe Fumimaro, to unite all political parties into a single structure to promote national unity.[125] He was an influential advocate of economic control in both the prewar and wartime periods, and in this sense his activities in the first half of the 1930s are significant.[126] After the war, Mukai returned to academic life, teaching at Aoyama Gakuin University and Chūō University, among others, and he also served as head of the Japan Society of Commercial Sciences.[127]

Mukai's activities took place against the backdrop of his academic achievements as an economist. In 1929 he published *Keiei keizaigaku sōron* (Introduction to business economics), focusing on joint-stock companies and the participation of workers in management from the point of view of business economics. Two years later, following a tour of the United States, Great Britain and Germany in 1930, he put out *Sangyō no gōrika* (Industrial rationalization), describing the moves towards rationalization in Great Britain and Germany. His ideas about the controlled economy developed from this, and he elaborated on them in his contribution to the "Collected works on the Japanese controlled economy", *Tōsei keizai genri* (Principles of the controlled economy). This overview occupies an important position in the development of the later debate about the controlled economy, and his arguments for restructuring capitalism were linked ideologically with Ryū Shintarō's views about the reorganization of the Japanese economy

---

124 The Central Society of Commercial Associations was founded in 1935 and became a corporation in 1938. It was the central organization of commercial associations of small and medium traders, and in 1938 it consisted of about 2200 associations with 180,000 members. Mukai joined it in 1940 and became its managing director the following year. The main task of the Society was at first to support the commercial activities of Japanese tradesmen by supporting regional associations. Under the war economy the Society and the regional associations were required to work with the government and all traders were required to belong. Thus in 1939 there were around 4000 associations with 3 million traders. Mukai played an important role, conveying government policy to the associations.

125 For details about the Imperial Rule Assistance Association, see Tipton 1997, p. 214, Itoh 2003, pp. 67-70, de Bary ed. 2008, p. 621.

126 Mukai published a stream of books between 1926 and 1934 dealing with his research on stocks and commodity transactions. He also published a number of books on the distribution system (see References).

127 For a detailed biography, see *Keiō gijuku daigaku hyakunenshi, bekkan (daigakuhen)*, p. 145 et seq.

that impacted on plans for a New Economic Order, especially on the views of reformist bureaucrats on the Cabinet Planning Board.

A second important figure in the early debate about the controlled economy was Hon'iden Yoshio. Like Mukai, he was concerned with the practicalities of the controlled economy, outside the university environment. He had served in the Agriculture and Commerce Ministry until 1921, when he returned to his alma mater Tokyo Imperial University to teach economics. In 1939 he had protested the suspension of Hijikata Seibi, a fellow professor in the Economics Faculty of Tokyo Imperial University in the so-called "Hiraga Purge"[128] and resigned. The same year he was appointed to the Central Price Control Cooperation Council (*Chūō bukka tōsei kyōryoku kaigi*), and successively filled posts as head of the economic policy section of the Imperial Rule Assistance Association and of the Cotton and Staple Fiber Control Association.[129] In 1946, under the Occupation, he was legally prohibited from entering public affairs, but after the purge was rescinded, he became a professor successively at Risshō, Meiji and Dokkyō Universities.[130]

The Central Price Control Cooperation Council brought together representatives from economic groups from around the country. In 1940, when the New Economic Order became a subject of discussion, the Council advocated structural improvements for such economic groups, based on the priority of the public interest and the leadership principle (the authority of a single leader with absolute power). As the only full-time director of the Council, Hon'iden contributed greatly to the drawing up of these ideas. His understanding of the controlled

---

128 The Hiraga Purge refers to the expulsion of a number of professors of the Faculty of Economics at the Tokyo Imperial University by its president, Hiraga Yuzuru, in an effort to overcome factionalism. For further details, see Marshall 1978, 1992, Barshay 1998.

129 Control associations were established under the Important Industry Association Law of 1941. Nominally, they were responsible to, and under the control of, ministries. Twelve industries were organized into control associations in October 1941 (iron and steel, coal, foreign trade, mining, precision machinery, automobiles, vehicles, industrial machines, electrical machinery, metalworking, cement and shipbuilding). The Cotton and Staple Fiber Control Association was set up in the second wave in 1942 and Hon'iden was appointed to head it. It consisted of around thirty large textile companies as well as all regional textile associations. It became the central state organ for controlling the production and sale of textiles. Control Associations enjoyed great autonomy in practice, and received broad powers to allocate raw materials and regulate output. Hon'iden occupied a very important office. See Cohen 1949 [2000], pp. 59 ff.

130 Katō ed. 1979. For his wartime activities, see Hon'iden zeminaaru no kai 1971, pp. 85-91 (Iwazawa, Kan'ichi).

economy appears within them as a course of action representing the stance of business circles in response to the new conditions.

In 1938, while still a professor at Tokyo Imperial University, he had published *Tōsei keizai no riron* (Theory of the controlled economy) with the intention of "compiling into a single work theories associated with the controlled economy as it has been conceived". Both Mukai and Hon'iden shared common ground in their ideas about the controlled economy in that basically they both wanted reform as a premise for anything concerning the capitalist system as it stood. Hon'iden did not have a plan for reform like Mukai, but his actions were more politicized. In his 1938 work, he called on economists to "set up countermeasures for, and research into, political awakening, national enlightenment and postwar economic policies in Japan and abroad."

He set up an organization called the Kakushinsha (Reform Group) with financial assistance from Kagakushugi kōgyōsha, a publishing and advertising company belonging to the Riken combine managed by Ōkōchi Masatoshi. This company published many books and pamphlets concerning the development of production and enterprises, especially about the scientific management ideas of Ōkochi. Among the economists who answered Hon'iden's call and joined were Tanabe Tadao (1891-1967), Nakanishi Torao (1896-1975), Hijikata Seibi, and Hashizume Akio (1899-1975), all from Tokyo Imperial University; Tanaka Seiichi (1911-1998) and Nabeshima Tatsu (1907-1990) from Rikkyō University; Ono Takeo (1883-1949) and Matsumoto Nobutsugu (1904-1984.) from Hōsei University; Sugimori Kōjirō (1881-1968), Hayashi Kimio (1883-1947) and Nakamura Saichi (1891-1978) from Waseda University; Kada Tetsuji (1895-1964) and Kinbara Kennosuke (1897-1959) from Keiō Gijuku University; Ueda Tatsuosuke (1892-1956), Igaya Yoshikazu (1901-1980), Itō Hanya and Yamaguchi Shigeru (1893-1974) from the Tokyo University of Commerce; Sakuta Sōichi, Taniguchi Yoshihiko, Yagi Yoshinosuke (1895-1944) and Shibata Kei from Kyoto Imperial University; Kawada Shirō (1883-1942), Fujita Keizō (1894-1985), Hori Tsuneo (1896-1981) and Asaka Sueki (1896-1971) from Osaka University of Commerce; Kitayama Fukujirō (1901-1984) from Taihoku Imperial University (Taiwan); Akamatsu Kaname, Miyata Kiyozō (1896-1977) and Sakai Shōzaburō (1901-1981) from Nagoya Higher School of Commerce; Nakamura Tsunejirō (1907-1980) from Fukushima Higher School of Commerce; and Furuya Yoshisada (1893-1966) from Kansei Gakuin University.[131]

131 Katō ed. 1979, p. 258. For Kakushinsha, see Naimushō keihokyoku ed. 1938, p. 359, *Tokyo Asahi Shinbun*, July 24, 1938, *Kokushi daijiten*, "Kakushinsha". The list of names of taken from *Tokyo Asahi Shinbun* July 24, 1938.

Though Hon'iden left the group after he resigned from Tokyo Imperial University, he continued the ideas behind it in his 1940 work *Shintaiseika no keizai* (Economics under the New Order), which played a practical role linking the new trends in the world of economics with Konoe's New Order movement.[132]

(3) The liberal economy, rationalization and organization

At the beginning of his "Theory of the controlled economy" (1938), Hon'iden wrote: "At the present time, the death-knell of the *laissez-faire* economy is ringing everywhere. Some people are shedding copious tears and are waiting for the miracle of resurrection to occur. Others rejoice at the dawn chimes that announce the birth of a new age. But in either case, simply to deny the splendid contributions the *laissez-faire* economy has made to humankind for more than a century is to deliberately close one's eyes to the facts." (p. 1)

Underlying the debate about the controlled economy was the conviction that the *laissez-faire* economy had reached its end. What "contributions" had it made? Hon'iden understood the *laissez-faire* economy to be a market economy, based on unfettered competition among firms to secure profits, and so technological improvement and rationalization in production were inseparably related to it. Because the purpose of capitalistic "rationalism" was "to make money", it led to industrial concentration (the dominance of a few large firms) and mergers, but also gave rise to "abuses". In other words, while the point of the controlled economy is to correct these abuses, the "contributions" of capitalism, that is the rationalization of production, must be preserved and promoted.

Managerial and industrial rationalization was a very important policy issue in Japan at the time, and a core topic discussed by the Temporary Industrial Rationalization Bureau. Mukai Shikamatsu too had a great interest in the question, particularly regarding the development of specialization, the evolution of a managerial body to organize it, and the growth of technological rationalization. He consolidated these interests in his theory of a controlled economy. As we have seen, Mukai, as a member of the Temporary Industrial Rationalization Bureau, had been involved with drawing up the draft for the Important Industries Control Law, and a large task that had confronted him was how to reconcile plans to strengthen cartelization with policies to encourage rationalization.[133]

---

132 Hon'iden 1940 (6th edition 1941).

133 Miyajima 1984. Refer also to *Sangyō gōrika* 1 (1930), and Kishi 1934.

Let us first summarize Mukai's views about rationalization.[134] Rationalization was the conscious employment of rational means and it was implemented primarily in order to lower actual production costs. "Technological rationalization" (the rational use of the means of production and of labour) was particularly important and basically meant the standardizing (or "patterning," Jap. *kata*) of machines, parts, the work process, and finished articles. All economic activity should be part of such "patterning", which included standardization, streamlining, and the unification of standards.

Rationalization, as control towards a uniform purpose, developed in the form of fit-for-purpose organization and control in the technological, managerial and industrial fields. (a) Technological rationalization meant rationalizing the work process; this involved analysing, streamlining and standardizing each phase of the process and introducing automation and mechanization on that basis. (b) Managerial rationalization consisted of analyzing the components of the management system (workers, products, job functions), then standardizing and "patterning" them to achieve mechanization (division of function, piece work, streamlining) and a planned and rationalized system of management. Mukai pointed out two examples of this: the Scientific Management of Frederick Winslow Taylor (1856-1915) and the assembly line production method of Henry Ford (1863-1947). (c) Industrial rationalization, on the other hand, involved the rationalization of both management and business within a particular industry; it was expressed by agreements over product standardization, unification of standards, and standardization of trading conditions, against a backdrop of specialization (*Spezialisierung*). Mukai, who understood that such streamlining should be based on purposeful control by people, paid close attention to studies of Taylor's Scientific Management in the United States (for example, decreasing waste

134 See Mukai 1933, chapters 5 and 6. In March 1930, Mukai gave a lecture on rationalization to members of the influential Japan Industrial Club and then studied rationalization in the United States and Europe until autumn that year. He was particular interested in the German case, and his stay there was the longest. He spent three months in Berlin, supported by Fritz Reuter of the Reichskuratorium für Wirtschaftlichkeit, editor of *Handbuch der Rationalisierung* (Berlin 1930). During his stay he visited large factories, such as Siemens, AEG and Borsig, under his guidance. He published the results of this investigation first serially in the Osaka Mainichi newspaper and the Tokyo Nichinichi newspaper, and then as a book (*Sangyō no gōrika*, 1931). His analysis and evaluation of rationalization, especially in Germany, was thus widely known, not only among academics but also among business leaders, bureaucrats and intellectuals.

through time-and-motion studies, saving time and space, achieving standardization for such practices, dividing brain work from physical work, and improving the labour system) and to the diffusion of scientific management throughout industry as a whole through the work of the Taylor Society. At that time, Mukai differentiated this Taylorist scientific management from the Ford system. He recognised that Fordist mass production and mechanization were based on mass consumption, while Taylor's scientific management could be applied unconditionally. Thus the Taylor method seemed much more suitable in Japan, where the scale of consumption was very different to that of the United States. This fact encouraged Mukai to look at the development of rationalization in Germany, where the market was significantly smaller than the American.

The German rationalization movement differed from that in the United States. It had developed out of an emphasis on reconstructing German industry as a whole, and was characterized by a tendency to involve society overall, which extended down to discrete units of management. Its aim was to diffuse scientific management and mass production, and it was promoted as a "cooperative endeavor" for industry as a whole, over and above the level of individual management. Four areas were of particular importance: (a) allocation and specialization of firms to designated sections and work processes in the industry; (b) creation thereby of the possibility of mass production for specialized firms; (c) concentration and cartels among production units to achieve this; and (d) agreements between firms to streamline and unify planning. By this means, it would be possible to overcome Germany's lack of conditions for mass consumption.

Despite the differences in industrial conditions between Germany and the United States, the Fordist method was thus pursued also in Germany. Mukai pointed out further that it could be achieved on the one hand by doing away with inefficient management through the fusion of firms by large corporations in the same industry, combining related manufacturing processes, and introducing automation in large enterprises, and on the other, by controlling the administrative side of things through industrial agreements.

Of the three types of rationalization mentioned above, Mukai favoured the industrial, that is, associations and agreements, understanding this to be a feature of German-type rationalization and he recommended that Japan look to this model.[135]

---

135 Contemporary literature in English concerning German rationalization includes Warriner 1931, National Industrial Conference Board 1931, Brady 1933 (1974), Bonn 1934, 1935 (reprint). Bonn wrote: "The term rationalization was first popularized in Germany, where indeed it became a catchword for any and all forms of

Such industrial rationalization, depending on combinations and cooperation among firms, meant in actuality cartels and trusts. Mukai drew attention to the fact that a distinction had to be drawn here with rationalization simply for the purpose of industrial concentration, in particular for liquidating enterprises, improving financial affairs and controlling markets. The idea that rationalization meant cartels and trusts was an English way of thinking, he said, and Japan had been influenced by it, but he criticized it as not being appropriate.[136] This point is related to what later became a significant problem, the relationship between the reason for promoting cartelization, as contained in the Important Industries Control Law, and the evaluation of state regulation. In any case, the questions of associations among enterprises, state regulation and economic cartelization to bring them about, and state control over them were fundamental discussion points during the early period of the debate about the controlled economy. It is significant that discussion about industrial rationalization was presented as belonging to this debate, in terms, for example, of specialization and the division of labour through agreements among firms, and of the unification of standards.

Mukai was not the only person to draw attention to rationalization and scientific management, for many Japanese scholars in the prewar period shared his interest. There was increasingly widespread popular interest in scientific management at the time, and Watanabe Tetsuzō pointed out in his 1930 work *Sangyō gōrika* (Industrial rationalization), that the term 'industrial rationalization' "showed signs of becoming widely known" (p. 1). The activities of the Temporary Industrial Rationalization Bureau were a clear expression of this. This interest strengthened substantially during the period of war as the most important topic

---

industrial reorganization. Scientific management and industrial combination were to be merged in a new system of industrial organization" (*Ibid.*, p. 117).

136 German rationalization attracted considerable attention in Britain. This interest focused chiefly on scientific management. However, the economic crisis of 1929 caused large-scale stagnation of rationalization. Referring to the steel industry in the early 1930s, Aldcroft stated, "To assist the process the central organization of the industry was strengthened by the establishment of the British Iron and Steel Federation, whose chief duty was to foster schemes of reorganization… Thus suppression of competition rather technical reconstruction and rationalization of industry appears to have been the primary objective of the controlling authorities". Aldcraft 1970, p. 173. Kishi Nobusuke (see Note 121 above), a leading member of the Bureau, pointed out that "in the United Kingdom, the word "rationalization", an important issue there, is taken to mean creating combinations or "cartels"." Kishi 1932, p. 47.

in the policy to expand productivity as a condition for establishing a wartime economy.[137] In other words, the debates about rationalization and the controlled economy were not opposed to each other, but rather inseparably bound together. This however posed a conundrum for scholars: how can the controlled economy, with its regulations about profit-making activities, be melded with rationalization, bound up as it is with the pursuit of profit? Resolving it was a very difficult task.

Industrial rationalization did not simply concern technology and labour; it was also related to the circumstances of management and of the enterprises through which rationalization would be brought about.[138] This is why one of the most fundamental discussion points in the debate about the controlled economy was the separation of ownership and management in joint-stock companies and the dissociation of stock-holders (owners) from management, and the subsequent expansion of the role of managers. Mukai Shikamatsu attempted to solve the problem of the lack of interest by stock-holders in rationalization through his idea of the autonomous corporation, where functioning managers were the mainstay of the company (see Chapter One). Herein too lay a difficult problem concerning the relationship between profit-making and rationalization. Several years later, Ryū Shintarō of the Showa Research Association emphasized the importance of technological universality, the "liberation" of technology from "subordination to the free economy" and "autonomy" in regards technological progress in the manufacturing process. His perspective on rationalization was linked with a criticism of the primacy of profit maximization, and he understood that the "standardized production" and "a functional organization" that

137 A large number of studies concerning production control and labour management were published for an enthusiastic readership. *Sangyō nōritsuron* (On industrial efficiency) by Ueno Yōichi (1883-1957) of the Industrial Efficiency Institute (Sangyō Nōritsu Kenkyūjo) in Osaka was published in 1929 and had gone through thirty reprints by 1940, and *Seisan kanri* (Production Control) by Muramoto Fukumatsu (1890-1973) was published in 1937 and had reached its fifteenth reprinting three years later. See Sasaki 1998 for the expansion of scientific management in Japan. In English, see Tsutsui 1998, chapter 2.

138 Magnus W. Alexander, President of the National Industrial Conference Board in the United States, stated: "Rationalization, or putting reason into industry, is understood in Europe to refer to the organization of technical processes in individual establishments and the co-ordination of these units in various co-operative forms to regulate production and distribution. It thus includes all that is known in the United States under the term of scientific management, but it goes beyond this into the problems of economic organization and combination." National Industrial Conference Board 1931, vi.

were central to management, as opposed to profit-making, were at the core of control and planning.[139]

The debate on the controlled economy was indelibly associated with rationalization and the relationship between ownership and management. Hon'iden Yoshio stated that rationalization was not a matter of private interests but had to be linked to the "public interest" (*kōkyō no rieki*), and he pointed out that "the controlled economy is one element in the rationalizing of production." Kojima Seiichi also linked the two discourses in his *Sangyō gōrika* (Industrial rationalization) of 1929.[140]

(4) Towards Corporate Concentration, the Formation of Monopolies, and Economic Organization

The capitalistic economy gives rise to corporate concentration and monopolies. Hon'iden Yoshio drew attention to this phenomenon, understanding it as follows: Free competition among firms demands improvements in production for the cheaper cost of the product within the individual firm. This brings a growth of fixed capital that makes capital transfer difficult, and hampers automatic regulation in the market through a price mechanism. As capitalistic expansion into foreign areas reach a bottle-neck, the economic sphere for capitalism becomes satiated. In this way the harmful effects of free competition make themselves felt. Business leaders should work together to safeguard themselves from the disorder of free competition, forming monopolistic groups such as cartels, trusts and combines (*Konzern*), and so arrive at an age of monopoly capitalism. The price of products will no longer be decided through free market competition among enterprises, and determined by large firms in a monopolistic position. Self-regulation of business activities by large companies and private monopolies in the market will result. Hon'iden asserted that as people gained greater realization of the "serious repercussions" (*jūdai na eikyō*) of monopoly pricing, enterprises would become more self-critical (*jiko hihan*). Business leaders of monopoly economics realized the contradictions associated with the capitalistic economy, such as confrontations between monopolies and antimonopolies, and between capital returns and earned income, consumer poverty, and straitened circumstances among workers and farmers. They perceived, in particular, the danger that this would lead to a prolongation of the crisis that intensively manifests the evils of

139 Ryū 1939, p. 128 et seq. Nakamura and Hara 1973, p. 83. In English, see Fletcher 1982, Gao 1997, p. 101.

140 Kojima 1929.

capitalism. Hon'iden pointed out that in such circumstances, there emerges the "possibility of organizing the economy through conscious regulation".[141]

Mukai Shikamatsu also drew attention to an aspiration towards economic stability and a tendency towards economic organization on the part of enterprises as a means to combat the harmful influences of the *laissez-faire* economy. He attached great importance to the American situation where society's opinion about monopolies and combines was in the process of changing from criticism to approval. His chief concern was the equilibrium between economic stability and monopolies and their rationalization. Thus we see both Mukai and Hon'iden concerned about the impasse in the *laissez-faire* economy and tending towards a controlled and planned economy.

What kind of response did Mukai consider it necessary to make, from the viewpoint of economic stability and rationalization, as monopolies like cartels and trusts began to appear and economic systematization take place? This was a question that affected him personally, in that he had been closely involved with the drafting of the Important Industries Control Law. He recognized that cartels and trusts fell under industrial rationalization for the industries concerned, but he thought that the combination of firms only for market regulation was not rational. On the other hand, he agreed that such associations among enterprises did create stability at a time when there was an impasse in free competition and economic instability. He had taken note of the Swope Plan in the United States, which he regarded as a typical American strategy to reorganize capitalism, and he highly appreciated the efforts of Gerard Swope (1872-1957), the president of the General Electric Company, to organize the economy by means of trade associations as a way for capitalists to plan for the autonomous regulation of the economy. Swope introduced the basic principles of his plan as follows:[142]

(1) Every effort should be made to stabilize industry and thereby stabilize employment to give the worker regularity and continuity of employment, and when this is impracticable, unemployment insurance should be provided.

(2) Organized industry should take the lead, recognizing its responsibility to its employees, to the public, and to its stockholders – rather than that democratic society should act through its government.

(3) There should be standardized forms of reports so that stockholders may be properly informed. As a result of the steady increase in number and size of corporations and number of shareholders, there has been much discussion

141 Hon'iden 1938.

142 Frederick 1932, chapter XIV, especially pp. 316 ff.

of the uniformity, frequency, and regularity of reports of corporate activities, and considerable criticism of the form of these reports.

(4) Production and consumption should be coordinated on a broader and more intelligent basis thus tending to regularize employment and thereby removing fear from the minds of the workers as to continuity of employment… This should be done preferably by the joint participation and joint administration of management and employees. These things cannot be done by an individual unit – organized industry must do them.

(5) If organized industry is to undertake this work, every effort should be made to preserve the benefits of individual originality, initiative, and enterprise, and to see that the public is assured that its interests will be protected, and this can be done most effectively by working through the agency of the Federal Government.

Mukai attached a great deal of importance to the Swope plan to organize trade associations that recommended:

1. All industrial and commercial companies (including subsidiaries) with 50 or more employees, and doing an interstate business, may form a trade association which shall be under the supervision of a federal body referred to later.

2. These trade associations may outline trade practices, business ethics, methods of standard accounting and cost practice, standard forms of balance sheet and earnings statement, etc., and may collect and distribute information on volume of business transacted, inventories of merchandise on hand, simplification and standardization of products, stabilization of prices, and all matters which may arise from time to time relating to the growth and development of industry and commerce in order to promote stabilization of employment and give the best service to the public.[143]

Mukai responded to the Swope Plan, and to legislation in the United States to limit free competition in terms of trends in Japanese business circles following

143 For Mukai's opinion of the Swope Plan, see Mukai 1933, pp. 195-198, 425-430. For an outline of Swope's trade associations, see Loth 1958, pp, 204-205. See also Sutton 1975, McQuaid 1977. For the Swope Plan, see Sutton 1975, Appendix A. The Swope Plan attracted wide interest in the United States. A contemporary American wrote: "Immense interest has been shown in the Swope Plan, presented September, 1931. Not only has it been more widely discussed than any other plan, but it has received praise from a wider variety of political and social opinion. Both Left and Right have received it with great interest and considerable approval. Several editions of a book giving it in detail, plus comment, have been exhausted, and the electrical industry has taken decisive steps to adopt a considerable part of it." (Frederick 1932, p. 313).

the outbreak of Depression in 1929. Over and above that, the Important Industries Control Law had as its purpose the provision of stability and organization to the business community, and so it was "a step towards industrial rationalization", but he was critical of the fact its enabling legislation incorporated the "desires of the capitalists" and so was little better than a law to promote cartels. It was necessary, he asserted, for "cartels to organize the economy for a new age": unifying cost accounting, applying general rules for calculation cartels (organizations for calculating the normal cost of the products of member firms), protecting workers, making cartel agreements public knowledge, and publishing company reports and research results. He placed his hopes on Clause Three of the Important Industries Control Law to order alteration or abrogation of agreements that were inimical to the public interest.[144]

Hon'iden Yoshio, who regarded monopolies more highly than Mukai, expounded their necessity as a prerequisite for economic organization. He wrote: "The regulation of monopolies in a controlled economy does not mean that monopolies themselves are being rejected. Because we recognize the profit of the whole in organizing the economy, we cannot destroy the positive results of a system possessing monopolies by rejecting them." While the Important Industries Control Law promoted the organization of monopolies on one hand, Hon'iden considered that it also acted "to remove the harmful effects contingent on the organization of monopolies." He regarded it as corresponding to the amendments made by the new Nazi government in July 1933 to the 1923 Cartel Law.[145]

Arisawa Hiromi too pointed out the correspondence between the purport of the Important Industries Control Law and the 1933 German law. The Japanese legislation had grown out of "the realization that unregulated defects in Japanese industry had come to light" during the period of over-production after World War I. He stressed two points. The first was bringing stability to

144 Mukai 1933, pp. 198-207.

145 Hon'iden 1938, p. 36. Cartels were allowed to continue under the Nazi regime but they were controlled much more than previously and were used as a tool within the economic system. The first cartel decree allowed the Reichsminister of Economics to "constrain the economic freedom of action" of firms considered to be unreliably managed. The second statute of July 1933 gave the Minister the competence to create compulsory cartels, "to compel outsiders to attach themselves to existing cartels, to prohibit the erection of new enterprises and the extension of existing enterprises either in size or capacity, and to regulate the capacity of existing plants". Neumann 1942 [1944, 1967], pp. 265-267. See also Reich 1990, pp. 23-24.

industry by placing controls on it and removing the abuses of excessive competition. The second was that the law provided guidelines for governmental regulation of industry in cases of a "misuse of economic power" in business circles, and so the sound development of the national economy as a whole could be planned. However, Arisawa criticized the fact that the provisions of the law to curb the misuse of their power by cartels had been kept to a minimum. He recognized that the "initiative of businessmen" was the starting point of the law.[146]

The issue of the controlled economy was thus closely associated with the formulation of the Important Industries Control Law and it was discussed in relation to the law. The largest point of contention to emerge was the concentration of capital and its regulation. Hon'iden pointed out: "A controlled economy is required because of the present economic distress. However, if it is not based on older systems, it will end up as no more than a pipe dream. The way to bring about a new system must be conditioned by our present social foundations." Thus he understood the development of corporate concentration, especially cartels, to be the "socialization of the enterprise" (*kigyō no shakaika*). In the broadest sense, "socialization" refers to the development of the social division of labour and the productive cooperation of society as a whole, which is accelerated by production growth. Hon'iden uses the expression to refer to cartels as a combination of industrial enterprises, a form of cooperation of the productive power of the large corporations.[147]

Hon'iden regarded corporate concentration to be the basis of industrial regulation and analyzed its development in detail.[148] Corporate concentration developed together with a growth in industrial and manufacturing cooperative associations (*kyōdō kumiai*). Hon'iden recognized the significance of organizing agriculture and small industry in terms of the distribution process, and also turned his attention to state and municipal managed businesses, noting that "they were advancing steadily, and were already right in the middle of the capitalist economy." He said this offered an organizational device for the controlled economy.[149]

---

146 Arisawa 1937b. section 1, chapter 3.

147 For the definition and description of "socialization", see the entry by G. D. H. Cole on "Socialization" in Seligman ed. 1934, pp. 221-225.

148 There was a considerable amount of research into corporate concentration at this time, for example Fujita 1936, Kunihiro 1939, Takamiya 1942 (which had gone to its third printing of 5000 copies four months after publication), Shizuta 1943.

149 Hon'iden 1938, chapter 5, sections 2 and 3.

The Influence of the German Discussion about the Transformation of Capitalism

A fundamental element in the early debate about the controlled economy was, as we have seen, the recognition that the capitalist economy was in the process of transformation, and discussion about modifying capitalism developed on this basis. At that time, the arguments were grounded on economic theories and ideas about the economy developed in Europe and the United States. Particularly influential were John Maynard Keynes (*The End of Laissez-faire*, 1926), G. D. H. Cole and R. H. Tawney (guild socialism), Alfred Marshall (economic chivalry), American Fordism and Taylorism, the Swope Plan, the example of the Soviet planned economy and the discussion engendered at the World Social Economic Congress held in Amsterdam in August 1931,[150] and German and Austrian theories and ideas. All of them influenced scholars and intellectuals concerned with the subject in some form or another. However, it was German and Austrian scholarship that particularly influenced the understanding of capitalism by Mukai, Hon'iden and others.

The work of the German economists Werner Sombart and Eugen Schmalenbach left a significant imprint on the understanding of Mukai and other Japanese scholars regarding the impasse of the free economy, and the move to a bound economy or partially controlled economy. Sombart was already well-known for his research into economic history (for example, *Luxus und Kapitalismus*, translated into Japanese in 1925) and economic methodology (for example, *Die drei Nationalökonomien*, translated into Japanese in 1933). But for Mukai and others interested in the debate on the controlled economy, it was the short pamphlet *Die Zukunft des Kapitalismus* (The future of capitalism, 1932), translated into Japanese the following year, which had the greatest impact. Here Sombart summarized his lecture entitled "Wandlung des Kapitalismus" (The transformation of capitalism) that he gave at the conference of Verein für Socialpolitik (Social Policy Association) in Zurich in 1928. Analyzing trends and stages in the development of capitalism, he saw the post World War I period as being marked by the slow decline of capitalism, a stage he called Spätkapitalismus ("Late Capitalism"). At such a time, he asserted, a controlled economy that was independent and

---

150 The subject of the Congress was social economic planning and the necessity for planned adjustments of productive capacity and standards of living. H. S. Person of the Taylor Society, New York, spoke on "Scientific management as a philosophy and technique of progressive industrial stabilization". World Social Economic Planning (1932).

self-sufficient (autarkic) was necessary. A debate about these views subsequently developed in Germany, into what might be called a dispute about capitalism. Mukai and other Japanese scholars understood the situation fairly accurately, and evaluated Sombart's opinions positively against the stance of critics of Late Capitalism, like the liberal economists Christian Eckert (1874-1952) and Alfred Weber (1868-1958), and Emil Lederer (1882-1939) and others who advocated social democracy.

Christian Eckert, the first Rektor of the College of Commerce (Handelshochschule) in Köln (1919), became president of the Verein für Sozialpolitik (Social Policy Association) in 1930. He was suspended as Rektor in 1933 (to return in 1945). Alfred Weber was a professor at Heidelberg University, and was a co-founder of the German Democratic party after the First World War. He opposed National Socialism and voluntarily resigned from his academic offices in 1933 (he returned after the war). His theory of industrial location was widely known in prewar Japan. Emil Lederer was appointed an assistant professor at Heidelberg University in 1918, and a full professor in 1920. From 1923-1925 he was a visiting professor in the Faculty of Economics at the Tokyo Imperial University, at which time he was assisted by Arisawa Hiromi and Ōmori Yoshitarō (1898-1940) and instructed students such as Takayama Yokichi (1901-1975). He succeeded Sombart at Humboldt University, Berlin in 1931, but was dismissed in 1933, when he emigrated to the United States and became a professor at the New School for Social Research in New York. His books were widely translated into Japanese before and during World War II.[151]

In *Die Zukunft des Kapitalismus*, Sombart gave a number of examples of substantial changes in the capitalism of his time: a decline in the capitalistic spirit due to a diminished will to strive after profit in a speculative and adventurous way as a result of the rise of a rationalistic spirit; the move from a free and individualistic economic order to a more binding one (bureaucratizing management, "de-spiritualizing" (*Vergeistung*)[152] undertakings where a system of regulation holds sway, corporate associations such as cartels, state control, control by workers), and the elimination of the old market mechanism and its replacement by a rigid system (price fixing by cartels and the state, wages fixed by trade unions). While these all contributed to the decline of capitalism, Sombart pointed out that together with the parallel rise of a new economic system that was characterized by management by state and municipal bodies, old patterns also survived. "The

151 Kocka 1979, Brandt 1993, Janssen 2000. See References for a list of translated works of Lederer.

152 See Chapter 1, footnote 65.

late epoch of an economic system is characterized inasmuch as it must share its dominance with the economic systems that have cropped up anew," he wrote.[153]

Together with the changes in the national economy noted above, capitalism was also affected by conditions abroad. "It is obvious that the substance of the economy is not only fixed by the external value and the inner structure of the different economic systems having a national economic body, but also by their relationship to foreign economic bodies."[154] The global trading mechanism ("barter, compensation and adaptation") of the prewar world economy of the age of "High Capitalism" (Hochkapitalismus) had been based on free trade and the regulated exchange of foreign currency centring on the City of London allowing European capital to flow overseas and the countries of Europe to purchase raw materials and foodstuffs and pay for them with manufactured goods and capital derived from loans. This mechanism had been dismantled in the postwar period and the former system of High Capitalism was foundering at its very foundations, as customs barriers were raised, credits recalled, and the gold standard failed. As well, with the industrialization of formerly agricultural, non-European countries and the growth of capitalism in the emerging countries, the traditional pattern of exchange between Western Europe and those countries would cease, as the new countries retained their foodstuffs and raw materials for their own use and were in no position to export them to the older industrialized nations. Thus the markets for European industrial products would disappear and European countries would find it increasingly difficult to import agricultural products and raw materials. Moreover they would have to compete with the products of the new countries on the world market. "The extra-European countries have liberated themselves in every respect from the ... system of exploitation exercised over them by Western Europe", Sombart remarked. "The 'domination of the white race' on Earth is definitely at an end".[155]

In the face of such a situation, Sombart saw three possibilities for the future as far as the old industrialized countries were concerned: maintaining the status quo (the conservative viewpoint), returning to a free economy (the reactionary viewpoint) or building a planned economy (the reformative-revolutionary viewpoint). He evaluated the third possibility in a positive light. This "planned economy" would not be according to the Soviet model, but rather permitted a certain amount of freedom and diversity. It was an economic system that

153 Sombart 1932, p. 12. He thus distinguished "Late Capitalism" from that of the former period, which he called Hochkapitalismus, "High Capitalism".

154 *Ibid.*

155 *Ibid.* p. 40.

provided for the coexistence of both private and state ownership and of varied economic forms and devices.

Mukai adopted Sombart's viewpoint above in his own chapters about the "reform of the world economic mechanism" and the "reform of the economic system and the planned economy." Hon'iden too took up Sombart's "three viewpoints" (conservative, reactionary and reformative-revolutionary) regarding the impasse in the economy; he criticized the first two, but like Sombart himself, chose the third. Thus the way was open for state control of the economy.

How about the second option, a return to the liberal economy? Both Mukai and Hon'iden were aware of the criticism of the planned economy and interventionism by the liberal Austrian economist, Ludwig Edler von Mises (1881-1873). Commenting on the tendency towards socialization and socialism in postwar Germany and Austria, von Mises said that a socialist planned economy would not work, because it lacked a market price system and therefore would engender confusion. Many prewar Japanese non-Marxian economists agreed with him and his arguments were used to form the basis of the criticism of socialism. Mukai and Hon'iden were no exception, as their criticism of the socialistic planned economy makes evident. In his *Kritik des Interventionismus* (Critique of interventionism) of 1929, von Mises pointed out that there existed a "third way" between socialism and capitalism, "an ideal system which... is neither capitalistic nor socialistic, (and) is based neither on private property in the means of production nor on public property... a system of private property that is hampered, regulated, and directed through government intervention and other social forces, such as labor unions." However, though this "economic policy [of] *interventionism*" was intended to eliminate the flaws in capitalism, it had in fact caused the present economic depression by creating monopolies, and so von Mises advocated a return to liberalism. Mukai and Hon'iden both completely disagreed with this. They criticized him for overlooking the fact that "the development of liberalism within the economic mechanism was necessarily premised on change" and that a return to a liberal economy "went against the historical current".[156]

A fundamental premise for understanding the structural transformation of capitalism was the accumulation of capital and the expansion of the scale of management. In 1928, Eugen Schmalenbach, a professor at the College of Commerce in Cologne, gave a speech at the Business Economists' Conference in Vienna

156 Mises 1929, Preface, Mukai 1933, pp. 231, 276-85, Hon'iden 1938, p. 28 et seq. For a theoretical refutation on von Mises's view, see Sugimoto 1943.

entitled "Die Betriebswirtschaftslehre an der Schwelle der neuen Wirtschaftsverfassung" (Business Economics on the Threshhold of the New Economic Order) in which he pointed out that the expansion of capitalism had been accompanied by an enlarged scale of management and a growth of the management apparatus, and in particular, by rising fixed costs and capital intensification. However, this has deprived the economy of the means to bring production and consumption into equilibrium and given rise to various harmful effects, such as parasitism, bureaucratism, the loss of the entrepreneurial spirit, and monopolies such as cartels.[157] In other words, rising fixed costs would propel the economy towards becoming a state-run cartel. Schmalenbach, as an authority on business administration, was very important to Mukai, also a scholar of management. Mukai's understanding of the transformation of capitalism as it appeared in his discussion of the controlled economy owed a very great deal to Schmalenbach and Sombart.[158]

The New Order: the Supercorporation and the Controlled Economy

(1) The controlled economy

Mukai regarded the retreat of the liberal economy and moves toward a restricted economy and national economic regulation as part of a global tendency. He considered the deliberately planned regulated (or "bound") economy (*gebundene Wirtschaft*) based on a unified purpose to be one kind of economic system, which he classified in three types: self-controlled (i.e. cartels), controlled, and planned. The present time represented, in his opinion, a trend towards the second and third of these.

The controlled economy (type 2) can be divided into individual economic policies and a controlled economy with some form of planning, while the planned economy (type 3) can be classified as the perfectly planned economy, the partially planned economy and the controlled economy with some form of planning. This last item obviously overlaps with the second item in type 2. The perfectly planned economy, the very culmination of the planned economy, is the socialist compulsory, managed economy, a system entirely subject to government

157 Schmalenbach's lecture, "Die Betriebswirtschaftslehre an der Schwelle der neuen Wirtschaftsverfassung" appeared in *Zeitschrift für handelswissenschaftliche Forschung*, Jg. 22, H. 5. It was translated into Japanese after World War II (1960). For a summary of this speech in English, see Forrester 1993, pp. 307-309.

158 Mukai 1933, pp. 230-38.

control that rejects any notion of the rights of individual ownership of production capital. Mukai excluded this as being utopian, and instead advocated both a partial planned economy to operate in a particular environment, detaching "specific industries and economies" within the national economy from the free, competitive market, and a controlled economy with some form of planning that "permits, within the national economy, economic systems whose governing principles are different, though controlling them however under a unified plan according to national economic policy".[159]

Measures of both direct and indirect control could be applied. Direct control included the private and public ownership of industry, moves toward a national monopoly of specific types of economic activity and a licensing system, aid for particular industries (in the form of subsidies and government orders for products), and the banning of businesses harmful to the public interest. Indirect control comprised such things as the transfer of national government functions to particular economic organizations (for example, granting rights of quality inspection to the various export associations[160]), granting powers of compulsion (for example, granting special rights of compulsion to cartels through the Important Industries Control Law of 1931), monetary control, and other means such as trade policy regarding customs duties, etc., and currency policies.[161]

Mukai attached great importance to the coexistence of diverse economic forms and systems and to joint applicability of various means of control. He advocated the necessity of "synthesizing" these into "an economics with a new significance" and he looked to an "economic general staff" (*keizai sanbō honbu*) to determine and draft important economic policy. More specifically, he investigated the technical means by which to bring about the controlled economy, such as systems of management, the market system (particularly the distribution system) and state enterprises. Finally, he examined the situation in other countries concerning the "economic general staff". At that time, what particularly drew attention to Mukai's theory about the controlled economy were his ideas about the autonomous corporation and the autonomous economy.

---

159 Mukai 1933, chapter 9.

160 A variety of export associations existed, including for example the Japan Porcelain and Earthernware Export Association, the Japan Green Tea Export Association, the Kobe Marine Products Export Association, the Japan Brush Export Association, etc. etc. See *The Oriental Economist*, vol. 1, 1934 and *Contemporary Japan*, vol. 4, 1936.

161 Mukai 1933, pp. 294-296, section 2.

(2) The supercorporation and the separation of ownership and management

Mukai was convinced that the age of the free economy, where enterprises were run by owner-managers, whose activities, efforts, enthusiasm, initiative, ingenuity and creativity all went towards their own profits, through which they contributed to the community, was over, and in its place large-scale management, within a corporate system that separated ownership and management, was now in the ascendant. "Industrial absenteeism",[162] where the owners of the capital did not themselves assume the task of management, was based on the limited liability of stockholders, on converting stocks to bonds and on the possibility of trading and transferring those stocks, on an increase in the total number of stockholders who provided capital and a decrease in the number of equity shares held by one person, and on the delegation of management rights to directors. Stockholders were not interested in company management but simply wanted secure earnings so their investment would be safe. They lived on "unearned income" – "annuities and interest" – and, completely divorced from the "mindset of an entrepreneur", "periodically received a portion of the company's profits", "without taking any part in its activities" or "playing any role in it." This creates the possibility that through stock dispersion, companies will come under the control of large stockholders who own only a small proportion of the company's capital. The management of an enterprise should, however, be in the hands of directors who have sufficient motivation and talent regarding the affairs of the company, since technical problems (to do with production and administration of the business) increase and become more complicated as capital expands.

However, managers entrusted with the operations of the enterprise, unlike the case where owner-managers run the business, are not directly subject to economic interests. They preserve their position as long as they carry out their duties faithfully on a daily basis, but since they are promoted according to seniority, as time passes they not longer need to demonstrate their special ingenuity or talents. Mukai thus points out: "Company management, like individual management, will lose both originality and energy, and improved managerial efficiency is obstructed, as it becomes more regulated, impersonal, bureaucratic and mechanical. Moreover, it becomes easier for supervision and guidance of lower-ranking staff to become lax, for office work to back up, and dishonesty to be triggered."[163]

---

162 Mukai used the English expression "industrial absenteeism". It was probably based on Veblen's "absentee ownership" (Veblen 1923 [1997]). For further on the concept see Veblen *ibid.* pp. 209ff, 213, 215 ff. Also refer to the Introduction to the 1997 edition by Marion J. Levy, Jr.

163 Mukai 1933, chapter 12.

Mukai, who took a serious view about the loss of the good points of private companies when corporations took on a stronger bureaucratic character, questioned whether at the present time corporations any longer needed to continue to exist as private companies. "I think that in such activities [by the large corporations], the capitalistic enterprise has already completed its mission." Here he showed that his thinking was in line with the trend towards corporate autonomy and socialisation (where the autonomous corporation becomes like a semi-public enterprise). It was therefore a question of the existence of the company's business as a business: the risk borne by shareholders was limited with the establishment of a fixed amount for returns on dividends, and shareholders were detached totally (legally and economically) from the business. Thus company managers could specialize in the business, work to keep profits within the company, and devote themselves to developing business.

Corporations were no longer "instruments for profit-making" by capitalists but "had an intrinsic life of their own", with the same characteristics as a state, an autonomous body, or a foundation. Mukai called this the "supercorporation", corresponding to Rathenau's "autonomous enterprise" and "autonomous economy" (autonome Wirtschaft). It was from here that the idea of "enterprise-in-itself" arose.[164] The "new managers" (the directors), as trustees for such a business, take decisions independently of the capitalists and, with their own duties and position in place, create a new standard of management and new business ethics. They manage the business not for specific individuals but for everyone who is part of it (all the shareholders, all the workers, the consumers). They are thus in the position of "public officials". It is not a "business" existing to make profits, but a "profession" whose purpose is to discharge its responsibility.

The autonomous enterprise is not the traditional capitalistic concern. However, it does not reject the idea of acquiring dividends based on the proprietary rights of stockholders and remains premised on profit-making. The undivided attention to the business paid by the "new manager" is linked as a result to the growth of the "services" offered by the corporation and to the rise in profits. The autonomous enterprise is not "a purely private enterprise under capitalism", but, "since there has been no abolition of private wealth", it is neither "managed under socialism" nor is it a "public (state) enterprise". It is "intermediate between the private and the public company", and being so, "is inevitably an important constituent in the controlled economy, which is also a controlled economy with partial planning."

164 For "enterprise-in-itself", refer to footnote 53, Chapter 1.

Mukai's ideas about the socialisation and autonomy of corporations had already been developed in his 1929 *Keiei keizaigaku sōron* (An introduction to business economics). Mukai gave his attention to the fact that after World War I, people had begun discussing the class conflict between capitalists and labour in terms of "cooperation" and "partnership" in various forms. He made a close study of the participation of workers in the company through the acquisition of shares and of factory committees. He also looked at the participation of labour in management through the Whitley Councils in England, at the attempts to form industrial organizations, and at the German "Works Councils" (*Betriebsrat*). The Whitley Report of 1917, proposed in 1917 by J. H. Whitley (1866-1935), recommended setting up Joint Industrial Councils (called Whitley Councils) as regular consultative meetings between management and employees, with equal representation form both, District Councils, and factory Works Committees. Mukai compared the Whitley Councils with the *Betriebsrat*, which had begun as a result of an Act of January, 1920. They were to be set up in all firms where at least twenty persons were employed, and a trades-union representative was to be allowed to attend if more than a quarter of the members requested it. The Councils were to be funded by the employer and normally consisted of workers alone, who had full access to the firm's records. By contrast, the Whitley Councils were voluntary and the employer controlled the information given.[165]

It was as a counterproposal to these that Mukai proposed the concept of the autonomous enterprise, the supercorporation.[166]

(3) The influence of Rathenau's new economic order

As Japanese scholars focused on the importance of the corporation in modern society, they were very influenced by Western economic thought regarding the separation of ownership and management (or, the enterprise and management) and on managers (management) versus shareholders (capital). Mukai's ideas were most influenced by *The End of Laissez-faire* by J. M. Keynes and particularly by the economic thought of Walther Rathenau.[167]

---

165 Mukai 1929, pp. 279-307 (Whitley Councils). For contemporary discussion on English industrial organization, see Bloomfield 1919, Lee 1923.

166 Mukai 1929, chapters 10-12.

167 For further discussion, see Chapter 1. Concerning Rathenau, see Yoshida 1976, Ono 1996. For details of his life, see Pogge von Strandmann ed. 1985, "Biographical sketch", pp. 1-26. For Ratheau's ideas, see (in German) Solzbacher 1933, Laux 1998 and (in English) Pogge von Strandmann 1985, Michalka 2010.

Rathenau was the son of Emil Rathenau, the founder of the electrical combine Allgemeine Elektrizitäts-Gesellschaft (AEG) and together with Wichard von Moellendorf[168] and others he greatly influenced Japanese intellectuals through his conception and implementation of ideas about the cooperative economy (*Gemeinwirtschaft*) after World War I. Both Mukai and Hon'iden expressed great interest in the cooperative economy; Mukai's ideas about the autonomous corporation were enormously influenced by two of Rathenau's works written towards the end of World War I, *Von kommenden Dingen* (In Days to Come) and *Die neue Wirtschaft* (The New Economy). Rathenau believed that capitalist society would inevitably become "mechanized", "organized" and "specialized". As a way of countering the alienation of human freedoms that would ensue, he drew attention to the possibility of gaining independence from corporate ownership as a result of the depersonalization of ownership and the fragmentation and dispersion of property rights that had come about through securitisation and stock circulation. He presented the idea of a new kind of functional capitalism that was aware of its social responsibility rather than being motivated purely by the desire for profit.

Rathenau coined the term "autonomous" (*Autonome*) to refer to the condition marked by the depersonalisation of ownership, the objectification of the corporation and the dissolution of proprietary rights (the holdings would, depending on the enterprise, be bought back from the owner) that would eventuate in the enterprise becoming a foundation or a public institution. He linked his concept of the collective economy to his ideas about corporate functionalisation and the corporation without stockholders. In a collective economy, enterprises would form groups and syndicates based on product and process that would be under state supervision. This concept was summarized in *Autonome Wirtschaft* (Autonomous Economics) in 1919. His arguments about the "autonomous" enterprise and the "new economy", posed at a time of postwar confusion and incipient revolution, set out to counter Socialism and Social Democracy and the plan (and policy) of socialisation based on them. (Rathenau's economic thought and its international influence were discussed in Chapter 1.)

Cartels: The Independent Organization and the Public Interest

When speaking about the role of the corporation in modern society, Hon'iden Yoshio looked towards the development of managers and their "economic morality", referring to Adolf A. Berle and Gardiner C. Means, the authors of *The*

168 For Wichard von Moellendorf, see Barclay 1978, Bowen 1971 [1947], chapter 5.

Modern Corporation and Private Property (1932). At the same time, he was critical of the non-interventionist approach to the "profit-seeking business organization", and criticised Keynes's concept that a corporation should have a commitment to the public interest, saying "It is over-optimistic to expect that they [managers] will conduct their business unswayed by private profit, and work for the national and public interest".[169]

A characteristic of Hon'iden's theory about the controlled economy was that he brought the "public interest" of Mukai and others to the forefront. "The controlled economy has as its purpose the protection and enlargement of the public interest," he wrote. "Therefore the state can exercise its authority over each individual."[170] His words show that for Hon'iden, the public interest was the aim, to achieve which the state occupied a crucial position. From the perspective of the "public interest" that was his objective, state control was exercised in three stages: from the industry, to the industrial sector, and then to the whole economy. This would result in an economic system that sought to achieve a balance between production and demand.

This was not a purpose confined to a time of emergency, fighting depression and providing for national defence. Rather it was the "ultimate objective" that went beyond such issues. "Therefore even when the time of emergency passes, control will not be withdrawn" and "the highest social objective will shine radiantly forth, and the controlled economy will expand more and more." The "time of emergency" is therefore positioned as a period of "reform" and "rapid progress".

Hon'iden had great expectations that business leaders would at such a time become aware of the "national and social point of view". Subjectively, the enterprise was "a means for personal profit", but objectively it was to be "a body within the national economy having the duty to manage industry." Thus Hon'iden asserted that the controlled economy would develop into a "cooperative economy" through a change (a "mental revolution") in the "consciousness" of business leaders regarding the "twofold meaning of the enterprise", that is, the enterprise as a profit-making resource and the enterprise as the body whose duty it was to manage the industry within the national economy.[171]

It goes without saying that the importance given to the "public interest" did not mean that "private interests" were denied. But "private interests" could "only be allowed to the extent they were in harmony with the public interest." If there

---

169 Hon'iden 1938, p. 143 ff.

170 Hon'iden 1938, p. 55.

171 Hon'iden 1938, pp. 85-87, chapters 7 and 10.

was a conflict with the "public interest", the business leaders must practise self-restraint regarding "private interests". The core of Hon'iden's thesis on the controlled economy was the "self-restraint" of business leaders, the "organization" of "self-restraint", the resultant awakening of business leaders to the "public interest", and national control to back this. Neither Hon'iden nor Mukai denied capitalistic relationships, which were in fact a premise for their arguments, and even more than that. Together with the private enterprise described above, one of the foundations of Hon'iden's thesis about control was the development of state and public enterprises. However, as far as the national economy was concerned, the position occupied by private enterprise was far greater; self-regulation by private enterprises itself had to be regarded as the core of the controlled economy, and indeed as a method for realizing it. Hon'iden emphasized that when control was carried out through each industrial sector, the "autonomous control" of each had to be respected. The state "leaves control up to the particular body, and only takes over guidance or supervision in cases of necessity."[172]

For "autonomous control", an "autonomous body" has to be set up, and this takes the form of an "interface between industry and the purposes of the state." When that happens, "corporate concentration" exhibits a "firm foundation" for "industrial control for the sake of the public". Cartels, trusts and combines are utilized precisely for the "autonomous control" of the enterprise. Hon'iden wrote that "when the bodies are created in the private economy and are working for self-control, it is a fact that they can act as agents of state control, and this makes them the best way to facilitate control". "The Nazis," he continued, "in many respects give the impression, from outward appearances, of acting violently, but in the sphere of corporate control, their policy is moderate and autonomous." Thus he links his own ideas to those of German National Socialism.[173]

This "autonomous body" would both represent the enterprise and be an agent for the government. It would transmit government requirements to each entrepreneur, who would himself instigate controls. It is therefore a private organization that lays emphasis on the interests of the enterprise, but at the same time, it also has a public character.

The "autonomous body" is "an institution midway between the state, which desires economic control and is attempting to pursue it, and the economy, which

---

172 Hon'iden 1938, chapter 7. In 1934 the Nazi regime has set up "economic groups" (*Wirtschaftsgruppe*) in each sector of the economy; they were autonomous but also state controlled. The "control associations" (*tōseikai*) in Japan were modeled after them (see Chapters 3-5).

173 Hon'iden 1938, p. 219 ff.

is manifested through the individual company or private cartel that is subject of that control". It also has to be multi-functional: undertaking product inspection, technological research, the training of technical experts, industrial rationalization, and market regulation, and being an intermediary with the government, making proposals and referring problems to it, and so on. The government would require the autonomous body to come up with an agreement, to which it could give approval or direct changes, and also to receive reports concerning equipment capability, production, sales and warehousing, and to supervise and control the industry by dispatching its own officials and inspectors.[174]

The core of Hon'den's discussion about control was the creation of "autonomous bodies" on the foundation of the cartel system, the imposition of state regulation concerning them, and through this, having business leaders become aware of the "public interest". At that point, the autonomy of cartels had to be sufficiently respected. Of course, this had to be differentiated from the previous self-regulation for their own interests through industrial combinations of enterprises. However in terms of the restructuring of the capitalistic apparatus, it stopped short of state organization of the economy, and did not go so far as regulating basic principles of profit-making. Hon'iden's ideas were directly connected with opinion in business circles about the new economic order, to be discussed below.

In contrast to Hon'iden, Mukai's idea about the controlled economy on the basis of the "supercorporation" imposed much greater restraints on profit-seeking by capitalists. However, he shared Hon'iden's views about the organization of cartels. As part of his idea of a partially planned economy, he understood cartels to be a type of organization "controlled from above by the state".[175] This is why Sakisaka Itsurō, the author of *Tōsei keizairon sōkan* (General view of the debate over the controlled economy), the tenth volume of the *Collected Works on the Controlled Economy in Japan*, classified Mukai's position as being "the theory of the controlled economy as a smokescreen for intensifying monopolization". He wrote, "It is impossible to do away with the domination of monopoly capital. Whatever name is given to the social system, it does not eliminate monopoly capital control or the strengthening of monopolies. Indeed, there is no recourse but to join forces with it to promote it further."[176] This is even clearer in Hon'iden's stance.

---

174 Hon'iden 1938, chapter 7.

175 Mukai 1933, p. 290.

176 Sakisaka 1934, p. 97.

Nevertheless, at the same time we have to pay attention to the severity of the situation facing the capitalistic economic system, forced to raise a "smokescreen" over itself. Mukai conceived a controlled-type of economy as an "economic system" that was "midway" between capitalism and socialism, while Hon'iden perceived the need to organize capitalism on the basis of the public interest. What lay behind their ideas was the realization that capitalism itself was in danger. The controlled economy was conceived from the understanding that the *laissez-faire* capitalist economy was breaking down and monopolies were in the process of forming, and that capitalism needed to be revised in order to solve the various problems that had arisen. The "smokescreen" itself is significant as one stream in the history of capitalism, one that was realized in Germany as National Socialism and in Japan as the "New Order".

Chapter Three: Early Japanese Analysis of the Nazi Economic System

In January 1933 the National Socialist German Worker's Party (Nationalsozialistische Deutsche Arbeiterpartei: NSDAP) led by Adolf Hitler (1889-1945) seized power to form the Third Reich. In 1936 the Nazi Party set up a Four Year Plan to prepare for total war and in 1939 Germany invaded Poland, triggering World War II. Japan in the meantime consolidated its relationship with Germany by signing the Anti-Comintern Pact (with Germany) in 1936, the Anti-Comintern Pact (with Germany and Italy) in 1937 and the Tripartite Pact in 1940. This chapter seeks to shed light on how prewar Japanese scholars, especially social scientists, analysed and assessed the economic thought and the economic system of Nazi Germany, with a focus on the period immediately after the Nazi Party assumed power.

In 1935, Frederick L. Schuman wrote in a preface to a book published the following year that the phenomenon of Fascism had stimulated "the writing and publication of an impressive number of histories, descriptions, eulogies and indictments" and noted a vast increase in their number since the "political upheaval of 1933". He commented though, that "none of the studies of German Fascism thus far published, however, offers a comprehensive and definitive analysis of both the National Socialist movement and the new Nazi State", and that there was no "full and critical treatment available of the organization, philosophy, and strategy of the NSDAP".[177]

In fact, Japanese scholars had displayed an interest in the Nazi Party and Hitler's thought and actions well before the Nazi Party seized power. As previous studies have revealed, there was an animated debate, especially among Marxian scholars, about the nature of Nazism, particularly in connection with the growing nationalist movement and the inclination towards totalitarianism in Japan. In the process, the relation between Nazism and capitalism became an important point of debate.[178]

177 Schuman 1936. Despite this, he cited "useful treatises" written by Konrad Heiden (1934), Ernst Ottwalt (1932), Edgar Ansel Mowrer (1933), Calvin Hoover (1933), Mildred Wertheimer (1935), and other commentators.

178 Abe 1975 (new edition 1995), part 1, chapter 1, Yoshimi 1977, Kanda 1978. Abe and Kanda refer to discussions of fascism by non-Marxian scholars.

The economic theory that backed Nazi authoritarian political ideology began to attract academic interest not just from Marxists but also from a wide range of social scientists, especially after Hitler and his Nazi Party had progressed from being a mere political movement to becoming the party in power in a position to realise its ideology in the policies that were developed under the dictatorship. Japanese scholars of the time superimposed the development of Nazi Germany on to what was happening in Japan, and responded to the question of Nazism with even more urgency than before. It was in the years 1933 and 1934 that Japanese scholars first began examining Nazi economic thought in connection with the Nazi system.

From the numerous analyses of Nazi economic thought conducted during that period, I have chosen to examine in this chapter the pioneering works of Wagatsuma Sakae (1897-1973), a professor of civil law and later head of the law faculty of the Tokyo Imperial University, Kada Tetsuji a scholar of the history of economic thought and sociology and a professor in the economics faculty of Keio Gijuku University, and Chō Moriyoshi (1900-1971) of the South Manchuria Railway Company (Mantetsu), with an emphasis on how they understood and discussed Nazi economic thought.

None of the three conducted their studies from a Marxist point of view. Kada Tetsuji, who, along with Miki Kiyoshi (1897-1945) was to become an active member of the Showa Research Association (*Showa Kenkyūkai*), had been greatly influenced by Marxism, but was not a Marxist in a narrow sense, while Wagatsuma Sakae was critical of Nazism throughout his career, looking at it from the standpoint of Weimar democracy. Chō Moriyoshi, a student of Hijikata Seibi (also known as Shigeyoshi; 1890-1975), a professor in the faculty of economics at the Tokyo Imperial University who subsequently resigned his post, was an active sympathiser of Nazism and critical of Marxism. This chapter thus looks at analyses of Nazism conducted outside the Marxist context. Even after the government's crackdown on speech and ideas intensified and eventually put an end to Marxist discourse on fascism in Japan,[179] these three scholars, because they were not Marxists, were able to continue their studies on Nazism and publish their results, at a time when the Nazi regime was taking shape in Germany.

The studies of Nazism by non-Marxist scholars such as the liberal Christian, Imanaka Tsugimaro (1893-1980) and Gushima Kanesaburō (1905-2004) have already attracted scholarly attention.[180] They were both political scientists. Imanaka

179 Abe 1975, p. 23, footnote 7, Miyake ed. 1999, chapter 4. Fascism from a Marxist viewpoint was discussed again in terms of Japanese fascism particularly in the years 1935 and 36. See Yoshimi 1977.

180 Imanaka has been discussed in English in Tansman ed. 2009, pp. 34-41.

was a professor at the Kyūshū Imperial University until his resignation in 1942, though he was reinstated after World War II. Gushima was an assistant professor at Dōshisha University in Kyoto before taking up a post with Mantetsu; he was imprisoned, but became a professor at Kyūshū University after World War II. By contrast, the work of Wagatsuma, Kada and Chō has so far attracted little interest, and was not reviewed in the studies of prewar Japanese fascist ideology by Abe Hirozumi, Yoshimi Yoshiaki and Kanda Fuhito mentioned above.[181] Nor were they discussed in the histories of the academic study of Nazism or of Nazi intellectual history by scholars such as Yamaguchi Yasushi.[182] What has caused this oversight? Perhaps the following comment by Abe Hirozumi, a noted scholar of fascism who also paid attention, not just to Marxian scholars but to non-Marxians like Imanaka Tsugimaro, suggests an answer: "Although studies of fascism multiplied after 1932 and 1933, the quality of such research peaked in those years, because most work until that time had been undertaken from an anti-fascist viewpoint. As Japan started to lean more and more towards fascism and solidify its alignments with other fascist nations, studies about fascism were increasingly conducted from a pro-fascist standpoint."[183]

Studies about Nazism (fascism) in Japan have thus been assessed according to their objectivity and the quality of their socio-scientific analysis. The quality of the study is measured against the author's stance towards fascism, as if the former corresponds to the latter. Abe is saying that the anti-fascist standpoint was dominant before 1932-1933 and this made an objective analysis possible, thus elevating the quality of studies. However, though the number of such studies multiplied with the rise of fascism in Japan, Abe implies they lacked any critical analysis of fascism and thus their objectivity suffered. This is probably why studies of Nazism done in Japan after 1933-1934, particularly when totalitarianism was taking hold, have not so far attracted serious attention.

But it was precisely because Japan was leaning more and more towards fascism and because totalitarian nations were strengthening their international alignments, that Nazism, as the ideology and policies of Nazi Germany, was introduced in a positive way to Japan and had a great impact on the growth of totalitarianism there. Nazism was both an object for comparison with the Japanese situation, since it was occurring in parallel with similar circumstances in Japan, as well as one element in the formation of totalitarianism.[184] At issue here was not only the issue of the essential nature of Nazism, but also the burning questions

181 See Footnote 178.

182 Yamaguchi 1976. For other studies, see Kurihara 1981, Nakamura 1990.

183 Abe 1975, p. 23, note 7.

184 See Chapters 5 and 6 below.

about how its ideology was given shape in practice, and what was the content of policies under the Nazi system.

The question of their academic quality aside, the studies of Nazism made during this period should be examined in terms of how their perception of Nazism compared with the reality, and how they were connected with Japan's precipitous march towards fascism and the tensions caused by this. Pro-fascist studies should be closely scrutinized all the more because of their pro-fascist stance. If we assess research solely by its academic quality, we run the risk of excluding this important point. Moreover, the studies of Nazi Germany that were made at this particular time contain much that should be recognised today as valuable pieces of socio-scientific research. Especially notable is the fact that they examined Nazism not only as a political movement before the party seized power, but also as an ideological tool for dominance and for its ideas about policy connected with an actual economic system.

Ideas proposed when the Nazi party was seeking political power changed even before it seized power, and further modifications were made during the process of establishing a new system of government. The Nazi Party's seizure of power in Germany prompted Japanese intellectuals to reassess their initial observation of Nazism primarily as a political struggle for power. Now in a position of rule, Nazism required examination as a political system. And a further point of interest was how its ideology had been systematised, since it affected how Japan perceived and accepted Nazism. Inevitably, analyses of Nazi Germany conducted by Japanese scholars were deeply intermeshed with the circumstances under which those scholars lived.

This chapter will look into studies about the Nazi political system that were carried out around the years 1933 and 1934 by Wagatsuma, Kada and Chō. Their studies focused on Nazi ideas about the economy and policy, and they laid the foundation, and served as a springboard, for future research. Wagatsuma published important papers in 1938 and 1942 and Kada in 1940 and 1941, while Chō published a book in 1939.

Wagatsuma Sakae

(1) Analysis of Nazi thought

Wagatsuma Sakae published his first study of German National Socialism, "Nachisu minpō riron" (Theory of Nazi civil law) in two parts in 1934.[185] His

185 Wagatsuma 1934a. For Wagatsuma's works before and after World War II, see *Jurisuto: Wagatsuma Sakae Sensei tsuitō* 1974. See also Hirowatari 1979. Hirowatari,

understanding was further extended in "Nachisu no shoyūken riron" (Nazi ownership theory) in 1938 and "Nachisu no keiyaku riron" (Nazi contract theory) in 1942.[186] "Nachisu minpō riron" was included in its original form in the 1934 co-authored volume *Nachisu no hōritsu* (Nazi law) and a summary of it, entitled "Nachisu no shihō genri to sono rippō" (Principles of Nazi civil law and its legislation), appeared in the journal *Hōritsu jihō*.[187] Wagatsuma's first studies of Nazism thus appeared in forms accessible not only to experts in law and related fields but also to those outside academia, including bureaucrats.

Throughout his career, Wagatsuma looked at Nazi law from the viewpoint of the "relationship between changing capitalism and private law".[188] His analysis had both legal characteristics but also, when it concerned "changing capitalism", elements of economics and economic thought as well. It was because of this outlook that his contemporary, Nishihara Kan'ichi (1899-1976), a scholar of corporate law at Keijō Imperial University, acclaimed Wagatsuma's work as a careful and detailed analysis of "how the Nazi Party handled economic life and economic legislation".[189] Thus Wagatsuma's studies of Nazi legal thought also had the effect of shedding light on Nazi economic thought.

Wagatsuma was particularly interested in the relationship of Nazi thought with the guiding principles of the Weimar Constitution as they concerned social life, both in terms in what they had in common and how they differed. Although he acknowledged that the Nazi Party had trampled on the democratic principles and state structure of the Weimar Constitution during its first year in power, and set up a totalitarian political structure in its place, he noted that there still remained traits shared by both regimes. For example, the Nazis attacked the theory of private law that was rooted in liberal individualism, and attached importance to restrictions imposed by the state in accordance with the party's fundamental assertion of the "subordination of private to public interests". The Weimar Constitution, too, recognised the active responsibility of the state towards family life, and, in accord with the principles governing social and communal life,

---

however, does not review in detail Wagatsuma's research on Nazi law, which is thought to have had a vital bearing on Wagatsuma's views on Nazism.

186 They were published respectively in *Makino Sensei kanreki shukuga hōrironshū* 1938 and *Sugiyama Kyōju kanreki shukuga ronbunshū* 1942. Both are reprinted in Wagatsuma 1966, I.

187 Wagatsuma 1934b.

188 See preface, Wagatsuma 1966, I.

189 Nishihara 1936, p. 117. Chō Moriyoshi (Chō 1934) included Nishihara's essay in his list of references, and commended it as "a detailed introduction to Nazi economic law".

imposed certain restrictions on such individualistic principles of the civil law as freedom of contract and private ownership. The Nazi Party, while denouncing the Weimar Constitution, recognised private ownership, on the premise of the large number of guiding principles regarding private law in relation to social life that they held in common.

All the same, the gap between the two was considerable, and the following three points can be considered particular characteristics of Nazism. (1) There was to be autocratic discipline in relation to social life. Emphasis was placed on the leader-subordinate relationship and the spiritual unity of the participants in relationships such as those between landowners and tenants, and employers and employees, and among colleagues and fellow tradesmen, eliminating the principles of negotiation and collaboration among equals. (2) Society was to be based on the purity of the German race, not for the co-existence of all human beings. (3) Society was to give priority to farmers and to medium and small traders and manufacturers.

Wagatsuma explored those points in depth by examining the Nazi 25 Point Programme of 1920, Feder's Manifesto of 1918, the March 1930 declaration about agrarian policy,[190] and other pieces of legislation.

(2) Analysis of Nazi economic ideas

Wagatsuma defined Nazi economic thought as having two main objectives. First, it aimed to change the current structure of society and the economy geared towards satisfying individual self interest and bring into being a society that aimed to satisfy the collective economic and cultural needs of its citizens. Second, to fulfil this aim, the Nazi Party valued individual economic initiative and promoted economic activity based on individual economic freedom and responsibility, while imposing state control in order to make those individual economic activities congruous with the ideal of satisfying the needs of the people.

The Nazi Party did not disown the capitalist economy itself, but rejected the form it had taken, geared solely towards the pursuit of private interests. Loan capital or finance capital was a case in point; its dominance resulted in the "shackles of interest" (*Zinsknechtschaft*) – an excessive burden of interest payments. In exchange for a monetary loan, finance capital seized the fruits of labour of the borrower and thus reaped unearned income, in the process exploiting the debtor, whether it be a farmer, an industrialist or a state. Wagatsuma paid particular attention to Point

190 "Parteiamtliche Kundgebung über die Stellung der NSDAP zum Landvolk und zur Landwirtschaft". See Feder 1934, pp. 9 ff., Holt 1936, pp. 185 ff., also: Farquharson 1976, chapter 2.

11 of the Nazi Twenty-Five Point Programme that stipulated "the breaking of the bondage of interest" (*Brechung der Zinsknechtschaft*); he regarded this as the objective of the Nazi economic policy and of the Nazi political movement itself.

Set against the bondage of interest and the pursuit of private interests was "demand-sufficiency" (*Bedarfsdeckung*), a guiding principle that, while valuing individual initiative, looked to impose restrictions and controls for the public and collective interest. This principle was linked with the following policies.

(1) Protection of the rural population, who were "the sound blood and spirit of the race".
(2) Sound management of enterprises as a whole based on individual freedom and responsibility, and the protection of medium and small traders and manufacturers who were their backbone.
(3) Sanction of the large-scale management of enterprises by industrialists like Krupp and Siemens who were in sympathy with party objectives and were regarded as economic leaders.
(4) In the case of joint-stock companies, investors tended only to pursue their own profits and to pay scant attention to the company's social mission. Such companies could become a target for speculation by finance capital, and so be a contributing factor in industrial domination and debt-slavery by finance capital. The Nazis distinguished large enterprises as being firms under individual direction on the one hand, and dehumanised joint-stock companies that would make easy prey for speculation, on the other. The Nazis approved the former but denounced the latter.
(5) The nationalisation of all trusts, or associated industries (Point 13) was linked with policy (4). The criticism of unearned income and interest exploitation from the viewpoint of citizens' welfare (Point 11) could be understood as a criticism of the concentration of finance capital.
(6) The demand that profits from all large industries be divided (Point 14) did not imply joint management by capital and labour, but simply consented to the continuance of the existing workers' councils as advisory groups. Nazi economic thought did not attach importance to the position of workers' groups; rather it was concerned with maintaining the leading position of the industrialist within the leader-subordinate hierarchy.
(7) The 25 Point Plan demanded the abolition of unearned incomes, the prevention of all land speculation (Point 17), the ruthless confiscation of war profits (Point 12)and abolition of speculative profiteering (Point 18). However, under the existing economic system it was very difficult to eliminate the unavoidable consequences arising from the workings of capital.

Wagatsuma further examined how these proposals were legislated after the Nazi Party seized power in 1933. Legislation directed at farmers included the Reich Inherited Freehold Act (Reichserbhofgesetz; 29 September 1933), which forbad the sale, mortgage or division of small holdings, an order protecting farmers from forcible eviction, and a law to set up a foodstuff marketing organization (Reichsnährstand) and impose price controls on all commodities and services (13 September 1934). Legislation aimed at medium and small businessmen and retailers included the Law for the Protection of the Retail Trade (12 May 1933), which banned the expansion of department and chain stores, and the small industry credit guarantee law (31 November 1934). Laws were also passed concerning the Preliminary Construction of German Handicrafts (29 November 1933) to create handicraft associations. There were significant changes too made to the organization of labour. Examples of legislation regarding them include a law concerning corporate representative committees and economic associations (4 April 1933), a law for trustees of labour (19 May 1933), and the Labour Organization Law (20 January 1934). Cartel legislation included a law to modify the existing cartel law and one for compulsory cartelization (15 July 1933), while laws concerning interest-bearing capital included a compulsory eviction act (26 May 1933)and a law for capital transactions standards (10 December 1933).

Wagatsuma cited the principle of "the subordination of private to public interests" as the fundamental principle lying at the heart of Nazi economic thought and policy-making. This principle, coupled with the regulation of domestic industries, led to the compulsory formation of business organisations and a state supervisory system to oversee them. At the same time collective agreements based on employment contracts between the employers' associations and labour unions were eliminated. In their stead a new order in industrial relations was created in line with the enterprise community of employers ("leaders") and employees ("followers") that was founded according to the "leader principle" and under state supervision. Wagatsuma concluded that all of the new laws were working together to create an "economy akin to a totalitarian national economy."

(3) Criticism of Nazism and advocacy of a democratic solution

Wagatsuma criticised Nazism on three counts. First was the Nazi racial and ethnic stance that advocated the superiority of the German race while denouncing everything that was either Jewish or non-Germanic. Wagatsuma contended that the Nazi rhetoric was highly ambiguous and its logical foundation was full of holes both regarding the demand that Roman law be replaced by German common law (Point 19) and also the relationship between ethnicity and race and between the race and nation. The Nazi economic viewpoint also suffered the same defect. The word *gemein* (common) in the phrase *Gemeinnutz geht vor Eigennutz* (the common good comes before self-interest), a founding principle of Nazi economic thought, did not mean "common" as being universal for all people but a community consisting of one race. Thus it was no more than narrowly-defined racialism. This racial and ethnic viewpoint was connected with the principle of maintaining and carrying on the community of families, which formed the foundation of race and ethnicity. Policies like those designed to protect farmers were inseparable from this principle. Wagatsuma sharply criticised this "narrowly-defined racialism", Aryan supremacy in particular, as arbitrary and groundless.

Second, Wagatsuma questioned the practicability of Nazi ideas. He expressed "grave concerns", pointing out the contradictions intrinsic to some Nazi proposals: between the aim to secure for the farmers ownership and management of agricultural land and broader financial policy, between the goal of sustaining medium and small retailers and businessmen and of favouring big business, between emphasizing the importance of big business and denouncing the joint-stock corporation system, as well as the unrealistic target of eliminating finance capital ("the breaking of the slavery of interest"). He concluded that these objectives were pushing the capitalistic economy "one step back" on its natural and inevitable course of development.

Third, Wagatsuma focused on the leader principle (*Führerprinzip*) as a means of state control. How could this dictatorial principle, which rejected majority rule, guarantee each citizen the right to fair economic activity and improve the efficiency of industrial organisations? Above all, he raised strong doubts about whether the hierarchical "community" principle in labour-management relations bound by loyalty could sustain rationality regarding labour contracts.

Of the second point, Wagatsuma commented: "I don't think that the developmental stage of capitalism as described here is either inevitable or irredeemable. I think that the most appropriate and feasible course would be to bring capitalism gradually back to be within democratic regulation, while letting it follow its natural course of evolution." He thus recommended "democratic" solutions to the problems of capitalism. He also suggested democratic measures to improve industrial relations, his third point: "While a cross confrontation [between employer and employee] can be perceived in modern society, a policy that promotes gradual and democratic cooperation between them will probably prove to be more comprehensive and less flawed."[191]

191 For Wagatsuma's criticism of National Socialism, see Wagatsuma 1934a (1966), I, pp. 644 et seq., and II, pp. 889 et seq., especially the concluding remarks in chapter 4. See also Wagatsuma 1934b and his concluding remark, "Nazis, where are you going?"

Wagatsuma pointed out the lack of universality in Nazi policies, but refrained from making a final judgement, considering there might be "special circumstances" related to "the national emergency" in Germany. He wrote: "In short, I have observed an attempt to modify the theory of individualistic liberalism in the Nazi theory of civil law. Their reasoning is questionable in parts and contains contradictions, but at the same time I cannot flatly deny that there is nothing enlightening or suggestive. Furthermore, a series of changes and additions are being made to the theory as it is put into practice by a giant political power in Europe. I will watch how things will unfold with great interest, as I am a student of civil law and believe it inevitable that individualistic democratic theories will undergo certain changes."

This understanding of National Socialism laid the foundation for Wagatsuma's future studies. His articles, "Nachisu shoyūken riron" (Nazi ownership theory) (1938) and "Nachisu keiyaku riron" (Nazi contract theory) (1942), were both argued from the viewpoint of legal theory and were even more critical of Nazism than his earlier ones. He denounced most vehemently the idea of a "Volk" community forming the basis of the Nazi legal system and social order, and the irrationality of its racial standpoint. He did not try, however, to deny the significance of the principle of community itself. He had no objection to making the community principle the foundation of the ownership system, as long as the immutable autonomous status of the "individual" was guaranteed in the social structure, and that the community was defined as that which integrated "individuals" into a "whole", so as to achieve an organic union between them. He wrote: "If it is a just criticism of democratic ideology, the direct heir of modern individualistic liberalism, that democratic thought can be accused of having defined the 'individual' as an abstract everyman who is then lost in the masses, and ignored the worth of each 'individual' and denies it an autonomous status, I do not hesitate to support the idea that the theory of 'community' should replace that of democracy."

The Nazis, however, defined community (*Gemeinschaft*) as "the natural reality arising spontaneously from the blood linkages of the German Volk". Wagatsuma pointedly warned that if the Nazis expanded this idea and forced it upon an array of complex social relations often beset with sharp conflicts of interest, which had arisen in the process of developmental of the capitalist society, they would run the risk of uncritically endorsing existing but unjust powers, so robbing the "individual" of its autonomy and exposing the community to the arbitrary dominance of a powerful person. In particular, the Nazi attempt to modify the relationship between employers and workers through a works (or enterprise) community (*Betriebsgemeinschaft*) modelled on the leader principle posed a grave danger for the worker, for as a subordinate he would be forced to swear loyalty to the industrialist who was the designated leader.[192]

Wagatsuma dismissed the Nazi race-based reasoning as quasi-mysticism and a quasi-religion, scathingly criticising its irrationality while stressing the importance of the rational, critical spirit that "confronted reality". He had stated this view in his article of 1938, and he reiterated it in his 1942 paper, saying: "I feel strongly that I have no choice but to repeat the same warnings with even more urgency."

We should pay attention to the fact that the Nazi idea of the "Volk community" (Volksgemeinschaft), and especially the works community modelled on the leader principle with the employer as leader and the employees as subordinates, was then exerting a great deal of influence on Japan. It was just at that time that a "spiritual movement", sponsored by the Greater Japan Industrial Patriotic Association (*Dai Nihon Sangyō Hōkokukai*, ("Sanpo"), set up in 1940 to replace labour unions), was greatly expanding. This movement called for "the industrial prosperity of the empire" through "contributing to the state through the cooperation of every member of industry" (*zensangyō ittai hōkoku*) based on "the cardinal principle of the national polity (*kokutai no hongi*)", the "enterprise-family" (*jigyō ikka*) and "public service" (*hōkō*).[193] It is not at all difficult to see in Wagatsuma's censure of the Nazi idea of the Volk community a veiled criticism of contemporary Japanese ideas about the national polity and racial consciousness as well as their offshoot, the "enterprise-family", and understand it as being directed towards what was then happening in Japan, such as the application of the traditional, familist spirit to the employer-employee relationships, which was further strengthened by ideas about the national polity.

Wagatsuma strongly accused Nazi thinking of lacking a logical and critical spirit, but the suppression of logical and critical thinking was exactly the most conspicuous trait that characterized Japan's dominant thought and studies at the time. His denouncement of Nazi thought as "an ideology as irrational as a quasi-religion" could well be a covert manifestation of his scathing criticism towards the thinking dominant in contemporary Japan, which stressed the superiority of Japanese race, union by blood and spirit with the Emperor at the centre, and a "national structure" based on family, home town and the national polity.[194]

---

192 Wagatsuma 1938, p. 444 (Wagatsuma 1966, I, pp. 384 et seq.), Wagatsuma 1942, pp. 166 et seq.(Wagatsuma 1966, pp.454 et seq.).

193 Morito 1941, preface. See also Chapter 6 below. For *kokutai no hongi*, see Gauntlett and Hall 1949.

194 See Chapter 7 below.

Through his analyses of Nazi thought, he gained an important key to the prevailing political, social and ideological realities that he faced at home. It is probably not an exaggeration to say that his criticism of the Nazis was superimposed on his criticism of what seemed to be happening in Japan.

Wagatsuma accepted "the theory of community in the true sense of the word" and "community in its original sense". He acknowledged in daily human relationships the existence of communal dealings that fall outside contract theory, and recognised peasant family and peasant associations (not to be confused with the agricultural village community) to be original examples of community. He wrote: "The theory of community that lies at the base of Nazi ownership theory must shed the irrationality of the quasi-mystical and quasi-religious elements that are based on its racially defined legal view. This process is essential for Nazi ownership theory to acquire universality and rationality, and to become a guiding principle that is both realistic and critical."[195]

Kada Tetsuji

Studies of Nazism

A scholar of social economic thought and sociology, Kada Tetsuji (Tadaomi, 1895-1964), who taught at Keio Gijuku University and resigned after World War II, had early on developed an academic interest in Nazi economic thought and started to publish his critical analysis of it even before the Nazi Party rose to power.[196] His studies on Nazism appeared in the university bulletin *Mita gakkai zasshi* (Mita Academic Journal) and in general magazines, as well as in books. Kada joined the Showa Research Association soon after it was founded in 1937, and was very active as the chairman of one of its committees, the Research Association for the Study of the Economy of the East Asian Bloc (*Tōa burokku keizai kenkyūkai*) and as a member of another, the Research Association for Cultural Studies (*Bunka kenkyukai*) [initially named the Research Association for Cultural Issues (*Bunka mondai kenkyūkai*)]. Members of the former included Yukawa Morio (1908-1988), a Foreign Ministry official, Kinbara Kennosuke, Wada

195 See Wagatsuma 1938, pp. 446 and 386. It is clear that Wagatsuma had a vision of a rational community based on the firm autonomous status of the individual, and his view may well have had a certain bearing on Japanese post-war reforms, legislation for which Wagatsuma was involved in. See also Wagatsuma 1948.

196 For details about Kada Tetsuji, see Masui 1998, pp. 101 et seq., Ikeda et al eds 2001. For Kada's views on the idea of an East Asian economic community, see Hatano 1980, pp. 38 et seq., Takahashi 1980.

Kōsaku (1907-2006), a Mantetsu official who joined the Cabinet Planning Board in 1937, Yamazaki Yasuzumi, Itani Zen'ichi, Tomooka Hisao (1899-), Miura Tetsutarō (1874-1972), Matsui Haruo (1891-1966) and Ryū Shintarō. The latter was headed by Miki Kiyoshi and its members included the leftist intellectual Saigusa Hiroto (1892-1963), the journalist and scholar Shimizu Ikutarō (1907-1988), Nakajima Kenzō (1903-1979), Sugai Jun'ichi (1903-1982), Fukui Kōjun (1898-1991) and Funayama Shin'ichi (1907-1994); Sasa Hiroo (1897-1948), Ryū Shintarō and Yabe Teiji (1902-1967) joined later.[197] Kada Tetsuji was one of the foremost authorities on Japanese nationalism and the Nazis; it is easy to imagine how significant a role his expert opinions played in discussions amongst those enthusiastic leading scholars.[198]

Kada published two noteworthy studies of Nazism in 1932, the year before the Nazi Party rose to power, *Kokuminshugi to kokusaishugi* (Nationalism and internationalism) and *Nihon kokka shakaishugi hihan* (Criticism of Japanese State Socialism). In the former, he asserted that Nazism (National Socialism) was a movement with more emphasis on action than on ideas, which had yet to work out a comprehensive ideology, but he warned that National Socialism was "an issue of the day, whatever ideological forms and details it took". The phenomenon of National Socialism had originated in Germany and was characteristically German in its form, but it would be wrong to say that it was a phenomenon limited to Germany. Rather, it had the potential and inevitability to emerge in any country at the present stage of world history. German National Socialism was "a pioneer" and "a prototype" of this movement.[199] Based on this premise, Kada attempted to draw a connection between Nazism and various movements in contemporary

---

197 Sakai 1979, p. 135 and pp. 154 et seq. Founded in 1938, the Research Association for the Study of the Economy of the East Asian Bloc published the fruits of its research in 1939 in a book entitled *Burokku keizai ni kansuru kenkyū* (Research on Bloc Economics) by the Shōwa Research Association. Kada was in charge of theoretical and overall aspects of chapters 1 and 6 (see below). The activities of this committee are outlined in the "references" attached to chapter 1 of the above work. As a member of the Research Association for Cultural Studies, Kada reported on "Nihonshugi to sono naiyō ni tsuite" (Japanism and its various aspects). Ryū Shintarō also reported here on "Keizai saihensei no mondai ni tsuite" (Restructuring the economy). Miki reported to the group on "Shin-Nihon no shisō genri" (Ideology of the new Japan) in January 1939; this paper was also discussed in the Research Association for the Study of the Economy of the East Asian Bloc (See note 10 of chapter 1 above.)

198 Yonetani 1997. For the idea of an East Asian Community, see Itō 1998, Fletcher 1982, pp. 115, 135. Also. Young 1998, p. 223. See Chapter 5.

199 Kada 1932a, pp. 238 et seq. and p. 243.

Japan such as state socialism, national socialism and Japanese-style socialism. His analysis of Nazism was closely connected with socio-scientific studies of Japanese fascism, as was the case with others of his contemporaries such as Imanaka Tsugimaro.

As its sub-title, "On Japanese fascism" (*Nihon fashizumu-ron*) suggests, his "Criticism of Japanese State Socialism" was a pioneering work of socio-scientific criticism of a Japanese state socialism that had distinct fascist leanings. Here Kada understood the movements of Japanese nationalism and state nationalism that had been on the rise since the Manchurian Incident to be part of a universal trend towards fascism to counteract Marxist social thought and the Marxist movement. He advocated the necessity of conducting an objective review and criticism of Japanese state socialism in the fascist mould. He closely studied Japanese ultra-nationalism as well as the basic principles of state socialism advocated by Takabatake Motoyuki (1886-1928) and Akamatsu Katsumaro (1894-1955), and compared them with Nazism in Germany.[200]

Through these studies, Kada came to define fascism in the form of four characteristics:[201]

(1) Nazism is a nationalistic ideology aiming to overcome the myriad problems that arose when capitalism hit an impasse. It has two aspects: internationally it is engaged in a political confrontation and struggle with imperialist countries; and domestically it is engaged in a struggle against leftist and socialist movements.

(2) Fascism takes a totalitarian stance in its struggle against the class system. It thus presupposes the existence of social classes, and the middle classes are at the core of the movement.

(3) It is not simple traditionalism. It opposes capitalism, but only up to "a certain point". It plays up external problems to maintain this ambivalence.

(4) Kada summed up the situation in Japan in three points. (a) Problems in foreign relations are more conspicuous than domestic problems, while domestically more emphasis is placed on the fight against Marxism than the struggle against capitalism. (b) Japanese fascism glorifies the military, advocates nationalism and denounces the multiparty political system, thus accommodating the ideology held by the middle-class majority. As its members become more economically hard-pressed, fascist sympathisers will increase to some degree. (c) Considering the characteristics

200 Kada 1932b, preface. For Takabatake, see Hoston 1984.
201 Kada 1932b, particularly pp. 186 et seq.

of fascism, the fascist movement will not succeed in establishing a new, ideal society. Kada concluded by saying: "I can predict this with absolute certainty".[202]

Studies of Nazi economic thought and its various currents

Kada defined Nazism through the emphasis it placed on the race, the spirit of community (putting public good before private interests) and the abolition of interest/debt slavery. In 1933 he published an article called "Doitsu kokuminshugi no keizaikan" (The economic thought of German National Socialism), in which he attempted a comprehensive examination of Nazi economic thought.[203] It was included, virtually in its original form, in his book *Tenkanki no seiji keizai shisō* (Political and economic thought in changing times) published in 1940, through which his analysis of Nazi economic thought was made widely known. The book went into a second impression within a month of its initial publication.

Kada analysed the distinct Nazi traits of "Volk" nationalism and racialism from an economic viewpoint through his examination of the 1920 Twenty-Five Point Programme, two commentaries on it by Gottfried Feder,[204] and contemporary writings on the Nazis. He understood that the Nazis placed the people of the race in the highest position as the group conducting economic life, and set out a number of objectives from that viewpoint: the economic independence of German citizens, harmony among the social classes, and cooperation among citizens. All of these could be summed up by the Nazi principle of *Gemeinnutz geht vor Eigennutz* (the common good comes before self-interest). Points in the party program, such as the right to self-determination, racial independence and

202 Kada 1932b, p. 60.

203 Kada 1933. Kada had been avidly collecting Nazi-related materials, and they formed the basis for an exhibition of Nazi reference materials that was held in June 1934 in the library of Keiō University. The list of exhibits appeared in the *Mita gakkai zasshi*, vol. 38, no. 7 (July 1934) and it attests to the impressive range of the collection.

204 Gottfried Feder (1883-1941) published a manifesto called "Breaking the Bonds of Interest" (*Brechung der Zinsknechtschaft*) in 1919 and was involved in the formation of the German Workers' Party (which later became the Nazi Party). He was Hitler's main economics advisor and drafted the Twenty-Five Point Programme. In 1924 he published *Der Deutsche Staat auf nationaler und sozialer Grundlage. Neue Wege in Staat, Finanz und Wirtschaft*, and in 1927, *Das Programm der N.S.D.A.P. und seine weltanschaulichen Grundlagen* (The NSDAP programme and the world views that underpin it). These works of 1924 and 1927 book are the main commentaries by Feder on the Programme; Kada's understanding is based on Feder 1924, 1927.

the demand for land and territory to maintain the people and to provide settlement of the surplus population, signified "the *autarky* of national economy". To achieve economic *autarky*, the Nazi Party emphasized the importance of agriculture as the supplier of food and raw materials, and devised a series of agricultural and land policies, which eventually led to the Agriculture First policies.

Kada then examined how Nazi economic ideas treated issues such as private property, the abolition of interest slavery, capital, socialisation, finance, taxes and policies regarding workers. His analysis shared much in common with the studies of Wagatsuma and Chō. Kada was distinct from them, however, in pointing out the existence of various currents of thought within the Nazi Party, and linking changes in economic thought with shifts between competing factions within the party. Today, the fact that the Nazi Party was not monolithic and that there were differences and conflicts in both ideas and practice within the party, is well understood. Kada had already gained an accurate grasp of this fact at the time the Nazis seized power.

Kada pointed out the differences between the minority faction of Otto Strasser and his followers, who supported a revolutionary form of National Socialism, and the majority faction of Hitler and his followers.[205] Hitler was in favour of capitalism, while Strasser was opposed to it, demanding a more radical planned economy as well as the re-agriculturalisation of Germany in order to secure economic independence. As a premise for a planned economy, Strasser and his followers contemplated the elimination of the economic privileges of private property, thus distancing themselves from the majority who, in principle, supported private ownership. They opposed the state's gratuitous confiscation of land in the name of the public interest outlined in point 17 of the Twenty-Five Point Programme ("We demand an agrarian reform in accordance with our national requirements, and the enactment of a law to expropriate the owners without compensation of any land needed for the common purpose"). In 1928 they restricted its application to land that had either been acquired illegally or was deemed to be in inappropriate hands from the "standpoint of national welfare", and took a stand against Hitler's attempt to confiscate the land of Jewish companies involved in land speculation. Kada took a keen interest in the

205 Otto Strasser (1897-1974) was a left-wing member of the NSDAP, which he joined in 1925. He led a socialistic faction within the party and supported strikes and the nationalisation of industries and banks. After he was expelled from the party he set up his own party, called the "Black Front". He left Germany after the left-wing was smashed in the Night of the Long Knives (1934). Kada referred to his *Aufbau des deutschen Sozialismus* (1932).

differences and conflicts between Strasser's radical views and the majority group led by Hitler.

Like his contemporaries, Kada considered Point 11 of the Programme, the "breaking of interest slavery", the most important item in the Nazi economic agenda. This demand, advocated by Gottfried Feder and supported by Hitler, was an attack on banks and finance capitalists for their practices of levying heavy interest on farmers and the industrial middle classes and paying high dividends to shareholders, and it went so far as to include a sweeping demand for the abolition of all unearned income. Since opprobrium was, however, concentrated on international financial capital and Jewish loan capital, Kada criticised it as smacking of extremely emotional anti-Jewish sentiments and viewed it as a good example of how Nazism incorporated racial elements into the economic life.

He paid particular attention to Hans Reupke (1892-1942) and his opposition to the abolition of interest slavery on the grounds that it might be understood as part and parcel of the demand made in Point 11 that "all unearned income, and all income that does not arise from work, be abolished". Reupke took a pro-management stand and Kada was of the opinion that his revisionist approach, aimed to "modify Nazi ideas so as to better accommodate the interests of the "propertied bourgeoisie" was gradually gaining ground within the Nazi Party (see below for further on Reupke).[206]

This had ramifications for the Nazi view of capital. The Nazis divided capital into two categories: the first, productive or industrial capital and the second, finance or loan capital that was solely concerned with interest and dividends. They regarded the former as useful for the national economy, and the latter as exploitative and harmful. Their criticism against finance capital, however, was confined to the elimination of "Jewish loan capital", and was never directed more generally. Moreover, the nationalisation of trusts and large banks and the communalisation of large stores, which had been demanded in the Twenty-Five Point Program (Nos. 13, 16),[207] were modified as the "new (pro-)capitalist policies" advocated by

---

206 Kada 1933, pp. 25 et seq., p. 41 and pp. 45 et seq.

207 Kada's understanding derives from Feder 1924, probably the section on pp. 20-22 which states "Die Banken müssen die Diener, nicht die Beherrscher der Wirtschaft sein". Thus the national-socialist state will have its banks and another monetary institutions, but they will no longer be the "Beherrscher" of the national economy but its "Diener". Concerning the "zinskapitalische Raubwirtschaft", Feder pointed out "die Begrenzung des Eigentums nach oben"(p. 22). I think Kada interpreted these as a programme of "bank nationalisation". He seems not to have distinguished too clearly between "nationalisation" and "socialisation".

Reupke gained ground, and subsequently it became increasingly difficult to act on the demand made in Point 18 that "ruthless war be waged against … profiteers".

Nazism advocated cooperation between industrialists and workers, but since it considered employers to be leaders and their employees followers, management was characterised by the absolute control of employers over workers. Kada considered that this model displayed the very essence of fascism as it actually worked to solidify the existing class system.

Observing that fascist movements tended to undergo fundamental changes of characteristics in the course of their evolution from the initial to the late stage, Kada defined such a transformation as a general tendency of fascism that Nazism shared. As the Nazi Party consolidated its power after its successes in the General Election of September 1930, when it became the second-largest party in the Reichstag, it was in the process of transforming the style of its movement. The ensuing changes were reflected in the retreat of elements critical of capitalism and the ascendance of a pro-capitalist stance within the party. The "conservative ruling class", noting the totalitarian and anti-proletarian stand taken by the early Nazi movement, supported by the middle classes, adopted a similar stance, and it began to move closer to the Nazis. Kada predicted that while the Nazi movement still retained its foundations and its initial ideology, this ideology would go through a major transformation following the Party's accession to power.

As Kada's analysis of Nazi economic thought shows, he shared many points of similarity with the Marxist interpretation of fascism. He not only examined Nazi economic thought in specific detail, but also succeeded in shedding light on certain characteristics of the Nazi Party, the movement, and the course it might take in the future, pointing out confrontations and conflicts within the Party, such as between the minority group of Otto Strasser and the majority faction of Hitler, and between the pro-capitalist stance taken by pro-industrialists such as Reupke and the tenor of the demands of the Twenty-Five Point Programme. Compared with the standard of modern studies of Nazism, Kada's analysis was obviously approximate and incomplete, but considering the time when he made his study – in the period just preceding and just after the Nazi rise to power – his work should be valued highly for its pioneering role and for its lucid perception of phenomena that were just unfolding.

In relation to the fate of the Twenty-Five Point Programme, modern studies provide us with detailed information about the activities and ideas of Otto Strasser and Hans Reupke. Reupke was a lawyer on the staff of the National Association of German Industry (Reichsverband der deutschen Industrie); he had been a member of the NSDAP since 1930, but was expelled in 1934. In 1930 he published *Das Wirtschaftssystem des Faschismus*, based on research conducted in

Italy, in which he asserted that in the economic system of Italian fascism, private enterprise and the individual entrepreneur were protected by the regime. His book won him a private commendation from Hitler and a favourable review in the newsletter of the Reichsverband. He published *Der Nationalsozialismus und die Wirtshaft* the following year.[208] The Japanese historian Kurihara Masaru clearly interprets Reupke's function as "suppressing elements of anti-capitalism and anti-big business within the Nazi Party in order to secure support from industrial circles". Forty years before Kurihara's paper was published, Kada had already drawn attention to Reupke, who had just emerged on the scene, and his observations turned out to be more or less correct when set against modern historical research. Chō Moriyoshi also showed greatest interest in Reupke, although, unlike Kada, he viewed him in a positive light.

Criticism of Nazi racial nationalism: the concept of the "cooperative economic union"

Kada focused on the fascist aspects of Nazi ideology in his socio-scientific and critical analysis of Nazism, and this was closely connected with his analysis and criticism of Japanese fascism. This viewpoint remained unchanged in his later work "Political and economic thought in changing times" (1940), in which he gave critical attention to the pro-capitalist and anti-labour characteristics of fascism, as well as its ethno-nationalistic and racial-imperialistic traits. These traits were interconnected, and Kada went on to develop a strong interest in Nazi racial theory and ethnic nationalism. His thorough analysis and criticism of Nazi racialism characterise his studies on Nazism, and, unlike those of Wagatsuma Sakae, they were closely linked to his own activities in response to the situation in Japan at the time.

From the beginning Kada defined fascist ethnic nationalism as an imperialistic stand against foreign countries, and therefore understood it in the context of an international conflict among the world powers. He continued to conduct studies of Nazism sharply critical of its explicit totalitarian traits as well as its racialist and ethnic nationalism, denouncing in particular its discriminatory nature and its irrationality. He expressed this criticism repeatedly in two works,

208 Kurihara 1974. For Reupke, see Kurihara 1974, part 2. Also Turner 1985, p. 136-137. In the 1931 work, "He assured his readers that once in power National Socialism would, as a dynamic movement, feel no more bound by doctrines or programmatic pledges than had Mussolini and his followers. The Nazis could also be counted on to follow the example of the Fascists by breaking the Marxists' hold on the minds of the workers and thereby restoring national unity" (Turner 1985, p. 137). See Hoepke 1968, pp. 149 ff. Kada's view on Reupke is based on Reupke 1931.

Jinshu, minzoku, sensō (Ethnicity, race and war, 1939) and *Seiji, keizai, minzoku* (Politics, economics and ethnic groups, 1940). Here Kada made a socio-scientific examination of Nazi policies and practices such as the promotion of the racial superiority of the German race, the persecution of the Jews and other ethnic groups for their perceived racial inferiority, and territorial expansion and the acquisition of colonies to improve German living standards. These policies he connected with debates on general ethnic and racial problems, and pointed out the inherent irrationality and contradictory nature of Nazism.

Kada linked the Nazi claim of German racial superiority to white supremacy theory, with which the imperialist powers justified their domination of the world, and connected it with criticism against colonial and semi-colonial rule by the Western powers. He considered it a pressing contemporary issue that the imperialistic ruling structure be changed by encouraging the dependencies to extricate themselves from the system and form cooperative unions based on reciprocity and united in their opposition to imperial rule and racial and ethnic discrimination. This is the idea of the "cooperative economic union" (Jap. *keizai kyōdōtai*). As is widely known, this concept (derived from the German *Wirtschaftsgemeinschaft*) was linked with the creation of a cooperative New Order in East Asia to justify Japan's military advancement into Asia, especially the Second Sino-Japanese War (1937-45).

"Cooperative economic union" was closely related to discussions held by the Research Association for the Study of the Economy of the East Asian Bloc (within the Shōwa Research Association). It was thought that the creation of an Asian-style "cooperative economic union" that did away with the ruler-ruled relationship depended on the reform of capitalism (domestic reform) in Japan itself, the nucleus of the cooperative union. "Reform" meant a shift from "the capitalist spirit of prioritising private interests" to "total communalism for the benefit of the whole community".[209] There is considerable overlapping here between Kada's argument and *Shin-Nihon no shisō genri* (The ideological principles of new Japan), a paper by the Research Association for Cultural Issues (later "Cultural Studies") of the Shōwa Research Association, which is said to have been authored by Miki Kiyoshi.[210] Kada's criticism of Nazi economic thought and racial and ethnic theories was not only connected with his criticism of National

209 Shōwa Kenkyūkai 1939, especially ch. 6.

210 Yonetani 1997, pp. 85 et seq. Kada subsequently came to regard the successful outcome of Japanese military action as a necessary step for the liberation of Asia, and he began linking the idea of cooperation among Asians to the spirit of nation building. He continued to publish books, including *Sensō honshitsuron* (The true nature

Socialist movements in Japan but was also inseparable from the principles of an Asian "cooperative economic union". The idea of Japan's being "a core country" in the "cooperative economic union" and the reality of Japan's military advances and dominance over other people were two sides of the same coin. Herein lies the serious contradiction in Kada's argument.[211]

Chō Moriyoshi and the Nazi controlled economy

Evaluation and analysis of Nazism

Chō Moriyoshi worked in the European office (located in Paris) of the South Manchurian Railway from 1941, and, after returning to Japan in 1946, taught at Chūō University and Kanagawa University. His first book *Nachisu – Hittorā undō, shisō, seisaku* (Nazis - Hitler's movement, thought and policy), published in April 1933 right after the Nazi Party had assumed power, was among the earliest publications in Japan containing a comprehensive analysis of Nazi economic thought and policy.[212]

Chō had a close relationship with Hijikata Seibi, his mentor at the Tokyo Imperial University Graduate School. As Hijikata acknowledged in his foreword to *Tōsei keizai seiji kikō* (Political organization of the controlled economy), the seventh volume of the "Collected Works on Japan's Controlled Economy", Chō contributed a great deal to the book.[213] At the time of its publication in July 1933, Hijikata was leaning towards an anti-Marxist and anti-liberal approach to economics in Japan, and probably it was owing to the influence of his mentor that Chō also took an anti-Marxist stand, and regarded Nazism positively. He analysed the contemporary situation as follows:[214]

(1) It is true that capitalism has many defects, but I cannot support Marxism, as it is trying to destroy capitalism by focusing solely on its defects while discounting its merits.

---

of war) and *Nihon keizaigakusha no hanashi* (Stories of Japanese economists), both in 1942. For more about Kada, see Itō 1981.

211 Hatano 1980 and Takahashi 1980.

212 Wagatsuma cited this book in a footnote of his first paper, saying: "It gives a good view of Germany under the Nazi regime." He also referred to it in the translation of the Nazi 25 Point Programme.

213 Hijikata 1933b. Hijikata published *Fashizumu* (Fascism) in 1932, an analysis of Italian fascism.

214 Chō 1933.

(2) By contrast, fascism and National Socialism do not attribute the cause of the crisis facing capitalism to the capitalist system itself, but to its ideological background, namely individualistic liberalism, and they plan to reform society from a universalist standpoint for the well-balanced good of all citizens.

(3) Thus far, the Nazi Party has been regarded as a thuggish group and its platform has been dismissed simply as demagogic or reactionary, but National Socialism is now taking "firm root" among the German people, and so we need to examine closely the thought, policy and platform of the Nazi Party.

Chō maintained that fascism aimed to achieve the reconciliation of interests of all citizens within the framework of capitalism, which was full of defects and facing a crisis. His view matched Kada's almost completely in this respect except that Kada had a critical stance towards fascism while Chō regarded Nazism in a positive light.

Chō's works served as a comprehensive introduction to Nazism and its movement, the first of its kind in Japan, giving a detailed explanation about social democracy and its demise, about the ideology and movement of National Socialism, Nazi political theory and Nazi ideas about the economy and policy, and about National Socialism in relation to fascism.

(a) Chō presented a sociological analysis of Nazi supporters, saying that they mainly comprised the middle classes, such as white-collar workers and medium and small traders and manufacturers as well as farmers and young people, and that currently even labourers and the masses were converting from social democracy to Nazism. He also examined the characteristics of the new and old middle class referring to the writings of Johannes Wernicke (1863-?),[215] a company lawyer in Berlin who was an expert in the study of middle class movements and policies, and Rudolf Hilferding, the foremost theoretician of the Social Democratic Party during the Weimar Republic.

(b) Chō pointed out that the surge of support for the Nazi Party among German citizens refuted the dismissive view of the Nazis as a seditious and thuggish group without an ideology, and that the spread of Nazi sympathisers proved the appeal of certain aspects of Nazi ideology to the German people. He further examined Nazi ideology, and found diverse aspects of Nazism

---

215 His chief work was *Kapitalismus und Mittelstandspolitik* (1907). Chō referred to his article (Wernecke 1925).

reflecting the influences from many ideas and movements from the past, such as the Romantic Movement,[216] state socialism,[217] academic socialism (Kathedersozialismus),[218] Christian socialism[219] and ethnic nationalism.[220]

(c) Chō concluded that Nazism had also internalised traits of other ideas and movements such as nationalism, ethno-statism, racialism, anti-Semitism and national socialism.

The dichotomy between the subordination of private to public interest and the promotion of private initiative

Chō observed that Nazi economic thinking aspired to an ideology distinct from either individualistic and liberalistic economic theories or socialist theories, but it had yet to formulate a system for its various ideas. He positively evaluated Nazism's focus on the power of spirit and will, saying that Nazism contained "passions rarely found elsewhere" and "ethical elements". In particular, he examined in detail the items of the Twenty-Five Point Programme, as delineated in Feder's commentary on the Programme.

Like Wagatsuma and Kada, Chō noted that the core idea of Nazism was the principle that "common good comes before self-interest", a concept based on "the spirit of community" that was the "absolute order" of the Nazi Party, and upon which various policy ideas were formulated. Especially important were

---

216 Chō mentioned the names of Johann Gottlieb Fichte (1762-1814), Friedrich Schlegel (1772-1829), Josef Goerres, (1776-1848), Adam Müller (1779-1829) and Friedrich List (1789-1846); and Houston Stewart Chamberlain (1855-1927), Oswald Spengler (1880-1936) and Othmar Spann (1878-1950) as his contemporary followers.

217 A movement associated with Karl Rodbertus-Jagetzow (1805-1875) and Ferdinand Lassalle (1825-1864) to create a new society not by revolution but through the support of the state.

218 Social reform through government legislation, associated with Adolph Wagner (1835-1917).

219 Chō mentioned the names of Rudolf Todt (1839-1887), Adolf Stoecker (1835-1909), founder of the Christian Socialist Party (Christlichsoziale Partei) in 1878, and Friedrich Naumann (1860-1919), cofounder of the German Democratic Party in 1919.

220 Chō pointed out in this context the movement of Georg Ritter von Schönerer (1842-1921) and Friedrich Naumann's Nationalsozialer Verein (National Social Association), a progressive offshoot of the Christian Socialist Party. He introduced Naumann's views from his 1897 pamphlet, *National-sozialer Katechismus*, and his 1915 work *Mitteleuropa*.

demands for the elimination of unearned income and the abolition of interest slavery, which should be understood in the context of this basic principle. He maintained that the Nazi Party singled out the lack of an "ethical element" that gave precedence to the common good as being a grave defect in the liberalistic and individualistic system that was based on individual self interest and the pursuit of private profit. Thus, he said, the Nazis had introduced "a new ideology" of the common good taking precedence over self-interest in order to correct this defect. He concluded that the "spirit of community" was the fundamental idea of Nazism. Focusing on the decisive role that ethical and spiritual elements played in Nazism, Chō reviewed the Nazi principle of "the common good over self-interest" in the context of economic ethics and ideology. He also regarded the so-called "anti-capitalist" ideas that demanded, among other things, the abolition of interest slavery, not as practical measures but as part of an "ideology". He correctly understood that the basic characteristic of Nazism was its emphasis on its own "world view".

Chō wrote that "despite its anti-capitalist stance, Nazism did not oppose the capitalist system itself",[221] but valued individual initiative, acknowledged private ownership and recognised the contribution of the entrepreneur to society as a leader of the economy. He concluded that Nazi economic theory embraced private ownership and individual initiative but, by enforcing certain restrictions on them, aimed to eliminate excessive competition characteristic of a *laissez-faire* economy. Like Wagatsuma and Kada, Chō regarded private ownership and individual initiative as the basic aspects of Nazi economic thought.

Further, he regarded the abolition of interest slavery and unearned income simply as ethical requirements. This observation was based entirely on Hans Reupke's interpretation of Nazism, to which Kada Tetsuji also paid close attention, though from a different point of view. Kada regarded Reupke as playing a part in steering Nazism towards a pro-capitalist stance, while Chō held that Reupke's stance was aimed at watering down demands for the abolition of interest slavery. Chō internalised Reupke's views within his own interpretation of Nazism. If Kada was right in conceding that Reupke's pro-capitalist stance defined Nazi practice, Chō's take on Reupke's views correctly reflected what was happening in Nazis Germany. On this score, Chō and Kada shared their perception of what the Nazi Party was around the time of its ascent to power.[222]

221 Chō 1933, p. 224.
222 Chō 1933, chapter 5.

Analysis of the Nazi controlled economy and its significance

In his *Fasshoteki tōsei keizai* (The fascist controlled economy) published in 1934, a year after his first book *Nachisu* (The Nazis), Chō Moriyoshi gave a detailed review of Nazi economic policies immediately after the party seized power. He first focused on the worldwide trend of an increased control over the economy by the state and examined it from the standpoint of the "controlled economy" (*tōsei keizai*). He cited two models of a controlled economy: the Soviet-style socialist economy; and the totalitarian German- and Italian-style (fascist) economy, distinct from either socialism or individual liberalism. He attempted to shed light on the latter fascist-style, controlled economy.

Chō noted, concerning the fascist-style controlled economy of Nazi Germany, that under the principle of "the subordination of self-interest to the common good", individual enterprises had a wide scope for their activities and their autonomous decisions were largely respected. This was very different from the Soviet model. He identified two new "organizations" as being at the heart of the economic system based on the Nazi principles, in other word, the New Order that was implemented after the party's rise to power.[223] These were the German Labour Front (*Deutsche Arbeitsfront*, DAF), into which the trade unions had been united by the National Socialists, and the organization of business associations. This was in accordance with the Nazi concept of an organic corporate state (*Ständestaat*).

Chō detailed the characteristics of these organizations as follows:[224]

(1) The idea of forming a state made up of associations stood at the opposite end of the spectrum from the concept of nuclear individuals in a class-divided state. The idea was greatly influenced by Othmar Spann (1878-1950), a conservative Austrian sociologist and economist who advocated a corporate state (*Ständestaat*) based on a hierarchical structure of associations. This kind of *Ständestaat* did not, however, have medieval or traditional state characteristics, but was an autonomous organization formed in accordance with economic conditions and with the objective of protecting the common interests of its members.[225]

---

223 Chō 1934, especially p. 122.

224 Chō 1934, chapter 3, para. 2.

225 Chō's understanding of the corporate state is interesting, and seems quite modern. For the corporate state, see Bowen 1971 (originally published 1947), Cox and O'Sullivan eds 1988 (especially Berghahn 1988). For Spann's *Stände* and *Ständischer Staat*, see Spann 1921.

(2) The constituent units were supervised and given guidance by the state. However, state intervention did not uniformly or bureaucratically apply to individual economic activities. Rather, state control was exerted only during the process of deciding the direction and goal of economic activities or eliminating legal and systemic contradictions. Basic autonomy rested with the units. The plan entailed the formation of economic units such as the National (Reich) Food Estate (which organized agriculture), an autonomous agricultural association recognised by public law, the Reich Estate of Handicrafts (which supervised small businesses), the Reich Groupe of Industry and the Reich Groupe of Commerce. Economic groups of enterprises in industry and commerce were then organized according to the Law for the Organic Upbuilding of the German Economy (March 1934).

(3) Labour unions were abolished and reorganised as the Labour Front (DAF) in May 1933. This was closely related to the basic labour law of the Third Reich, the National Labour Organization Law (Gesetz zur Ordnung der nationalen Arbeit) that was promulgated in January 1934.[226] This law outlined the principle of the "enterprise community" (*Betriebsgemeinschaft*) built on relations bound by "loyalty" between entrepreneur, staff and workers together with principles of the "leadership" and "high performance" or "achievement" (*Leistung*). Simultaneously, the state supervised salaries and protected of social honour. In the "enterprise community", the entrepreneur, as leader (*Führer*), was charged with aiding the workers, while the workers, as his followers (*Gefolgschaft*, lit. "the followers"), had to swear absolute obedience and loyalty. Together they were to strive for the growth of the company and the welfare of the state and its citizens.

(4) The leader principle (*Führerprinzip*) was an all-encompassing principle applied not only to company management but also to all aspects of the economy. Leadership was linked with individual responsibility and was to be exercised from the standpoint of the national economy and the state. It was emphasized that all should be aware of their responsibility to serving the whole (the *Volk*). It did not, however, deny individual initiative. On the contrary, the individual was strongly required to engage in creative activity and to exercise his ability to the full. The "performance" principle (*Leistungsprinzip*) – the recognition and protection of "gifted and creative individuals" – went hand in hand with the leader principle. The salaries of

226 For the DAF and the 1934 Labour Law, see Noakes 1980, pp. 81-83, Linder 1987, pp. 109-110, Rimlinger 1989 pp. 593-594, Mason 1995.

> the workers and administrative staff in the "enterprise community" were no longer to be decided uniformly by "*combative labour unions ignorant of how to run a business*" (my italics)), but determined by the performance principle.[227]

Chō Moriyoshi thus understood Nazism as the machinery of the state to control economic activities. On the one hand, he saw the Nazi system as the organisation of industry and labour by the state, that is, the organic formation of the national economy, and on the other, as individual "enterprise communities" imbued with the leader principle and a merit system in the context of totalitarianism. He repeatedly emphasised the significance of an entrepreneurial spirit and individual creativity and initiative being prized in the state controlled economic system, as well as the autonomy and initiative granted to the economic associations.

Chō went on to describe in detail how the state had extended its control over various branches of the economy, such as agriculture, industry, medium and small businesses, international trade, finance and unemployment in the framework of the controlled economy. Lucid and specific, his commentary is a fine pioneering analysis of Nazi economic policies immediately after the party came to power. More importantly, Chō's depiction of the Nazi Party, and the specific picture that he drew of the Nazi controlled economy, coincided with the transformation of the Japanese economy that followed, particularly regarding the development of a wartime economy. It is clear that the Nazi economic thought and its controlled economy that Chō studied and favourably assessed was to have a great impact on the debate about how to organise a defence economy for Japan and its New Economic Order. The basic ideas in the Outlines for the Establishment of a New Economic Order, presented in December 1940, such as the initiative and responsibility of the entrepreneur, the subordination of the private to the public interest, the leader principle, and the creation of an organic national economy by creating business associations, correspond exactly with the Nazi economic ideas that Chō evaluated positively in his analysis. (see Chapters IV and V below).

Summary

Wagatsuma Sakae, Kada Tetsuji and Chō Moriyoshi studied Nazi economic thought at the time the Nazi Party moved from being a political movement into a position of power and began structuring its machinery of governing machinery. We have reviewed those three scholars' pioneering socio-scientific analyses,

227 Chō 1934, p. 144 and pp. 119 et seq.

examining their characteristics and significance. Wagatsuma made his critical analysis from the standpoint of the legal thought of the Weimar democracy. Kada Tetsuji, a leading member of the Shōwa Research Association, criticized Nazism in connection with the concept of the "economic community" (*Wirtschaftsgemeinschaft*). And Chō Moriyoshi, taking a stand close to his mentor Hijikata Seibi, looked on Nazism favourably, and he closely observed the evolution of the Nazi regime. His portrayal happened to overlap with the process of the transformation of the Japanese economy itself into a controlled economy. I hope that this chapter has made it clear that their analyses of Nazi economic thought, all conducted around the same time but from different viewpoints, are valuable not only for their pioneering merit, but also for the quality of their socio-scientific research.

Their studies of Nazi Germany not only shed light on German fascism to gain a better academic understanding if it, but also had ramifications for a number of issues facing Japan at the time, as a country was falling towards fascism. Here I will once again outline the framework and viewpoints that the three scholars shared in their analyses of Nazi ideology.

(1) They did not view Nazism merely as anti-Semitism, ethnic nationalism (ethno-centrism) or totalitarianism, but examined it in the context of the evolution of capitalism and recognized it as a response to the crisis caused by the impasse that capitalism was in due to its excessive emphasis on individualistic liberalism. By studying the Nazi movement and regime in connection with this crisis, they came to look at Nazism not only as a political phenomenon, but also in the context of its responses to economic problems, and so evaluated it giving emphasis to Nazi economic policy and ideas among the myriad traits and phenomena surrounding the movement. These problems included the decline of medium and small traders and manufacturers, the issue of self-management of farmers, and the dominance of finance capital. They also discussed in the same context such general Nazi traits as racialism and ethnic nationalism, anti-Semitism and totalitarianism.[228] By putting emphasis on the economic issues, they were able to recognize parallels and points in common between Nazism and burgeoning Japanese fascism, and other contemporary phenomena arising in the evolutionary process of capitalism. Their viewpoint had a great socio -scientific significance.[229]

---

228 It is also important that Nazism was understood not just as an ideology for war or total war.

229 Recognizing points in common comes with recognizing uniqueness. They are like two sides of the same coin. This fact was recognized even more acutely when the New Economic Order was being established in Japan, a time when Nazi ideas like

(2) Of all Nazi economic ideas, in the broadest sense of the word, the three scholars all agreed that the guiding principle was that the common good took precedence over self-interest (*Gemeinnutz geht vor Eigennutz*), over and above others such as the promotion of private initiative and anti-capitalism. This understanding, which was shared by most of their contemporaries in Japan, was based on the interpretation of Nazi thought by contemporary Germans, who defined this principle as the Nazi "categorical imperative". The strong influence of Nazi thought led to this principle being adopted as a fundamental principle of the New Economic Order in Japan at the end of 1940, but the stage had already been set in the early 1930s. Unlike the liberal economic system with the pursuit of private profit takes priority, this Nazi economic principle gave priority to the overall interests of the race and nation. "*Gemein*" in the phrase *Germeinnutz* refers in National Socialism to the nation or race, and so it placed the focus clearly on the German race, and on its identity with political totalitarianism.

The principle of prioritising the interests of the whole, however, did not deny either private property or private economic activity, but rather valued private initiative and integrated it into the economic system. Wagatsuma, Kada and Chō all recognized private ownership, individual initiative in economic activity and individual responsibility as fundamental Nazi principles. Their interpretation that the Nazis did not deny the profit principle or the capitalist principle was later taken up in the debate on the New Order by the Japanese business community who used it in an effort to join their standpoint to that of the Nazi Party. The phrase "...granting the entrepreneur a right to autonomous management based on his initiative and responsibility" in the "Guidelines for the New Order" might well have been taken from Nazi literature. (see Chapter V)

Wagatsuma, Kada and Chō all cited "the abolition of interest slavery" (*Brechung der Zinsknechtschaft*), point 11 of the 25 Point Programme, as an attempt to suppress the pursuit of private profit for the benefit of racial and national welfare. The inclusion of this point was a result of the perception that the heavy burden of interest on people had resulted from the single-minded pursuit of private profit, and that it now posed the most serious threat to people's welfare, and so must be eliminated for the good of the whole race and nation. Wagatsuma went so far as to say about this that "It is no exaggeration to say that this is what

---

the subordination of the private to the public interests were being considered for introduction or application to Japan. See Chapters 5 et seq.

Nazism stands for."[230] In theory, the abolition of interest slavery means the end of the dominance of banking and finance capital, and consequently the end of the pursuit of excessive profit by speculation in land and stock, and war profiteering. In actuality, though, this vehement opposition to finance capital and the worship of money that should have taken centre stage in Nazi "socialism" was linked to anti-Semitism and used as a tool to attack Jewish economic activities, especially those of Jewish finance capital. Wagatsuma, Kada and Chō all saw it in this way.

More recent historical research has placed a particular emphasis on "anti-capitalist" elements, particularly the abolition of interest slavery and unearned income, as being a characteristic of Nazism. But even as early as 1933 and 1934, Wagatsuma, Kada and Chō had already made an accurate analysis of those so-called "anti-capitalistic" elements. They all agreed that around the time of its rise to power, the Nazi Party took a basically capitalistic stand and its criticism of finance capital was concentrated on the elimination of Jewish capital. It should be said though that they made little attempt to define the overall nature of Nazi economic thought from an "anti-capitalist" viewpoint.

(3) They all noted an anti-democratic trait in labour relations, though how they evaluated it differed. From a Nazi ethnic nationalist and totalitarian standpoint, the capitalist-worker relationship was regarded not as a class -based relationship but as one defined by a racially-united community. Within the framework of the leader principle, which defined the entrepreneur as a leader and the workers as subordinates, labour-management negotiations and other democratic principles underpinning labour relations were eliminated, while the leadership of the entrepreneurs was strengthened. Chō regarded this favourably. Kada, on the other hand, denounced it as a dictatorial tendency on the part of the entrepreneur, and criticising it vehemently as being a fundamental aspect of fascism and an agent for entrenching the existing social system even more firmly. Wagatsuma also warned that the Nazi idea of community would result in the uncritical approval of existing unjust powers, the deprivation of individual autonomy, and arbitrary control by those in power.

(4) The three scholars also shared the observation that there was a close relationship between Nazism and the middle classes, but they differed on how they were connected. Kada regarded Nazism as "appearing from the outside to be a middle-class movement", and pointed out its inherent contradictions, predicting that it was fated to be used by the members of the ruling apparatus, that is, "monopoly capitalism" and he placed particular stress on the development and

230 Wagatsuma 1934a 2, p. 837.

transformation of the Nazi movement. "Today [1932]", he said, it "is no longer a middle-class movement", but had become "a movement for Germany's large bourgeoisie". Kada predicted that such ideas as the abolition of interest slavery were responses to the demands of the middle classes, and though they might remain as an ideology, they would inevitably undergo change.

Also focusing on the relationship between the middle classes and the Nazis, Chō, unlike Kada, deemed important the fact that under the Nazi regime legislation was proposed for farmers as well as medium and small traders and manufacturers. Chō noted that the policies for the middle classes had been carried over from the Nazi movement to the Nazi regime. Like Chō, Wagatsuma also noted that the principles for the maintenance and protection of farmers and medium and small traders and manufacturers were stressed not only in the party platform, but also in laws that were enacted after the party came to power, the inherent contradictions of which Wagatsuma also pointed out. Chō did not find any particular problem in this development under the Nazi regime, whereas Wagatsuma, who believed in the inevitability of the evolution of capitalism, harboured strong doubts about the possibility of carrying out such policies.

Given the circumstances, the studies of Nazism by contemporary Japanese were inevitably lacking in accuracy and in the thoroughness of their assessment of the historical facts, and this affected the overall quality of their work as academic research. Their studies are nevertheless valuable for their pioneering role and their socio-scientific quality, and we need to recognise them as trailblazers in the study of Nazism. More important still is the fact that these contemporary studies of Nazi Germany by Japanese scholars were superimposed onto and entwined with the current situation in Japan, and it was inevitable that they contained a tension *vis-a-vis* the realities arising from Japan's slide towards fascism.

Chapter Four: An Economy for Total War: Japan and the Nazi Model

Fascism emerged as part of the state organization in Japan in the period following the February 26 Incident of 1936 and the outbreak of the Second Sino-Japanese War in July 1937. It was imposed from above as a means of control by the military, and comprised the civil bureaucracy and senior statesman on one hand, and large capital and the political parties on the other.[231] It was also during this period, when an international and totalitarian system was coming into being, that Japan concluded Anti-Comintern Pacts with Germany (November 1936) and Italy (November 1937). In Japan, people were experimenting with the theoretical constructs of an economic system based on national defence and preparedness for total war, and in 1938 the National Mobilization Law was drawn up as the basic law to allow such a system to be put into effect. In this chapter, I shall examine the influence of Nazi thought on ideas about defence economics and the principles of the National Mobilization Law in order to elucidate connections between German and Japanese totalitarianism in policy ideas at that time.

As research into Japanese economic history has shown, the period between the Manchurian Incident of 1931 and the flare-up of war in China in 1937 was a watershed in the move towards a controlled, wartime economic system.[232] The prime purpose of introducing a wartime economy was to facilitate the war against China, though it was also intended to serve as a system able to make ready for the

231 Maruyama 1964, pp. 32, 38 et seq., Maruyama 1969, p. 2 (in English), Maruyama 1995 (vol. 3), pp. 262, 269 et seq.

232 For example, Kindai Nihon kenkyūkai ed. 1987, Hara ed. 1995. Hara points out (p. 5) that "Japan started its aggression against China in 1931 with the Manchurian Incident. At this time, the Japanese economy was on the road to recovery from the Depression that had begun in 1929. The move of the economy as a whole towards a wartime economy began in earnest with the Sino-Japanese War that erupted after the Marco Polo Bridge Incident of July 1937. From the point of view of political and military history, war lasted fifteen years, from 1931 to 1945, but in terms of economic history, the wartime economy is considered to have been in place only from 1937; between 1932 and 1936, the period associated with the Manchurian Incident, there was very little military influence and in general it can be considered a peacetime economy."

expected total war in the future. Thus it was essential that a structure to expand productivity, especially in the munitions industry, and to mobilize all aspects of economic power, should not simply be a response to the pursuit of war in China, but also a preparation for total war. Such a structure was in effect a wartime economic system, readying for total war, to be adapted when future conditions made it necessary.

From our present perspective, it is obvious that the system put in place to mobilize the economy for war, both the present one in China and the total war to come, was simply the first step in a series of measures leading towards a wartime economy, but it was not so apparent to those concerned at the time. Their ideas of modern war were based on their experience of World War I which led them to understand that the military was now mechanized and technology-driven, and that war had become long-term and general. Nevertheless, even in a situation where another such all-out, large-scale war was being anticipated, it was not at all clear how a system should be constructed during peace-time that could be easily transformed into a total war economy when necessary. World War I, as the first instance of total war, had taught people about the nature of modern war, and it was based on this experience that questions were raised afterwards about how to organize the economy in preparation for total war if one were forecast, so the economy could quickly respond to the situation. As people observed the intensifying global crisis, they felt the necessity of conceiving and planning an infrastructure to prepare the ground to mobilize economic power and increase production capacity to support the military strength that would be crucial when total war occurred (or was caused) some time in the future.

The military authorities and the Cabinet Resources Bureau (*Shigenkyoku*) began thinking along such lines in the 1920s.[233] The Cabinet Resources Bureau had been established in 1927 to plan a national system to mobilize civilian and military resources for war. It was essentially a research body staffed by elite bureaucrats who held their positions in it concurrently with those in their own ministries.[234] The Depression of 1929 encouraged a global move towards military expansion and bloc economics among the world powers, and this momentum was accelerated by military incursion in Asia. In 1938, the year after the

---

233 Katō, Toshihiko 1977, 1979, Yui 1978, Fujimura 1981, Kōketsu 1981, Andō 1987, etc. Also, Suzaki 1997. The phrase "total war" is associated with General Erich Ludendorff. His memoir *Der totale Krieg* (Munich, 1935) sold more than 100,000 copies in its 1939 edition. It was translated into Japanese in 1938. See also Miyake 1996, section 1, chapter 1.

234 For the Resources Bureau, see Johnson 1982, p. 118, Mimura 2011, p. 20.

outbreak of the war between China and Japan, Japan legislated the National Mobilization Law (*kokka sōdōin hō*). The period around the beginning of the war in China thus saw the ideas about an economic system of defence and preparedness in the face of total war brought to actuality.

The National Mobilization Law

The Cabinet Resources Bureau studied the idea of preparing a system of mobilization for the expected total war during peace-time in conjunction with the concept of "national general mobilization" (*kokka sōdōin*). The idea was actualised in May 1938 as the National Mobilization Law. This legislation was intended to make it possible to control and utilize on a national basis "human and material resources" for "the purpose of national defence". It later became the legal basis for a variety of measures to control the economy. The Law was set up as an enabling act to carry out government decisions without going through parliamentary deliberation, and it is well-known as an important landmark in the establishment of a Japanese-style fascism. However the thinking behind the law as such was not uniquely Japanese. In Europe and the United States too there were similar plans, and the Japanese concept had been devised making reference to European and American discussion about war "preparedness" and "procurement", and about planning for industrial mobilization.[235]

A study of the morphological changes in, and modernization of, warfare that had occurred during the Great War led the Cabinet Resources Bureau to strengthen its conviction that early military and industrial mobilization was vital for the pursuance of a future total war, and that "preparation" for it was necessary.[236] It made a detailed study of instances abroad of planning for total war, looking for example at American plans for industrial mobilization. Industrial mobilization and military procurement planning in the United States was promoted through the Office of the Assistant Secretary of War, as a result of the 1920 National Defense Act, and through the War Policies Commission, a joint

235 There is a considerable amount of research concerning the National Mobilization Law. I have made particular reference to Honma 1978, Nagao 1982, Kikakuin ed. 1989(reprint). However, Honma does not refer to connections between ideas regarding the Japanese National Mobilization Law and those found in Europe and the United States, and so overlooks the common global context of the thinking behind the law, with the result he understands it only in terms of Japanese distinctiveness. See also Berger 1977, pp. 149-157.

236 Bōeichō bōei kenshūjo senshishitsu 1967, Abe 1975, part 2, chapter 1, Andō 1987, Yamaguchi 1979, also Mikuriya 1996, p. 18 et seq.

congressional-excutive body set up in 1930 to study how to reduce war profiteering.[237] The former body published an Industrial Mobilization Plan in 1931; this was revised in 1933[238] and finalised in 1939.

The American Industrial Mobilization Plan as it was revised in 1933 consisted of an Introduction, Part One (Procurement planning), Part Two (Control of economic resources and mobilization of industry) and Appendixes. The Introduction stated that "complicated weapons and machines are used up rapidly in war. Armies and navies must not only be well supplied initially, but maintenance must be adequate and continuous. Thus, the success of a modern fighting force is directly and immediately dependent upon the ability of the Nation's resources to satisfy promptly its requirements in munitions. In addition, throughout the duration the war, the Nation must continue to provide all the material things upon which the health and well-being of its population depend. War is no longer simply a battle between armed forces in the field – it is a struggle in which each side strives to bring to bear against the enemy the coordinated power of every individual and every material resource at its command. The conflict extends from the soldier in the most forward lines to the humblest citizen in the remotest hamlet in the rear." Thus industrial mobilization plans must be set up during peace-time. "Experience in modern war has demonstrated that lack of adequate plans for industrial mobilization and for military procurement is the source of many evils in war." It is therefore suggested that "a large unit of specially qualified officers in the War and Navy Departments should be devoted in time of peace to studies of supply programs for hypothetical military undertakings. As these programs would always have to be based upon the obtainability of the supplies outlined, the two Departments should be required to go deeply into a study of the industrial resources and possibilities of the country as they relate to war needs. Mobilization and maintenance of armed forces (in peace-time) result in a decrease in the number of citizens available for productive purposes at the same time that a great increase in the output of productive establishments is required in order to provide the necessary munitions in war. Two methods are available: First to increase the aggregate volume of output; second, to divert labor and raw materials from the production of nonessential items to the production of those things absolutely necessary to the successful conduct of the war. In a major

237 Smith ed. 1959, part 2, chapter 4, Kawamura 1998, part 2, chapter 1.

238 "A revision of the plan for industrial mobilization submitted by the War Department in 1931 to the War Policies Commission appointed under the authority of public resolution no. 98, Seventy-first Congress". United States Government Printing Office, Washington, 1935.

conflict both methods must be used." Part One lays out the above principles, the development of Army procurement plans and their features, and steps in planning. Part Two deals with the control of economic resources and the mobilization of industry, which included the priority of control of industrial products, price controls, commandeering, the control of foreign trade, the organization of government corporations, and the application of control measures as well as organizational plans, especially within the executive branch of the government of the United States.

In 1931 too, the Army Chief of Staff, General Douglas MacArthur (1880-1964), presented "The War Department Mobilization Plan" before the War Policies Commission.[239] In the concluding section, he summarised the policy recommendations of the War Department in what he called Group A: "Those policies which will assure practical and efficient peace-time preparation for the emergency of war, promulgated and published in such a way as to have a serious, sobering effect upon every man, woman and child when he or she contemplates the possibility of war."[240] However, unlike in Japan, the Army needed to have the approval of Congress and the President, and so MacArthur stated: "The problem consists in making all pre-arrangements necessary to insure effective use of material resources in war. The system evolved must incorporate the views of the Army, the Navy, and of industry, and must receive the approval of Congress and of the President. The ramifications of the pre-arranging process are almost endless."[241]

The Cabinet Resources Bureau translated the industrial mobilization plan, as revised in 1933, together with MacArthur's presentation and a statement by Bernard M. Baruch of the War Policies Commission about eliminating war profiteering and made it public in 1933 under the title, "General Mobilization Plan of the United States" (*Beikoku sōdōin keikaku*).[242] In the introduction, the Resources Bureau demonstrated its understanding of the global situation and the necessity to prepare for mobilization. Since it is of interest, I will summarise it here.

"Even in the United States, which sets the diplomatic agenda for the maintenance of world peace, institutions to prepare for general mobilization in the

---

239 "The War Department Mobilization Plan. The measures necessary to insure an efficient defense system", presented before the War Policies Commission. In *Army Ordnance*, vol. XII, no. 68, 1931.

240 *Ibid.* vol. XII, no. 69, 1931, p. 183.

241 *Ibid.* vol. XII, no. 68, 1931, p. 86.

242 Shigenkyoku ed. 1933. Part of it was excerpted in *Shigen*, the journal of the Bureau (vol. 2, no. 1(August 1932), no. 3 (November 1932), vol. 7, no. 10 (October 1937).

case of war in the future, are gradually being put in place. Concerning plans for industrial mobilization, which are fundamental in terms of preparing for mobilization, the Assistant Secretary of War is responsible for procurement under the revised 1920 National Defense Act: 'The Assistant Secretary of War, under the direction of the Secretary of War, shall be charged with supervision of the procurement of all military supplies and other business of the War Department pertaining thereto and the assurance of adequate provision for mobilization of material and industrial organizations essential to war-time needs.'[243] His duties thus incorporate setting up systems and methods for the speedy and economical acquisition of large amounts of military supplies in an emergency, and also preparing plans to advise the President in a time of war about mobilizing economic resources and managing the economic efforts of the populace. Planning was undertaken to expedite these duties: procurement districts were set up, plans for industrial production were made, and various schemes to put into effect an educational ordering system[244]."

It is plain that "preparing to mobilize" for "future wars" was seen as a global trend, and that the "fundamental prerequisite" for it was "the provision of industrial mobilization". The text then included a direct translation from the concluding section of MacArthur's statement quoted above.[245] "The problem consists in *making all pre-arrangements necessary* to insure effective use of material resources in war. The system evolved … *must receive the approval of Congress and of the President*." (my italics).

The Cabinet Resources Bureau was also interested in the French situation, and reported on it twice in its Research Reports (*Kenkyū shiryō*, January 1930, May 1937).[246] The latter report described "national mobilization" as the total "control and utilization" of "human and material resources" and pointed out that, with military force, it was indispensiable for waging "future wars", and that it was necessary to prepare for a conversion between the "two times" of "peace and war". This was the trend of legislation in various countries.

Japan's National Mobilization Law (*Kokka sōdōin hō*) of 1938 was thus legislated to a backdrop of the development of similar mobilization plans in Europe and the United States that were studied in the course of the law's preparation.

243 41 Stat. 759 (June 4, 1920), 764-765.

244 This means that during peacetime, the government would order armaments, etc. from enterprises producing non-military goods in order to give them experience in military production.

245 Shigenkyoku ed. 1933, p. 72 et seq.

246 Shigenkyoku ed. 1930. Shigenkyoku ed. 1937.

Article 1 reads: "National mobilization as termed in this Law means the control and operation of human and material resources in such as way as to enable the State to give full scope to the efficient use of its strength for national defence in time of war, or armed incidents that are equivalent to war". Not only was this law "preparatory" in the sense that it provided a legal basis ahead of time to operate national mobilization for war during a time of peace, but it also served as a basic law for setting up "preparatory" measures to control and operate human and material resources at a time of ostensible peace when "armed incidents that are equivalent to war" occurred. The following quotation is taken from *Kokubō keizaihō taisei* (The national defence economy law system), a work that appeared in 1942, coauthored by Suekawa Hiroshi (1892-1977), which focused on the National Mobilization Law.

> Basically considered, the National Mobilization Law is the fundamental law for determining the broad lines of the economic control of resources "in a time of war" and particularly for the purpose of "national defence". In this sense it can be said to be an emergency law, having an extraordinary nature, that is, pertaining to wartime. However, "wartime" does not refer only to specific, definite times of war like the China Incident but also includes more broadly all times of war that may possibly occur generally in the future. Furthermore, since there are aspects concerning the preparations that should be put in place already *during peace-time in order to prepare* for such a time, in this sense it is a law having *permanency* to be applied to times of *normality*. For this reason, it forms the basis of a broad law of the national defence economy.[247] (my italics)

This comment is concerned with the "peace- and wartime" as prescribed in the Mobilization Law (Articles 21-26, 31): "In terms of the National Mobilization Law, the government can when necessary act .... according to imperial decree." Controls were placed on inquiries into human resources, the training of technical experts, the possession of materials, the planning and practice of operations, examination research, fostering enterprise, report collection and official inspections and audits. The "human and material resources" that were the subjects of these were stipulated in Articles 2 and 3 as "materials for mobilization" (*sōdōin busshi*) and "operations for mobilization" (*sōdōin gyōmu*). The former referred of course to munitions, but also more widely to necessary consumer items for daily use and materials for their supply, as well as other items designated as fitting, not on the list of specified items. The latter, "operations", referred to everything necessary for national mobilization, including production, repair, distribution, import and export, and storage; this could extend beyond munitions to "all matters pertaining to living".

---

247 Suekawa 1942, p. 20.

While Japanese plans for mobilization during peace-time shared points of similarity with ideas about preparing for total war in France and the United States, they also differed from them in a decisive way. There, "mobilization" was predicated on democratic processes, like the approval of the parliamentary body, but in Japan, such a method was denied. The "force of public opinion" had been emphasized in the American Industrial Mobilization Plan translated by the Bureau: "Having determined upon the proper uses for materials and services, the next problem is how to assure that they will be so used. Plans for this must be concrete, definite, and practical. There must be considered methods for utilizing efficiently the war powers of the President, the authority likely to be acccorded by Congress, the war-time power of commandeering, and, above all, the force of public opinion. The support of public opinion is so essential that anything that may appeal to the majority of the people as unnecessary, unfair, or unjust cannot be permitted to creep into the plans."

Tamaki Hajime of the Cabinet Planning Board (Kikakuin, the body that was constituted in 1937 combining the Resources Bureau and the Planning Agency) understood the differences between the American and Japanese situations as follows.[248] First, there is at present, he said, no will in the United States to prosecute war. Second, in the United States, military action and the production of munitions are seen from the viewpoint of industry in general; this is in contrast to the general case of industry in other countries [i.e. Germany and Japan, author's note], in view of the expansion of military activities and the production of munitions. In the United States at present, stated Tamaki, industrial expansion has the greatest importance, and it can even be said that the best policy is considered to be to make every effort to avoid war. In "countries needing to be actively engaged in war, that is, countries regarding their industries to be on a military standing", "wartime organization occupies an incomparably more important position" than the peacetime organization of ministries, government offices and economic associations. In addition, he commented that "it seems that a wartime machinery has to perform a guiding role towards industry". The third distinctive feature Tamaki brought up was "industrial democracy" within the system for industrial mobilization. This refers to the appointment of directors of the War Resources Administration and other government offices concerned with the economy from among the private sector, and also to the fact that the decisions of the wartime labour bureau and the committee to control prices would have no legal force. Fourth, the most focused expression of democratic features was that the author-

248 Tamaki 1938, p. 202 et seq.

ity of the president was prescribed as "the duty of controlling the economy based on public opinion" "according to the constitution, according to Congress". In other words, "the wartime economic framework is not organized under the autocratic powers of dictatorial rulers".

Tamaki thus understood that the American national mobilization plan had no interest in prosecuting war and lacked a positive attitude towards military matters. Furthermore, its framework was democratic, not autocratic. This meant it was different to the German and Japanese situation. The dissimilarity with Japan was in the importance attached to republicanism; it is probably safe to say too that the same could apply to the French case, where close attention was paid to the role of the League of Nations.[249]

Japan's National Mobilization Law was very different to those in Europe and the United States, in that it rejected democratic methods and adopted the principles of totalitarianism. This is apparent by the wording of the Law that "the government can, when necessary for national mobilization in times of war, act according to imperial decree" and "the government can, when necessary for national mobilization, act according to imperial decree". The government could implement the National Mobilization Law to prescribe control measures through according imperial decrees and supplementary ministerial ordinances, without relying on parliamentary legislation. Also, only abstract and general fundamental principles has been laid down regarding preparations for, and the enforcement of, national mobilization, and so the law had to be very comprehensive in its scope.[250]

Tsumagari Kuranojō (1900-1969), a professor of Civil Law in the Tōhoku Imperial University and author of *Nihon tōsei keizai hō* (Japanese economic control legislation, 1942), wrote, "To achieve its purpose of national defence, this law should be termed a powerful national control law for a time of war, carrying out the control of material and human resources. It is also a kind of enabling act, a standards law."[251] Indeed, the Japanese National Mobilization Law was an "enabling act",[252] in the sense of the German "Ermächtigungsgesetz" (formally

249 In France nationalization of the munitions industry was planned. Fukuda Yoshiharu (1905-1983) of the Cabinet Planning Board pointed out its unsuitability, and also spoke of the ideology of nationalization and the popular front. Fukuda 1939, p. 200. For military planning in France, see Challener 1965, chapter 6 and Young 1978, chapter 7.

250 Suekawa 1942, Honma 1978.

251 Tsumagari 1942, p. 73. See also Nagao 1982, p. 14.

252 Honma 1978.

"Gesetz zur Behebung der Not von Volk und Reich", Law to Relieve the Distress of the People and the Reich) of March 24, 1933. As is well-known, this law formed the basis of the Nazi dictatorship, in that it gave the government broad authority to enact legislation without the approval of the Reichstag.

Kikuchi Haruo, who was tasked with examining the Nazi national defence economy for the Cabinet Resources Bureau, and later its successor, the Cabinet Planning Board, described the "Ermächtigungsgesetz" as follows: "On the basis of this Enabling Act, the Nazi government was endowed with the power to enforce laws ranging over a broad range of national policy, and it was able to press forward without legal hindrance towards the establishment of the Third Reich. It was an important piece of legislation, equivalent to the first article of a Nazi national mobilization law."[253] The Japanese National Mobilization Law, as legislation for total war preparation, rejected the democratic mobilization methods of the United States and France, and consciously adopted the 1933 Nazi Enabling Act that allowed the organization of "a wartime economic framework under the autocratic powers of dictatorial rulers".

The National Mobilization Law begun to be implemented wholesale following the decision by the Cabinet in January 1939 to embark on a four-year (1938-1941) plan to increase industrial strength that had been drafted by the Planning Board in 1938. A number of ordinances followed, enabling various articles of the Mobilization Law to be put into practice; these included the National Service Draft Ordinance (*Kokumin chōyō rei*, for Article 4), the Employee Recruitment Restriction Ordinance (*Jūgyōsha yatoiire seigen rei*, for Article 6), the Ordinance for Wage Control (*Chingin tōsei rei*, for Article 6), and the Corporate Profits, Dividends and Financing Ordinance (*Kaisha rieki haitō oyobi shikin yūzū rei*, for Article 11). In addition, there were a number of ordinances regarding prices (Article 19), such as the Price Regulation Ordinance (*Kakakutō tōsei rei*), the Ordinance to Control Land and Housing Rents (*Chidai yachin tōsei rei*) and the Farm Rent Control Ordinance (*Kosakuryō tōsei rei*), and various others, like the Land Transportation Control Ordinance (*Rikuun tōsei rei*), the Marine Transportation Control Ordinance (*Kaiun tōsei rei*), the Ordinance for the Control of Electric Power (*Denryoku chōsei rei*) and the Rice Hulling etc. Control Ordinance (*Beikoku tōseitō seigen rei*).[254]

The "China Incident" of July 1937 marked the outbreak of the Second Sino-Japanese War, the first of the "incidents" (*jihen*), armed clashes without any

253 Kikuchi 1940, p. 7.
254 Tsumagari 1942, p. 75 et seq.

formal declaration of war, which conformed to the definition of "war" as contained in the Mobilization Law, and from 1938, it was clear that these had become long-term. Nevertheless, this Law was understood as a national defence economic system preparing the total war predicted for the future, not simply as a measure to cope with "incidents". This understanding continued through the New Economic Order and the resulting (or planned) outbreak of the Pacific War (a full-scale total war) in December 1941. If we consider the Pacific War to be all-out total war, then the period leading up to it was the first, and preliminary, stage.

While the National Mobilization Law was based on a capitalistic economic system, this system needed to be changed. It is for this reason that the issue of a new economic order arose, concerning the restructuring of the Japanese economy.

The Japan-Manchuria Financial Economic Research Group and the Soviet and German Economic Models

The term "defence economy" in itself simply means an economy for defending one's own national borders, but here it indicates a particular type of economic system that is capable of moving easily to one of total war, one that could change from a peacetime economy to one supporting a war of aggression in Asia at the same time as assuming, and preparing for, total war. This is why a defence economy can simultaneously be called a war-preparedness economy. A pioneering role in the formulation of the concept of the defence economy was played by the Japan-Manchukuo Finance and Economics Research Group (Nichiman zaisei keizai kenkyūkai), set up in 1935 by Ishiwara Kanji (1889-1949). Ishiwara, a strategist on the General Staff of the imperial army and the leading figure in the creation of the state of Manchukuo, charged Miyazaki Masayoshi (1893-1954), a director of the Economic Research Association (ERA) of the Manchurian Railway (Mantetsu keizai chōsakai), to form the group to study the economic strength of both countries in view of the need to increase armaments in the face of the looming global crisis. The scheme that members came up with was later inherited by the Cabinet Planning Board and, in revised form, was used to establish a wartime economic system as World War II approached.[255]

---

255 *Nichiman zaisei keizai kenkyūkai shiryō* 1970, vols. 1-3, Nakamura and Hara 1970, Yamazaki 1987, 2002 and 2011. etc. For more general works, see Kobayashi 1995a, 1995b and Kobayashi et al eds. 1995. The group was assisted by economists such as Hijikata Seibi, Konno Genpachirō, Koshimura Shinzaburō and Koga Hidemasa. Concerning the general situation at the time of the war with China, see Matsuura

The Japan-Manchuria Financial Economic Research Group (hereafter JMG), in conceiving and planning a national economic framework for "national defence", carried out extensive surveys and investigations whose results were used in the compilation of the plan. Kobayashi Hideo, who has made a close study of both the JMG and Miyazaki Masayoshi, emphasizes the fact that they referred to the Soviet Five Year Plan when making their own. "The Japanese structure for total war was formed in imitation the Soviet Five-Year Plan, but it outstripped it and improved on it."[256] Okazaki Tetsuji too draws attention to "the permeation of planning within government and the military" and pointed out that the blueprint for the five-year plan made by the JMG "was the premise on which government plans to expand productivity were based". He draws our attention to the fact that the original plan had already been drawn up in August 1936, a year before the outbreak of war with China, and this indicates its close relationship with the Soviet five-year plan.[257]

How valid is it to link the Japanese economic system for total war with the Soviet planned economy? The Soviet plan was based on the socialist formula of abolishing private ownership as a means of production. Since Japan did not subscribe to this theory, applying the Soviet model for state economic control was restrictive. The JMG chose, not a socialist-type centralized control of the economy that rejected private enterprise and management, but rather a form of state control that assumed a capitalist economy. And the precedent for such a system was not to be found in the Soviet Union but rather in Germany. For this reason, the JMG turned its attention to the controlled economic system of Nazi Germany, regarding it to be on a par with, or even superior to, the Soviet model. It would seem very likely then that the JMG took note of Nazi policy and ideas from a variety of angles, in order to decide on the formula for a state system of economic control and to build a theoretical construct for a defence economy as an independent stage in the preparation for total war.[258]

The JMG included both scholars, such as Hijikata Seibi, professor at the Tokyo Imperial University, and Koga Hidemasa (Nanjō Norio, 1908-2004), a teaching

---

1995. For Ishiwara Kanji, see Peattie 1975, pp. 208 ff. See also Berger 1977, pp. 111 ff., Gao 1997, pp. 107 ff.

256 Kobayashi 1995b, Introduction.

257 Okazaki 1991, p. 378 et seq. Okazaki points out that the Cabinet Planning Board also used the Soviet Union "as a model for economic management".

258 For the diplomatic relationship between Germany and Japan in this period, see Miyake 1975, Yoshii 1987. See also Sommer 1962, Krebs 1984, Tajima 1992, part 2, Sprang and Wippich eds. 2006, Kudo and Tajima eds. 2008.

assistant at the same university (and in the postwar period a professor at Chūō University and a novelist), as well as army men, such as Nagata Tetsuzan (1884-1935), but its driving force was Miyazaki Masayoshi. Immediately after the outbreak of war with China, Miyazaki described its planning as follows.[259]

(1) The implementation of the "Five Year Plan for Expansion of Key Industries industrial development in Japan and Manchukuo" was a watershed in terms of economic control. It resulted in a "great leap forward", from a stage where planning guidance by the state regarding the economies of Japan and Manchuria was simply a matter of indicating general policy, to one where guidance came in the form of specific plans for economic construction. This Five Year Plan was "the first example" of planned economic guidance by the state in accordance with "the requirements of national defence".

(2) The first plan was drawn up at the beginning of 1936 under the direction of the Army General Staff, as an appendix to the Fiscal Five-Year Plan that centred on attaining military preparedness. In the course of the following year, an "original combined plan incorporating both Japan and Manchuria" was finalized as a result of a study of four drafts. After the plan was passed to the governments of both countries for study, it appeared first as a bill of the Manchurian, and then of the Japanese, Government.

Miyazaki added a note about the Japanese government bill, that he "had heard detailed bills were being formulated by the Cabinet Planning Board," and he pointed out that the policy for the expansion of productivity later "came to occupy a very important position in my economic policy. I think that the Five Year Plan for the Expansion of Key Industries in Japan and Manchukuo opened up *a methodological space for planned economic guidance in a system preparing for war.*" (my italics)

Nakamura and Hara have made a detailed study of how the JMG drew up the original plan and of the scrutiny it later came under (see Note 255, this chapter). For Miyazaki, this "Five Year Plan" was the "first example" of planned economic guidance by the state in accordance with the demands of "national defence", and he understood it to have opened up "a methodological space" for planned economic guidance in a system preparing for war.

It was inevitable that there was a strengthening of state control over various sectors of economy in order to expand the munitions industry and other related industries and to mobilize all aspects of economic power. When considering the nature of

259 Miyazaki 1938, p. 93 et seq.

the planned "economic guidance" linked with such control, Miyazaki and his colleagues looked to the planned economy of the Soviet Union, making a close study of the "funding problems" of the First and Second Five Year Plans and of the production statistics for heavy industry, as Kobayashi and Okazaki have emphasized.[260] The items in the plan drawn up by Miyazaki and the other members of the JMG and the detailed statistics and estimates were very likely derived from their research into the techniques and methodology of Soviet planned economic management.

A more important question, though, concerns the basic method through which non-socialist Japan could bring about state economic planning based on a capitalist economy. This went over and above technical issues, being concerned with the principles and framework for state "economic guidance". And this has a very close connection with the concept and nature of a defence economy preparing for total war.

Miyazaki pointed out that "a war-preparedness economy requires, as I have mentioned already, planning over a broad range of economic sectors, though *there is absolutely no need for a so-called state planned economy to go hand in hand with state-operated enterprises* [my italics]. In some countries, for example the Soviet Union, a war-preparedness economy takes the form of a socialist planned economy, whereas in others, for example Germany, Italy, the United Kingdom and France, it does not."[261] Thus Miyazaki saw two models for such an economy, socialist and non-socialist. He rejected the former, saying of the Soviet model that "the economy is a sensitive construct and does not permit rash turbulence. The Soviet experience shows very clearly the unsuitability of deliberately daring to destroy the framework of the bourgeois economy based on a particular ideology. In moving towards a socialist system, the planned economy brought about the ruin of the national economy." In place of the socialist model of the planned economy he looked to the systems of Germany, Italy, the United Kingdom and France that were based on a "bourgeois economic framework". And of these, it was the German model he adopted.

In 1936, Hitler announced a series of economic reforms called the Four Year Plan. Miyazaki wrote: "In Germany, as the Führer's speech and the party's fiscal manifesto show, a war-preparedness economy and a planned economy are not necessarily the same thing. 'The state does simply require of itself that it guides the economy in the direction necessary for national policy; it entrusts the pursuit of individual economic lines of policy and economic initiative to free, individual

260 JMG Report, in *Gendaishi shiryō* 8 (Sino-Japanese War), p. 701; Kobayashi 1995b, p. 118 et seq.

261 Miyazaki 1938, p. 100 et seq.

judgement and to the free private economy." Thus "guidance for a planned economy" meant "guiding" the economy in the direction necessary to meet the needs of state policy. It assumed "economic initiative" based on the free judgement of the individual and on a free private economy. Miyazaki recognized the duality inherent in Nazi economic thought between the principle of state control and the recognition of the importance of individual initiative and autonomy, and evaluated this positively. From the standpoint of the appropriateness and reasonableness of "control", he asserted that in Japan people acknowledged that a "continuation of the private economy" was an important pattern in the national economy, with the state considering that "the most appropriate way to extend planned economic guidance was in the form of a war-preparedness economy". Miyazaki increasingly used the expression "national defence economy" in place of "war-preparedness economy" as he formulated an economic pattern that seemed to be superimposed on Hitler's speech. "Thus we can say that purposeful and planned *economic guidance* by the state of the national economy is the essential constituent part of our country's present defence economy. The aim is to expand to the greatest degree, in order to prepare for war, the function of the economic system as a single organism by extending, through powerful state authority, a planned nature to the whole range of the economic framework, while *leaving the operation of the various enterprises within the private economy* to the *voluntary efforts of efficient businessmen*. This is the form taken by the present defence economy."[262] (my italics)

Studying the German Model

(1) Attention moves to Nazi Germany

As we have seen, the JMG looked to the Nazi German defence and controlled economy premised on capitalism as the actual model for Japan rather than the Soviet model based on socialism,[263] and so it pursued a very close study of Germany. Miyazaki and his colleagues actively studied the Nazi economic system, policy and ideas, including the Nazi economic law, Hitler's Four Year Plan of 1936, and the situation of the German munitions industry. They also gave a great deal of attention to German ideas about a wartime economy that underlay them, particularly the theory of Wehrwirtschaft (literally, defence economy).

262 Miyazaki 1938, p. 103.

263 See JMG Report, in *Gendaishi shiryō* 8 (Sino-Japanese War). Andō 1987 gives attention to German influence, pointing out that "the Nazi German model was applied even at the time of the promotion of the mobilization system after the Manchurian Incident" (p. 392).

In June 1937, the JMG published the fruits of its research into the Nazi economic system as *Nachisu keizaihō* (Nazi economic law). This work was a selection and translation of important laws related to the economy in Nazi Germany that had either been used in the JMG's research or had been recommended for publication.[264] Translation work of the German original and content checks probably began around 1936, the same time the JMG was drawing up its Five Year Plan. Just how important the Nazi example was for Miyazaki and his colleagues, who were hard at work on a design for "planned economic guidance" by the state, can be surmised from the opening paragraph of the Introduction to *Nachisu keizaihō*.

"There are few instances in the history of the development of the modern state of a government enacting regulating legislation over a broad swathe of the national economy, as Germany has done since 1933 (and the Soviet government did on its inception). It is clear from statistics attesting to the German economic recovery that, if not all, at least most Nazi legislation has functioned effectively. Of course, the economic legislation of a country has to be constructed and carried out according to the specific economic and social situation of the country concerned. The Nazi economic legislation, which has been constituted for a uniform purpose under a well-ordered system, is a model of a controlled economy. By studying it, we should be able to receive virtually infinite suggestions regarding the structure of economic policy."

The JMG thus judged the Nazi economic legislation to be "a model of a controlled economy" and spoke of it in the highest terms as giving "virtually infinite suggestions" about "the structure of economic policy".[265]

(2) Analysing the Four Year Plan of 1936

Just as the JMG was drawing up its Five Year Plan, Hitler publicly announced the German Four Year Plan at Nuremberg on September 9, 1936. Miyazaki and the others hastily studied it with the intention of comparing it with their own ideas. They gave their attention first of all to Hitler's announcement of the plan in Nuremburg,[266] according to which Germany would be made self-sufficient in raw materials and fuel, and the savings made on foreign exchange would be

264 See Introduction, Nichiman zaisei keizai kenkyūkai ed. (1937a). This work is based on Hoche 1933-1939, focusing on the laws of 1933 and 1934. According to the Introduction, the translation was undertaken by Iwano Chōjirō (1902-1945) and Takehara Hachirō.

265 *Ibid*. See also Chapter 3 above.

266 Miyazaki 1938, pp. 94 ff. Hitler's announcement was included in Nichiman zaisei keizai kenkyūkai ed. 1938. This work was a mimeographed copy of a translation of

used to secure the supply of food and buy the raw materials it could not produce itself. Miyazaki quoted Hitler's words: "Next, I [Hitler] give you today a new Four Year Plan. In [the next] four years, Germany will become completely independent of foreign raw materials to the extent that we can produce them through our own efforts in our chemical, mining and machine industries." Miyazaki and his colleagues attached great importance to this plan for greatest possible self-sufficiency in the chemical, mining and machine industries, and the concomitant independence from reliance on foreign countries, because it was closely linked to German rearmament and the concept of a national defence and war-preparedness economy anticipating total war in the future. Koana Tsuyoshi (b. 1906), an expert on the German economy, pointed out. "By means of the Four Year Plan begun in the late autumn of 1936, Germany has moved forward towards setting up a full-scale national defence economy".[267]

The JMG gave a great amount of attention to an analysis of the German munitions industry. This study resulted in *Doitsu ni okeru gunju kōgyō no taisei* (The general situation of the munitions industry in Germany), brought out in August 1937 when the JMG was in the middle of preparing the Japan-Manchukuo Five Year Plan. It analysed German plans for military expansion as follows: A general phenomenon in the world of today is the prevalence of an 'enthusiasm for military preparedness'. This is the key to the 'reconstruction and regeneration' of the world economy. In particular, this tendency is illustrated quite clearly in Germany, 'one of the weakest economies in the world'". It then summarized the process of German military preparedness. "Hitler's domestic policy since assuming power has developed in four stages. The first was the eradication of unemployment beginning with the first Four Year Plan of 1933; the second was Schacht's New Plan of 1934; the third was the effort to rearm after 1935; and the last was putting into practice the second Four Year Plan of 1936. The year 1935 was the turning point, when Hitler's financial policy changed from being one of national relief to one of war-preparedness. Germany had taken a decisive step towards re-armament."[268]

However, Germany lacked raw materials, a vital factor in its policy of military growth, and so it had to work towards autarky. "The demand for autarky is in itself the objective condition necessitating policies of economic control and a

---

Kolbe et al. 1936 (also 1939). For the German Four Year Plan, see Schweitzer 1964, Petzina 1968.

267 Koana 1938, Introduction, p. 48. Arisawa Hiromi pointed out the same thing (Arisawa 1937a, p. 327).

268 Nichiman zaisei keizai kenkyūkai ed. 1937b (mimeograph), p. 3 et seq.

war-preparedness economy in Germany", said the report. By studying the policy -making process and its various stages, the JMG came to see the Four Year Plan not simply as bloc economics but as a policy for rearmament and military expansion, in other words, as a plan for a war-preparedness economy, and understood self-sufficiency in raw materials and autarky as being one with it.

Organization of the economic framework

The strategy for the JMG's "planned economic guidance under a war-preparedness system" did not derive from the Soviet model of state planning but on planned guidance by the state authority on the basis of the continuation of private enterprise acting on its own initiative. A typical model of this was the method found in Nazi Germany, a fascist type of control. But how can planned economic guidance work if premised on a private economy? This necessitates the idea of the economy as an organic body, in other words, the organization of private enterprise and its organic restructuring. Miyazaki and his colleagues sought the model for this in Nazi Germany and so paid particular attention to Germany's "Law for the Preparation of the Organic Structure of the Economy".[269]

This law came into effect in 1934. It was an important attempt to restructure the German economy from the standpoint of corporatism, with a clear distinction of occupational status. Miyazaki paid particular attention to the following points: (1) the formation of economic associations (*Gruppe*) based on the organization of different sectors of the economy, other than agriculture. As a result the group became the single representative of the particular sector represented; (2) the leader principle was the fundamental rule regarding the activities of constituent members, and a leading entrepreneur in each sector was appointed Führer; and (3) the economic demands of business leaders and businesses were fundamentally protected.

This was related to cartel-type organization. Miyazaki superimposed cartelization based on Nazi compulsory cartel laws onto the Japanese Important Industries Control Law. Making cartelization national policy, of the type seen in Germany, depended on a changed kind of cartel (not monopolistic, but a rational and regulated organization) that was employed in a positive way to seek technical link-ups within the same industry. There did not exist in Japan a strict and compulsory cartel system, but the Important Industries Control Law had the power to mandate limits on investment and to compel outsiders to enter into

---

269 Miyazaki 1938, p. 103 et seq. For the law, see Barth 1939, Neumann 1942 (part 2), Nathan 1944.

cartels. By enforcing the law, cartels could be organized to be "part of the national defence economy" and the free activity of cartels would be permitted only within those bounds. This is method by which "cartels would become part of state policy" and at that stage, "the word cartel would no longer be appropriate".

Miyazaki's understanding was in line with the views expressed in the Commentary section of the JMG's "Nazi economic law" (*Nachisu keizaihō*). The Commentary gave importance to this law as being the bedrock of the Nazi system and its controlled economy. "The structural transformation of a class state to a corporative state (*Ständestaat*; Jap. *dantai kokka*) is the fundamental idea of the Nazi controlled economy. For a corporative state, it is important to organise the national business associations. [Thus] the Law for the Preparation of the Organic Structure of the [German] Economy [of 1934], through which enterprises in various sectors are organized into autonomous associations, should be the most basic decree in the economic legislation of National Socialism."[270]

The "fundamental idea" of the Nazi controlled economy was first of all perceived as the "structural transformation" from a "class state" to a "corporative state". (The *Ständestaat* was understood as being not based on an old-fashioned estate system but on modern corporatism.) Over and above that, these laws were decisively emphasized as organizing the economy for a particular purpose. Miyazaki directed his attention to the laws organizing the economy that were the pivot of Nazi economic law as being the basic means for economic control under a national defence economy. The guiding principle of economic organization according to the Nazis was in this instance a "corporative and autonomous order". Individual, separate economic entities were recognised as being central while at the same time being constituent members of the group, and they were required to act as organic parts of the national economy. Economic associations represented various groups, and the leader principle was the fundamental rule for the activities of members.

The understanding found in "Nazi economic law" about Nazi policy concerning monopolies such as cartels and combines also agreed with Miyazaki's.[271] Cartels were positioned from the standpoint of the fundamental Nazi principle of the corporative state (*Ständestaat*). They were tolerated as being a branch of the autonomous associations connected with the public interest and free activity was permitted as long as it coincided with the profit of the entire national economy. It was in such terms that the July 1933 revision of the Cartel Law and compulsory

---

270 Nichiman zaisei keizai kenkyūkai ed. (1937a), p. 2.
271 Nichiman zaisei keizai kenkyūkai ed. (1937a), p. 5 et seq.

cartelization were interpreted. “Nazi cartel laws did not have the purpose of the socialization and nationalization of monopolies that occurred under Social Democrat rule, but allowed each monopoly complete freedom in terms of its economic activities (for example, competition in production), as long as they contributed to the public good, in other words, to the welfare of the total national economy. Here too the leader principle applied.”

Of course this understanding of Nazi policy was not confined to Miyazaki and other members of the JMG from the first. For example, Chō Moriyoshi, a student of Hijikata Seibi, a JMG member, displayed much of the same understanding in drawing attention, as we have seen, to measures for an organic regeneration of economic associations and for legislation regarding cartels.[272]

The characteristic features of the Nazi controlled economy that Miyazaki and others evaluated positively, such as corporative autonomy, the perspective of self-regulation, the leader principle, and the government control of cartels, were made reference points at the time of the Japan-Manchukuo Five Year Plan, and it was thought that they had been absorbed as basic constituent elements in the framework of Japan's national defence economy.[273] For example, the “Industrial Control Policy” contained in the Policy Outline regarding the implementation of the Five Year Plan for Key Industries (10 June 1937) advocated that, through “strong” government guidance, the “state and private sectors should agree and capital and labour should cooperate”; it also emphasized the “self-regulation” of private enterprises, together with the “mobilization” of “valuable persons”, based on “the present economic structure”. This was because various policies were being considered, such as the revision of the “General Cartel Law” within the Important Industries Control Law, “guidance regarding new investments” through the application of the Article concerning controls on the establishment or expansion of firms, and a strengthening of regulations concerning the public good.[274]

A more detailed plan appeared in the Guidelines to National Policy (*Kokusaku yōkō*) drawn up in February 1937. They exhibited a tightening of control from the standpoint of national interests, proposing (1) the establishment of “large associations of leading firms” from among the oil, coal, steel, automobile and chemical industries and (2) the formation of autonomous cartels (enforced cartelization) within other key industries. Next it was planned to organize industries all over the country by forming trade associations in the various industrial sectors, in a pyramid structure with a national federation with regional

272 See Chapter 3 above.

273 See also the short comment in Kobayashi 1995b, p. 130 et seq.

274 *Gendaishi shiryō* I, p. 13, p. 248.

associations at the centre.[275] We can conjecture that a Nazi-type controlled economy method was referred to as a model for this.

The most important issue for capitalistic economic control different from the socialistic Soviet model was the organization of economic associations. This was premised on the interests of economic circles, who emphasized business autonomy, and was a vital condition in their ongoing subsumption by the state. However, the business community violently opposed control and organization from above and asserted "autonomous control". The issue of the organization of economic groups would later become a critical question when the New Economic Order was being discussed.[276]

The defence economy: Japanese and German theories

(1) The defence economy as the preliminary stage for total war

The series of proposals beginning with a programme to expand key industries in Japan-Manchukuo sought a planned increase in the production of munitions and in associated basic industries (the heavy and chemical industries) together with the mobilization by the state of its various economic strengths. The proposals were strongly characterized by military concerns and military preparedness, and were connected with an understanding that modern war had changed qualitatively – that war had become a battle of collective national strengths, total war – and therefore it was necessary to expand the munitions and related industries, as well as total economic strength, and to mobilize all resources accordingly. Miyazaki expressed this idea through the terms "an economy for wartime preparedness" (*junsenji keizai*) and "national defence economy" (*kokubō keizai*), and these terms expressed the fundamental concept about the situation at that time. What exactly did they imply?

Miyazaki explained the meaning of "national defence"[277] saying that "the system of a country with powerful defences" was prescribed through a "qualitative and quantitative buildup of national strength" in order to continue the war against China and prepare for the expected coming total war, in view of the national interest. Planned state direction was essential on the economic front for attaining "a country with powerful defences", and Miyazaki considered that this in itself was an important topic in the "national defence economy". He and

275 *Gendaishi shiryō* I, p. 318 et seq.

276 See Chapter 5 below. Refer also to Matsuura 1995, p. 180 et seq.

277 Miyazaki 1938, p. 60.

others also used the terms "war preparedness" (*junsen*) and "semi-wartime preparedness" (*junsenji*) for "national defence", and "war preparedness economy" and "national defence economy" were equivalent.

These terms were used with a specific meaning, referring to a system of national military mobilization (controlled economy) to respond to the prosecution of the war in China and to "prepare for the expected coming total war". Studies of economic history have hitherto not necessarily grasped this clearly. For example, Nakamura Takafusa, a representative figure in modern Japanese economic history, writes, "The term 'wartime (semi-wartime) preparedness" economy is said to have been used by Baba Eiichi, the Finance Minister in the Hirota Cabinet. Following the February 26 Incident [of 1936], Baba tried to cooperate with the demands of the army, which had become the strongest political force in the country, and had to approve a vast increase in military expenditures, the issue of public bonds, and a large tax increase. The reason for this was that 'wartime (semi-wartime) preparedness ' took precedent over 'time of emergency'."[278] Here, the term "wartime (semi-wartime) preparedness" is understood simply as a vogue word, used in the same category as "time of emergency".

However, at the same time, Arisawa Hiromi cautioned against using the term as a vogue word, arguing that it should be employed as a concept expressing the situation of a particular time.[279] "When we talk about a war-preparedness system for our country, some think that it simply means preparing for armed warfare and in particular for its financial support. This however is a superficial understanding. Since the time Finance Minister Baba said that the dramatic increase in taxation announced under his tax reform bill was a so-called wartime (semi-wartime) preparedness order, this term has been regularly used in a variety of situations. Its true meaning, however, should not be understood simply as being restricted to the sense of preparedness for war in the financial institutions; rather, it must imply *organization of the total national economy to prepare for war*. This is because the predicted war will be a total war, and to limit preparation for it to financial institutions would simply be to retrogress to the time before the Great War, for example, to the time of Professor [Jacob] Riesser.[280]" (my italics)

Arisawa explained his reasoning as follows. It is clear that war in the future will be a total war, a war of material. Severe tensions are raising questions on a

278 Nakamura 1987, p. 1.

279 Arisawa 1937a, p. 7.

280 Jacob Riesser (1853-1932) was a German jurist and banker, who became a professor of law at the University of Berlin. He helped found the Hansabund in 1909 to promote industrial policies in face of the government's pro-agrarian stance.

daily basis in various countries around the world relating to the war preparedness of the economy. Issues concerning the wartime preparedness economy and the national defence economy are a manifestation of this, he said. Here, "wartime preparedness economy" and "national defence economy" have the same meaning. In a situation of extreme tension, they represent a specific system that makes economic preparation for the total war expected in the near future. This does not apply to Japan alone, but was a phenomenon common among all the world powers.

The characteristics of modern warfare – advances in the technology of war, mechanization, the enormity of scale, the totality, the long duration – had become common knowledge as a result of the experience of World War I. This knowledge led to the question of how to expand and mobilize the necessary economic power to engage in total war. Before World War I, the question of how to convert a peacetime economy to one of total war had not existed; it was after this experience of total war that it was first recognised and discussed as a key issue.

In his important work, *Senji tōsei keizairon* (On the wartime controlled economy, 1933), Mori Takeo, a doctor of economics and a teacher in the Military Paymasters' School, had already analysed the situation in various countries regarding the building up of industry and national defence. In doing so, he referred to the significance of economic preparation for war through the intensification of plans for organizing the munitions industry together with those for military mobilization, and through state regulation. However, Mori's view was based on a demarcation between the peacetime economy and the wartime economy, and he understood the latter simply as a modification of the former to meet the requirements of war. Thus he was not sufficiently aware of setting up a distinctive stage of preparedness.

In contrast, Miyazaki and other members of the JMG were one step ahead in that they recognized a distinctive stage between the economies of peacetime and (total) war, the war preparedness economy and the national defence economy. This was not direct total mobilization of the peacetime economy towards one for total war, but a system with a special meaning – to make preparations as far as possible for the expected total war, premised on the peacetime economy. The outbreak of the second Sino-Japanese War in 1937 added a further element: an acceleration of conditions that might potentially lead to total war. The national defence economy did not mean simply "defence"; it acquired an added sense of a positive expansion of military operations abroad in the name of defence and preparations for the impending total war in the near future that such actions would bring. The national defence economy was literally a "war preparedness economy", positioned as a system possessing elements of a wartime economy and so showing indications of already having moved towards one.

What was this conception based on?[281] For this we must look to the German theory of "Wehrwirtschaft", which appeared following virtually the same course as the 1936 Four Year Plan.[282]

The JMG made concerted efforts to study the wartime economy. German discussion about "Wehrwirtschaft" provided the most important point of view in this. A 1936 work by Guido Fischer (1899-1983) of the University of Munich, *Wehrwirtschaft. Ihre Grundlage und Theorien*, was translated into Japanese the following year and printed in mimeograph.[283] In 1938, four essays by Kurt Hesse, a major in the German army, and others that were carried in the *Kriegswirtschaftliche Jahresberichte* (published by Hesse) were translated as *Sensō keizai ni kansuru kenkyū* (A study of the war economy) and published in mimeograph. Hesse was seen in Japan as an instigator of the debate about the national defence economy.[284] The JMG translated "Wehrwirtschaft" as both "war-preparedness economy" and "national defence economy". This is in accordance with the terminology used by Miyazaki, as discussed above. Miyazaki's study of "a methodological area for planned economic guidance under a war-preparedness system" took place around the same time as this translation work was going on. Let us next look at the distinctive points in the discussion about the national defence economy by Guido Fischer, which Miyazaki noted closely.

(2) German theory of the defence economy

Fischer made a division between the "national defence economy" and the "war economy". The "national defence economy" takes into account the satisfaction of the economic demands (procurement of military equipment and supplies,

---

281 Andō 1987 mentions that Nazi Germany was the model (pp. 292, 295) but does not develop this observation any further.

282 This term was generally translated into Japanese as *kokubō keizai* (defence economy), for example Kobayashi 1942. The German term "Reichswehr" (the armed forces of the Weimar Republic) that was stipulated in the Treaty of Versailles was translated into Japanese as *kokubōgun* (army for national defence). A law of May 1935 changed "Reichswehr" into "Wehrmacht" (armed forces), and this too was translated as *kokubōgun*.

283 This work was also translated by the Marxian economist Itō Kōdō (arrested in December 1937) and published in 1940. Fischer was a scholar of business administration; after the war he developed the theory of Partnerschaft (partnership) based on the idea of equal rights between management and workers.

284 Arisawa 1937a, p. 8 et seq. Also Kikuchi 1940, p. 19. Debate about the national defence economy may be found in Akamatsu 1942, chapter 1. See also Carroll 1968, especially chapters 1 and 2, Herbst 1982, pp 95 ff.

materiel) of the army of national defence, and is the system making preparation for mobilizing the economy. In other words, in a situation where total war is a possibility, preparations have to be in place for converting the existing peace-time economy into a wartime one. This is not the opposite of the peace-time economy but rather the form taken by the peace-time economy in the present.

"The new form of defence of the people and the realm that the total war (der totale Krieg; JMG translation: *zentai sensō*) of the future has brought about [means] there must be preparation and training in advance, from the time of peace (Friedenszeiten). The duty of a national defence economy (Wehrwirtschaft; JMG translation: *junsen keizai*) is to construct all the economic policies that total war brings about, making total war possible. However, a national defence economy should not be regarded as an exceptional circumstance or as a preparation for a war economy (Kriegwirtschaft). This is because the total war of the future will deploy the various strengths of all the people already during peace-time, and these must be protected for war. Therefore, a national defence economy organized for the purpose of total war cannot be called the antithesis of a peace-time economy (Friedenswirtschaft; JMG translation *heiwa keizai*), or evaluated as one. The *national defence economy is rather the new form of the peace-time economy conditioned by the present age.*"[285] (my italics)

Fischer's view that the national defence economy was the modern form of the peace-time economy was consistent with an understanding that preparations for total war were an expression of new conditions in international relations and of new political and social developmental stages. For Fischer, the combination of the peace-time economic conditions prevailing before World War I and the requirements of a defence economy of preparation for the new stage of total war led to the formation of a new type of peace-time economy. Consequently, the circumstances of a peace-time economy could no longer take a traditional form and there could be no return to the peace-time economy of the nineteenth century.

The reason was as follows. Preparations for total war gave an impetus to the conversion of the national economy, that is to one of national defence, and this brought about a change in the quality of established international economic relations. The transformation to a national defence economy was taking place in conjunction with the conversion of the pattern of the laissez-faire economy then in progress and the dismantling of the self-regulatory balance of the market economy; structural transformation through planned state control and economic reorganisation were two sides of the same coin. Economic restructuring, in the form

285 Fischer 1936, p. 23, JMG Japanese translation 1937c, p. 31, Itō translation 1940, p. 37.

of countermeasures against external factors, such as protective tariffs, an import and export licensing system, and exchange controls, and a state response to the problem of unemployment had a reciprocal relationship with the conversion to a national defence economy. However, in the case of Germany, this conversion did not mean the wholesale seizing of economic management by the state, as was the case in socialism. There the state was important simply because it steered the economy in the direction necessary in terms of national policy, and the economic initiative remained with the free decisions of individuals and the private economy.

Based on this understanding, Fischer presented two concrete spheres as topics of the "national defence economy". One was satisfying economically all military demands. The other was economic mobilization, that is, converting the existing peace-time economy to a national defence one, and the preparations for doing so. This national defence economy was conditional upon structurally converting the national economy.

The national defence economy at that time passed through two stages. The first stage was a plan for economic mobilization. This meant to prepare economically for national defence. This consisted of safeguarding the ability to satisfy the demands of the military, to draw up plans to commit economic strength to the war effort, and to raise awareness within industry and among individuals. The second stage was economic mobilization in the narrow sense of the term, that is, to change the national defence, peace-time economy to a war economy. This was necessary once there was a strong danger of war.

Fischer said that for this to happen, there needed to be an accurate understanding of current economic conditions and strengths. He placed importance on the use of statistical information, on setting up particular facilities for guidance and enforcement and utilizing existing systems, on establishing one's own munitions industry and becoming independent of foreign countries, of not relying on other countries for necessary commodities, machinery and raw materials, of converting sectors of the economy to this purpose, and having an import system that laid stress on important raw materials. He also proposed setting up specific measures such as the standardization and technical development of goods associated with military demand, methods of combining private and public management in the procurement of munitions, control over cyclical fluctuations due to ordering and distribution, organization over ordering, the elimination of monopolies and special rights, and a public tender system, an examination of estimates, etc., and impartiality of profitability through the regulation of the calculation of costs.

Junsen keizai to senji keizai (The war preparedness economy and the wartime economy) was the JMG's translation of Fischer's *Wehrwirtschaft*. It is very easy to surmise that this work played an important role in the "pioneering" of the JMG plan for a war-preparedness and national defence economy, and in its methodology.[286]

The JMG, which embarked on the conversion to a peace-time, national defence economy as a preliminary stage for total war (that is, Fischer's Stage 1), moved its emphasis, with the outbreak of the Second Sino-Japanese War, to the concept of more of a wartime economy, as in Fischer's Stage 2, the national defence economy strongly imbued with elements that could in emergency become a wartime economy. This corresponded with the "transitional economy" leading towards war and the "war economy" proposed by Kurt Hesse in his theory of the defence economy that had drawn the attention of the JMG. Hesse however, while making a division between the peace-time economy, the national defence economy, and the war economy, firmly believed that once war was over it would be possible to return to the peace economy. The national defence economic system was wholly concerned with war and so to that extent was only a temporary phenomenon. Fischer, on the other hand, understood the national defence economy as a modern form of the peace economy: as the structural change of the national and global economies and a new stage in political and social developments in international relations. He denied any possibility of returning to the original peace economy. He considered that, while the national defence economy was a preparation for total war, it was not simply a stage; rather, war preparation itself was an intermediate but constant condition. The national defence economic system did not simply pertain to the current situation but was one modern stage in the economic system that characterised the age and in its historical development.

Miyazaki Masayoshi described his ideas about the national defence economy as agreeing with just such an understanding.[287] The collapse of the market economy after World War I in Europe came to a head with the global depression of 1929, into which Japan too had been drawn, being part of the world economy. Following this, there was a dismantling of the laissez-faire equilibrium that was the governing principle of the exchange economy internationally, and this led to a period of competition among the national economies, as they scrambled for markets and resources. The trend of the century was the decline of the laissez-faire international economy and the emergence of national war-preparedness economies. Japan, he said, now needed a fundamental modification and qualitative conversion of its economic policy.

---

286 For example, see Miyazaki 1938, p. 97.

287 Miyazaki 1938, p. 86 et seq. Fischer's views would also be helpful in understanding the defence economies under the Cold War, though in a different sense.

Arisawa Hiromi, as we have seen, criticised those who understood the terms "war-preparedness (semi-war) economy" and "national defence economy" simply as vogue words, stressing that they were objective concepts with their own meanings. Analysing the theory of Wehrwirtschaft as discussed by Hesse and others, he viewed the two terms as the "organization of the war economy" (*senji keizai no taiseika*), which he explained as follows. Total war is a war of weapons, but over and above that it has the character of economic war. In order to pursue an economic war, mobilization of both the military and the national economy was necessary. This is what is meant by "organization of the war economy". This is born out by the fact that various countries, learning from the experience of World War I, were setting up, not just munitions industry mobilization laws, but also national mobilization laws. The peace-time economy would not be switched over to a war economy upon the outbreak of war, for the modern tendency was for the existence of an intermediate, transitional stage in the conversion of the one to the other. During this stage, the way is paved for the wartime economy; this transitional stage is none other than the "war-preparedness economy" or the "national defence economy". At this stage, the standpoint of national defence is fundamental; economic policy has to concentrate on it, and the state must guide the economy directly. Therefore the stage of the national defence economy is qualitatively close to a wartime economy, though wartime conditions do not prevail directly.

Arisawa thus stipulated that a "national defence economy" was "already the prior stage for a wartime economy, and is thus a system for a time of war-preparedness, even though the country is not directly in a situation of war".[288] He wrote this in 1937, when the Second Sino-Japanese War had broken out. The following year in February he was arrested with a group of fellow Marxist economists in the so-called Professors' Group Incident (Kyōju gurūpu jiken) and relieved of his post in the Economics Faculty of the Tokyo Imperial University.

Japanese characteristics of the national defence economy

Koana Tsuyoshi, a specialist in Nazi economics, characterised the Germany of his time in the following way. "The Nazi economic makeup is ultimately founded on a war economy and a national defence economy that makes preparation during peace-time for a war economy."[289] He stressed how much Japan had paid attention to this system and how much it had referred to it.[290] The Nazi

288 Arisawa 1937a, p. 7 et seq.
289 Koana 1938, p. 46.
290 Koana 1940, p. 6 et seq.

war-preparedness policy "was adopted, revised and reinforced to apply to the situation in our country [Japan]". The reason for this was "not only the closeness between the German and Japanese peace-time economic structures, but also because the wartime economy practised by Germany and its present national defence economy provide a valuable model, from a global point of view, and because it has furnished [us] with proven and respected data."

Of course, the model referred to for specific planning methods to expand productivity in key industries, centring on the munitions industry, was not the just the German one, but also the First Soviet Five Year Plan, beginning in 1928, as well as the Second Five Year Plan, beginning in 1932, which focused on the expansion of the heavy and chemical industries. Also studied were techniques to calculate the productivity of the Russian national economy. Nevertheless, however advanced and technically skilled the methods employed in Soviet economic planning were, the fact remained that they were premised on the abolition of capitalism. The Soviet method, that was aimed at the expansion of socialism, was essentially different to Japan's, whose planning was based on a capitalistic economy. There thus existed institutional limitations difficult to overcome if Soviet methods were to be applied. The Nazi model, by contrast, was presented, not in terms of its technical expertise, but as a theory and a more suitable "methodology" regarding basic viewpoints, directions and a framework for a national defence economy of large-area autarky and ideas about economic control and mobilization.

Nazi-type economic ideas had not been accepted just as they were from the outset. As Koana pointed out, many were "adopted, revised and reinforced" while there were others that were not used, but rather eliminated or rejected, such as the "anti-capitalistic" demands associated with Nazism that could be boiled down to the item in the 25 Point Programme to "break the bonds of debt slavery". Miyazaki pointed out that "the distinctive feature of Nazi monetary policy, whose slogan was freedom from Jewish supernational finance capital and breaking the bonds of debt slavery, is that we cannot yet catch even a glimpse of legislation to that end."[291] In Germany, the Nazi slogan of "breaking the bonds of debt slavery" was virtually eliminated from the party's economic platform after the Nazi rise to power. Miyazaki too excluded such notions of "anti-capitalism". However, this did not mean rejecting the idea of "limiting the profits" of private industry. Indeed, he saw this as an important issue for the war-preparedness economy, and drew attention to the German Capital Investment Law (Kapitalanlagegesetz)

291 Miyazaki 1938, p. 105.

of March 29, 1934 and the Dividend Limitation Act (Anleihestockgesetz) of December 4, 1934. This placed a ceiling of six percent on dividend payments by companies (eight percent under certain conditions). Profits exceeding that amount were to be transferred to the Gold Discount Bank for investment in government bonds or Reich guaranteed bonds. Miyazaki considered this policy to be linked to the "purposes of fostering the sources of capital", rather than to "restricting profits for the common good". He said that the question of restricting dividends in Japan, an issue revolving around the implementation of Clause 11 of the National Mobilization Law,[292] which should be understood from "a political and social standpoint, [as] the equal division of burden and sacrifice among all classes of the nation under a policy of control." Opposition to the implementation of Clause 11 was probably related to whether "our country" had become, "as expected, a strong nation of national defence". The problem was the "want" of "political power able to realise a total national defence".

The issue concerning the national defence economy was closely related to the question of national "political power" to bring economic control into effect. For Miyazaki and others, the way such "political power" should be exercised was not the same as the dictatorship of Nazism or Fascism. Rather, it was connected with what the "sentiment of the Japanese people" should be. The JMG prepared "Guidelines for National Policy" (*Kokusaku yōkō*) of December 1937 opened with the words "unification of national sentiment" (*kokumin shisō no tōitsu*) and went on to say: "Establishment of the philosophy of the Japanese race: We will establish a rich national philosophy permeated with the true essence of our national polity (*kokutai*), as opposed to systems of thought like Marxism and Liberalism, which run counter to our national polity (*kokutai*), and German and Italian Fascism without modification."[293]

Thus the JMG made its basis the concepts of "national polity" and the "character of the race". From this standpoint, Marxism and liberalism were disavowed, and at the same time "German and Italian fascism" without modification was to be excluded. But fascism and totalitarianism, if revised, were attractive to Miyazaki, and in fact, the elimination and the thorough-going suppression of

292 See Nakamura 1994, p. 95. "Article 11 was to create problems later. This article empowered the government to restrict or ban the establishment of corporations, increases of equity capital, mergers, changes in purpose of business, flotation of corporate bonds, and second and subsequent paying in of shares. It also allowed the government to issue orders concerning management decisions, such as the disposal of profits, and the manner in which financial institutions deployed their funds."

293 *Gendaishi shiryō* I, p. 311.

Marxism together with liberalism and individualism were distinguishing features of totalitarianism essentially shared with German Nazism. A contemporary expert in political science, Kinoshita Hanji (1900-1989), a professor at Meiji University in the postwar period, defined the term "totalitarianism" as follows: "In the narrow sense, totalitarianism (*zentaishugi*, Ger. *Totsalitätsprinzip*) is synonymous with German Nazism, and in the broader sense it is used in the sense of the principle of groupist and dirigist reform, opposed to individualism and liberalism. In the latter sense, there are many possible forms of totalitarianism in different countries, and this can be said to apply to Fascism in Italy, Nazism in Germany and nationalism (*kokkashugi*) or ethnic nationalism (*Nihonshugi*) in Japan."[294]

Kinoshita described Nazism as "placing importance on the whole over the individual, and placing the greatest value on the race as the specific manifestation of this whole". The Nazi system as anti-Marxist and anti-liberal "totalitarianism" had much in common with Japanese "totalitarianism", also anti-Marxist and anti-liberal, which had taken the form of "nationalism" and "ethnic nationalism". The German model of the controlled economy, based on a totalitarian "national defence economy", was linked conceptually by the JMG with the idea of a Japanese "national polity" based on the emperor system (Tennoism). In order to put a national defence and war-preparedness economy into practice, a particular "political strength" was indispensable, one that would be supported by the concept of the "national polity" of the Japanese people, that is, the ideology of the emperor system. This had to be a Japanese form of totalitarianism based on Tennoism, different from that of Nazi Germany, nothing other than a Japanese version of "Fascism as the state".

294 Kinoshita 1941, p. 115 et seq.

Chapter Five: The Japanese New Economic Order and Nazi Economic Thought

In this chapter we will bring together various debates concerning the New Economic Order (*keizai shintaisei*) of the Second Konoe Fumimaro Cabinet which prepared the economic system for the full-scale war that began in December 1941. We will consider the form in which Nazi economic ideas and policy were received in the process of designing the "Outline for the Establishment of a New Economic Order" (*Keizai shintaisei kakuritsu yōkō*), approved in December 1940, and how those ideas were combined with Japanese-style traditionalism and views about the emperor system (Tennoism).

The Second Konoe Cabinet was inaugurated in July 1940, three years after the outbreak of the Second Sino-Japanese War, and plans for the new economic system were put in the hands of the reform bureaucrats of the Cabinet Planning Board. The idea behind the plans was to seek, in view of the drawn-out war in China, a new type of economic system in order to set up a wartime economy, as well as a national defence economy to prepare for total war. This was not, however, simply a temporary reponse at policy level to the exigencies of wartime, but was also a response to issues arising from changes in the global economy, such the Depression, the bloc economy, and rearmament, as well as to the impasse that had originated in the *laissez-faire* capitalistic economies.

The significance of the New Economic Order and other associated issues have been thoroughly discussed by Nakamura Takafusa and Hara Akira.[295] The proposed changes, which were part of Konoe's "New Order", brought about a confrontation between reform bureaucrats and business leaders; Nakamura and Hara have shed light on how this strong resistance evolved and moved from opposition to compromise. However, they only indicated a possible connection between the New Economic Order and Nazism, and did not include it within the scope of their study.[296] But nevertheless, we cannot deny the importance of the subject of the reception by Japan of Nazism and Nazi economic thought, and particularly their influence on the discussion surrounding the New Economic Order.

---

295 Nakamura and Hara 1973, p. 71 et seq.

296 Ibid. p. 72.

Andō Yoshio (1917-1985), a pioneer in the study of modern Japanese economic history who also experienced prewar and wartime conditions, has pointed out the relation between the New Order movement and Nazi thought from the standpoint of economic history. He states that trends during the period of the New Order were an "important signpost in the formative process of [Japanese] fascism", and that the period represents a watershed in the development of "a fascist system dominated by the military and the bureaucracy". This transitional period clearly demonstrates the distinctive features of Japanese fascism, which include the pivotal role of the emperor system (Tennoism), the preservation by the military and bureaucracy of their superior position, and the decisive voice held by business leaders and financial capital in issues related to the economic system and government policy.[297]

For Andō, the ideology of the New Order, which played an important role in these developments, was nothing but an "imitation of Nazism". He pointed out that "reformist" tendencies had come to be understood as Nazi-type anti-capitalism, or as a reform of capitalism, and as such were opposed by business circles and the "ideological right wing". This opposition weakened the spirit of reform and the end result was compromise. Speaking of the "Outline for the Establishment of a New Economic Order", Andō wrote: "Slogans like 'the primacy of the public good' and 'the service of one's calling for the nation' were woven into the [Outline], but we are given the impression that they were the product of an ideological compromise between state socialism and the Japanese business world."[298]

Andō's understanding is important. First, a fundamental element within the concept of the New Economic Order was the ideology of German Nazism, or more accurately, Nazism as it was defined in Japan, and of state socialism. This was an important determinant in the New Order movement, which he called an "important signpost in the formative process of [Japanese] fascism". Second, the ideology of state socialism or Nazism was opposed to "the ideology of Japanese business circles", but the two reached a compromise, and this compromise was absorbed into the "Outline". Third, Andō concluded that "The New Order and Japanese Fascism thus ended up within a framework that did not touch at all upon the essence of 'national polity' (*kokutai*), that is, the emperor system, or of capitalism (especially Japanese capitalism) or their pain points" (underlining Andō's).[299] In other words, the ideology of a Nazi-type New Order had been

297 Andō 1963, p. 253 et seq.

298 Ibid. p. 248 et seq.

299 Ibid. p. 255.

changed and weakened, and was incorporated into the framework of the national polity (the emperor system) and Japanese capitalism.

What though is the ideology of Nazism? Nazism has many dimensions; what we are interested in here is its economic thought, concerning capitalism and profit-making. Andō, like many modern historians, saw Nazism as being "anti-capitalistic state socialism", and placed importance on its "reformist spirit" vis-à-vis capitalism. How accurate, though, is this commonly accepted view?

It is of course true that Nazi economic thought, with its anti-capitalistic elements, played an important role in the early campaign of Hitler and the Nazi party in Germany. However, the economic ideas previously professed by the party underwent a change, and once the party seized power in 1933, were revised and watered down in the process of policy construction. In Japan, the Cabinet Planning Board and the reform bureaucrats, considering the concept of the New Order and how it should be put into practice, understood, as contemporaries, the facts of such changes to Nazi ideas. How then did they interpret and receive the reality of Nazi Germany, and its policy and economic thought? And what was the relationship with the slogans Andō mentioned, like "the primacy of the public good" and "the service of one's calling for the nation"?

This issue is also related to the understanding of Nazism among business circles, which opposed the reformist bureaucrats. The leaders of the business community strongly resisted "anti-capitalistic" tendencies that denied the profit principle. However, they noted that in actuality the Nazi economic system sanctioned the profit principle and stressed the autonomy of enterprises, and so they interpreted it in such a way as to bring it close to their own point of view. Therefore just as we cannot say that the New Order ideas of the reform burau-crats equalled Nazi-type state socialism (=anti-capitalism), neither can we say that business circles were anti-Nazism. In fact an understanding of Nazism was something both sides held in common. Just as we need to examine the Nazi-type "ideology" of the reform bureaucrats more closely, we should also investigate the "ideology" of business circles in greater detail.

Furthermore, was Andō correct in setting up Nazi economic thought and the ideology of state socialism against the ideology of the emperor system? For example, the Nazi "primacy of the public good" and the "Führer principle" were in essence conflated with the Japanese idea of Tennoism, and were considered complementary as elements making up the ideology of Japanese fascism.

How has later historical research dealt with these issues? A great amount of fine studies have been made concerning both German fascism and Japanese fascism, which have tended, down to the present, to focus on a comparison between the two. The biggest concern has been to filter out the points of similarity and difference between the two by comparing German Nazism and the totalitarianism of the Japanese emperor system. However, there has been unexpectedly little study done on internal "connections", in terms of ideas or policy. What was the intrinsic influence of Nazism and the Nazi system on the actual process of fascism itself in Japan? How did those contemporary Japanese who were connected with policy formation respond to Nazism and what parts of it did they accept or reject? Fascism in Germany and Japan has been interpreted only as an independent and parallel phenomenon, and at the most descriptions of Nazi influence in Japan have been kept to the the level of "Nazi-like", "Nazi-type" or "imitation Nazi".[300]

Of course, a few studies have dealt with the issue. For example, Furukawa Takahisa, while basing his work on the studies of Nakamura and Hara, notes the role of reform bureaucrats of the Cabinet Planning Board like Minobe Yōji (1900-1953) at the planning stage of the ideas behind the New Economic Order and points out that the policy of heavy industrialization centring on the manufacture of munitions under state guidance seen in the original draft of those ideas "followed the same course as economic planning in the Soviet Union and Germany".[301] Discussing the thinking behind the draft, Furukawa expresses concerns about the importance placed by Nakamura and Hara on Ryū Shintarō's *Nihon keizai no saihensei* (Reorganizing the Japanese Economy) of December 1939. He draws attention to the originality of the thinking of the reform bureaucrats, in contrast to "Ryū's economics, which carried on Marxian economics affirmatively", and says that "Nazi-like totalitarian economics" were a strong influence on their ideas.[302]

---

300 For example, Hirschmeier and Yui 1981, part II. Recent research in European languages has drawn attention to the influence of the "German model" on Japanese prewar and wartime economic policy, but they all lack detailed corroborative proof. See Gao 1997, pp. 12, 25-28, 69, 96-101, Lehmbruch 2001. When speaking of the Nazi influence on Japan, most works in Japanese stop at expressions like "Nazi-style" and "Nazi-like", and do not in general clarify the specific nature of the influence or how it occurred. Hayashi 1971 recognises the influence of a Nazi-style ideology in Japan in the 1930s but stresses the differences between the two countries, as well as the differences in the political stuctures between them from the ideological dimension, and so rejects applying the concept of fascism to Japan. As a result, there is no connection between his article and the questions brought up in this chapter. Other studies are similar in that they stress the distinctiveness of the political conditions of the time in Japan as compared with Nazism in Germany, and avoid applying the concept of fascism.

301 Furukawa 1992.

302 Ibid. p. 178 et seq.

Here, Furukawa attempted to link these ideas with Nazi policy according to Mōri Hideoto and other reform bureaucrats, to German geopolitics, to citations drawn from Friedrich List (1789-1846) and others, and to the ideas of Othmar Spann and Friedrich von Gottl-Ottlilienfeld (1868-1958).[303] However, he was unable to deepen his examination regarding what specific form these ideas had on the content of their plans and so his study does no more than give background to the ideas of the reform bureaucrats, and is unable to elucidate the connection between Nazi economic thought and the ideas of the reform bureaucrats about a new economic order, in terms of content.[304]

To what extent the economic thought of the German Neue Ordnung was appropriated and absorbed into the Japanese economic "new order" is an extremely important issue. It concerns the way the economic system of German "fascism" in the form of Nazism was consciously received and absorbed into the economic organization of Japanese "fascism" (the emperor system) in the form of the state, and consequently the intrinsic contemporary links between German and Japanese facism. This is a fundamental standpoint that has obviously to be taken into account when comparing fascism in the two countries. This chapter will attempt to study these points.

The "Outline for the Establishment of a New Economic Order" and Nazism

1. Contemporary understanding among Japanese social scientists

We will begin our study of the relationship between ideas about the New Economic Order and Nazi economic thought by looking at how contemporary social scientists and economists looked at the question.

Ueda Tatsunosuke, a professor of the Tokyo University of Commerce (later Hitotsubashi University) and a scholar of economic thought and history, stressed that the concepts behind the New Economic Order were not the product of Japan alone, but were part of a contemporary "global community of ideas".[305] "As

---

303 Ibid. pp. 119, 178.

304 A similar point is made in Kerde 1999. Concerning the intellectual position of Ryū Shintarō, who emphasized the connections between the ideas about the New Economic Order, and those of the Shōwa Research Association to which he belonged, see Fletcher 1981 and 1982. Fletcher sees the influence of Nazism in the ideas of Ryū Shintarō and Miki Kiyoshi (1897-1945). However, he does not analyse deeply their views about Nazi economic thought and policy.

305 Ueda Tatsunosuke 1941; 1942a p. 129.

for the conception behind the New Order, there are many clauses that appear to have been born of an effort to build a new world order, of which Japan was one part, rather than as products of pure Japanese originality. Thus, in our country's New Order we can detect a tendency towards what might be called a global community [of ideas] regarding the course of action in parallel with originality in terms of specific content."

In this way, Ueda drew attention to a global community of ideas in the New Order as well as purely Japanese elements. This was due to the fact that ideas about "systematic coherence" in the conception of the New Order were shared with the "*Ständestaat* [corporate state] system, Nazi Germany's New Order" and the "*corporazione* system that represented the New Order in Fascist Italy". Specifically, Ueda paid attention to the organization of economic associations in the ideas of the Japanese New Order, and to the principles underlying their functional formation, and understood this to be a point of commonality with policies in Germany and Italy.

Next Ueda pointed out the importance of the "primacy of the public good" and the "leader principle" in the conception of the New Order, and he detected a point of common here too with German and Italian thought.[306] "The core of the issue may be apprehended in that the New Economic Order conforms to the global view of a new order and that the establishment of this new order requires that preparations be necessarily made for an advanced defence state. This basic fact can be expressed in the slogan 'primacy of the public good'. In addition, 'the service of one's calling for the nation' shows how this is to be done." "The leader principle too has frequently been been called forth in recent years. Like 'primacy of the public good', it is an idea that has come from abroad."

In this way, Ueda observed, regarding the New Economic Order, that the ideas about structural reconstruction in terms of organizing economic associations, the 'primacy of the public good', and the leader principle had similarities with German and Italian thinking. Furthermore, he understood them to have been introduced from Italy and, in particular, Germany in order to promote the "building of a new world order, of which Japan was one part".

Azuma Mitsutoshi (1903-1973) of the Tokyo University of Commerce, a jurist who dispassionately analysed Nazi civil law, ironically criticised exclusionist tendencies towards foreign law held within Japanese legal circles as being a result of the irresponsible introduction of Nazi ideas. "I see the most outstanding example being the importation of Nazi ideas. As economic control has tightened, Nazi

306 Ueda Tatsunosuke 1942a, pp. 129, 139, 149.

slogans such as the 'primacy of the public good' and the 'Führer principle' have been imported with great vigour from Germany, where such control is advanced, without their meaning begin closely examined. Again we have adopted a foreign law system. Those who call into question, as if it were something new, our dependence on foreign law since the early years of the Meiji period must surely be prepared to have a critical attitude regarding the recent situation (sic)."[307] Here, Azuma, basing his comments on his specialist knowledge of Nazi Germany, was asserting that 'primacy of the public good' and the 'Führer principle' were Nazi slogans that had been imported into Japan from Nazi Germany as economic control tightened.

Nazi influence, in terms of such slogans, is apparent in an explanation about the New Economic Order made to an audience of businessmen in 1941 by Takemura Tadao (1905-1987), a economics professor at Keiō Gijuku University who had close connections with the military and who wrote for many general magazines. Taking the position that enterprises should not just pursue their own profits, but "serve the public good and work for the productivity of the whole national economy", he asserted that businesses should operate in accordance with the "various functions occurring in the reproductive process of the whole national economy." Here Takemura was of course alluding to the principle of the "primacy of the public good". He explained its meaning as follows: "The expression 'primacy of the public good' was originally a slogan of the Nazi controlled economy, which was transferred to Japan. Thus some might consider it to be a term belonging exclusively to Nazism, but in fact, the idea of the primacy of the public good has existed since ancient times within the spirit of the Japanese people."[308] The term "primacy of the public good" had indeed originated within the Nazi controlled economy. Takemura went on to quote from the *Kokutai no hongi* (Principles of the national polity)[309] to strengthen his argument that this Nazi principle was one with the Yamato spirit, the essential quality of the Japanese race.

Of equal importance to the "primacy of the common good" as ideology for the New Economic Order was the leader principle. This too was an import from Nazi Germany, known in Japanese transliteration as *fyūrā shisutemu* and *hyūrā purinchīpu*, from the German *Führerprinzip*. Kojima Seiichi, author of the 1940

307 Azuma 1942, Preface, Minemura 1942, p. 181.

308 Takemura 1941, p. 40. For Takemura's relationship with the Navy, see Itō Takashi 1981. For the debate about the controlled economy, see Chapter 2 above.

309 *Kokutai no hongi* was published in 1937 by the Ministry of Education (Monbushō) to clarify the orthodox ideology of the Japanese.

work *Nachisu tōsei keizai dokuhon* (new edition; A reader in the Nazi controlled economy) and a commentator on the economy well-versed in Nazi matters, linked the leader principle of the New Economic Order with the control associations and their "Nazi-type *fyūrā shisutemu*".[310] "The *fyūrā shisutemu* as advocated in Nazi Germany, deriving from a particular Nazi social and political environment, has been strikingly effective there", he wrote. Kojima raised a voice of caution about the effectiveness of the leader principle as it existed in the New Economic Order and as it was related to the control associations within the various branches of heavy industry as a way to organize economic associations.

Thus, contemporary social scientists and economists noted that the conception of the New Economic Order was greatly influenced by Nazi thought and that there were three basic principles that could be identified as Nazi-type policy ideas: the principle of the primacy of the common good, the Führer principle, and the organization of economic associations (the plan to organize more efficient labour). These principles were mutually connected, as we will discuss below.

2. The three principles and the "Outline for the Establishment of a New Economic Order"

Let us examine how the three principles that the commentators had identified as Nazi-type elements were expressed in the "Outline for the Establishment of a New Economic Order" approved by the Cabinet in December 1940.

The basic objective of the "Outline" was to set up a self-sustaining co-prosperity sphere in East Asia, incorporating Japan, Manchuria and China, to establish an autonomous national defence economy based on the resources available within this sphere, and to implement an integrated planned economy centred on heavy industry managed through the collaboration of government and the private sector.[311] To do so, it was first essential to set up a corporate system. This meant creating an organic unity of capital, management and labour in firms, positioning firms as constituent parts of the national economy under an integrated state plan. Management should seek to expand productivity autonomously based on its own ingenuity and responsibility. Second, the "Outline" sought to unify the national economy organically by guiding it and by organizing economic associations, based on the primacy of the common good, the leader

310 Kojima 1941, p. 151 et seq.

311 See Chapter 4 above for the important influence exerted by Nazi policy ideas on the conception of a self-sufficient and broad-area national defence economy.

principle and 'the service of one's calling for the nation'. These measures would display the national strength and accomplish the national objective of a high degree of national defence.

The first purpose of the "Outline" was to establish a national defence economy: state control and economic organization to expand the productivity of heavy industry, expecially the munitions industry. This was not to be done through state-run industries or government-controlled corporations, but on the basis of the autonomous management of private enterprises, where the wider needs of the nation went hand in hand with the profit principle. The "Outline" thus accepted the continued existence of private enterprise and private interests. However, enterprises were ranked as constituent parts of the national economy and required to assist state purposes ("the common/public good"). Limits were thus placed upon the pursuit of profit: the criterion was a fair profit – profits from speculation and monopolies were banned – and there were restrictions on dividends. Because of the very fact that private profit was allowed, the common good had to be stressed. This accorded with the above-mentioned principles of the primacy of the common good and the service of one's calling for the nation. This clearly originates in the Nazi slogan *Gemeinnutz geht vor Eigennutz* (The common good before the private good") referring to the subordination of the economy to the national interest.

To realise the state's objectives – expansion of productivity and economic mobilization – it was vital to organise the economic structure by systematising economic associations, which were to act as intermediaries in directing enterprises towards meeting the requirements of the state while at the same time coordinating the points of view of enterprises and conveying their interests to the government. They were thus a mechanism for bringing about cooperation between the official and private sectors and creating them was a central task of the New Economic Order. Indeed, close to half the provisions of the "Outline" concerned these economic associations, together with the form enterprises should take, a point indicative of their centrality to the structural changes conceived by the New Order. The model for organising enterprises nationwide according to industry and product was the Nazi *Gesetz zur Vorbreitung des organischen Aufbaues der deutschen Wirtschaft* (Law for the Preparation of the Organic Constitution of the German Economy) of February 1934 and its Enforcement Ordinance of November the same year, providing regional and industrial control offices.

The "Outline's" "enterprise (or business) associations" (*kigyō dantai*) later came into being as "control associations" (*tōseikai*). Minobe Yōji, a central figure in the Cabinet Planning Board which helped draft the "Outline", explained "control associations" as follows: "The control associations were organized on a

German model, and there was much discussion about whether they fitted the Japanese national character. *However, in character they are by no means a direct imitation of the German [model].* We need to give clear and ample thought to this point" (my italics). The systematization of economic associations under the New Economic Order may not have been a direct import from Germany but it was certainly based on a German model.[312]

Economic associations were to be regulated according to what was considered the Nazi-type leader principle. The "Outline" made explicit reference to the leadership of the state over the enterprise, to the leadership of the directors within economic associations, and to the leadership of important industrial organizations over subordinate organizations and affiliated firms. It was an up-down hierarchy consisting of the state, the economic associations (the directors), subordinate economic associations and the firm, with the economic associations positioned as intermediaries between the state and individual firms.

The leader principle denied the democratic principle of majority rule, and implied a style that characterised the totalitarian system of Nazi Germany of heavy-handed command from top to bottom with the leader taking responsibility. It was the basic principle that underpinned directives about state intentions to subordinates, and, inseparably linked with the principle of the primacy of the common good, was accepted as the principle of Japan's New Economic Order. In this way, the "Outline" united the three principles: the primacy of the common good, the Führer principle, and the organization of economic associations.

Growing Interest in Nazi Economic Thought

Japanese interest in Nazi economic thought and policy ideas grew significantly in the period around the outbreak of the Second Sino-Japanese War. One indication of this was the study undertaken by the Japan-Manchuria Financial Economic Research Group (JMG) of the Nazi economic system (see Chapter Four). This section introduces two other trends in order to examine the extent of Japanese

312 Minobe 1942, p. 91. Also, Tsūshō sangyōshō ed. vol. 11 (1964), p. 465 states "There were two types of control organization in heavy industry: *tōseikai* and *tōsei kumiai*. The former were national, industry-wide contol associations and the latter represented medium and small businesses on a local basis. What are of particular importance here are *the control associations (toseikai), modelled on the Nazi,* whose main role was to participate in government planning related to production, distribution, etc. in a particular industry and to guide and control the industry regarding production, distribution, activities, etc." (my italics).

interest in Nazism immediately before the introduction of the New Economic Order. One was the semi-official translation into Japanese and publication of the majority of the introductory works compiled in Nazi Germany, and the other was the critical study of Nazi structural reform undertaken by the Shōwa Research Association, which influenced the thinking of the reform bureaucrats.

1. Presentation of the Nazi System

In 1936, Germany began compiling a series of pamphlets aimed at public service personnel and others with official responsibilities to give them an overall picture of the Nazi system. They were bound in three volumes. Their translation into Japanese, mooted in 1938, was published between 1939 and 1941 in the 12 volume *Shin Doitsu kokka taikei* (Survey of the new German state). A support group was formed for the translation and publication under the chairmanship of Godō Takuo (1877-1956), President of the Japan Chamber of Commerce and Industry, a former naval ordnance vice-admiral, president of Shōwa Steel Works in Manchuria, a director of the South Manchuria Railway Company, and minister of commerce and railways in the Hayashi Cabinet of 1937. There were twelve honorary advisers, including the Minister of the Navy, Yonai Mitsumasa (1880-1948), other ministers, men connected with Japan-German cultural cooperation, the head of the Cabinet Planning Board, the jurist Makino Eiichi (1878-1970) of the Tokyo Imperial University and Otto Koellreutter (1883-1972), a professor of Munich University and head of the Japanese-German Cultural Institute in Tokyo (1938-39). General advisers included Hozumi Shigetō (1883-1951) and Suehiro Izutarō, both experts in civil law at the Tokyo Imperial University, as well as Kanokogi Kazunobu (1884-1949), professor of the Kyūshū Imperial University, visiting professor at Berlin University, and later secretary-general of the Great Japan Patriotic Writers Association (Dai Nihon genron hōkokukai) and an ultranationalist, and Fujisawa Chikao (1893-1962) of the Institute for the Study of the National Spirit and Culture (Kokumin seishin bunka kenkyūjo[313]). The task of translation and publication, a semi-government cultural undertaking, took place against a background of German and Japanese anti-communist and cultural pacts and was linked with a positive appreciation of Nazism.[314]

---

313 Created by the government in 1932 under the supervision of the Ministry of Education in order to foster the study and dissemination of information about Japanese culture and Shintō and combat Marxist ideology and eventually any kind of liberalism.

314 The German original was presented by Helmuth Wohlthat, head of the Ministerial Department, special representative of Hermann Göring and German representative

We should note the following points about this project. First, the German pamphlets, made into three volumes, were an official introduction to, and interpretation of, the structure and organization of law, government and economics in Nazi Germany, since the party seized control. At the same time, they were intended to inform the German people about the principles of Nazism. In other words, they were both an introduction to the current situation in Nazi Germany and a primer for spreading Nazism.[315] The official nature of the work is apparent in the names connected with it: its editors were Hans Lammers (1879-1962), Head of the Reich Chancellery and a man close to Hitler, and Hans Pfundtner (1881-1945), State Secretary of the Ministry of the Interior, who was close to Wilhelm Frick, the Interior Minister, while the Preface was written by Rudolf Hess and Frick. The first volume," Die weltanschaulichen, politischen und staatsrechtlichen Grundlagen des nationalsozialischen Staates" (The conception of the world, political and constitutional principles of the national socialist state), has 29 sections, the second," Der Aufbau des nationalsozialistischen Staates" (The structure of the national socialist state) has 21, and the third," Die Wirtschaftsordnung des nationalsozialistischen Staates" (The economic system in the national socialist state) has 23, making a total of 73. Leading members of the government and the academic community contributed essays to this large work. They included Alfred Rosenberg (1893-1946), Nazi Party dogmatist and author of *Der Mythus des 20. Jahrhunderts*, Otto Dietrich (1897-1952), chief press officer of the Nazi party, Walter Darré (1895-1953), Reich Minister for Food and Agriculture 1933-1942, Fritz Reinhardt (1895-1969), tax expert and NSDAP member since 1923, Otto Koellreutter, a constitutional lawyer, Ernst Rudolf Huber (1903-1990), professor of jurisprudence, Universities of Kiel,

---

in the conferences for the commercial agreement between Japan and Germany (1937-1938) to Nagai Alexander, Japanese commercial attache in Germany. It was taken back to Japan in the autumn of 1938 by two visiting members of the House of Peers, Baron Yasuba Yasutake (1888-?) of Shibaura Transportation and Count Gotō Ichizō (1893-?), president of Iwate Nippō. For conditions at the time of publication, see Mainichi shinbunsha ed. 1972, p. 291 et seq. Concerning Hirano Yoshitarō (1897-1980) and others connected with the translation and publication, see particularly Akisada 1996, also Suzuki Asao 1998, p. 256 et seq. See also Sugiyama 2001. For the Germany-Japan Agreement, see Sommer 1962.

315 The title of the earliest published work was *Die Verwaltungs-Akademie. Ein Handbuch für den Beamten im nationalsozialistischen Staat* (The Administration Academy. A Guide for Functionaries in the National Socialist State). This book was published in pamphlet form, chapter by chapter. Those who bought the pamphlets would keep them in a binder. There are no continual page numbers. A guide to reading the book was included at the top of the first volume.

Leipzig and Strassburg, Karl Haushofer (1869-1946), geopolitician and president of the Deutsche Akademie (1934-37) and the Volksbund für das Deutschtum im Ausland (1938-41), Justus Wilhelm Hedemann (1878-1963), professor of civil and economic law at Berlin University, and many others.

Second, the Japanese translation, *Shin Doitsu kokka taikei*, in 12 volumes, has a preface written by Eugen Ott (1889-1977), the German ambassador to Japan between 1938 and 1942. Its fifth volume, first published in 1941, went through seven printings. A large number of articles and books had appeared in Japan about the Nazi economy and Nazi economic thought since Hitler came to power,[316] but this work was the official, *de facto* German government explanation of the Nazi system, and its size and detail made it a valuable aid for understanding the realities of the Nazi system.

Third, it is significant that leading scholars of the time (and in the post-war period) were mobilized to contribute to the translation. They included Imanaka Tsugimaro, a political scientist of the Kyūshū Imperial University; Sumiya Etsuji (1895-1987), an economist of the Matsuyama Higher Commercial School and later president of Dōshisha University; the diplomat Kurusu Saburō (1886- 1954); a number of professors from the Tokyo Imperial University, including Kawashima Takeyoshi (1909-1992; civil and social law), Yamada Akira (1908- 2003; public law), Kaneko Hajime (1906-1973; civil proceedings), Miyazawa Toshiyoshi (1899-1976; constitutional law), Tanaka Jirō (1906-1982; administrative law), Sugimura Shōzaburō (1900-1991; administrative law), Suzuki Takeo (1905-1995; commercial law), Ishii Teruhisa (1906-1973; commercial law), Ōkōchi Kazuo (1905-1984; economic and social policy), Kondō Yasuo (1899-2005; agricultural policy), Yasui Takuma (1909-1995; economics) and Kamikawa Hikomatsu (1889-1988; international politics); professors from the Tokyo College of Commerce, including Azuma Mitsutoshi (labour law), Itagaki Yoichi (1908-2003; economics and economic policy) and Uehara Senroku (1899-1975; history); professors at the Tōhoku Imperial University, including Kimura Kameji (1897-1972; criminal law), Hattori Eitarō (1899-1965; economics and social policy) and Yanase Yoshimoto (1905-1985; administrative law), as well as Kazahaya Yasoji (1899-1989), a professor of social policy at the Kyūshū Imperial University, and Kobayashi Ryōsei (1898-1975), professor of economics and later president of Senshū University in the postwar period. Together with these social scientists, a number of bureaucrats from the Cabinet Planning Board also helped with the translation, including Nakajima Seiji, Fukuda Yoshiharu, author of *Doitsu keikaku keizai* (The German

316 See Chapter 3 above.

planned economy, 1938, see below), and Minoguchi Tokijirō (1905-1983), later a professor at Hitotsubashi University. At the centre of the actual translation work were Hirano Yoshitarō (1897-1980), head of editing on the publication committee, and the above-mentioned Kobayashi Ryōsei. Both were Marxian economic historians of the Kōza-ha ("Lectures Faction") who contributed to the compilation of the best-selling seven-volume *Nihon shihonshugi hattatsushi kōza* (Lectures on the history of the development of Japanese capitalism; 1932-1933).[317]

Fourth, each volume of the *Shin Doitsu kokka taikei* had a preface written by a leading person in government circles. Many exhibit the writer's own understanding of Nazi Germany. The preface at the beginning of the first volume was written by Godō Takuo, chairman of the translation support group. As the President of the Japan Chamber of Commerce and Industry, and a former Minister of Commerce and Industry, he was a powerful figure in business circles and was one of their representatives when questions about the New Economic Order were being discussed. It is worth noting his close connection with this semi-official translation and publishing project. Godō judged that, together with the Four Year Plan and the accompanying reform of the economic system, factors in Germany's prosperity were the Nazi world view, the spirit of leadership and prioritizing the common good over that of the individual. He thought highly of Nazi ideas and structural reform, stating that it was imperative that their roots be studied, since "there is a pressing need for Japan to continue to build a new order in East Asia".[318] Similarly, the author of the preface to the section on the economy in the translation was Matsui Haruo, formerly of the Cabinet Resources Bureau, and then a director of the Japan Chamber of Commerce and Industry and a supporter of Godō.[319] Matsui also paid attention to the controlled economy of

---

317 For Marxian economic historians and the Lectures Faction, see de Bary et al ed. 2005, p. 1236 et seq. For the publication of the translation, see the recollections of Mimasaka Tarō (1903-1989) in Mainichi shinbunsha ed. 1972, p. 291 et seq. Nazism and Fascism were two of the most pressing issues at the time. It is very possible that the scholars associated with the translation work saw their task as being linked with their own academic interests regarding contemporary questions. For further on the case of Kawashima Takeyoshi, who was working on Hedemann's property law, for example, see Kawashima 1949 (foreword) and its new edition of 1987 (afterword). See also Sugiyama 2001, Barshay 2007, p. 180.

318 *Shin doitsu kokka taikei,* vol. 1. Concerning Godō, see Matsuura 1995, p. 181 and Matsuura 2002, pp. 106, 207. Also Godon 1991, p. 322.

319 For Matsui at the Cabinet Resources Bureau and later, and for his ideas about the controlled economy and the Economic General Staff, see Itō Takashi 1989, p. 338, p. 349 et seq. and Mikuriya 1996, I.

Nazi Germany and, although he took Japanese distinctiveness into consideration, judged that there were an extremely large number of points that could be "an example for us to adopt". He stressed in particular the role of Chambers of Commerce and Industry and Economic Chambers in the German controlled economy. He wrote: "The German controlled economy does not depend upon state management like the Soviet Union, nor does it depend on corporatism like Italy. Permitting in large measure the activities of individuals and the links with industry of existing economic associations, banks and companies, it seeks to restructure the economic world organically, for a specific purpose and in a specific direction, based on the so-called leader principle. Thus, the organization of the German economic world comprises the organization of each of the sectors, and the cartel-like association of each of these organized sectors has the right to control the main economic markets, all under state direction. The task of the individual economic chambers is to integrate economic associations and the economic relationships among the various sectors. All are brought together under the Reich Economic Chamber and thus economic control of the whole country is regulated without contradiction or conflict to operate with maximum efficiency."[320]

Matsui understood the German controlled economy as an organic organization of the economic world based on the leader principle and individual activity. Building on this understanding, he presented the organic reorganization of the economic world as being centred on the economic chambers and a methodology for economic control based on the requirements of business circles. He set this against "control through paper plans" (i.e. bureaucratic control) that did not "accord with the realities of business circles". Since "national sentiment and a totalitarian leader principle were common to both Japan and Germany", he asserted that there should not be any great obstacle to transplanting the "system of guidance and organizational practices" of the German controlled economy to Japan. This understanding of Godō and Matsui and their plans for the organic organization of the economic world through the Japan Chamber of Commerce and Industry coincided chronologically with the undertaking of the translation of *Die Verwaltungs-Akademie*.

2. Critical Study by the Shōwa Research Association

As we have seen, the outbreak of the Second Sino-Japanese War and the strengthening of state economic control made economic restructuring a necessity. The

320 *Shin doitsu kokka taikei*, vol. 9 (Preface to section on the economy).

earliest ideas about ordering private economic associations organically came from the Shōwa Research Association (SRA), the brain trust organised to support Konoe Fumimaro. As soon as it was formed in April 1937, a number of sub-committees were set up, and study began on the organization of key economic associations in the United States, Great Britain and Germany, in order to establish a pivotal organ to integrate the strengths of the private economic associations. In December that year, a draft plan for a central organ of the private economy was drawn up. In contrast to the Japanese Federation of Economic Organizations (*Nihon keizai dantai renmei*), which had been set up the previous September simply to bring together all existing business organizations, this draft plan called for establishing a "Japan Industrial Federation" (Nihon sangyō renmei) as both a parent body and a systematic pivotal organ.

In thinking about the draft plan, the SRA paid great attention to the methods employed by Nazi Germany to organize the economy. However, it distanced itself from introducing German ideas for reform as they were. Rather, it wanted to draw up a plan that was fundamentally different from the "so-called Nazi commercial and industrial control system" and its "framework". The system of control, according to the "Law for the Preparation of the Organic Structure of the German Economy", was "on the surface autonomous", but in actuality "the Nazi party gives orders to the whole of German industry through this system" with "the purpose of spreading Nazi economic policies throughout the whole of industry." This is the "organization of industry as a whole from above", based on the "Führer principle", the "Nazi ideology" of making the supreme directive the "responsibility of the subordinate towards the power of the state". In character, such organizations should be seen as "extensions of the state machinery" rather than as private industrial associations. By contrast, the SRA envisaged its proposed "Japan Industrial Federation" as "organizing heavy industry through its own strength, autonomously from below completely independent of the state", functioning in a complementary and cooperative relationship with the state and the government authorities.[321]

---

321 Shōwa kenkyūkai (1937), especially pp. 4, 22. The Shōwa Research Association thus made a distinction between the Nazi position and their own and tried to hammer out a contrasting idea. Cf Fletcher 1982. Concerning studies of ideas about policy for industrial control, etc. held by the Shōwa Research Association, see Matsushima 1978. On contemporary ideas about the reorganization of economic associations, see Miura 1939a. Miura Testutarō was the chief editor of the *Tōyō keizai shinpō* (The Oriental Economist). In this connection, see also Kazahaya 1939a and Ryū 1939, p. 159 et seq.

This did not however mean the adoption of a system of economic associations as existed in Great Britain and the United States. In terms of the total organization of industry into associations based on both economic sector and particular category of business, compulsory membership, and the coexistence of associations and cartels, the draft plan clearly shows, in how their functional elements were incorporated, the degree to which Nazi-type methods of restructuring were absorbed.

In August 1940, just as the problems associated with the New Economic Order were coming to the surface, the SRA drew up a "Draft Plan for the Reorganization of the Japanese Economy" (*Nihon keizai saihensei shian*).[322] It is contained within the "Documents of the Research Association for National Policy" (Kokusaku kenkyūkai bunsho) connected with Minobe Yōji and the Cabinet Planning Board, which suggests Minobe and the other reform bureaucrats referred to it when discussing the New Economic Order, although it too was conceived as a critical study of Nazi-type modes.

It regarded the development of a "production economy"[323] as the main issue in the reorganization of the Japanese economy and so placed great weight on "management", as the basic unit of such an economy. Enterprises have a double nature, it stated: the capitalist function of seeking their own profit and a "public (social) function". Profits are the concern of the owners of the capital and investors, while the public function (that is, production maximization) is connected with the activities of managers, who shoulder the administrative function in enterprises. There is a gap, and a contradiction, between the two. What is necessary today, it went on, is to "control" the "selfish pursuit" of private profit, and bring the function of management into full play. How should this be done?

The draft plan considered that new factors were required to "bring out the self-power" of management. This "new drive" was seen to be what was known as the Führer principle in Nazi Germany. This principle had an integral connection with the "spirit" of national socialism (*minzoku shakaishugi*), and in Germany management based on the "Nazi principle" by the "leaders of industry" gave form to the "new drive" to manifest this management function. The plan

322 The full text is contained in Sakai 1979. See also "Kokusaku kenkyūkai bunsho mokuroku" (microfilm) 6209. Nakamura & Hara 1973 infers that the plan was produced around August 1939 and points out "it was easy to pull together a similarly impractical argument. However it is undeniable that the theory of the new economic order was later built upon it" (p. 84 et seq.).

323 The production economy is concerned with the management of technology, production and logistics processes in enterprises.

understood the leader principle to be the essential concept underpinning the actualization of the Nazi world view and its principles by Nazi economic leaders, and regarded it as the driving factor in the development of a Nazi-type system of management. Nevertheless, it did not view it as being suitable for Japan; what was needed was a "new system that accorded with the Japanese spirit".

"Nazism has adopted the leader principle as its driving factor. It is a system where leaders of industry who have absorbed the Nazi spirit follow Nazi principles and guide management to function appropriately. However, it is not possible to employ this leader system in our country, for it just does not suit. We must work to find a new system in accord with our national sentiment. Can we not create such a system?"

What was suggested as the Japanese way of doing things in place of the leader principle was, broadly defined, the "salary method" (*kyūryō hōshiki*). This meant that those responsible for managing enterprises be given a public character, and that a salary system be put in place to correspond with their professional activities. Specifically, this meant that company presidents and managing directors would have the status of civil servants, controls would be put on the amount of profit shareholders received while productive management would be increased, the abilitities, ingenuity and competitive spirit of managers would be utilised for the sake of the state, the potential and public nature of all employees would be recognized, and technology would be liberated. These views influenced the thinking of the Cabinet Planning Board in the early stages of the conception of the New Economic Order.

The Cabinet Planning Board, Reform Bureaucrats and Nazi policy thought

The Cabinet Planning Board and its Study of Nazi Germany

As we have seen in the previous chapter, the Cabinet Resources Bureau played a leading role in formulating the plan for the government to mobilise manpower and materials in preparation for war. With the outbreak of the Second Sino-Japanese War in 1937, the most pressing issue for the government was how to control the national economy. In September 1937, the first Konoe Fumimaro Cabinet, merging the Cabinet Planning Agency (Kikakuchō; formerly the Cabinet Research Bureau, Naikaku Chōsakyoku, 1935) with the Resources Bureau, launched the Cabinet Planning Board (Kikakuin) as the central body for instituting a war-preparedness economic system. It began operations the following month with Taki Masao as its head. In March 1938, the National Mobilisation Law was enacted, laying the legal foundation for state control of the national economy and the same year, the staff of the Cabinet Planning Board published the six-volume *Sekai keikaku keizai* (Planned economies of the world). Fukuda Yoshiharu (Research Department) wrote the first volume, *Doitsu keikaku keizai* (The planned economy in Germany) and the fourth, concerning France, Uchida Genbei (General Affairs Department) the second, about Italy, Naoi Takeo (Research Department) the third, about the Soviet Union, Okakura Koshirō (Finance Department) the fifth, about Great Britain, and Tamaki Hajime (Internal Affairs Department) the sixth, about the United States. All six volumes had the term "planned economy" in their title, next to the country name.

Here, "planned economy" did not signify the socialist planned economy, but was used more broadly to mean state control or planning of the national economy in the major countries. In the volume about the United States, the New Deal, legislated through NIRA (the National Industrial Recovery Act, officially known as the Act of June 16, 1933), was discussed as an example of a government-implemented planned economy. The staff of the Cabinet Planning Board had discerned a trend towards a "planned" or "controlled economy" within global economic developments in the two decades following World War I, from the Great Depression down to the subsequent formation of economic blocs and rearmament.

Countries had taken different approaches to implementing state control over their economies, and the staff of the Cabinet Planning Board recognised three patterns: the Soviet-style socialist economy; the German and Italian model of a "have-not" (resources poor) nation; and the British pattern of a "have" nation. Since Japan was a capitalist "have-not" nation, the Soviet socialist model was clearly incompatible, but the British model was too liberal, which left the German and Italian "have-not" capitalist models as the obvious choice. It was no coincidence that the first volume of the "Planned economies of the world" series dealt with Germany and the second with Italy.

In January 1938, the Cabinet Planning Board had launched a monthly report called *Kikaku* (Planning), which analysed in detail the major economies around the world with a focus on Great Britain, Germany, France, the United States and the Soviet Union. As recent studies have pointed out, *Kikaku* was particularly interested in the Soviet-style planned economy, introducing the preparation of its national economic plan and its administrative machinery in the fifth and sixth issues of volume one. The journal drew attention to two important elements of the Soviet-style planned economy: the dictatorship of the proletariat and the nationalisation of important resources and the means of production. The Soviet model was both a national economic plan and a national mobilisation scheme, made possible by the great political and economic power of the dictatorship of the proletariat. The Cabinet Planning Board realised that the way the Soviet national economic plan and its calculations had been made, as well as its administrative machinery, were an important technical means for a policy of control. However, Japan lacked the two crucial factors that had made the Soviet planned economy possible: the dictatorship of the proletariat and a nationalised production system.

Though the Soviet model was an important point of reference as a template for a planned economy for capitalist Japan in terms of the technical aspects of policy formation, it could not provide it with a fundamental blueprint for an actual framework to carry out state economic control in practice. European and American countries with a capitalist system presented more familiar models for Japan to emulate, especially resource-poor Germany, which shared many characteristics with Japan. Consequently, *Kikaku* made a remarkably detailed analysis of Germany. Among the important subjects that the Cabinet Planning Board chose to study were Nazi Germany's First and Second Four-year plans, its prices and labour policies, its state-run companies, its road construction policies, its war-time mobilisation plans and its food policy.

Kikuchi Haruo, a research officer with the Board, was among those most deeply involved in introducing Germany and translating German writings. He wrote two books, *Nachisu senji keizai taisei kenkyū* (A study of the Nazi wartime economy, 1940) and *Nachisu rōmu dōin taisei kenkyū* (A study of the Nazi labour mobilisation system, 1941), based on research conducted by the Board. Both works presented analyses that were equal in quality to those published in the United States and Europe around the same period, demonstrating that the Board's understanding of Nazi Germany was of a considerably high standard, despite the constraints of limited access to information at the time.

The Board's research was aimed at formulating a plan to expand and manage national strength in peacetime, and at coordinating administrative affairs among the various departments regarding the establishment and execution of a national mobilisation plan, even though the country was not formally at war.[324] The model that met these objectives was found in Nazi Germany's efforts to transform its economy from a peacetime one to a national defence economy capable of being transformed to one suitable for wartime, in anticipation of an expected total war. Kikuchi, as the most respected German specialist on the Board, outlined how Germany had established its national defence system by channelling national power into the defence of the country after the Nazi party's rise to power in

324 "Sōkan no ji", *Kikaku* vol 1 (January 1938), by Taki Masao.

1933, from the Second Four Year Plan down to the outbreak of World War II. He emphasised that in Germany the implementation of an "economic mobilisation" system had preceded that of a "military mobilisation" system, with the national defence system put in place as a new transitional stage from peacetime to wartime, specifically in preparation for total war. He said: "A national defence system geared towards modern total war was established to a large degree a few years prior to the outbreak of war."[325] Kikuchi drew his conclusions about the Nazi defence and wartime economy from the research conducted first by the Cabinet Resources Bureau and then by the Cabinet Planning Board, where his views were probably shared among its members.

Minobe Yōji's ideas about the war-preparedness economy and the New Economic Order

(a) The war-preparedness economy: Minobe Yōji, together with Mōri Hideoto and Sakomizu Hisatsune, played an extremely important role among the reform bureaucrats of the Cabinet Planning Board who designed the New Economic Order.[326] Let us now consider what connection existed between their conception of a new economic order and the Nazi New Order (*Neue Ordnung*).

In 1938, the year after the Second Sino-Japanese War broke out and before the discussion about the New Economic Order began in earnest, Minobe published a paper entitled, "Kōgyō seisaku no Nihonteki tenkan" (The Japanese-style transformation of industrial policy).[327] There he described the characteristics of the evolution of capitalism in Japan, pointing out the current world trend towards "developing and strengthening national defence systems", and emphasizing the importance of restructuring industry in general, and heavy industry in particular. He focused more on the establishment of a "war-preparedness economy" in anticipation of total war than on a wartime economy itself, thus distinguishing the "war-preparedness economy" not only from the "peacetime economy" but also from the "wartime economy". He wrote: "The war-preparedness economy and the wartime economy both aim at carrying out economic policies designed to defend the country. There is a difference, however. The former is a system to prepare for an imminent war, while the latter is a series of economic policies devised to fight an actual war." He makes this distinction drawing on Japanese experience, saying that the Sino-Japanese war had broken out before a

325 Kikuchi 1940, Preface, chapter 1 and p. 390 et seq. See also Kikuchi 1941.

326 Furukawa 1992, p. 176 et seq.

327 Minobe 1938.

war-preparedness economy was fully in place, which meant there was an urgent need to transform the national economy rapidly into a wartime economy and increasing pressure to strengthen state control.

Minobe deemed it important to establish an economic system designed to prepare the country for total war, rather than to move directly from a peacetime economy to a wartime one. He said that under a war-preparedness economy, the national economy undergoes a process of "planned control" with a focus on the systematic expansion of productive capacity in order to "upgrade and strengthen national defence capabilities", in other words, this was the stage where the economy transformed itself from a "peacetime economy" into a "wartime economy". As we have seen, the war-preparedness economy was also called the "national defence economy" at the time, and we have already discussed how this term corresponded to the German *Wehrwirtschaft*, a concept that was much discussed in Germany in connection with the Nazi Four Year Plan around 1936, which was itself closely surveyed and studied by the Japan-Manchukuo Financial Economic Research Group (JMG). The JMG had distributed the results of their study among those involved, and we can presume that Minobe's views were based on this report.[328]

Minobe linked this concept to the international situation. He observed that after World War I, countries across the globe had adopted "self-centred" policies and "nationalistic economic plans" while "increasing armaments" and "enhancing their national defence systems". As a result, each nation had "turned its economy to a large degree into one controlled (by the state)". As the Soviet Five Year Plan and the Nazi Four Year Plan had shown, this required countries both to establish their heavy industry and to restructure their domestic industries to centre on heavy industry.

Further, he pointed out that the need to establish a war-preparedness and defence economy made it inevitable that the nation would move away from *laissez-faire* capitalism. He said: "If a country lets capitalism guide its future economic development according to *laissez-faire* principles, it will have no chance in succeeding to restructure its industry. The Great World War has in this sense brought a revolutionary change to the concept of war, showing us that the outcome of a modern war is determined by munitions and materiel. A country cannot fight a modern war if it fails to establish a munitions industry during peacetime to provide the enormous amount of military supplies required. There is a huge discrepancy in the need for armaments in peacetime and wartime, yet when war breaks

328 See Chapter 4 above.

out, a country has to steer its industries smoothly from peacetime to wartime operations. In order to achieve a satisfactory transition, a country has no choice but to transform its peacetime economy into one prepared for war. The countries that fought in the Great War in Europe learned this the hard way."

According to Minobe, Japan had lagged behind the other developed nations in terms of the evolution of capitalism and was now faced with the "twin problems of underdevelopment and a scarcity of raw materials"; to overcome this predicament, it had to strengthen control of the economy and implement structural changes in all industries to "prepare industry for a future war". In the process, he asserted, the "capitalist economy of the past based on *laissez-faire* must be gradually rescinded and converted to a totalitarian, controlled economy centring on the state" and the country's existing industrial policies must undergo a drastic change and "assume the character of a state-controlled industry".

Minobe thus placed emphasis on the importance of establishing and strengthening a system to prepare for a future war. He observed that the Second Sino-Japanese war had broken out before such a system was fully in place, and this unpreparedness had forced "a hasty transformation into a war economy", strongly pressuring the government to tighten state control. The New Economic Order was conceived with a knowledge of the world situation and an awareness of the inevitability of the transition from a war-preparedness economy to a wartime one.[329] For this reason, there was a need to reverse *laisse-faire* capitalism and in its place adopt a state-centred, totalitarian controlled economy akin to the German model.

(b) The New Economic Order and studies of Nazism: Two years after Minobe's paper was published, dissension over the New Order came to a head during the second Konoe Fumimaro Cabinet. The draft plan drawn up by Minobe and his colleagues in September 1940 was leaked to the newspapers, which reported that plan intended the separation of ownership and management. The business community vehement opposed any such policy and debate escalated. The government adopted a modified version of the plan at the beginning of December, but the business community was not appeased. In early December,

329 Furukawa agrees with my analysis that proposals for the New Order were based principally on establishing a national defence economy and expanding heavy industry, centring on the munitions industry (Furukawa 1992, p. 177). It is considered that the basic framework of these proposals was constructed in 1938, before the debate about the New Order became an issue in 1940. We can therefore presume that the rationale for the necessity of a New Order grew out of the deliberations of the time.

the Japan Economic League and six other major business organizations handed Prime Minister Konoe a statement entitled "Opinion Paper Concerning the New Economic Order", which asserted that the plan of the reform bureaucrats risked driving the national economy into chaos, and recommended that matters concerning the economy should be left to business circles. The government should therefore cease its plans to impose control on the economy, since the pursuit of profits was key to increasing productivity; by restraining this drive, the government was jeopardizing companies' development. The business community denounced the draft plan both for its socialist tendencies and because it rejected the profit principle. Minobe countered what he called "the business community's misunderstanding" by publishing a paper entitled "Keizai shintaisei kanken" (A personal view of the New Economic Order)[330] immediately after the Cabinet approved the "Outline for the Establishment of a New Economic Order". His main points were:

(1) The most important reason for insisting on the establishment of a new economic system is to respond to what the business community's "Opinion Paper" calls "the crisis affecting the very existence of the [Japanese] Empire". It is by no means whatsoever a case of "making reforms for reform's sake". That is why the New Economic Order advocates "a planned national economy" and a "concerted national effort to expand industrial output by maximising productivity".
(2) However, it is not feasible to implement a comprehensive economic plan when the national economy is run by a "*laissez-faire* management rooted in a liberal economic system". Therefore, the existing economic system must change. This change is not, however, merely "to rectify the evils of the *laissez-faire* economy", but more importantly it is to manage the national economy based on a coordinated plan to meet the exigencies of war". It is this pressing need that has called for the establishment of a New Economic Order.
(3) Regarding the question of profit, "the Cabinet Planning Board has not the slightest intention of rejecting profit", but private interests must not override the public interest. That is why he and his colleagues had advocated "purifying the desire to pursue profit" in accordance with the principle of the "identification of public and private interests".
(4) The business community's "Opinion Paper" demanded that Japan follow the example of Germany. Therefore business leaders should know that

330 Minobe, 1941a, Minobe 1942, section 1, chapter 4; Mimura 2011, pp. 164-167.

Germany, more than any other country, has promoted the primacy of the public good. Article 10 of the "25 Point Programme" of the NSDAP demanded that "The first obligation of every citizen must be to work both spiritually and physically. The activity of individuals is not to counteract the interests of the universality, but must have its result within the framework of the whole for the benefit of all". Furthermore, Article 18 demanded a "struggle without consideration against those whose activity is injurious to the general interest".[331] The business community should study these points if it intends to make Nazi Germany its model.

Points (1), (2) and (3) are in line with Minobe's 1938 paper ("The Japanese-style transformation of industrial policy") published before the New Economic Order had become an issue. In his original plan for the New Economic Order, Minobe discussed his basic points in a logical sequence: first the nation must take heed of the worldwide escalation of the arms race and grasp the need to establish a war-preparedness economy and a national defence economy based on the German concept of a defence economy (*Wehrwirtschaft*); second, it must comprehend the urgency of restructuring the national economy with a focus on heavy industry, and the inevitability of reforming liberal economic policies. Minobe's recommendations denied neither the profit principle nor capitalism itself, but he emphasised it was necessary to "give priority to the public interest over the private interest" in order to realise these objectives. That is why he mentioned the priority given in Nazi ideology to the public good, and he used this as the basis for his counterargument. Minobe's ideas about the New Economic Order are clearly connected with both the Nazi economic principle of the public interest over the private, and Nazi ideas about creating a war-preparedness economy and a national defence economy, which necessitated the expansion of economic strength and the control of the economy.

Initially, inherent in the Nazi principle of the public interest over the private was a criticism of the capitalistic pursuit of profit, such as the profit principle of the *laissez-faire* economy, and the demand to abolish debt slavery and unearned income and suggestions how to correct those evils. These reflected the socialist elements of National Socialism, whose anti-capitalistic stance was best expressed in Article 11 of the "25 Point Programme" and its demand to break debt slavery. Minobe, however, completely ignored this Article, since it did not fit with his own view. In advocating a New Economic Order, he made no attempt to do away with the generally recognised defects and evils of a *laissez-faire* economy

331 Minobe 1941a, pp. 18 ff. and Minobe 1942, pp. 64 ff.

and capitalism, and so did not aspire to state socialism or national socialism, both of which had anti-capitalist tendencies. Minobe's was no more than a medium -term plan designed to bring the Sino-Japanese war to a successful conclusion, which envisaged a move towards a war-preparedness, defence economy and then an actual war economy. This unconcern does not mean, however, that his views deviated from Nazi economic thought. As we have seen, after they seized power, the Nazi party played down the anti-capitalist aspects of their economic ideology and made extensive revisions. Thus we can say that Minobe's plan for the New Economic Order was based on an accurate observation of the New Order (*Neuordnung*) of Nazi Germany as it was in reality.

Minobe's stance on capitalism was also manifested in his basic ideas about the need to systematise corporate management and economic organisations for the implementation of the New Economic Order. The business community demanded that "corporate management be led by the private sector". Rather than opposing their demands, Minobe countered them in his paper, saying that "this is exactly what I and my colleagues desire most". In his eyes, a Soviet-style planned economy based on a socialist political system could not serve as a model for Japan, since Japan was looking for a model for a controlled economy based on the principles of a capitalist economy. In reality, a wartime economy could not be established without the cooperation of the private sector, and the only possible way to bring this about was to build "cooperation between the private and public sectors" on "the premise that autonomy rests with the private sector".

In the same paper, Minobe also asserted that "for the state to take over corporate management by force from the private sector would be a worst case scenario in the present circumstances, and must be avoided at all costs". The government and the private sector must therefore resolve their current conflict and "work together" to manage "the national economy in a time of crisis". He stated that "the management of each corporation must have a clear sense of being a part of the national economy, strive to fulfil its duties, and contribute towards the ultimate goal of the nation within the framework of a coordinated plan for the national economy. The government in turn must fully understand its responsibility, perform its supervisory and directorial duties from a broad point of view, and also act as a coordinator for the economic associations, each of which has been formed by enterprises engaged in the same line of industry or dealing with the same goods".[332]

332 Minobe 1941a, pp. 19 ff. and Minobe 1942, pp. 66 ff.

It was therefore necessary to organise economic associations grouped together by industry and product, to coordinate their activities, and to establish the leader principle. As far as Japan was concerned, the best model for doing so, so as to bring about autonomous corporate management and cooperation between the public and private sectors and to promote an awareness of the national interest among business leaders, was neither that of the socialist Soviet Union nor liberal Great Britain or the United States, but of Nazi Germany. In Japan, economic associations categorised by industry (control associations in the case of important industries), modelled on the German *Wirtschaftsgruppe* (Economic Group), were expected to play a central role in supporting the wartime controlled economy as a mediator, by means of the leader principle, between the primacy of the public good and autonomous corporate management. Germany and Japan differed greatly from one another, however, in terms of their power structures, through which the leader principle was to be exercised. We will examine this last point below.

Reform bureaucrats and the principles of the public interest and profit

Minobe shared with other reform bureaucrats the two principles of the priority of the public interest and of profit. An article entitled "A round-table discussion about the New Order" featuring four leading reform bureaucrats, Minobe Yōji, Mōri Hideoto, Sakomizu Hisatsune and Kashiwabara Heitarō (1896-1952) appeared in a special New Year's edition of the magazine *Jitsugyō no Nihon* (Business Japan) dated January 1941. Here the participants criticised those industrialists who, they said, had misinterpreted the principle of the primacy of the public good as "communist", completely denying private interests and ownership. Minobe explained that "the notion of the public interest taking precedence over private interests by no means denies the private interest", and pointed out that "the expression comes from Germany", where it was taken to mean that "private interests cannot be divorced from the public interest".

In the course of the discussion, Mōri Hideoto equated the Japanese reform bureaucrats with Hjalmar Schacht (1877-1970) who served as President of the Reichsbank (1923-1930; 1933-1939) and was Minister of Economics in Hitler's government (1934-1937). He stated that "the planned economy is not in direct opposition to a liberal economy" and that "it would have no legs to stand on if the mechanism of the liberal economy itself were denied". He also asserted that "we have to accept the liberal economy for what it is, understanding its pluralistic nature and integrating it into the larger picture. Buraucrats must develop the sensibility and flexibility to do this task". Like Minobe, Mōri contemplated a reform plan that acknowledged capitalistic profit-making activities as a given and sought to integrate them into a totalitarian economic framework.

Sakomizu Hisatsune also criticised the business community for its misunderstanding about profit-making. "We are criticised for denying profit-making," he said. "This is a gross misunderstanding. We have used on occasion the expression 'denying the pursuit of profits', but our critics have overlooked the word 'pursuit' and jumped to the conclusion that we were denying profit itself. If we reject profits, extended reproduction will be impossible, since in a money economy, profit is its concrete expression." He said that, with pressure for the expansion of production mounting, it was now a pressing matter to undertake extended reproduction, and under these circumstances, it made no sense to deny the profit principle. He concluded by stating that what he and his colleagues had denounced were "cases of rapacious pursuit of profit, harmful to the national interest".[333]

To sum up, a war economy calls for the expansion of production and extended reproduction, and the profit principle is necessary for this. However, "acquisitive" profit seeking that hurts the public interest must be eliminated. Minobe emphasised that he agreed with Sakomizu on this issue. "We do not deny profit, whether generated from business or production. On the contrary, we believe that profit generation contributes to the national interest." He did however criticise "profits arising from speculation and monopolies".[334] He also stated that "a planned economy does not in itself deny profit, because we need profits generated by production so that we can expand our productive capacity and our extended reproduction. Denying profits arising from production denies the expansion of productive capacity, which makes it impossible to increase national wealth. At a time when the national economy must be managed according to a coordinated plan, profits earned by speculation and monopolies risk destroying the coordinated management of the national economy. These are the only type of profits we are seeking to eliminate."[335] Here the reform bureaucrats were advocating ideas akin to the Nazi demand in the 25 Point Programme for the elimination of self-centred profit seeking and the total confiscation of war profits.

---

333 *Jitsugyō no Nihon,* January 1941, pp. 55 ff., 58 ff., 65 ff., also Nagashima 1986, p. 291, Mimura 2011, pp. 167, 169. Many preceding studies regard the reform bureaucrats as "anti-capitalist" in their stance on the New Order, but their observations should be reexamined. See Shibagaki 1979, p. 302, Okazaki 1987, p. 193 and Miyajima 1993, p. 313.

334 *Jitsugyō no Nihon*, January 1941, p. 65.

335 Minobe 1942, p. 24.

Restricting dividends and Nazi legislation

In Japan an ordinance restricting dividends and finance (Corporate Profits, Dividends and Funds Accommodation Ordinance; *Kaisha rieki haitō oyobi shikin yūzū rei*) was promulgated in April 1939, enforced under Article 11 of the National Mobilisation Law of March 1938. It was revised in December 1939, and later incorporated into other legislation such as the Company Accounts Control Ordinance (*Kaisha keiri tōsei rei*) of October 1940. Previous studies have made it clear that the business community vehemently opposed putting restrictions on dividends, and denounced the ordinance as denying the "entrepreneurial spirit".

By limiting capital returns, the Company Accounts Control Ordinance aimed at promoting capital accumulation and rational corporate management, curbing consumption and purchasing power, and preventing production costs from rising, so as to increase internal reserves within corporations and thus strengthen their ability to finance themselves through their own capital. Sakomizu Hisatsune played a central role in drafting this policy. In the above-mentioned round -table discussion (*Jitsugyō no Nihon*, January 1941) he had emphasised that restricting dividends was not a denial of the profit principle; rather the action had been taken to promote an increase in the internal reserves of corporations and an expansion of production, which in turn leads both to increased profits and an expansion of productive capacity in the national economy, thus contributing to the public interest.[336]

The policy Sakomizu and his colleagues drafted corresponded to Nazi Germany's policy to curtail dividends and so control profit distribution. In 1934, soon after seizing power, the Nazi party passed two laws to limit dividend payouts – the Capital Investment Law (*Kapitalanlagengesetz*, March 29), and a revised version called "Profit Distribution in Joint-stock Companies" (*Gesetz über die Gewinnverteilung bei Kapitalgesellschaften*, December 4), also known as the Loan Reserve Law, *Anleihestockgesetz*), which provided that all firms distributing dividends of over 6 per cent must for a period of three years pay all such excess profits to the Gold Discount Bank, which invested the funds and held them in trust for the shareholders.[337] The law's initial goal was to have companies absorb public bonds in order to help reduce the national debt, which had been mounting as a result of unemployment relief measures and other related policies. The law forced high-performing companies to invest their profits in government bonds.

336 January 1941, the New Year's special issue of *Jitsugyō no Nihon*, pp. 59 and 65. Sakomizu 1942, pp. 17ff.; Mimura 2011, pp. 151 ff.

337 Neumann 1942, 1944, p. 316.

This law attracted attention in Japan, and was discussed in parliament during the premiership of Hirota Kōki (March 1936-February 1937). Exorbitant dividends issued by companies had become a social issue in Japan, then reeling under a recent coup attempt (February 1936), and many saw the legislation as a Nazi-type state control of capitalistic, profit-seeking activities. A specialist on this subject, Hasegawa Yasubei (1896-1942), a professor at Waseda University, connected it with the Nazi idea of the subordination of private to public interests, saying, "The leader principle, which is at the heart of the Nazi controlled economy, emphasises the public interest over the private and situates the principles of corporate management within the public interest, in order to correct the acquisitive capitalistic sprit that seeks to pursue private gain at all costs, even at the expense of the public interest…. If such conduct brings harm to the national economy through letting the private interest take precedence over the public interest, it is natural that the state should intervene forcefully to eliminate abuses."[338]

Sakomizu and his colleagues regarded such Nazi policy less as a way for the state to control profits than as a means to rationalise capitalist management. In other words, they regarded it as a measure to expand the productive capacity so as to establish a wartime economic system, thus to contribute to the public interest. The Nazi legislation also had the function of making companies absorb public bonds, and it was this aspect on which the reform bureaucrats focused their attention, regarding it as a way to expand production, a prerequisite for wartime economic planning. The business commuity, on the other hand, viewed the Nazi policy as no more than a form of state control on profits stemming from the principle of public over private interests, which to them meant a denial of the *laissez-faire* profit principle.

Restricting dividends did mean, in theory at least, state control on profits, but at the same time the policy could also be presented as an attack on unearned income, as Hitler did. The view then prevalent in Japan was that of Ryū Shintarō and others, which opposed the profit-first principle, placed emphasis on production and advocated the rational reconstruction of the national economy. The issue they had raised was inevitably connected with the relationship between the dividends paid to shareholders and business activities within corporations, and the relationship between the ownership of capital (stocks and shares) and management. It was in this climate that the reform bureaucrats proposed the separation of ownership and management in their draft of the "Outline for the Establishment of a New Economic Order". Business circles identified the legislation to

338 Hasegawa 1937, pp. 10ff., and 1942.

restrict dividends (the Company Accounts Control Ordinance) with the separation of ownership and management, and viewed it as dividend standardisation and state intervention in the capitalist profit principle. Thus the issue of restricting dividends became a point of contention between the reform bureaucrats and the business community.[339]

Views about Nazi economic policies within business circles

As we have seen, the business community denounced the "Outline for the Establishment of a New Economic Order", drafted by the reform bureaucrats of the Cabinet Planning Board, as "red". Business leaders not only took an anti-Marxist stand, but they also opposed any form of state control of profits. The Nazi party program that advocated restraining profits made the business community wary and critical of the National Socialism (or State Socialism) that the Nazi party espoused. Business opposition to National Socialist ideology did not however imply any outright denunciation of Nazism or fascism. In this section we will examine how Japanese business circles interpreted Nazi economic ideas.

The Japan Chamber of Commerce and Industry and its plan for structural reform

In 1938, the Ministry of Commerce and Industry unofficially presented to the Japan Chamber of Commerce and Industry a provisional draft of a bill to create a new "economic chamber" (*keizai kaigisho*) with broader functions than the existing Chamber of Commerce.[340] In response, the Japan Chamber presented its own reform plans, first that of Matsui Haruo and then that of Godō Takuo. The plan of Matsui Haruo, director of the Chamber, advocated expanding the functions for the Chamber of Commerce beyond its advisory capacity to play an active role in drafting state economic policies as the representative of the private sector, undertaking an official administrative role, and, in its capacity as an extra-governmental organization, acting as a bridge between the government and the business sector. Godō Takuo, president of the Chamber, added his own ideas for reform to those of Matsui, proposing that the Chamber be given the authority to coordinate communication and cooperation among the commercial and industrial groups associated with it, as well as to exercise control over

339 Nakamura and Hara 1973. See also Chapter 1 of this book.

340 Kimura 1939. See also Sunaga 2004. Regarding the transformation of business enterprises into economic organisations, see Yanagisawa 2012b, 2013, II.

them. He also proposed inviting economic associations nationwide grouped by industry and trade to join the Chamber, and thus establish it as Japan's central economic body.[341]

The Matsui and Godō plans, both aimed at creating a central economic body by restructuring the Chamber of Commerce and Industry and the economic associations, were closely related to the evaluation of Nazi Germany made in the recently published *Shin doitsu kokka taikei* (Survey of the new German state) with which Godō had been closely associated. Godō pointed out "strong similarities" between the circumstances under which Japan and Germany had found themselves, saying: "With a controlled economic system working well today in Germany, we should closely study its development, as this will be very useful for making projections about the future of Japan's controlled economy, and ironing out the details."[342]

Both Matsui and Godō focused on how Nazi Germany had organically restructured its economy and remodelled its Chambers of Commerce and Industry based on both economic control and the autonomy of economic associations. The Kyūshū University professor and Marxist theorist Kazahaya Yasoji, a translator on the *Shin doitsu kokka taikei* project, criticised the Godō plan for "proposing the formation of autonomous associations grouped by industry even more thoroughgoing than the original Nazi model", and concluded that "the Japan Chamber of Commerce and Industry has clearly endorsed, through its President Godō, a Nazi-style reorganisation of industrial associations".[343]

Matsui and Godō adopted the Nazi model, as it appeared in the Law for the Organic Constitution of the German Economy (March 1934) and the Decree Concerning Chambers of Industry and Commerce (August 1934), for restructuring economic organisations in Japan because they recognised the extreme importance of such restructuring if economic control was to work. Their

341 Kimura 1939, pp. 29 ff., Kazahaya 1939a, 4, pp. 5 ff., Sunaga 2004, pp. 27 ff.

342 Godō, June 1939 (5th ed. May 1944), p. 188.

343 Kazahaya 1939a, 4, p. 6. Shōkō keizai, 1938, focuses on the importance of this issue in an article on a round-table discussion attended by Kojima Seiichi, Arisawa Hiromi, Kawahara Jikichirō, Minobe Ryōkichi and Kimura Masutarō; Arisawa Hiromi stressed the need of a control mechanism; see p. 202 for the negotiations between the Tokyo Chamber of Commerce and Industry and the Ministry of Commerce and Industry on this issue. See also Kojima 1939, p. 154. For the organisation plans by the private sector including the Chamber of Commerce and Industry, and their significance, see Sunaga 2004 and Matsuura 1995 (unlike Yanagisawa, Matsuura sees this attempt to reorganise the Chambers as drawing on the American model.)

understanding of the Nazi system differed from that of the Shōwa Research Association. While the latter saw the formation of German economic organisations as a way to exercise strong state control, the Japanese Chamber of Commerce and Industry focused on the autonomous aspect. As we have seen, Nazi Germany's policies and institutions comprised a duality: initiative by enterprises and economic organisations and control from above based on the leadership principle. The Shōwa Research Association dismissed the leadership principle as typically Nazi, while Godō and Matsui looked favourably on the Nazi emphasis on corporate initiative, and adopted it as the basis for restructuring their own organisation. All the same, the Godō and Matsui plans themselves differed from the original Nazi plan on a number of points.

The German plan for the "organic constitution" of the economy consisted on the one hand of forming national and regional organisations grouped by industry, and on the other, restructuring chambers nationwide as regional associations comprising all trade and industry. Godō and Matsui envisioned a structure centred on the latter system, a network of Chambers of Commerce and Industry that absorbed local industrial associations. Their view went against that of the Japan Economic Federation which advocated the formation of economic organisations grouped by industry, particularly cartels.

The Chamber of Commerce and Industry had a strong connection with regional economies, and local small and medium-sized firms of various types were important components. Their interests often conflicted with those of the organisations of large corporations that were connected with the important industries, especially nationwide groups and cartels. As the Japanese economy moved towards a wartime system, direct suppliers, such as cartels and trade, commercial and industrial associations grouped by industry, assumed control of the allocation of raw materials and the distribution of commodities, as well as production, imports and exports, pricing and transportation. This was an issue of life and death for regional businesses, and the areas in which the Chambers of Commerce and Industry could participate were greatly curtailed.[344]

On 25 November 1939, the Japan Economic Federation held a panel discussion about the current economic situation, which doubled as a standing committee meeting, and invited Murase Naokai (1891-1968), undersecretary at the Ministry of Commerce and Industry, and other officials to participate. It used the occasion to present to the Ministry of Commerce and Industry a "Summary of grievances from affected parties concerning state economic control and

---

344 Koana 1939, pp. 7ff. Prior to the publication of this book, Koana had been a member of the Tokyo Chamber of Commerce and Industry.

proposals for improvement". This pointed out problems in the proposed measures arising out of the unequal relationship between "large, powerful corporations" and "powerless small and medium businesses", and reflected the interest of local businesses in Osaka, Nagoya and other areas.[345]

The plans drafted by Godō and Matsui, based on regional economic connections, represented local interests and those of small and medium businesses. Citing the principle of group autonomy, they saw the Chambers of Commerce and Industry participating in the process of policy making, with expanded authority by acting on the government's behalf regarding administrative affairs, and protecting its infrastructure to serve local interests. They represented a stand against the trend to strengthen the main cartels in the Japan Economic Federation and to form a vertical organisational structure based on the type of industry, through which the conventional model of "self-control" would be exercised.

Japanese intellectuals and government officials were well aware that the Law for the Organic Constitution of the German Economy and the Decree Concerning Chambers of Industry and Commerce acknowledged autonomous associations on the one hand and advocated the leadership principle by emphasising "the collective and national interest of commerce and industry" on the other. Having modelled their plans on Nazi ideas, Godō and Matsui focused on the autonomous associations, while regarding state control as inevitable, using it to their advantage in their campaign, not only to oppose the trend towards "self-control" by the cartels but also to integrate the system of "self-control" into their own plan. Their design was to lend support, from below, to the Cabinet Planning Board's policy of establishing a wartime economic system through the concerted efforts of both the public and private sectors. As Kazahaya Yasoji pointed out, it was based on "a plan to form Nazi-style autonomous industrial associations grouped by function". The plans aimed at integrating into the "national economy" the interests of small and medium enterprises rooted in regional economies, and in this sense they shared certain characteristics with those of the Nazi party, whose major support base consisted of the middle classes, including small and medium enterprises. The *Keizai dantai rengōkai zenshi* (A history

---

345 *Keizai dantai rengokai zenshi* (1962), pp. 288 ff. Mukai Shikamatsu, a leading authority on industrial unions and the controlled economy, had been appointed director at the Nagoya Chamber of Commerce and Industry after retiring from Keio University. For Mukai's view about the significance of Chambers as regional organisations and associations grouped by function across various industries, as well as their relations with small and medium enterprises, see Mukai, January 1943. Also see Sunaga 2004.

of the formation of economic organisations) looks at this movement from the viewpoint of the Japan Economic Federation: "Among the small and medium enterprises were those who opted for state control rather than having to yield to decisions made by large corporations under the name of self-control. Such dissenting voices resulted in disarray and consequently benefitted the progressive elements in the military and bureaucrats. This course of events was one of the factors that eventually necessitated the creation, in August 1940, of a separate organisation called the Conference of Control Associations of Important Industries (*Jūyō sangyō tōsei dantai kondankai*).[346]

The Japan Economic Federation, made up of the large corporations, naturally opposed any idea that the Chamber of Commerce and Industry should have any control over the economic organisations. Its director, Takashima Seiichi, criticised the Godō plan as premature. Thus Godō's plan was frustrated by the most powerful organization in Japanese business and its demands for a system of self-control and the implementation of cartels.

The Japan Economic Federation, the Conference of Control Associations of Important Industries and Nazi ideology

(i) The "Discussion Proposal Regarding the Outline of a Private Sector New Economic Order" and the primacy of the public interest

By the end of the 1930s, a much more positive attitude was emerging within the Japan Economic Federation towards both the wartime controlled economy and participation in government policy formation. In early 1940, its Current Affairs Committee began discussing economic control and in June drafted "An Emergency Proposal Regarding Measures to Improve the Industrial Control Mechanism" which it then presented to the government. The proposal included the idea of "overhauling the private economic control mechanism" by establishing a council of the control associations of the major industries which would reorganise and unify private economic organisations, strengthen and improve their

---

346 *Keizai dantai rengokai zenshi* (1962), p. 290. Matsuura Masataka (1995) points out the importance of the private sector's plan for economic control as opposed to the bureaucrats' plan. Matsuura, however, does not distinguish between the plan proposed by the Chambers of Commerce and Industry closely connected to regional economies and small and medium traders and manufacturers, and that of the Japan Economic Federation aiming to form organisations grouped by industry with large corporations and cartels as central players. Consequently, he overlooks the confrontational relationship between the two bodies.

autonomous controlling mechanism, and improve communications among the major industries. The Conference of the Control Associations of Important Industries (Jūyō sangyō tōsei dantai kondankai) set up in August 1940 was based on this idea and contained the germ of the control associations (*tōseikai*) that were established in August 1941.[347]

The Conference of Control Associations of Important Industries (known as Jūsankon)[348] consisted of the leaders of the major industries, such as steel, coal and shipping. It immediately set out to formulate the business community's conception of the new economic order, and in September drafted a "Discussion Proposal Regarding the Outline of a Private Sector New Economic Order", which it then presented to various sectors of the business community for approval. The proposal was to be forwarded to the government as the business community's position regarding the new economic order. It lays out the basic principle of its new economic order in its preamble: "With the purpose of our industry being the building a powerful national defence economy, in a spirit of ardent national consciousness we will establish a system that enables *the public and private sectors to work together* of their *own volition* and *autonomously, on the principle of the primacy of the public interest*, to design and implement national economic plans" (my italics).[349] This stresses the establishment and implementation of state economic plans through the cooperation of "the public and private sectors" "voluntarily and autonomously" while following "the principle of the primacy of public interest". In this sense, it corresponds to both Nazi economic thought and the ideas of the reform bureaucrats.

The proposal's preamble also states: "Industries will give the first priority to productivity and eliminate the evil of over-emphasis on profits. Enterprises and organisations will strive ardently to increase production for the advancement of the national interest. To this end, rather than having government agencies stepping up their intervention in individual enterprises, the private sector will cultivate a sense of publicness in the organisations grouped by industry and trade, and strengthen authority regarding the supervisory capacity of their leaders." The principles cited here – putting production first, eliminating the evil of placing excessive emphasis on profit, expanding production for national interests, nurturing the publicness of organisations grouped by industry and trade, and

---

347 *Keizai dantai rengokai zenshi*, pp. 296 ff.

348 Nakamura and Hara 1973, pp. 94 ff., Nagashima 1986, chapter 6., Miyajima 1993, pp.323 ff., Miyajima 2004, pp. 330 ff., Matsuura 2002, pp. 204 ff.

349 *Keizai dantai rengokai zenshi* (1962), chapter 3, pp. 524 ff.

increasing the supervisory capacity of the leaders of these associations – show strong parallels with Nazi economic thought.[350]

(ii) Hoashi Kei and his understanding of Nazi Germany

The Conference's plan of action had a complex influence on trends within the business community. Hoashi Kei (1905-1989), chief secretary of the Conference and later of its successor, the Important Industries Control Association Council (Jūyō sangyō tōsei dantai kyōgikai), drafted the discussion proposal and explained the views expressed there in a work published in 1941.[351] Economic conditions unique to Japan merit careful consideration, he asserts, and Japan must not rashly introduce the Nazi system. Nevertheless, he takes an interest in the mechanism of Nazi economic control and finds "there is a lot Japan can learn from its control structure". As a means to implement economic control, he favours the European and American model based on corporate responsibility and organisation that gives play to the private sector, and rates Nazi Germany highly for using this model better than anybody for the wartime mobilisation of national industry. He draws attention to the fact that Nazi Germany calls its control system "economic guidance (*Wirtschaftslenkung*)", differentiating it from the "planned economy". He explains that the Nazi "economic guidance" means promoting such strengths of the liberal economy as the creativity of an individual and the resourcefulness and inventiveness of an entrepreneur, and keeping the bureaucracy from intervening in business activities and limiting the government's role to guiding the national economy from a macro point of view in the direction of rational management. The Nazi party avoids using the term "planned economy" not simply because the term has "red" connotations, but because the Social Democratic Party, the political enemy of the Nazi party, traditionally favoured it, and also because it has the sound of being something

350 The research division of the Japan Industrial Club (Nihon kōgyō kurabu)(1940) analysed the state of the capitalist economy under the Nazi regime and published its results in December 1940. It summarised the leader principle in the Nazi economy as follows: "Concept of the Volk community (abolition of liberalism, individualism); primacy of the public interest (the elimination of the arbitrary pursuit of profit); the establishment of a controlled economy immune to recession (the abolition of free competition); all citizens granted the right to work (unemployment is not recognized as inevitable); dethroning financial capital; elevating production and labour; denouncing economic supremacy"(p.7).

351 Hoashi 1941, pp. 5 ff., pp. 11 and 17, pp. 29 ff., pp. 38 ff. For Hoashi, see Okazaki et al. 1996, chapter 1, Yanagisawa 2002, 2012a, 2013.

produced by civil servants rather than businessmen. As a result, the Nazi party came to use the more attractive and suggestive "economic guidance".

Hoashi links the government's "Outline for the Establishment of a New Economic Order" with Nazi "economic guidance", saying that it determined "the direction that Japan's industrial control should take in the future", and was "epoch-making" in that it stated clearly an intention to respect the creativity of the private sector and seek its cooperation in putting a control system into practice.

Hoashi regards Nazi economic thought as promoting a controlled economy with an emphasis on individual creativity. His interpretation corresponds to the view of the "Discussion Proposal Regarding the Outline of a Private Sector New Economic Order", which acknowledges the primacy of the public interest and demands maximum autonomy in corporate activity independent of both state and bureaucratic control. One of the key principles of Nazi Germany's economic thought is, as we have seen, the initiative, creativity and responsibility of each individual and, by focusing on this aspect, Hoashi attempts to connect these ideas with the introduction of state control in Japan. His understanding best represents the private sector's approach, receptive as it was to Nazi ideology.

The leader principle can be seen in the same light. A business association within the controlled economy mediates and connects individual initiative and public needs, while the state needs a mechanism that recognises and transmits its demands to industry. The leader principle in the economic association is indispensable to this mechanism. Hoashi sees its significance, not as a tool to exercise state control, but as a means "to rectify the evils of state control". He regards this approach as an appropriate way to introduce Nazi ideas to Japan, distinct from the act of mere "copying."

"Introducing the leader principle is not aping Nazism. Rather, it is an attempt to modify the good points of the liberal economy and incorporate them into the controlled economy so as to redress the weaknesses there. In other words, it is to respect the creativity and initiative of each individual, granting him the necessary and appropriate authority and clarifying where the ensuing responsibility lies. The leader principle enlists those factors so as to save the controlled economy from its natural tendency to head towards the pitfall of bureaucratisation."[352]

The character and abilities of the industrialist have an important meaning when he assumes a position of leadership that requires respecting the creative power and responsibility of the individual (enterprise or management) while

352 Hoashi 1941, pp. 29 ff. and pp. 50 ff.

controlling the strategic distribution of materials and labour according to national interests. Compared to Germany, a country more advanced than Japan, Hoashi remarks that "Japan does not have a Führer who embodies technical strengths, organizational skills and moral integrity", and so it is imperative to create brain trusts to support the leaders of the control associations and to train leaders within each industry.

Hoashi's understanding of Nazi Germany and the acceptance by economic circles of Nazi-type policy were largely influenced by a lecture given to the Japan Economic Federation by the industrialist and economist Emil Helfferich (1878-1972), head of the German Economic Delegation that was in Japan between March and April, 1940 and regarded as one of the leading economists in respect to Germany's controlled economy.[353] Hoashi's understanding and the acceptance of Nazism gave direction to the conception of the "New Order" held by the Conference of Control Associations of Important Industries and the Japan Economic Federation. If so, Emil Helfferich's lecture played a significant role in that it turned Japanese economic circles in a Nazi direction. We will discuss this lecture in detail below.

As we have seen, Hoashi repeatedly stresses that, when introducing Nazi policy ideas, Japan should not merely copy them but take into account the distinctive nature of Japanese conditions, different from those of Germany. By this, he means the backwardness of Japanese heavy and chemical industries. German heavy and chemical industries are at an advanced stage in areas like cartelisation and technical standards, the German economy has already advanced to the heavy industry stage, and small and medium enterprises and agriculture have been incorporated into this overall structure. Japan, however, is lagging far behind and is currently in a transitional stage, moving towards the heavy industry stage, and there are many problems it has to address regarding the merging and restructuring of small and medium industries as well as agricultural issues. He states that "the Japanese spirit of loyalty and devotion to country is incomparable" but Japan trails behind in science and organisational skills.[354]

The question of Japan's backwardness in the heavy and chemical industries was widely discussed among many scholars and officials. The reform bureaucrat Minobe Yōji also draws attention, in an essay entitled "Japanese-style transformation of industrial policies" (Kōgyō seisaku no Nihonteki tenkan), to the underdeveloped state of Japan's heavy and chemical industries and the high proportion of light industry. Japan's backwardness makes it imperative, he says,

---

353 Hoashi 1941, p. 33 and p. 11.
354 Hoashi 1941, pp. 5 ff.

to implement state control policies. In addressing the same issue, Hoashi's view focuses on the need for initiative and leadership in the business community. He envisions a structure in which the business community "cooperates" in implementing state control while maintaining its autonomy. For Japan to adopt Nazi Germany's economic policies and ideas and to make them work, Japanese leaders had to understand the similarities and differences between Germany and Japan, particularly those concerning economic development.

The "Discussion Paper" regarding the New Economic Order and the acceptance of Nazi ideas

(i) The Japan Economic Federation and the German Economic Delegation

The business community made clear their intention to actively cooperate in the effort to establish a wartime controlled economy while maintaining "autonomous control" in the form of cartels. Realising the need to study actual Nazi policies and ideas closely, business leaders decided to invite a German with a firsthand knowledge of the realities of the controlled economy in Germany to give a lecture.

In March 1940, soon after it began discussing economic control, the Japan Economic Federation invited Emil Helfferich to speak. Helfferich was, as we have seen, in Japan at the time with the German Economic Delegation. Originally from Hamburg, he had been a leading merchant in Indonesia at the beginning of the twentieth century, and he remained there until 1928. His elder brother, Karl Helfferich, was a financial expert who was successively director of the Deutsche Bank AG and undersecretary in the Ministry of Finance, and, as a deputy of the German National People's Party, was opposed to Walther Rathenau. Emil Helfferich was a founding member of Keppler-Kreis (Keppler Circle), a group of people, mainly from industry, formed at the suggestion of Hitler in 1932.[355]

355 The Keppler-Kreis was a group of businessmen brought together in 1932 at Hitler's request by Wilhelm Keppler, appointed his economics adviser the previous year. Founding members included Hjalmar Schacht, President of the Reichsbank; Albert Vögler (1877-1945), a director of Vereinigte Stahlwerke; and Kurt vin Schröder (1889-1966) of the Bankhaus J. H. Stein. It was "an orgaizational device that enabled the Nazis to bring leading businessmen close to the party leadership and thereby create the impression that the party had changed its economic policy". (Schweizer 1964, p. 101). This group, also known as Circle of Friends of the Economy (*Freundkreis der Wirtschaft*), was later taken over by Heinrich Himmler and called the Circle of Friends of Heinrich Himmler (*Freundkreis Himmler*). It then made large

He was sent to Japan by the German government to improve relations between Japan and Germany, which had cooled somewhat after the signing of the 1939 Nazi-Soviet Non-aggression Pact (*Deutsch-Russischer Nichtangriffspak*).[356] He met many Japanese leaders, including Gō Seinosuke, president of the Japan Economic Federation.

Helfferich's talk was entitled "Lenkung und Leistung der deutschen Wirtschaft" (translated into Japanese as "Guiding the German economy and promoting effectiveness in Germany").[357] He asserts that the new economic system in Nazi Germany is a "guided economy" (*Wirtschaftslenkung*), distinct from a planned economy, which is bureaucratic and impersonal. The new German economic system respects individuality and acknowledges ownership, but denounces the abusive use and disposal of property as well as the rapacious pursuit of profit, as clearly stated in the slogan of "common good before private good". According to the Japanese translation, he says: "While favouring the principle of community (*Gemeinschaft*) over individualism, National Socialism values highly the achievement of the individual, in other words his "abilities" such as initiative, responsibility and intention. It may sound contradictory, but it actually is not. An important task we had in establishing the new German economic structure was to find ways to incorporate two objectives harmoniously: implementing economic guidance and increasing productivity. We believe that as long as it does not get entrenched in bureaucracy, economic leadership will not negate freedom, therefore this new economic order we are constructing in Germany is none other than the principle of even higher freedom."

Having explained in detail how to organise industry in general, he goes on to elaborate on the dual nature of the task faced by business associations in Nazi Germany, stemming from their double identity as a public corporation and a private group. This allows them to be "autonomous bodies of industrial economy" and "a mechanism for the implementation of state policies", with the function

---

contributions to the SS. Originally, however, the Keppler-Kreis was an advisory body favouring conservative economic policies. See Turner 1985.

356 For Helfferich, see E. Helfferich, *Ein Leben*, 1948, vols. 1-3 [1964/1965, vols. 4 and 5 (for his sojourn in Japan, see vol. 4, pp. 158-159)]. He was an executive of the Straits & Sunda Syndikat, Deutsch-Amerikanische Petroleum-Gesellschaft (ESSO), and Hamburg-Amerika-Line. For his relationship with Gō Seinosuke, see Gō-danshaku kinenkai 1943 [1988], pp. 702 and 726. See also Yanagisawa 2008a, 2013, Kudo et aleds. 2008, 2009.

357 E. Helfferich 1940 [1965, vol. 5]. The Japanese translation of the lecture does not always correspond with ther German terxt as it appears here. The original text must have been revised. See also *Keizai jōhō*, June 1940, pp. 144 ff.

of bridging "the state and the economy". Each association has the duty to follow state laws and orders concerning the economy, but at the same time possesses the authority to act on its own initiative within the boundary of economic autonomy and to instruct and give orders to its members. Armed with these dual characteristics, the association can guard its independence against bureaucratic intervention and retain the freedom to engage in economic activities as long as it takes responsibility for its actions. The associations are an important component of the German economic structure, serving both the state and the business community, providing economic guidance and improving productivity.

According to an article in *Tōsei keizai* (The controlled economy), Helfferich's lecture "appears to have given guidance to the audience and left a lasting impression" on members of the Japan Economic Federation who had hitherto criticized the bureaucratic tendencies of the controlled economy.[358] Proof of the impact the lecture had on the business community can be gleaned from the fact that Hoashi based his views on the arguments in Helfferich's lecture in formulating his ideas about the controlled economy with an emphasis on the creativity and responsibility of the entrepreneur.

(ii) Exchanges with the German Labour Front

In November 1940, at a time when the issue of the New Economic Order was being hotly debated, the Japan Economic Federation invited two German officials to explain what was happening in Germany. The Germans, Claus (Nikolaus) Selzner (1899-1944), head (Organisationleiter) of the organising department of the NSDAP and the German Labour Front (DAF), and Otto Gohdes (1896-1945), national training leader in NSDAP and DAF, were invited as proxies for Robert Ley (1890-1945) of the German Labour Front to attend the Great Asia Recreation Rally (*Kōa Kōsei Taikai*), whose chairman was Godō Takuo. Among the guests were the Eugen Ott, German Ambassador to Japan, Kaneko Yōji, the Minister of Health, Ogawa Gōtarō (1886-1945), the Minister of Railways, Hoshino Naoki (1892-1978), president of the Cabinet Planning Board, and Nagai Arekisan, Commercial Attaché at the Japanese Embassy in Germany. Those attending from the Japan Economic Federation included its chairman, Gō Seinosuke (1865-1942), and its director, Godō Takuo. Selzner and Gohdes spoke about the current situation in Germany, a subject viewed as "containing many important suggestions relevant to Japan's current situation", and their lecture and subsequent question and answer session were published as a leaflet entitled

358 *Tōsei keizai*, September 1940, p. 140.

"The controlled economy in Germany" and distributed among the Federation members.

Gō Seinosuke acknowledged the necessity of economic control and asked the following question.[359] It is a little long, but as it is a good reflection of how the business community in Japan perceived Nazi Germany, I will quote it here in full.[360]

"When a country is waging war, as Japan is right now, its production is greatly affected and there are shortages of goods. Under those dire circumstances, the country must use what it has in the most effective way, and so there arises the need for a controlled economy. There are two types of controlled economy. One is what I will call the *Soviet model* of total control by the government, and the other is wat I will call the *Nazi model* of autonomous management through individual *initiative* and *creativity* under state supervision. It doesn't matter if we call this Nazism or fascism. As I understand it, firstly the Nazi model acknowledges *private property*, secondly respects *individual initiative*, and lastly *opposes Soviet ideology*. You have told us how the Nazi party has made a series of plans since taking power in 1933. I have heard that at one point socialism came on the scene and caused a great deal of headache for the government. I am most interested to know how socialist thought entered Germany and how the state countered it." (my italics)

Claus Selzner: "To be honest, your question has greatly surprised me. To my knowledge, Germany has not so far faced any type of Socialist movements, especially Soviet-style ones calling for the confiscation of private property.... Those of you who are used to a liberal economy might have felt there was a tinge of socialism in some of our policies such as control on profits and state taxes, but we have never adopted socialist policies. For instance, the income taxation system dictates that earnings over 100,000 marks are taxed at the rate of 50% and up; the cap on profits demands that dividends above 8% of the invested capital be used to purchase public bonds, and that part of the profits be reinvested into public bonds and redirected to the improvement of plant equipment and facilities. These government policies limit the freedom to dispose profit for the common good. They are not part of the socialist system. Profits are partly reinvested but will always remain in the hands of the corporations as materials or property."

359 *Keizai renmei*, February 1940. The Japan Economic Federation and seven other business groups held a reception at the end of October 1940 to welcome the two German officials and celebrate the signing of the Tripartite Pact of September 27. See *Keizai renmei*, January 1941, pp. 148 ff.

360 *Keizai renmei*, February 1940, pp. 10ff. For Gō Seinosuke's thought and actions, see Gō-danshaku kinenkai 1943, Matsuura 1995, 2002.

(iii) *Nazism and the "Opinion Paper" regarding the New Economic Order*

As we have seen, the business community drafted the "Discussion Proposal Regarding the Outline of a Private Sector New Economic Order" in the summer of 1940, and in December, when the dispute over the New Economic Order came to a climax, seven business groups drafted and presented to the government their famous Opinion Paper. Subsequently in January 1941, shortly after the "Outline for the Establishment of a New Economic Order" was passed by the Cabinet, the seven groups drafted an "Opinion Paper Regarding the Implementation of the New Economic Order" and presented it to the government.

Gō Seinosuke took the lead in this. The circumstances are recounted in his biography.[361]

"The Baron was concerned that even Cabinet members had failed to reach full agreement on the New Economic Order. He had watched closely the development of the discussions on the New Economic Order and their ramifications. He invited executive members of the Japan Economic Federation and heard their report on the matter. To make correct judgements, he also invited Hoashi, director of the Conference of Control Associations of Important Industries to his country house in Hakone, and held exhaustive discussions about the Conference's version of the New Economic Order for three hours both in the morning and afternoon for two days. Once a plan was agreed upon, the Baron speedily descended from the hills of Hakone. On December 4 he gathered the leaders of the business associations and had them present their opinions about the New Economic Order. The Baron then expressed his personal opinions. He suggested:

1. The New Economic Order should be in harmony with *virtues unique to Japan*, and should not stray from the *national polity* or destroy the *family system*.
2. The New Economic Order should strive to overcome difficulties posed by the current situation and to expand production. It should not deviate from the correct course and harm the effort to increase production.
3. The New Economic Order should stipulate that the *private sector* should take the *initiative, work hard* and assume *responsibility* for *managing business activities*, and that government offices should as a rule not touch matters directly, but just give *overall directions and supervision*. (my italics)

The Opinion Paper that had been drafted by the seven economic groups on December 5, and subsequently presented to the Prime Minister, declared that the business groups would accept a certain curtailment of "freedom" to correct "the

361 Gō-dashaku kinenkai 1943, p. 763 and pp. 766 ff.

evils of the liberal economy" with the aim of "constructing a national defence system" and "increasing production", but these measures must never upset "the foundation of the economic structure". It also demanded that the state sanction profits in so far as they were in accordance with the national interest, quoting the example of Nazi Germany: "*As in Germany*, we demand that the state advocate purifying the profit principle rather than castigating it, and that the state not denounce but encourage business activities so long as they do not harm national objectives and make fair profits, however large they may be". (my italics)

The "Opinion Paper Regarding the Implementation of the New Economic Order" drafted in January 1941 asserted that, in the face of total war, the private sector needed "to restructure itself voluntarily" under "state supervision" and this called for a "concerted effort" between "both public and private sectors". Its stated objectives were respect for the "way of economics" unique to Japan, "autonomy of the private sector" and "expansion of production". It also stated that business leaders must help expand production, since it is by serving the goal of building a powerful national defence system that they are best able to fulfil "their duties and functions". Further, the expansion of production requires "profit" and thus "profit" becomes "an integral part of the national production structure". Though the private sector accepts the principle of "fair profit", the Opinion Paper cautions, the state must be very flexible about setting restrictions on profits, for there are a range of factors that need to be taken into consideration, such as the need to procure funds to expand production, the risks inherent in running industries during a time of war, the hazards associated with developing new enterprises, and the effort to maintain, and increase, the competitive edge in anticipation of future, post-war foreign competition. Here again the Nazi model is held as an example, cited as "the way Nazi Germany handles corporate profit".[362] Plainly Nazi Germany served as a valuable model for the business community.

As the chairman of the Japan Economic Federation, Gō Seinosuke, had commented, the business community differentiated the Nazi-style controlled economy from the Soviet-model socialistic controlled economy. Japanese business leaders evaluated the Nazi-style controlled economy positively because of its recognition that profits should be made, its emphasis on individual initiative and its anti-socialist stand. As the Opinion Paper pointed out, during the transition to a wartime economic system, business leaders acknowledged the urgency of the national need for expanded production and the importance of cooperation with the government, which they associated with the need for corporations to

362 *Keizai renmei* 1941, vol. 11, no. 2, pp. 1 f.

maintain, and develop, their profit-generating activities. Thus they declared that they would accept the primacy of the public interest and agree to cooperate with the state on condition that initiative, responsibility and autonomy should rest with the enterprise. From then on, the main points of contention concerning the implementation of the New Order were to shift to such details as a demand for guidelines about "fair profit" to be set "with flexibility" and for autonomy to be granted to the economic control associations.

As we have seen above, Minobe expressed the reaction of the Cabinet Planning Board and reform bureaucrats to the Opinion Paper submitted by business leaders in December 1940 in his "A personal view of the New Economic Order". While acknowledging the importance of the profit principle and autonomous corporate management, he focused on the Nazi "model" that was the basis of the Opinion Paper's criticism of the Cabinet Planning Board's proposal, and pointed out that in fact this very model promoted the primacy of the public good. The "conflict" between the reform bureaucrats and the business community was not a serious disagreement on the fundamentals. Rather, it rested on a specific point – bureaucratic control versus corporate autonomy. Once they had agreed on the principal points, both sides were ready to work towards a compromise.

In their points of view and opinions about the New Economic Order, both the reform bureaucrats and the business community had come to accept Nazi ideas in various ways, based on their various interpretations of German economic policies and ideology. Their "dispute" was nothing more than that they had chosen to focus on different aspects of the Nazi model. Nazi economic policies and thought encompassed a broad variety of contradictory aspects and directions, and the conflicts and adjustments between them reflected the reality of the Nazi economic system. Seen in this light, the dispute between the reform bureaucrats and the business community in Japan and the subsequent compromise they reached mirrored what had happened between the Nazi party and the private sector in Germany. In this sense we can say that Japan had characteristics in common with Nazism as a fascist system.

Nazi principles and the ideology of Japanism and the Emperor System

Awareness of Japan's lack of the Nazi-style leadership

Expanding production and mobilising economic resources in order to establish a wartime economic system necessitate cooperation between the public and private sectors based on the principles of the primacy of the public good and the autonomy of corporate management. Such cooperation was to be realised under the New Economic Order through the formation of control associations among enterprises. The potentially conflicting principles of the primacy of the public good and the autonomy of corporate management would be mediated and consolidated by means of the leader principle (*Führerprinzip*) operating within these control associations. This channel of exchange would work, in other words, in two ways, top-down and bottom-up and its performance would depend on two points, how well those in a position of leadership were able to direct affairs as they balanced the interests of the business community with those of the public interest, and how well structured were the directive bodies that had the authority to order subordinate organisations to carry out state (public) objectives.

In Nazi Germany, the leader principle centred principally on the Nazi party and its memebrs under a dictatorial power structure headed by the Führer, Hitler. Japan, however, was not a dictatorship under one party and one leader, and not only was its leadership was weak but it lacked individuals with leadership potential. Minobe and the other reform bureaucrats who took part in the invited to the round-table discussion about the New Economic Order for the journal *Jitsugyō no Nihon* all agreed on this point. Kashiwabara Heitarō said: "It is not the title of leader that makes a man a leader. A true leader must be equipped with a firm ideological grounding, sound judgement and superb competence to lead. In this transitional period, Japan lacks such leaders in both the public and private sectors." Minobe agreed, pointing out that the difference between the two countries was in the fact that "Germany had most successfully established the *führer* system."

Around the same time, another round-table discussion was held between Minobe Yōji, Obata Tadayoshi (1893-1977), Kojima Seiichi and Kinbara Kennosuke, sponsored by the monthly journal *Kaizō* and published as an article entitled "What is the New Economic Order?" in its current affairs edition, *Jikyoku*14. The article opens with a discussion on the leadership issue.

Kojima Seiichi: "In Germany the Nazi party has powers that have enabled leaders to play their role fully, but it is not the same in Japan."

Minobe Yōji: "As you say, the Nazi party is the only power in Germany and so has been able to push forward it plans, but Japan has no equivalent. But in place of this, the Japanese have a strong sense of devotion to country, second to no other people. The Imperial Rule Assistance Association (Taisei yokusankai) has been founded to encourage the Japanese to perform their duties and to promote the spirit of one-hundred-million hearts beating as one. With the power of the Association behind it, the government should be able to give backing to leaders."[363] Thus Minobe focused on the sense of "devotion to the Japanese Empire" and the principle of "performing duties" and "the one-hundred-million hearts beating as one" to compensate for the lack of a powerful party like the Nazi party and its power structure. He had high hopes that the Imperial Rule Assistance Association would foster those ideas among the Japanese.

At that time, Obata Tadayoshi was assistant director at the Cabinet Planning Board and director of the planning department of the Imperial Rule Assistance Association; he was later appointed to the Industrial Patriotic Association ([Dainippon] Sangyō Hōkoku Kai) as managing director. When asked what he thought about the state's request to the business community for cooperation, Obata replied: "If we cannot hope for strong political leadership such as the Nazi party and fascism, we have no choice but to appeal to the national spirit." Kojima Seiichi agreed with Obata, saying: "It is very important to imbue business leaders with a sense of the national spirit. In Germany it has taken the Nazi party some years one way and another to install its ideas. Japan has a long way to go."

The issue of the leader principle revolved around control associations as the mechanism to implement state control in accordance with the principle of autonomous corporate management, and business leaders who understood it and could put it into practice. Success hinged on the dual requirement of a structure to channel government directives and competent business leaders in the private sector to put those directives into practice. The reform bureaucrats acknowledged that it was here that Japan lagged behind Nazi Germany, and they hoped that the traditional Japanese spirit would substitute for the Nazi leadership structure or complement its deficiencies. The directives to "perform duties" and "promote the slogan of the one-hundred-million hearts beating as one" were given to businessmen by the state through the control associations, and "the spirit of performing duties" was linked to the notion of "Empire" and so with the emperor system (the national polity).

Kashiwabara Heitarō, in the discussion reported in *Jitsugyō no Nihon*, had also pointed out the absence of the leader principle in Japan. Minobe Yōji responded by recalling the celebrations marking the 2,600th year after the (mythological) accession of the emperor Jinmu: "We all dined and drank in the presence of the Emperor and Empress, though most of us were seated far from them. I saw business leaders advanced in years and young people also with tears in their eyes. Prince Takamatsu then delivered a congratulatory address to the Emperor and Empress, on behalf of their subjects. We should all remember how we felt then

363 *Kaizō (jikyoku-ban* 14) 1941, p. 133.

for when we make a new start. I felt it was a turning point and I imagine you felt the same. If we all keep that feeling in mind when we contemplate Japan's future, I believe there will be nothing to worry about. I hope those of us present at the ceremony will make the most of our special experience."[364]

A nephew of Minobe Tatsukichi who challenged the Emperor Organ Theory and was persecuted for it,[365] Minobe Yōji speaks here about the very functions of the emperor system, albeit in deliberately vague terms and with great circumspection. The discussion thus concluded with what was virtually a political proposal, that the only way to make up for weaknesses in leadership in Japan was to make the best use of the sense of devotion and awe that Japanese subjects and businessmen felt regarding the emperor system and the national polity.

Utilising the traditional spirit and the ideology of the national polity

The leader principle thus proved to be a mediating device to bring together state control and autonomous management by businessmen. In terms of the primacy of the public good, its application hinged on an awareness of the mechanism employed to mediate between public and private interests, and on the level of understanding among those who received the state's directives. Minobe's suggestion above also implies supplementing such concepts about the primacy of the public good with the ideology of the emperor system. On another occasion, Minobe spoke of public and private interests being united under a "strong national defence system"; he regarded this unity as being none other than the traditional Japanese way. "*Japan has at its head an Emperor who is descended from the unbroken line. Loyalty and justice unite sovereign and subjects, and love and compassion the father and son. Our Empire, formed only of the pure Yamato race, is an object of envy for Germany; it has been Hitler's ideal.*"[366] (my italics)

Minobe called this traditional concept of emperor and empire the "Imperial Way" (*kōdōshugi*) and intentionally linked it to the "unity of public and private interests" (that is, the primacy of the public good). He concluded that the Imperial Way and slogans based on it, such as "assisting the imperial rule" (*taisei*

---

364 *Jutsugyo no nihon* (January 1941), p. 67.

365 Minobe Tatsukichi (1837-1948) was a professor of constitutional law at the Tokyo Imperial University. The Emperor Organ Theory (*tennō kikansetsu*) refers to the view that the emperor is an organ of the state (though the highest) and his prerogatives are delegated. It was a view widely accepted until the 1930s, when ultranationalists campaigned against it and Minobe himself. Minobe was forced to resign in 1935 and a number of his works were banned.

366 Minobe 1942, pp. 13 ff.

yokusan), "acting as a loyal subject" (*shindō jissen*) and "serving the state through one's calling" (*shokubun hōko*), constituted a "New Economic Way" that was the Japanese equivalent of Alfred Marshall's economic chivalry. In this, the Nazi leader principle and the primacy of the public good were linked with Japanese traditionalist ideas and the ideology of the emperor system in a complementary relationship.

How did the business community react to this? As we have seen, their Opinion Paper of January 1941 concerning the implementation of the New Economic Order stated that it should respect the "virtues of the Japanese way of economics that had had its unique trajectory of development". What they called the traditionalist Japanese "way of economics" was in fact their main argument against the plan drafted by Ryū Shintarō and others. Their blueprint for a new economic order did not concern economic reforms so much as it aimed at maintaining and fostering the "admirable customs and good practices" (*ryoshū bifū*) associated with traditional relationships. The ideology of "serving the state through one's calling" – that the people of Japan must willingly devote themselves to serve the country by performing their duties – had its roots in the tradition of "admirable customs and good practices" and was central to the Japanese "way of economics" that not only the reform bureaucrats but also the business community strongly advocated.

The ideal of "serving the state through one's calling" corresponds to the slogan "all industries as one serving the state" (*zensangyō ittai hōkoku*) advocated by the Greater Japan Industrial Patriotic Association (Dai Nippon Sangyō Hōkoku Kai; Sampō),[367] and also "enterprise as a family" (*jigyō ikka*) and "patriotism through labour" (*kinrō hōkoku*). The businessman serves the state, and his workers give their labour to the empire. "Serving the state through one's calling" requires that businessmen serve the Empire and their workers do their patriotic duty because all belong to the family of the enterprise. The slogan of "enterprise as a family" was later used to give management, as leaders of the enterprise, more power to restructure the workforce and increase its control. The Japanese "way of economics" was based on traditionalist familism, and subsequently linked to the state ideology of the emperor system, also founded on familism. This relates closely to the importance that Gō Seinosuke placed on maintaining Japanese virtues, the national polity and the institution of the family.

Godō Takuo met the Prime Minister when the Opinion Paper was submitted as a representative of the business community. In a lecture given later at the

367 Created in 1940 out of the Industrial Patriotic League set up to replace labour unions and establish patriotic associations in factories.

educational affairs section of the Ministry of Education, he emphasized the importance of what had been learned from Germany, which shared much in common with Japan, but also rated highly the uniqueness of Japanese totalitarianism and its significance. A controlled economy can only be implemented under a totalitarian regime, as the recent German experience attests. How about Japan? Some people here seem to think that totalitarianism is a new idea and the just apes fascism or Nazism, but they are wrong. Godō then went on to relate what Robert Ley, head of the German Labour Front (referred to as Dr. Ley in the original), had said to him when they had met,

"You have come to Germany to study about the German Labour Front, but why does Japan have to learn from our organisation? At a time of national emergency, the Japanese people will immediately form a united front whatever their class or occupation. Japan is a rare familial state centred on its imperial family. Germany is made up of one race, but because we have had from the past diverse ideologies and religions, we have had to set up an extensive range of institutions and spend a considerable sum to unite our people. We are very envious of Japan. I am planning to bring many members of my organisation to attend the 1940 Tokyo Olympics, but I am not coming simply to watch the games. I want to use the opportunity to study the Japanese national spirit."

Godō went on to say that the German leader had pointed out that what we call totalitarianism actually follows the example of the Japanese spirit. "For 2,600 years Japan has possessed a spirit of national foundation, and our ancestors repeatedly manifested this spirit at times of national crisis. What is needed today is not only individual initiative, but the unity and organisation of those individuals."[368]

He argued that a totalitarianism regime like fascism was indispensable for a controlled economy, and in fact the Japanese founding spirit based on familism had already created such a totalitarianism. German totalitarianism – Nazism – was modelled after it. His phraseology was exactly the same as that of Minobe Yōji, who stressed imperial ideology and the Japanese traditional way that was the unity of public and private, and declared that the Japanese empire was an object of envy for Germany and Hitler's ideal. It should be noted that both business leaders and the reform bureaucrats reiterated the myth that Nazi Germany had modelled itself on the traditional Japanese spirit.

---

368 After suffering a setback in plan to restructure economic organisations centring on the Chamber of Commerce and Industry, Godō drafted another plan based on Nazi-style economic organisations. See *Keizai jōhō (seikei-hen)*, March 1940. Regarding the Japanese controlled economy, Godō said: "Needless to say, the Japanese system is for the most part an imitation of the German model."

While their arguments started from totalitarianism, the point of similarity between Japan and Nazi Germany, they then turned to the differences in detail, focusing on the uniqueness of the Japanese model and defining it as the traditionalist emperor system, the crucial element that supported and reinforced Japanese-style totalitarianism. It did not matter for the Japanese leaders whether the claim that Nazi Germany held Japan as its model was true or false. What mattered was to propagate such a myth among the general public to stress the importance of the emperor system, stir up patriotism and mobilize the nation towards the war effort. The fallacy of Nazi Germany emulating Japan was deliberately drummed up to strengthen the grip of totalitarianism on a nation that lacked a Nazi-style one-party dictatorship.[369] The reform bureaucrats and the business community both recognized the significance of traditionalism and the emperor system, and their shared recognition served to unify them and so support a system of cooperation between the public and private sectors.

369 This myth was called "the Nazi party's move towards a Japanese-style national polity". See Nakagawa, 1944, chapter 8. For the interest that Goebbels and Hitler showed in Japan's State Shintō, see Miyata 1991 pp. 268ff. and Takeyama 1982, pp. 358 ff.

Chapter Six: The New Labour System and Nazism

The thinking behind the New Economic Order promulgated under the Second Konoe Cabinet revolved around restructuring the economic framework through a capitalistic business structure with businesses organised into associations. It was at the same time necessary to mobilize and regulate the workforce to underpin economic strength from the ground up, to set up a wartime economy able to respond to the war in China and to establish a system to prepare for total war. The "Outline for Establishing a New Order for Labour" (*Kinrō shintaisei kakuritsu yōkō*), determined in November 1940, one month before the Cabinet decision about the "Outline for the Establishment of a New Economic Order", laid out the basic direction for both the New Economic Order and the labour system that was so closely tied to it. This new system was based on the abolition of labour unions and the organization of workers by the state, on the principle that labour was a matter of state concern and of a corporative relationship between labour and management.[370] Here too we find that Nazi points of view had an important influence.

The Nazi Organization of Labour

In May 1933, soon after they came to power in Germany, the Nazis forcibly dissolved the trade unions and in their place set up the German Labour Front (Deutsche Arbeitsfront, DAF). The Law for the Organization of National Labour (Gesetz zur Ordnung der nationalen Arbeit) was enacted on January 20, 1934, thus laying down the ideology of the Nazi labour system. This ideology is apparent in its first two articles:

Article 1. In a business undertaking, the employer, as leader (*Führer*), and the employees, as his followers (*Gefolgschaft*; lit. "retinue"), shall work together to further the purposes of the undertaking, and for the common good of the people and the state.

Article 2. The leader is to take care of the welfare of the followers, and the followers are to keep faith with him in the spirit of solidarity in a joint enterprise.

---

370 See Okazaki et al eds. 1999, p. 115.

This was aimed at eliminating stances that arose from class conflict and placing relations between employers and employees on a communal basis. It clearly represented the introduction of the leader principle into industrial management. Labour conditions involving management, such as wages and so on, were no longer to be negotiated collectively but decided by a Trustee of Labour (Treuhänder der Arbeit), a public officer who acted as a supervisor of management.[371]

The Nazi Party Manifesto had demanded the elimination of the adversarial relationship between labour and capital based on class differences as well as the rejection of Marxism. The forcible dissolution of trade unions after the Nazi Party came to power and the organization of the DAF corresponded to the reorganization of existing employers' associations and various kinds of economic organizations, and to the organization of the economy by product and region under the Law for the Organic Constitution of the German Economy of February 1934. The Leipzig Agreement of March 1935 between the DAF (Robert Ley), the Ministry of Economics (Hjalmar Schacht) and the Ministry of Labour (Franz Seldte) sought to bring about harmony between the DAF and employers' organizations, and national and regional committees, called Chambers of the Economy (Wirtschaftskammer) and Chambers of Labour (Arbeitskammer), were set up.

By 1938, the DAF, under its head Robert Ley, had around 23 million members, and, on the financial basis of the assets of the old trade unions and compulsory membership dues, funded a wide variety of projects, including housing and housing settlements, insurance, publishing, ship-building, and the production of automobiles (Volkswagen). The Front also included an educational arm to provide training schemes and vocational training courses, and "Strength through Joy" (Kraft durch Freude) to provide benefits and amenities to German workers and their families.[372]

Strength through Joy was important in that it planned and subsidized visits to the theatre, concerts and exhibitions, sports and hiking, and foreign holidays for workers. Until then such cultural activities and pastimes had been exclusively the preserve of the middle and upper classes; now the working class too could gain access to facilities and opportunities previously denied them. Of course such actions had the purpose of maintaining and broadening support for the Nazi regime among workers and lower class urban dwellers. Strength

---

371 The Law for the Organization of National Labour (Gesetz zur Ordnung der nationalen Arbeit) has been widely studied. My main reference here is Mansfeld 1941. It had a print run of between 73,000 and 75,000 copies.

372 Mason 1993, pp. 3, 168-69.

through Joy also demanded, and supported, such things as the improvement by firms of the workplace and associated buildings, the provision of employees' canteens and sports facilities, and the improvement of hygeine and lighting. These activities, which were under the direction of the Schönheit der Arbeit (Beauty of Work), employed the results of modern management and labour studies, and with the above-mentioned leisure programme for workers had the purpose of raising labour productivity and reconditioning workers mentally and physically.[373]

The political scientist Maruyama Masao (1914-1996), while pointing out the similarities between Japanese fascism and Nazism, also drew attention to the "consideration of the working class" in Nazi Germany, commenting: "The divergence in this respect is clearly revealed in the difference between Japan's Industrial Patriotic Movement and Nazi Germany's Kraft durch Freude movement".[374]

Of course, there was a great difference between the labour systems of the two countries. However, it cannot be denied that Japanese ideas about the Industrial Patriotic Movement[375] and the labour system were influenced by Nazi Germany. Morito Tatsuo (1888-1984), a specialist in labour problems and social policy,[376] pointed out the connections between the Industrial Patriotic Movement and the German Labour Front (DAF): "… of the various systems substituting for a liberal order of labour, it is an undeniable fact that *the managerial communitarianism of the German DAF and the 'unity of labour and capital' (rōshi ittaishugi) of the Industrial Patriotic Movement in Japan are not only based on the same line of thought but that the DAF provided an important stimulus, suggestion and example to the conception and construction of the Industrial Patriotic Movement*". (my italics)

The DAF did indeed have a sigificant influence on the Japanese Movement.

---

373 See Mason 1974, Weiss 1993. See also Mason 1966, 1968, 1993.

374 Maruyama 1964, p. 56, 1995, p. 288. In English, Maruyama 1969.

375 The Industrial Patriotic Movement was launched by the government in April 1938 to restructure industrial relations, in view of the ongoing war in China and the need to stimulate production. Industrial peace and the conservation of manpower were vital towards this end. See Garon 1987, p. 215 ff.

376 An associate professor of economics at the Tokyo Imperial University, Morito was fired from his position in 1920 for having published a study of Russian anarchism, "Study of the social philosophy of Kropotkin" (the so-called Morito incident). Afterwards he became a member of the Ōhara Institute for Social Research, and in the postwar period became Minister of Education and president of Hiroshima University. For the Morito incident, see Mitchell 1976, p. 39, Barshay 1988.

Distinctive Features of the New Labour Order in Japan

In his *Kindai Nihon rōshi kankeishi no kenkyū* (A study of the history of relations between capital and labour in modern Japan), Nishinarita Yutaka gives as a distinctive feature of fascist capital-labour relations "the pseudo-communal composition of relations between capital and labour, through the reactionary 'sublation' (Ger. Aufheben) of the existence of class," and goes on to say: "The Industrial Patriotic Movement, which ideologically combined within itself both the idea of the unity of labour and capital as an 'organic and ethical communalism' (*kyōdōtai*) supported by the view of the familial state made up of all the people under one ruler (*ikkun banmin*), and the idea of industrial patriotism which aimed to support the prosperity of the imperial throne (*kōun*) through industry, rejecting laissez-faire principles and class struggle, is in this sense truly a fascist movement. The works councils (*rōshi kondankai*) that were at the core of the Industrial Patriotic Movement were the mechanism through which concrete expression was given to 'the pseudo-communal composition of relations between capital and labour'".[377]

Kawahara Hiroshi also points out that "during the war, Japanese ideas about capital and labour were divided into two streams. One was the "imperial labour theory", a direct descendent of the ideology of the emperor system. The other was the "totalitarian labour theory", a Japanese modification of suggestions received from German Nazism and Italian fascism. They were both mixed together, sometimes conflicting violently but on the whole functioning as an ideology to tighten labour during wartime".[378]

Neither Nishinarita nor Kawahara, however, went so far as to study precisely how Nazi, and more broadly fascist, ideology and views about labour spread to Japan.[379] Sheldon Garon, Andrew Gordon and Yasuda Hiroshi, on the other hand, have directed their attention to the question of the influence of the Nazi labour system on Japan.[380] They take particular notice of the ideas and activities of Minami Iwao (1900-1986), an expert adviser in the Cabinet Research

377 Nishinarita 1988, p. 425.

378 Kawahara 1978, p. 112. For connections with the Showa Research Association, see Arima 1983, p. 8, etc.

379 The content of Saguchi 1991 is very closely connected with this chapter, but there is no mention there of the relation between the Japanese labour system and Fascism.

380 Garon 1987, especially pp. 213-215, Yasuda 1991, Gordon 1991, pp. 321-322. For the totalitarian conditions of the time, see Miwa 1988 (for Minami Iwao in particular, see p. 182 ff.).

Bureau (*Naikaku chōsakyoku*),[381] regarding the ideology of the "unity of capital and labour" and "industrial patriotism" that developed around the years 1935 and 1936, and in this context refers to the influence of the Nazi viewpoint on Japan. Formative elements in Minami's thinking were a total economic system in regards policies to regulate and organize relations between capital and labour, the banning of labour unions, and the unity of capital and labour. They attach great importance to the fact that Minami's ideas were an amalgamation of Nazi elements and Japanist ideology, and investigate how, in the process leading to the formation of the Industrial Patriotic Movement in 1940, such a Nazi direction was received in Japan and how it was amended to do away with the leader principle, for example. However, their research looked almost solely at the Nazi influence through the figure of Minami (though Gordon also refers to Godō Takuo). We consider here the spread in Japan of the Nazi view of labour in relation to the new economic order and to the thinking behind the new labour system that was inseparable from it. It was this new labour system that sustained the Japanese wartime economy, through such basic ideas as the Industrial Patriotic Association.

The Nazi Law for the Organization of National Labour

Let us look first at the contemporary Japanese understanding of the German system of labour.

The Law for the Organization of National Labour (*Gesetz zur Ordnung der nationalen Arbeit*), enacted in January 1934, was the basic labour law in Nazi Germany, and as we have seen, it brought together various facets of Nazi ideology. Chō Moriyoshi, an expert in Nazi economics, promptly drew attention to the law in a book published the same year, pointing out four distinctive features of Nazi ideas about labour:[382] (1) corporative management erected on a basis of mutual trust between entrepreneurs, employees and labourers; (2) the leader principle and the principle of ability over social status; (3) state supervision of wages; and (4) preservation of social honour.

The 1937 volume on Nazi law edited by the JMG that had a great influence on politicians and bureaucrats placed great emphasis on the new law as a "charter

381 A supraministerial bureau set up by the Okada cabinet in 1935 as an organizational base for an economic general staff. It was headed by Yoshida Shigeru and many of its members were reform bureaucrats and army officers. Berger 1988, p. 103-104, Garon 1987, p. 196, Sims 2001, p. 201.

382 Chō 1934, p. 142ff. See Chapter 3 above.

for a new labour" and described its characteristics as follows. First, relations between entrepreneuts and workers were not founded on conflict, as ideas derived from the class society promoted, but on communal management, based on mutual trust between the two. Entrepreneurs are the leaders, who strive for the welfare of workers, while workers are their retinue, with the responsibility of being loyal to the communal management. Second, as a result of the dissolution of labour unions, collective bargaining was forbidden and decisions were made individually within each unit of management. Third, regarding the administration of units of management, while autonomous operations centred on the leader and the *Vertrauensrat* ("Council of Trust"), the total good of the national community was safeguarded through the strict jurisdiction of the state officials (trustees of labour, *Treuhänder der Arbeit*).

The Nazi Law for the Organization of National Labour also drew the attention of the Kyōchōkai (Harmonization Society), an important group concerned with research into industrial relations,[383] and the Sangyō Hōkoku Renmei (Industrial Patriotic League).[384] In 1936, the Kyōchōkai published *Nachisu rōdōhō* (The Nazi labour law), written by Inaba Hidezō (1907-1996). Inaba, who worked in the Research Section of the Kyōchōkai, was seconded to the Cabinet Planning Board in 1937 and arrested in the Planning Board Incident of 1941;[385] in the postwar period he was the assistant chief secretary of the Economic Stabalization Board and a director of the Sankei Newspaper Company. In his work, he translated the name of the German law as *Kokumin rōdō tōseihō* (National Labour Control Law). The Industrial Patriotic League in turn published *Kakkoku no kokumin soshiki to rōdō soshiki* (The organization of people and labour in various countries) in 1940, in which the first article concerned Germany. This was written under

383 The Kyōchōkai was an agency created with government aid in 1919 as an officially-supported think-tank to promote conciliation between employers and workers. It conducted important research into labour and social problems and published two journals. For further details and discussion, see Garon 1987, Kinzley 1991, Gordon 1991.

384 The Sangyō hōkoku renmei (Sanpo) was established in 1938 by a consortium of politicians, bureaucrats, managers and some workers. Its slogan was "the enterprise as one family" (Tsuzuki 2000, p. 375). See also Gordon 1988, Gao 1997, Nakamura and Odaka 2003.

385 The Planning Board Incident of January-April 1941 was the "discovery" of two leftist organisations within the Board which had allegedly taken advantage of the emergency situation to encourage official backing for policies intended to lead to a communist revolution. The incident grew out of the revelation by the Board that steel production had fallen. Board members were arrested for communist activities.

the direction of Tamarushima Takeo (1905-1990) and Aoki Jirō. Tamarushima had stayed in Germany for three months during his official visit to Europe and the United States from spring 1933 to April 1934 where he studied the labour movement under the Nazi regime and took part in a week's residential training of the DAF,[386] and in 1940 he was involved with setting up the Greater Japan Industrial Patriotic Association, and became deputy dirctor of the welfare section in its central office the following year.

The Law for the Organization of National Labour denied the principles of the organization of labour and collective bargaining with management and was constituted as a relationship between the state and individual units of management as the basis of industrial relations. As we have seen, Article 1 stipulated that in a business undertaking, the employer, as leader, and the employees, as his followers, should work together to further the purposes of the undertaking, and for the common good of the people and the state. This was understood as being the principle symbolizing the spirit of Nazi labour relations.[387] Here the Nazi leader principle was applied to a corporative relationship between management and labour in an undertaking, whose purposes were joined with those of the people and the state.

Article 35 indicates the importance placed on labour and management: "Every member of a workplace community bears the responsibility of fulfilling conscientiously the duties encumberted upon him by virtue of his position within the workplace community. Through his conduct he is to show himself worthy of the respect that arises from his position in the workplace community. In particular, he is to dedicate his full energies to the service of the enterprise, and subordinate himself to the common good, in constant consciousness of his responsibility."[388]

Japanese intellectuals of the time, and especially those involved in constructing industrial relations policy, had a good understanding of the Nazi conception of the workplace community as seen in the relationship between management and labour and of the dual purpose of management to fulfill the needs of the enterprise as well as the state. This was the condition that premised how Nazi labour ideology was understood and received in Japan.

The New Labour System and the Nazi View of Labour

In the establishment of the new order to respond to the war in China and to prepare for total war, labour was just as indispensable a condition as industry.

386 Tamarushima 1986, pp. 290-291.
387 Sugimura et al 1934, p. 349 ff.
388 Joerges and Ghaleigh eds. 2003, pp. 252-253.

Connected with this need was the "Industrial Relations Adjustment Plan" (*Rōshi kankei chōsei hōsaku*), drawn up and put forward in March 1938 by the Committee for Measures for the Current Crisis (Jikyoku taisaku iinkai) within the Kyōchōkai, which had been set up to consider social policy under a wartime system and was made up of bureaucrats and business leaders. Machida Tatsujirō (1893-1975), managing director of the Kyōchōkai, was chairman of the Committee. He had visited Europe and the United States between August 1934 and February 1935, and in an article about his experiences, wrote that "among the labour movements in various countries, that of Germany is the most interesting" and went on to describe the labour system under the Nazi regime, expecially the DAF, Trustee of Labour and the Labour Service.[389] Later, in an essay about the Industrial Patriotic Movement, published in November 1940, a month before he became managing director of the Industrial Patriotic Association, he stated that the new spirit in labour-management relations was characterized by "a new industrial spirit made up of the warp of 'the way of the subject is to assist the imperial destiny' and the weft of the practical idea of offering one's service to the enterprise-family'."[390] This Japanist "plan", that advocated "industrial patriotic associations" on the principle of the "workplace at one with the family", was based on the viewpoint that "an industry is an organic organization bound together by the various duties of entrepreneurs and workers", and that its "mission" was to "provide for the welfare of the people of the nation through its expansion and thereby to contribute to the prosperity of the empire and culture of humankind". To this end, "Entrepreneurs must provide for the welfare of their employees, taking full responsibility for administration, and employees must endeavour to work for the growth of the industry, in a spirit of familial harmony with the enterprise-family, thereby fulfilling their own specific duties in the service of the state".[391]

Here we see a view, that, though based on the existing Kyōchōkai philosophy of harmony between workers and employers, advocated "an organic organization" where relations between workers and employers were bound by their "duties" (*shokubun*). The relationship was not seen to be adversarial but as an organic workplace community, and the objective of both workers and employers was both the prosperity of the enterprise and the national good. This view

389 Machida 1935.

390 Machida 1940, p. 97 ff., especially p. 99 ff. For Machida Tatsujirō, see Umeda et al 2004, especially p. 147 ff.

391 Kyōchōkai kaiwakai 1945, Machida 1965, p. 93 ff., *Shiryō nihon-gendaishi*, 7 (*Sangyō hōkoku undo)*, ed. by Kanda 1981, p. 13 ff.

employs ideas common with Nazi ideas about labour and capital. One entrepreneurs' group, the Chūbu Sangyō Dantai Rengōkai, criticized the Kyōchōkai "Industrial Relations Adjustment Plan", and, comparing it to Nazism, commented on the points that the two seemed to have in common.

"What is called the unity of labour and management is the same way of thinking about labour and management as in Nazi Germany." In the case of Nazism, "both employers and workers are equally constituent members of the enterprise community", and "their interests are totally dissolved within the interests of the nation". "This point nears a strong resemblance to the spirit of leadership found in the Kyōchōkai."[392]

The Chūbu Sangyō Dantai Rengōkai made the following conclusions.[393] First, the "Industrial Relations Adjustment Plan" had received a great deal of direction from the ideas and movements related to labour and capital in Nazi Germany. Second, despite this, the German "leader principle" had not been adopted. As a result the fundamental spirit of the "unity of capital and labour" was a matter of talk rather than action. Thus on their side, the entrepreneurs considered that a Nazi-type leader principle that looked to managers as leaders within the workplace was absolutely necessary and they criticised the Plan for lacking it.

Ideas about the new labour system were, as far as the government was concerned, basically put forward by the Cabinet Planning Board. They were considered and studied by the First Section of the Board in connection with organizing the economy under the New Order. The Draft Outline for the Reorganization of the Economy (*Keizai kikō seibi yōkō an*) drawn up on August 8, 1940 by the Board represented one of the earliest conceptions about the New Economic Order. Here the Board incorporated the "principle of the workplace community (or "cooperative management body", *keiei kyōdōtai*) and proposed an "industrial patriotic movement" (*sangyō hōkoku undō*) to unite "leaders and workers" (*shidōsha oyobi rōmusha*). The proposal of August 17 added to this the clear statement of the establishment of "an organization for leaders in management" (*keiei ni okeru shidōsha soshiki*).[394] In other words, within this proposal of the First Division of the Cabinet Planning Board, "leaders" was used instead of "managers", and the plan was to have a "workplace community" which would "unite" them with the "workers". The influence of the Nazi Law for the Organization of National Labour seems unmistakable here.

---

392 *Shiryō Nihon-gendaishi*, 7, 1981, p. 22 ff.

393 *Ibid.* p. 24.

394 Kokusaku kenkyūkai monjo (microfilm) 6196, 6230.

Research into a new system for labour thereafter shifted to the Third Division of the Cabinet Planning Board. A researcher in that division, Minoguchi Tokijirō, later a prominent professor of economics at Hitotsubashi University, wrote a great deal about the New Order and in the autumn of 1940 stated that "the demand of the times for the building of a highly developed national defence state" required "a new premise, a system of labour". The biggest issues here were, together with strengthening the system to reallocate labour and augmenting labour productivity, "creating a new outlook on labour" and, based on that, "establishing a new labour system". "Without regarding labour simply as a means of gaining the resources of private life, we must establish a spirit of industrial patriotism, where we serve the state through our labour, and set up a new labour system that gives concrete expression to that spirit."[395]

In October 1940, the Third Division of the Cabinet Planning Board drew up a number of bills concerning the new labour system. Based on these, on November 8 the same year the General Plan for Establishing a New Labour System was ratified at Cabinet level. It was made up of a preamble, and of sections concerning the establishment of a proper spirit of labour, the establishment of a labour system based on the "unit of the managing body", the establishment of a federation of labour organizations, the relationship between this federation and other bodies, the administrative structure, and the system in Japanese overseas territories. Emphasized here were labour's connection with the state, its character, and its productivity, and what was asked for was the responsibility of the people of the nation, and their honour, a display of efficiency, obedience to the system, creativity and initiative. The labour relations of individual management bodies were specified; management was prescribed as "a special corporative organization composed of the managers of the enterprise as commanders (*shikisha*) and all workers affiliated with the management body".

It is significant that the management body of an enterprise was regarded as fundamental. It was positioned as "an organic unity [comprising] capital, management and labour". The viewpoint was adopted in its entirety in the "General Plan for Establishing the New Economic Order" that was determined a month later; it denied prior understanding about relations between capital and labour, seeking to create an "organic unity" in management between employers and employees. Further, company managers were clearly described as administrative "commanders". Such ideas had a strong Nazi flavour. This becomes particularly noticeable when we review the process by which the various drafts were drawn

395 Minoguchi 1940, p. 76 ff.

up. This is clear from the fact that the Third Division of the Cabinet Planning Board had stipulated in the drafts of October 3 and October 18 regarding the General Plan for Establishing a New Labour System that "the organization [proposed] would be an organization of leaders, one that was directed by leaders (*shidōsha*)". Here the Nazi-type expression "leader" was used in place of the more common designation of "commander" (*shikisha*). Then in the draft of October 21, this was further revised to the above-mentioned "special corporative organization composed of the managers of the enterprise as leaders (*shidōsha*) and all workers affiliated with the management body". This change brings the wording very close to that of the first article of the Nazi Labour Organization Law that begins, "In a business undertaking, the employer, as leader (*Führer*)…." This shows clearly that the Nazi-type leader principle relating to the superiority of management had been adopted. This was a point desired by the aforementioned Chūbu Sangyō Dantai Rengōkai. The expression was used as it stood in the Cabinet Planning Board draft of the General Plan for Establishing a New Labour System and in the draft implementing the Fundamental Policy Outline (Kihon kokusaku yōkō) of October 28, and was assimilated into the bill. Though the word "leader" (*shidōsha*) was replaced by the word "commander" (*shikisha*) when the plan was ratified at Cabinet level on November 8, the tenor of the legislation clearly reveals, as the above process shows, that the Nazi concepts of the workplace community and the leader principle in the workplace had been taken on board.[396]

Following the ratification of the General Plan for Labour, the Dai Nihon Sangyo Hokokukai (abbr. Sanpō; Greater Japan Industrial Patriotic Association) was set up on November 23.[397] As in Nazi Germany, trades unions were dissolved, and the Association, like the German Labour Front, was a nation-wide body of those involved in industry, including both workers and employers. And again like the DAF, which had as its prime purpose the training of leaders and education into the Nazi world view based on the categorical imperative of the common good over self interest (*Gemeinnutz geht vor Eigennutz*), the Association had as its chief objective the promotion of the "spirit" of "industrial patriotism", and educating and training people in it. It included in its activities "public welfare, life guidance

---

396 Kokusaku kenkyūkai monjo (microfilm). Documents concerning the General Plan for Establishing a New Labour System (Nos. 6690-3, 6696, 6702, 6931, 7070, 7104).

397 "The Sanpo program, while drawn up within the Home and Welfare Ministries, and discussed among Kyōchōkai members and business leaders, was conceived in a broader context of tremendous enthusiasm, among important intellectuals and many of the nations most powerful rulers, for an all-encompassing New Order in Japan that drew on Fascist or Nazi models" (Gordon 1991, p. 322).

and the improvement of 'work culture' (*kinrō bunka*)", which corresponded to the function of Kraft durch Freude. After the war, the aforementioned Tamarushima Takeo recollected: "With the leading members of the Industrial Patriotic Association I made speeches in many parts of Japan as the person responsible for investigating the German Labour Front and for introducing it into Japan as the Industrial Patriotic Movement".[398] But all the same, Sanpo was not a mere copy of the German model. Andō Yoshio, a specialist in modern Japanese economic history, correctly points out that "Sanpō was an imitation of the Nazi German DAF, and there was also a Nazi odour about the General Plan. But it was also an expression of the 'imperial economics' that ran through the ideas of the extreme right-wing. Here too we find characteristics of Japanese fascism manifested."[399]

The reproduction and training of the workforce are the most fundamental conditions for a wartime economy. To this end, not only working conditions at the workplace and in the work process had to be considered, but also modes of living outside the workplace, in the worker's free-time. In this sense, Kraft durch Freude was an object of interest to contemporary Japanese. In 1938, the newly-established Ministry of Health and Welfare created the Japan Recreation Association (Nihon kōsei kyōkai) to promote physical health and to manage leisure.[400] Appointed as its chairman was Godō Takuo, the then president of the Japan Chamber of Commerce and Industry and a keen advocate of the activities of Kraft durch Freude following a visit to Germany. At the first annual convention of the Association in Tokyo in 1938, Godō described the aim of the public welfare movement (*kōsei undō*) was to reform the daily life of the people, to maintain their environment, especially so that workers might put their free time to good use, to eliminate uneconomic and immoral luxuries, to recommend healthy amusements, to train people mentally and physically and to reform the culture of sentiment to bring about friendly relations among people. He described how the movement for the promotion of public welfare began to grow up in many countries after the [First] World War. He gave two particular examples: the Italian Dopolavoro ("After Work") movement, led by Mussolini,

---

398 Tamarushima 1986, p. 293. Tamarushima was purged after the war because of those facts, but later became head of the administration office of the Japan Productivity Center (Nihon seisansei honbu), and then chairman of the Financial and Economic Investigative Committee.

399 Andō 1963, p. 252. However, Andō himself does not explain the grounds of his argument.

400 See Tansman ed. 2009, p. 127. For a detailed history of the Association, see Sawamura 1988.

that aimed to improve the lives of people both spiritually and physically by resolving the problem of free time, so that workers were brought together into the new Italian nation, and the German Kraft durch Freude. This latter movement emphasises, he said, the meaning of labour, denying the distorted view that the labour is unpleasant and low, and it endeavours to give work a cultural value that brings joy into the lives of labourers. "It aims to build a Nazi society where people can enjoy labour and feel pride in the nobility of the worker. Recently in our country too, there has been a growing interest for this movement, and I am delighted that the Japan Recreation Association was established this spring and that its first convention is now being held."[401]

In Ocober 1940, the East Asian Recreation Convention was held in Osaka, to which representatives from all over Asia were invited as well as those from the Italian Dopolavoro and the German DAF and Kraft durch Freude. Claus Selzner, the Kraft durch Freude delegate, wrote in his report to Ley: "The convention was held between the 16th and 20th October 1940 in the large city of Osaka. It was carried out brilliantly by the mayor of this city of a million people in the presence of 2000 delegates. In all respects the convention was a copy of the annual meeting of Kraft durch Freude in Hamburg and its themes were essentially those decided by the International Centralbureau [of DAF] through Dr. Ley.[402] The final resolution adopted by the convention contains the words *kangi rikkō*, the Japanese translation of "Kraft durch Freude". But though the Japanese recreation movement received this idea from Germany,[403] it was not put into action in the same way as it was there.

Of course, circumstances were different between Germany and Japan. Yoshizaka Shunzō (1888-1958), a director of the Japan Recreation Association, while agreeing that the Italian and German movements could provide points of "reference", rejected any idea that they could be "translated as they were". Godō, too, emphasized that there should be agreement with Japan's specific "national conditions" and "national traits". He linked this with the Movement to Mobilize the National Spirit (Kokumin seishin sōdōin),[404] which stressed the idea of

401 Nihon kōsei kyōkai 1939. Ishikawa ed. 1990, vol. 16.

402 "Bericht über die Japanreise der Parteigenossen Reichshauptamtsleiter Claus Selzner und Reichshauptamtsleiter Otto Gohdes, 30 Januar 1941", presented to DAF / R. Ley and to Adolf Hitler, 11 February 1941. Bundesarchiv Berlin R43 II/ 1456a. Yanagisawa 2008a, 2013, II.

403 For a detailed reconstruction of the process, see Yanagisawa 2008a, 2013 II.

404 A movement first initiated by the Konoe cabinet in 1937 to rally support for the war in China. The National Spiritual Mobiliation Central League was set up in

supporting emperor-centred rule. The East Asian Recreation Conference linked Kraft durch Freude to the Japanese notion of service to the country (*hōkō*), and this in turn was combined with ideas about the emperor system and "serving the imperial well-being" (*kōun fuyoku*), a phrase found in the Imperial Rescript on Education, 1890.[405]

December 1937 and reorganized in April 1940 into the National Spiritual Mobilization Headquarters. Its functions were eventually taken over by the Imperial Rule Assistance Association. See Havens 1978.

405 See Yanagisawa 2008a, 2013, II.

Chapter Seven: Nazi Germany and Japan in the Eyes of Contemporary Economists

This chapter focuses on the period in from the start of the Sino-Japanese War down to the establishment of the New Economic Order in 1940 and the outbreak of the Pacific War in 1941. It looks at how leading Japanese economists of the time perceived Nazi Germany and Nazism, and how critically or favourably they viewed the realities and particularities of the situation in Japan in relation with what they observed about Nazi Germany.

In the preceding chapters, we have looked at studies of Nazi Germany made by Japanese social scientists at the time when the Nazis rose to power.[406] This chapter turns to the second half of the 1930s, a period marked by Japan's Anti-Comintern Pact with Germany in 1936, its Anti-Comintern Pact with Germany and Italy in 1937 and the Tripartite Pact in 1940, and an ensuing shift to a war-time economic system. During this time, a "fascist state" was coming into being in Japan as totalitarian tendencies strengthened and the New Economic Order was being implemented. In Germany, meanwhile, the Nazi regime effected the second Four Year Plan in 1936, and, forwarding a rearmament programme, invaded Poland in 1939 thus triggering World War II.

By this time, Japanese economists no longer viewed Nazism simply as a variant of fascism and its ideology, but rather as a system of government, and they were particularly interested in the totalitarian characteristics of its economic system. This chapter looks closely at the work of two major economists of the period in the field of social policy, Kazahaya Yasoji and Hattori Eitarō, and a scholar of Japanist economics, Naniwada Haruo (1906-1991), known for his efforts to construct the principles of national rule under the emperor system.[407] Linked to the realities of Japan at the time in one form or another, their studies of Nazism involved both comparisons between Japan and Germany as well as a

---

406 See Chapter 3 above.

407 For the ideas and activities of scholars and intellectuals in the field of economics in prewar and wartime Japan, see Shisō no kagaku kenkyūkai ed. 1959-62, particularly the article on Ōkōchi Kazuo and Kazahaya Yasoji by Takabatake Michitoshi, Chō and Sumiya eds. 1971, Ishida 1984, Yamanouchi 1996. None of these, however, follows the analysis undertaken here.

close look at the peculiarities of Japan. This chapter draws particular attention to how their comparative analyses gave them a better understanding of Japan's totalitarian system, whether or not they felt favourably towards it, as, in anticipation of a total war, the country attempted to set up a war-preparedness economy.

Kazahaya Yasoji

Kazahaya Yasoji was an expert on criminal law and social policy who had studied at the Tokyo Imperial University and then, from 1924, in France, Germany and Italy. On his return in 1926, he took up a position as a professor of criminal law at the Kyūshū Imperial University. A pioneering scholar of Marxian law, he was arrested and imprisoned in 1933, the same year Hitler seized power in Germany. In 1937, after his release, Kazahaya published "A History of Social Policy in Japan" (*Nihon shakai seisakushi*),[408] a pioneering work that examined the formation of Japanese social policy in terms of the developmental process of social reproduction, casting light on its modern universality and distinctive forms. A characteristic of his analytical method was that he not only studied the concrete details of social policy, but examined that policy in connection with both the typical and atypical factors found in the historical development of capitalist society in Japan.

In analysing Japanese social policy, Kazahaya examined it against German social policy theory and its historical development.[409] His knowledge of the German situation was drawn largely from a 1936 book by Ōkōchi Kazuo about the development of German ideas on social policy, and a 1934 paper by Hattori Eitarō about the collapse of social democratic theories about it.[410] Kazahaya examined the historical characteristics of Japanese social policy formation from

---

408 Kazahaya 1937a, 1938 (4th printing), 1951. For an evaluation of argument about the "third way" (in his *Rōdō no riron to seisaku*, 1938a), see Takabatake 1960, pp. 226 ff., Totsuka 1971, pp. 197 ff., Yamanouchi 1993, pp. 144 ff. and Yamanouchi 1996, ch. 2. Regarding how Kazahaya practised his theory, see Moriya 1982, ch. 6.

409 It should be understood that in Japan "social policy" (*shakai seisaku*) was associated with the "distributive functions of the market place" rather than the "redistributive functions of the welfare state" (Notar 1985, pp. 313-314). Almost synonymous with "labour policy", it derives from Bismarck's *Sozialpolitik*. It "anticipates state intervention to maintain an efficient market" and "recognized the relationship between maldistribution and social tension" (ibid.).

410 Ōkōchi Kazuo, *Doitsu shakai seisaku shisōshi* (An intellectual history of German social policy, 1936); Hattori Eitarō, "Doitsu shakai minshushugi shakai seisaku riron no hōkai katei" (The breakdown of German Social Democrat social policy theory, 1934).

the standpoint of these social-scientific studies about the historical development of social policy in Germany, covering the collapse of the Weimar Republic and the rise of the Nazi regime, and studied the problems Japan faced through a comparison with contemporary reality in Germany.

Kazahaya wrote: "I think that one can illustrate most clearly the characteristics of Japan's capitalist system, the basis for the formation of its social policy, through a comparison with German capitalism under Bismarck and then under the Nazi regime, rather than a comparison with British capitalism."[411] Two years after the publication of "A History of Social Policy in Japan", he published an article in four parts about restructuring Japan's industrial system, analysing the overall formation of industry in Japan and its structure.[412] Studying Japan through a comparison with Nazi Germany, he attempted to classify industrial organization into a "Japanese type" and a "German type". Thus for Kazahaya, there was an inseparable relationship between the study of Germany and that of Japan, in that he understood Japan through a comparison with Germany. His article therefore focuses on the history and contemporary situation of Germany. Let us examine the nature of the comparisons that he made.

Transplanting Nazi-style policies to Japan and the distinctiveness of Japanese-style capitalism

We have seen that the Japanese began to pay serious attention to Nazism and Nazi policy after Hitler's rise to power in 1933. Very soon after that, Japan began to make attempts to transplant Nazi policies. Kazahaya mentioned this in the "History of Social Policy", pointing to the distinctive nature of what was transplanted.[413] He discussed two pieces of 1936 Japanese legislation from this perspective: the Labour Union Control Law that allowed the army to order workers in its arsenals to withdraw from unions and banned them from acting collectively,[414] and a local financial adjustment subsidy system, which was a temporary supplementary fund to finance towns and villages. Some people regarded these measures as the Japanese version of the Nazi national labour law

411 Kazahaya 1937a, 1938 (4th edition), p. 474, 1951, p. 535.

412 Kazahaya 1939a. The articles, all entitled "The reorganisation of the Japanese industrial structure" (*Nihon sangyō kikō no saihensei*), appeared between July and October 1939. He had already published two articles in the same publication (Kazahaya 1937b and Kazahaya 1938b).

413 Kazahaya 1937a, 1938, chapter 10, pp. 474 ff., and 1951, vol. 2, pp. 535 ff.

414 See Garon 1987, pp. 208-215.

and the local government system.[415] Ōuchi Hyōe (1888-1980) wrote that "the dependence of communities on the prefectural government, and the subordination of the local government of the prefectures to the Ministers for Home Affairs and Finance are greatly strengthened (by the new law). Our system of local government resembles the new Nazi local government system".[416] Kazahaya by comparison was critical of such views and contended that while the Japanese legislation possessed some aspects of similarity with Nazi policy, it had its own unique characteristics arising from its Japanese background. Social conditions existed in Japan that engendered phenomena similar to Nazi Germany, yet there was "another principle" at work, one special to Japan.

Kazahaya understood German Nazism as a form of government that had emerged after the rise and subsequent fall of social democracy: it was thus a modern and evolved form of a capitalist society. A distinguishing feature of Japanese society, by contrast, was that while it shared certain modern aspects with Germany, it retained features of a society at an earlier stage of development than Germany. Capitalism had been dominant in the world economy, and Japan, as part of that economy, had also been ruled by more or less liberalistic principles. It was therefore undeniable that the principles of Nazi-type control that were the antithesis to such liberalistic principles might become an issue in Japan. In Japan, however, capitalist and pre-capitalist systems functioned closely together; the "restrictions" of pre-capitalism still exerted considerable power alongside the law of value of capitalism. Here, regulation, taking into account the limitations imposed by liberalism, coexisted with the shackles imposed by the restrictions of pre-capitalist society. To increase production, it was crucial to right the ills of the pre-capitalistic economy by eliminating its "restrictions" and thus realising "freedom".

---

415 The Nazi local government system was set up as a result of the Gemeindeverfassungsgesetz of December 1933 and the Deutsche Gemeindeordnung (German Local Government Statute) of January 1935. This legislation brought a uniform system of local government to the country.

416 Ōuchi 1937a. Rōyama Masamichi, a leading professor in political science at the Tokyo Imperial University criticised Ōuchi's words as a misunderstanding (Rōyama 1937). In reply, Ouchi again pointed out the similarities in the development of state policy for local government between Nazi Germany and Japan (Ōuchi 1937b). Ōuchi Hyōe taught economics at the Tokyo Imperial University from 1919, but lost his position in the Morito Incident (1934). He was reinstated in 1936 and became a professor in 1937. He was ordered to take a leave of absence because at the time of the Popular Front Incident (1938). He was later a member of the Ōhara Institute for Social Research and president of Hosei University (1950-1959). See Hoston 1986, pp. 251, 261, etc., Barshay 1988, p. 44. etc.

To the extent it was a capitalist country, Japan, like Nazi Germany, had a basis for allowing the principle of "control" on liberalism to arise. Unlike Germany, however, once transplanted to Japan, "control" was apt to become the pre-capitalistic "restrictions". In Japan, the "control" that came before "freedom" and the "control" that came after it reinforced, and merged into, one another. The "restrictions" of pre-capitalism had existed in Germany before Bismarck's German Empire, and in this sense, Japan combined Nazi-type elements, which post-dated Hitler, and pre-capitalist factors that had existed before Bismarck.

Kazahaya wrote: "Nazi Germany has come into being by passing through the stages of Bismarck and the Weimar Constitution. Japanese capitalism, on the other hand, combines elements that existed before Bismarckian Germany as well as those that arose after Hitler came to power. This is the basic and important precondition of Japanese capitalism. Missing this important point, some commentators erroneously regard Japanese policies as being analogous to Nazi ones, and others believe Nazi-style social policies should be transplanted to Japan now or in the near future."[417]

Kazahaya concluded that one has to look closely at the pre-Bismarckian and post-Hitler elements in Japanese capitalism to see "which type of element is the more predominant and how they are intertwined". In Japan, there had been a certain shift from the former to the latter in the second decade of the twentieth century, particularly during World War I, but in the process the two had become even more intertwined.

"Pre-Bismarckian" elements in Japanese capitalism

Kazahaya understood Hitler's Germany to be at the stage of state "control", a phenomenon responding to the development of liberalistic capitalism and confrontational relations between capital and labour. To him, Nazism was a modern form of control arising from the evolved stage of capitalism, while the pre-Bismarckian system was a pre-capitalist form. Kazahaya regarded Ōkōchi's 1936 work "An Intellectual History of German Social Policy" (*Doitsu shakai seisaku shisōshi*) highly, and based his understanding of Bismarckian social policy and its demise, and the shift to a social democratic social policy on it.[418] Bismarck adopted a carrot-and-stick policy, proposing the first Anti-Socialist Law (1878) while at the same time implementing legislation such as the Health Insurance Bill of 1883, the Accident Insurance Bill of 1884 and the Old Age and Disability

417 Kazahaya 1937a, 1938(4.ed.), p. 474.

418 Kazahaya 1937 and 1938(4.ed.), p. 1, and also footnotes on page 1.

Insurance Bill of 1889. He was backed by the power of the Junkers, but with the rise of monopoly capital and the expansion of the regional power of the Social Democratic Party, Bismarck fell from power and the Anti-Socialist Law was not renewed. The enactment of the Anti-Socialist Law demonstrates that under Bismarck, the workers had already gained enough strength to stand up to the capitalists. The social policies of the professorial socialists (*Kathedersozialisten*), who had developed in Germany by the 1870s, targeted the modern labouring class, and a precondition for them was labour-management relations. The suppression of workers' rights by the Anti-Socialist Law went with the protection given by the social welfare policies.

Japanese social policy before World War I, by contrast, completely prohibited workers from combining in any form or taking part in self-help activities, while at the same time providing no legal protection but only "aid" in the traditional sense of "charity". The poor and needy were not to be protected against the capitalist but merely "pitied". Social policy at this time did not acknowledge the existence of the working classes as such, and did nothing more than extend "religious benevolence" to "those to be pitied"; it was in fact designed to stunt the growth of the "autonomy" of the masses. This state of affairs corresponded to the situation in Germany "before Bismarck".

World War I, however, brought changes to Japanese capitalism. The social status of the working classes improved and so did their self image, and a series of social policies was enacted. Japan thus reached the Bismarckian stage, but the content of those policies was insubstantial, and the autonomy of the working masses was suppressed. Those policies were continued after the Great Depression. A distinguishing feature in the Japanese case was that there was a large swathe of the populace who had not joined the ranks of workers; such people included semi-proletariat tenant farmers and those engaged in cottage industries in the manufacturing sector. They had no awareness of belonging to any particular social class, and were at the mercy of a "charitable" policy not bound by law. Capitalists too preferred to maintain the practice of benefiting the needy, under the banner of "good morals and manners". It was the intention of management to try to nullify the "industrial burden" imposed by social policy.

In this way, Kazahaya drew attention to the traditional aspects of Japanese capitalism, such as the continuation of "restriction" and relief as charity, which were made good use of by capitalists, as well as the modern "control" and a denial of liberalism. He then focused on how the old and new elements overlapped. What was the situation in Germany? In post-Bismarckian Germany, enterprises were able to bear the industrial burden imposed by social policy, but under the exigencies of the Versailles Treaty after the defeat of World War I, small and medium sized firms buckled and were subsequently swallowed by giant corporations who had the means to sustain the burden. There was a sharp contradiction between production policy and social policy. The latter was sacrificed to realize the former, and in the process, Nazism stripped workers of their autonomy: Hitler had snatched away the autonomy labour had gained under monopoly capitalism. Something similar had also happened in Japan, but with the difference that there it had occurred in connection with traditional restrictions.

The organisation of industry under state control in Germany and Japan

(i) Unionization and the reconstruction of the national economy: Following the publication of "A History of Social Policy in Japan", Kazahaya was involved in the translation of a three-volume *Grundlagen, Aufbau und Wirtschaftsordnung des nationalsozialistischen Staates* (Fundamentals, Construction and Administration of the National Socialist State), a semi-official encyclopaedic work compiled of sixty-six pamphlets edited by Hans Lammers and Hans Pfundtner. Kazahaya translated two of the pamphlets, *Gewerbe und Gewerbepolitik* (Trade and business policy) authored by Paul Berkenkopf (1891-1962) and *Arbeitseinsatz und Arbeitsbeschaffung* (Deployment of labour and job creation) authored by Friedrich Syrup (1881-1945).[419] Around the same time he published his own paper "The reconstruction of the Japanese industrial framework" (*Nihon sangyō kikō no saihensei*) in the monthly journal *Kagakushugi kōgyō*, a comparative study of the reconstruction of the national economy in Japan and Germany, and its transformation into a controlled economy (then underway in Japan).[420]

Kazahaya's paper noted that a controlled economy was coming into being in Japan and attempted to explain the mechanisms for state control over industry and changes within them, the formation of control mechanisms for the major industries, the relationship between the bureaucratic control of industry and the autonomous control by the business sector, how the business sector functioned within the national economy, and the direction the reorganization of industry was taking on the basis of these. He maintained that a rapid expansion of production was imperative if Japan were to carry out its "historic mission" to "build a new East Asian State over the long term", and so the industrial mechanism had to be restructured to support and propel this expansion of production. It was thus necessary to "keep up the action to a suppression of

419 Berkenkopf and Syrup 1936. Kazahaya's translations are included in *Shin doitsu kokka taikei*, 1939: the former in vol. 9 and the latter in vol. 10.

420 Kazahaya 1939a, pp. 5ff.

the profit-seeking aspect of economic activities" and to "promote the aspect of the national economy to the maximum". This objective should be achieved by integrating "the state, capital and labour" into "the one-and-only national economy" through the medium of "the national power as the political driving power".

Kazahaya's view reflects his positive appraisal of "Theory of, and Tentative Plan for, the New Economic Order" (*Shin keizai taisei no riron to shian*) published by Miura Tetsutarō in 1939.[421] A liberal journalist, Miura advocated that there should be a system that gave the business sector the right to play a direct role in industrial administration and participate autonomously in it, in order to have joint planning by the public and private sectors. He also suggested that labour unions be organised and that workers be permitted to join them. Kazahaya set great store on the point that Miura's plan was connected with "a new labour system embracing all citizens" having a non-bureaucratic, national orientation that aimed at "industrial administration by those in charge of running the industries". However, he was not satisfied with the way Miura placed administration, labour and industry in a pluralistic and parallel relationship and urged a system of communication between them on the basis of such a relationship. Kazahaya proposed that the three parties should be formulated into "an organic, integrated unit of the national workforce" in order to create "a racial community" (*minzoku kyōdōtai*,[422] Ger. *Volksgemeinschaft*) that "united" the three parties as "organic components".

Kazahaya's ideas revolving around the formation of labour unions and their participation in state administration had Nazi elements in so far as Kazahaya spoke of coordinating the nation's workforce organically to establish "a racial community". Kazahaya's main object, though, was to organise labour unions and strengthen the autonomy of workers in a Japan backward in this respect, and, based on this, to realise a Japanese version of corporatism.

(ii) Restructuring industry in Germany and Japan (1938): In his paper, Kazahaya focused on the contemporary issues of the state's total mobilisation plan, particularly the materials mobilization plan and the plan to expand production, and the transformation of the industrial mechanism and the formation of

---

421 For Miura's view on this, see Yanagisawa 2013, II. For Miura, see also Hara 1998 and Matsuo 1995.

422 Dower 1986 comments that this term may be translated in a variety of ways, including "a collectivity of peoples", "racial community" and "racial cooperative body" (p. 279). It has also been translated as "communality", "cultural collective", "racial collectivity", "ethnos community", etc.

control associations. Kazahaya attempted to understand these crucial issues by comparing the situation in Japan with that in Nazi Germany.

He maintained that an impasse in the liberalistic economic system, a shift to heavy industry and more control mechanisms were phenomena inevitably experienced by all capitalist countries; however, since such a system was less well entrenched in Germany and Japan than in the United States, Britain or France, there was a greater need there to strengthen economic control. However, despite this shared trait, there were important points of difference between Germany and Japan regarding the setting up of an industrial mechanism under state control, differences distinctive enough to form two separate models, German and Japanese, differentiated in four ways.

a. The historical moment: The German restructuring of its industrial mechanism necessitated the rejection of both its liberalistic and social democratic systems in order to allow the establishment of a Nazi-style new economic order. At the time the Nazi party seized power, capital structure was highly developed, and there was already a high degree of heavy and machine industrialization. Therefore, Nazi policy centred not on expanding heavy industry but increasing agricultural production to secure food resources, and labour was allocated to the non-industrial sector to achieve this goal. As a result, a distinctive feature of the Nazi New Economic Order was its plan to restructure industry by function – to divide all industry, including agriculture, into groups, each operating as an autonomous, functional organisation in accordance with the leadership principle, permeated from within with the Nazi spirit. Thus the true objective of restructuring German industry was not to expand production by expanding heavy industry, but rather dismantling the traditional, liberalistic and social democratic system and installing in its place a "new structure for management and labour in the framework of the new social and economic order". By contrast, structural reforms in Japan aimed to increase the production of munitions, to regulate the supply and demand of goods, and to exercise price controls. As light industry was still predominant in Japan, a move to heavy industry was of the utmost importance for creating a new industrial structure. The country needed to achieve "heavy industrialisation" and the "industrial restructuring" simultaneously.
b. The initiative to restructure and the major players: The Nazi party took the initiative in dividing all industries into groups according to their function, assigning to each group a leader – a Nazi party member, in actuality – who would put into practice the leadership principle from within. In Japan, the

lead was taken by the government, particularly by bureaucrats from the Ministry of Commerce and Industry, who were in charge of administering most economic policies, and by the Cabinet Planning Board, which might be called the headquarters of economic planning. This means that the industrial structure was run by bureaucrats "from outside". The practice of bureaucrats taking the lead is a fundamental Japanese characteristic, but, in fact, such bureaucratic guidance "from outside" was not guidance in the real sense of the word but simply orders and instructions.

c. The nature of guidance: The functional, autonomous organisations in Germany were entrusted with economic and social responsibility. Their economic duties included overseeing production and allocation, supervising industrialists and workers, and providing technical education. More important, however, was their social mission of instilling the Nazi spirit into the members of the organisation, notably the maxim that the common good comes before self-interest, which was the embodiment of the totalitarian economic spirit as well as the spirit of contributing service and labour to the state. In Japan, however, the role of the control mechanism was concerned above all with distribution technology, price controls and technical improvements. If the German model had an economic and ethical mission, the Japanese one focused on production and technology, not simply because of the obvious need to expand productive capacity, but rather because it was tied in with the structural characteristics of the Japanese economy. Of course in Japan too the national spirit was being guided through the Campaign for National Spiritual Mobilization (*kokumin seishin sōdōin undō*), but this too was imposed "from outside". Moreover, there was a large gap between this spiritual guidance and the economic guidance performed by the industrial control mechanism. The slogan of the German functional structure, "the integration of economy and ethics", should, Kazahaya commented, be instructive for Japan to map out its future course, whether or not one approves of Nazism.

d. Control organisations, industrialists, cartels: Like Japan, the Nazi regime did not eliminate free competition. Rather, the Nazi party promoted free competition, while at the same time laying down regulations about economic ethics and denouncing the unfair pursuit of profit. These were not enforced by laws or orders but took the form of the education of the industrialist himself. The policy towards cartels and other types of combination was the same; monopolies themselves were not eliminated but any abuse of them was checked, not through state intervention but by educating industrialists or by adopting voluntary sanctions. The functional industrial organisations, especially the national economic *Gruppe*, and cartels existed side by side: the cartels were still allowed to control prices but they came under the supervision of the *Gruppe* and the National Economic Chamber. In Japan an attempt had been made to reorganise the existing cartel system so as to use it as an organ of state control over such things as distribution and prices. This however had met with opposition from the business sector and was not able to function fully, due to the fact that autonomous control had not fully developed within the private sector. In the future Japan needed to develop both autonomous and governmental control mechanisms simultaneously. Kazahaya concluded: "By comparing the new control mechanisms in both countries, I conclude that the German model is designed to exercise control from within and is concerned with the issue of leadership and economic ethics, while the Japanese model functions as an outside, bureaucratic mechanism and deals mainly with production and technology."[423]

Kazahaya's comparison between Japan and Germany was made in the context of the move towards a wartime controlled economy following the outbreak of the Sino-Japanese War. As a result, it was closely linked with questions about how, and in what direction, the national economy should be restructured. His analysis is an important example of a study of the contemporary economic situation by a former Kōza-ha economist that was made public at a time when the state was actively suppressing Marxism.[424] He characterized Japan as a combination of modern factors similar to those that arose after Hitler came to power and pre-modern factors akin to those that existed before Bismarck, and as a combination of a modern denial of liberalism and pre-modern anti-liberalism.[425]

423 Kazahaya 1939a, p. 11.

424 The Kōza-ha ("Lectures faction") was a Marxist faction that engaged in a debate over the nature of Japanese capitalism with the rival Rōnō-ha ("Worker-Farmer faction") in the early 1930s. The names came from the journals each published in: the former in the *Nihon shihonshugi hattatsushi kōza* and the latter in *Rōnō*. The Kōza-ha, who focused on the quasi-feudalistic aspects of Japanese capitalism, called for an agrarian revolution and argued critically against enforced industrialization by the state to achieve militarization, while the Rōnō-ha regarded the Meiji Restoration as a bourgeois triumph, so that the state rested on a capitalist foundation. Members of the former were arrested in 1936 and the latter in 1938. See Morris-Suzuki 1989, pp. 16-17. See also Hoston 1986.

425 Among the characteristics of Japan's industrial structure that Kazahaya focused on, the fact of the high proportion of light industry and the relative underdevelopment of heavy industry was generally recognised at the time.

This understanding is closely related to his division between German and Japanese models, the former restructuring the industrial mechanism "from within" following the "principles of leadership and economic ethics", and the latter, one of bureaucratic restructuring of the control mechanism "from outside". Post-war studies of fascism in Japan define German Nazism as fascism that was "bottom-up" and "from within", and Japanese totalitarianism as "top-down" state fascism. Kazahaya may be said to have been the pioneer of this interpretation.[426]

In contrast to Japan, with its strong pre-modern elements, Kazahaya saw Nazi Germany as a developed, modern form of a controlled economy. He focused on the advanced state of the Nazi economic system, especially the restructuring of industry, but he also regarded Nazi social policies and its labour system as having modern characteristics, and so were "policies that Japan should emulate".[427] He had a great interest in, and high expectations of, a series of Nazi policies, including the massive infusion of labour during peacetime and the continuing training of workers to increase skilled labour, the apprentice system for scientific and technical education, the planned allocation of labour (job centres dealing with employment unemployment insurance), the maintenance and nurturing of labour (regulations on wages and working hours, recreation facilities for workers, fundraising for this purpose by accounting control and capping profits), and the establishment of a new German-style labour system.

In particular, Kazahaya positively evaluated a rational Nazi labour system with the Law for the Organization of National Labour of 1934, the German Labour Front (DAF) and the "Strength through Joy" organization, and pointed out how they encouraged a voluntary effort among workers to be more productive. By contrast, Japan's national mobilisation system was too abstract and too concerned with trivialities, while the Patriotic Industrial Associations were no more than a spiritual movement. There was no evidence in either of any voluntary participation of workers to improve production. While his interpretation of the differences in the Japanese and German labour systems was inherited in part by Japanese scholars of fascism after World War II, it has a crucial flaw in that it concealed serious problems in the Nazi system, such as the repudiation of labour unions and the labour movement, anti-Semitism and the suppression of Marxism and democracy.

---

426 Maruyama 1964, especially 2 and 3, Maruyama 1995.

427 Kazahaya 1939b.

Hattori Eitarō

Morito Tatsuo[428] and Hattori Eitarō[429] were the two scholars of the prewar and wartime periods who showed the greatest interest in the social policy of Nazi Germany. Here we will look into Hattori's study of Nazi social policy and his comparative study of social policy and the labour system in Japan and Nazi Germany.

In 1934, soon after the Nazi seizure of power in Germany, Hattori, an economist at the Tōhoku Imperial University, published a long paper on the formation of a social democratic social policy under the Weimar Republic and its subsequent dismantling. Shortly after that, he wrote another paper on the history of Nazi totalitarian and functional social policy.[430] A few years later when the shift to a wartime economy and the New Economic Order were being hotly debated, he actively discussed issues concerning the Japanese labour system in comparison with the Nazi system. Kazahaya Yasoji was again arrested in 1940, leaving Hattori's critical analysis of existing conditions in Japan, based on a comparative study of the Japanese and Nazi systems, to occupy, together with the works of Ōkōchi Kazuo, a special position within Japanese socio-scientific research as one of the few Marxian economic studies from a time when Marxism was being repressed.

The ideological aspects of Nazi functional social policy

Based on the premise that the form of social policy changes as the capitalist mode of production evolves, Hattori defined social policy in a capitalist society at the current stage of development as a policy for expanding labor chances combined with a forcible, state-led labour policy and a policy of economic stimulation. This is reflected within social policy theory as ideology.

---

428 Morito 1941 represents his research of this period. For Morito at this time, see Mitani 1997, 1, especially pp. 62 ff., and Takahashi 2001, part 1, analysis 3. Morito, then teaching at the Tokyo Imperial University, was a central figure in the Morito Case of 1920 when he and Ōuchi Hyōe were indicted for publishing an article about the Russian anarchist Kropotkin. He then joined the Ōhara Institute for Social Research. See footnote 376.

429 Hattori was a professor at the Tōhoku Imperial University until his arrest in 1942; he returned to his position following the war. For his career and research, see *Hattori Eitarō chosakushū* supp. hokan (1976), and the vol.1(1967) explanatory note by Hattori Fumio. For his views before and during the war, see vol. 2(1968), explanatory note by Nishioka Yukiyasu, and for his standpoint after the war, see vol. 5(1969), explanatory note by Ujihara Shōjirō.

430 Kazahaya 1937a, 1938(4.ed.), p. 1. and 1951, vol. 1, p. 29. Hattori 1934, Hattori 1935 (both papers included with slight modifications in Hattori, 1966-1976, vol. 1.)

Following World War I, Germany had already demonstrated its current stage of capitalistic development to be the characteristic form of monopoly capitalism. Ideologically it was sociototalitarian, divided by status, and functional, based on the efficiency of labour, according to Hattori. It opposed labour unions as self-seeking organisations representing class interests, and also opposed social democratic labour union policy. Hattori studied, in the context of the intellectual history of social policy, works by German scholars such as Walter Weddingen (1895-1978), Othmar Spann, Otto von Zwiedineck-Südenhorst (1871-1957), Alfred Amonn (1883-1962), F. A. Westphalen (1899-1989) and Gerhard Albrecht (1889-1971), recognising them to be steps on the way to bringing theory to reality. These included labour-management cooperation versus labour-management confrontation, the organic unification of the people's community (*Volksgemeinschaft*) and the works community (*Betriebsgemeinschaft*), incorporation into the social community and grouping by social and professional class, the priority of economic policy over social policy and an emphasis on productivity and efficiency, and the formation of national community that transcends individual and class interests. Meanwhile, the functional transformation of works councils was already underway.[431]

Based on an observation by the Soviet economist Eugen Varga (1879-1964), Hattori declared that the Nazi "national revolution" of 1933 was "the entrustment of political power to the Nazi party by the German capitalist class". He observed that the capitalist class in Germany deemed it necessary to introduce a "constraining" social system and policy to replace the "liberalistic" social system and policy of the Social Democrats, and turned to the Nazi party, which advocated a new order of society defined by social and professional class. Thus the Nazi regime emerged as the natural heir of the Weimar Republic in the guise of a modern form of capitalism. The German Labour Front (DAF) set up in May 1933, the Law for the Organization of National Labour of January 1934, the Law for the Organic Constitution of the German Economy of February 1934 and the Leipzig Agreement of March 1935 were examples of how the Nazi party put into practice an ideology revolving around social and professional class. The German Labour Front relied on re-education to achieve its objectives: nurturing the idea of a "national and racial community", putting into practice the principle of the common good over self-interest, elevating an awareness of, and the ability to achieve, a conciliatory, cooperative, responsibility-sharing relationship between employers and employees, and, more importantly, eradicating Marxism and transcending class consciousness.

431 Hattori 1935.

This Nazi-style totalitarianism differed, Hattori said, from the totalitarian social policy ideas of the Weimar Republic, which were also oriented towards social and professional class. In Weimar ideology, "the whole" was not "the state" but "society" itself, and the state's responsibility for social policy took back stage. The Nazi party, by complete contrast, took the standpoint of the authoritarian and totalitarian state; the theoretical knitting together of a social order marked by work status and the totalitarian state was truly a feature of the Nazi system, Hattori concluded.[432]

The possibilities of the Nazi-type social state and the backwardness of the Japanese labour system

In 1941 Hattori published a paper entitled "The future prospects of the Nazi Social State" (Nachisu "shakai kokka" no tenbō), concerning the possibilities of the "social state" under Nazi rule.[433] He discussed this in connection with the issue of structural reform and "its implementation in society" at a time when the government was trying to set up a wartime system to wage war in China, and used his understanding of Nazi Germany to better analyse and criticise the conditions in Japan. Unlike in his earlier paper, where he emphasised the problems inherent in totalitarianism and Nazi Germany's social policy based on socio-professional status, here he completely held back his previous critical assessment of the Nazi regime, and focused instead on the modernity of the Nazi labour and policy system, attempting thereby to throw into relief problems about the conditions that existed in Japan and how the country was lagging behind in terms of developed thinking.

(i) Nazi social state (*Sozialstaat*): Hattori attached great importance to the fact that Nazi Germany had, as part of the "postwar social contract", drawn up plans for a national old age pension scheme and for subsidised housing, measures that Hattori saw as steps towards a new "social state". He recognised that they offered the possibility of unifying sets of objectives generally deemed antinomic, such as defence expenditure and social expenditure or a defence state and a social state, and he saw this as pointing the way for a social state to be established under the national defence system. He tried to show its potential by comparing the Nazi model with the traditional form of the social state.

A social state (or socialisation of the state) traditionally meant the expansion of the role played by social policy in a modern capitalist society, with a particular

432 Hattori 1935, pp. 194 ff. For the views of German economists on "Sozialpolitik", see Janssen 2000, pp. 265 ff.

433 Hattori 1941a., Hattori 1966-1976, supp. vol.(1976), and vol. 4(1974).

emphasis on the redistribution of wealth and the reallocation of national income. In economic terms, it was thought to increase the purchasing power of the masses and to expand the domestic market, and in political terms, to ensure the sound development of democracy with support from the working classes. However, from an economic viewpoint, the development of the social state could only be possible based upon the excess profits that came at the stage of imperialism. Enormous profits for monopoly capital and high wages for labour aristocrats, made possible in the social states of advanced capitalist countries, came at the expense of workers in underdeveloped capitalist countries, quasi-colonies and colonies. The enormous sacrifice of these workers helped the advanced countries push the limits of their social policies ever further. Closely connected with imperialism, those social policies required as a prerequisite the existence of gaps among nations in their developmental stage.

Now, though, a new situation had arisen. The advanced capitalist countries, characterised by an organised and powerful working class, with improved labour conditions and higher living standards thanks to various types of social policy, had suddenly found themselves in competition for the share of world markets with less developed or quasi-colonised capitalist countries and colonies, which could take advantage of workers willing to work for low wages and under inferior conditions. This competition had grown into a fierce battle over production costs, and the advanced capitalist countries, burdened with high social costs, were now in danger of defeat. This state of affairs had become apparent after World War I. Focusing on what had ensued from the subsequent uneven development, and on changes in the imperial system and the instability they had brought, Hattori pointed out the contradictions inherent in the Nazi expanded economic sphere.

If, he asserted, the Nazi-type social state and its "postwar social contact" are to be made possible by excess profits from agricultural countries in southeastern Europe and the colonies that Germany intends to acquire, there will be no change from the traditional social state, and the Nazi social state will reveal its inherent contradictions. This applies also to Funk's new European economic order. The limitations of the new social state, he wrote, will become apparent if it is designed according to the traditional view of social policy and redistribution.

However, at the same time, Hattori also drew attention to the historical process by which the social state evolved in close connection with war, looking closely at socialism during World War I, the nationalisation of the economy, and state control over production and labour in a total mobilisation system, as sought by the Hindenburg Programme of 1916, an effort to double industrial production, especially of munitions, at the expense of agriculture. Many such policies and systems were inherited by the postwar Social Democratic social state, and were made manifest in forms such as job centres and unemployment insurance, the public acceptance of labour unions, labour agreements and arbitration committees. Hattori emphasized that within the basic structure of the German Social Democratic social state there were already the germs of the transformation to the Nazi social state, and without this legacy the new Nazi-style social state could not have come into existence.

He asserted that the new Nazi social state has made a concentrated effort first to overcome the social crisis triggered by the Great Depression and then to establish an effective national defence system. The new social state was based on the leader principle and the ideals of the racial community (*Volksgemeinschaft*) and the workplace community (*Betriebsgemeinschaft*). The system was built around (1) the planned allocation of labour, control over working conditions including wages, and organisations in charge of state programmes such as social insurance, and (2) the German Labour Front, in charge of social policy to bring to realisation the workplace community and assisting the carrying out of state social policies. State control of working conditions, especially the autocratic position held by those entrusted with wage controls, characterised the Nazi system, but to counterbalance such top-down control, it was crucial to have cooperation "from below". The support provided by the German Labour Front to implement the state's social policy was integral to the Nazi system, Hattori stated, and it distinguished the Nazi social policy from that of Bismarck. "Social cooperation from below" had not yet been fully institutionalised as a system, but there were already prospects of that happening, he suggested, and in this sense there was a possibility that the new social state might transcend the limits set by imperialism.

Thus, though he had reservations about the imperialistic tendencies within Nazi military expansionism, and pointed out the autocratic character of the Nazi-type social state, Hattori maintained the hope that the Nazi state, having moved to a national defence system, might still develop a new type of social state, on the premise of cooperation "from below" from the German Labour Front.

Hattori's appreciation of the possibilities of the Nazi labour system is revealed even more clearly in his comments about the Nazi vision of a wider European economic sphere, particularly the ideas of the "New European Economic Order", attributed to Walther Funk.[434] Hattori no longer regarded Nazi military

434 Hattori, 1941a., Hattori 1966-1976, supp. vol. Funk (1890-1960) was the Minister of Economics (1938-1945) and President of the Reichsbank (1939). Herbst 1982, pp. 127-130.

aggression, which had started with the invasion of Poland in September 1939, as imperialistic expansion, but as part of the "social policy for a new Europe", and as such, an "advance" that looked towards "the future labour (order) of Europe" and "the advancement of social policy".

Hattori looked at the "National Revolution" of the Nazis in the same way. He understood the principles of Nazism mainly from the viewpoint of the "Organization of National Labour" (enacted in January 1934), linked with the importance given to labour and "performance" in the racial community. He considered that, unlike the "liberal economy", Nazi economic ideas would help eliminate the "power of capital" and improve the "status of labour". He also thought that labour would become a "public duty" in the real sense of the word, subjected to the state's "guidance and protection", and that "providers of labour" would be brought into line with the coordinated state system (*Gleichschaltung*). Hattori had previously connected the Nazi regime with monopoly capitalism, but this critical stance is now absent.

Moreover, he regarded Nazi military aggression against other countries as a means of replacing the "profit principle of private capital" in those countries with the Nazi principle of "labour and performance". He hoped that "the new economic direction" given to Southeastern European countries would grow into a broader European economic bloc including France, and help release Europe from the grip of class struggle. While admitting that there was room for "objective criticism" of the Nazi idea of a continental European *Grossraumwirtschaft* (organized economic space)[435], he said: "What follows the advance of the German defence forces is not the 'advance' of capital, let alone the 'advance' of the pursuer of private gain. What ensues is the 'advance' of social policy. Requisition means requisitioning for the implementation of social policy, and the protectorate seems to have the salient characteristics of social policy. On the whole, the Nazi military advance signifies the 'advance' of the 'ordering of national labour'".[436] Hattori's view had shifted radically, from critical to affirmative.

---

435 "Europe was perceived in terms of an 'extended economic space' onto which the Nazi dream of autarky, self-sufficiency and racial supremacy was projected… This *Grossraumwirtschaft* was to be an 'organized economic space' governed not in the name of a community of equal and independent states but that of the German *Volk*" Walters and Haahr 2005, p. 8.

436 Hattori, 1941b, p. 91 and p. 178. His high expectations for the Nazi regime are also expressed in his 1942 paper *Yōroppa kōiki shakai seisaku no tenkai* (Hattori 1967-1976, Hokan). Hattori had a high regard for Nazi Germany's "social policy considerations" for its regional bloc, and stressed that Japan must likewise take "practical

(ii) The backwardness of the Japanese labour system: Hattori too linked his study of the Nazi labour system to his critical analysis of that of Japan. He commented that "the architects of the wartime state control over the economy and labour, as well as their critics" have long turned to Nazi Germany for "examples of precedents".[437] That is why, he said, the Japanese labour ordinances based on the National Mobilisation Law appeared similar to their German counterparts. However, in such areas as the labour system and social policy, Japan lagged far behind Germany, and he illustrated his contention as follows:[438]

(1) The state regulation of wages and working hours legislated in 1939 was the first time Japanese firms and their employees had experienced any form of social policy. This demonstrated, said Hattori, the historical lack of any sort of social policy in the Japanese labour system. In fact, Japan had never had a proper labour system before.

(2) He pointed out that the various new laws and regulations contradicted one another, and that confusion would therefore ensue when they were implemented, since there was a total absence of any basic law for a new labour order that might serve as a basis for legislation or as the core of the labour system. Japan's backwardness was demonstrated by the fact that its government had never moved to legislate a basic labour law such as the Nazi Law for the Organization of National Labour or the Italian Labour Charter. In Japan, therefore, a law regulating labour and a labour system should, he recommended, be brought into being simultaneously with the implementation of the New Economic Order, with the objective of reforming an industrial system that obstructed labour law because of its single-minded pursuit of profit. Only when the Japanese equivalent of the Law for the Organisation of National Labour reflected the ideals of both the General Plan for Establishing a New System of Labour and the New Economic Order would the path be set towards achieving an advanced national defence system.

(3) This backwardness stemmed from a traditional disregard for the autonomy of workers and from the powerfully entrenched, patriarchal authority of the employer. The New Order advocated a cooperative relationship between management and labour in industry, but this had been misunderstood as the subjection of employees to patriarchal authority, and was often exploited by

---

care" upon "establishing the Greater Asia Sphere". See Hattori 1942e, Hattori 1966-1976, vol.4(1974), conclusion.

437 Hattori, 1942b, p. 33, Hattori 1966-1976, vol. 4, chapter 3, part 2, p. 240.

438 Hattori 1941c., Hattori 1966-1976, vol. 4, introduction.

the entrepreneur to strengthen his power to manipulate society. Unlike Nazi Germany, Japan needed to fight against these "traditional, systemic defects".

(4) In order to release labour from arbitrary manipulation by capital and to implement state regulations for the allocation of labour and state control of working conditions, there was a need to establish a state-backed, central organ and to reform the existing organisational structure. Following the example of Nazi Germany, Japan needed to adopt its own version of the Ministry of Labour and the system of Trustees of Labour (*Treuhänder der Arbeit*). Thus it had to reinforce its newly-established system of "Labour Officials" (*rōmukan*) by permitting Labour Officials to intervene in the management of private business, and at the same time allowing the state authority direct involvement with management.

(5) A state with an advanced national defence system is characterised by state control of labour, Hattori stated, but labour is comprised of individuals with their own independent will. It was therefore essential that those who provided the labour were responsibly mature and consciously cooperative in order to increase munitions production. To secure, maintain and nurture workers and to instil in them a sense of responsibility and autonomy, the Industrial Patriotic Association (*Sangyō hōkokukai*) should be given the status of a socially autonomous organisation working to control labour and engage directly in a range of labour-related problems.

Hattori's analysis emphasises the importance of promoting the New Economic Order and the New Labour Order simultaneously. Central to the former were the control associations (*tōseikai*), cartels to impose economic control comprised mainly of the important industries; they were an umbrella group to promote the expansion of production and the nucleus for high-priority industrial reformation. The Industrial Patriotic Association played an important role in the latter as the structural focus of the labour system. Things did not stop there: it was of utmost importance that the two organisations should always work together. The Nazi German model served as a valuable example for this. Hattori looked to Nazi Germany as a structural model for both. He wrote that "Japan can learn a lot from studying the organisational and structural linkages that connect the key organs of the Nazi economic system, commercial and industrial groups and the labour system with the German Labour Front. Lacking an institutional foundation, Japan may not be ready to emulate the German model faithfully. Nonetheless, the Nazi example provides very valuable ideas and suggestions."[439]

439 Hattori, March 1942a, p. 142, Hattori 1966-1976, vol. 4, chapter 2, part 3, p. 200.

In principle, issues concerning social policy and the control of labour in Germany had rested with the institutional support provided by the German Labour Front (DAF), as the central organ of the New Labour Order. Economic groups, as well as private sector self-government organisations, such as chambers of the economy (*Wirtschaftskammer*), did no more than participate in implementing state economic policies, the Four Year Plan and wartime economic controls: they were denied direct involvement in questions of social policy and labour control. However, with the Leipzig Agreement of March 1935, Hjalmar Schacht, the Minister of Economics, sought to bring DAF activities regarding economic policy under the control of the chambers, and new organisations were instituted to handle communication between them: the Reich Industry and Labour Council, Chambers of the Economy and of Labour, and local and occupational labour committees. Hattori was particularly interested in the rapid development of the functions of the labour committees, the lowest ranking of the three.[440]

In Japan, though, unlike Germany, the authority of the control associations, the core institution of the New Economic Order, penetrated the labour force. Moreover, control associations also functioned as cartels. This dual authority was linked, according to Hattori, both to Japan's low level of cartel development and to the underdevelopment of labour unions as well as the suppression of their productive functions. This illustrated for Hattori the structural characteristics of the Japanese economy. Being underdeveloped, Japan needed to set up Nazi-style labour and economic systems and implement a mechanism connecting them. To this end, there should be legislation equivalent to the German Law for the Organisation of National Labour, the Industrial Patriotic Association should be given more power, and both organisations should construct a cooperative relationship. If this was done, the control associations (cartels) would cease to monopolize the control of labour.

Like Kazahaya, Hattori was arrested in November 1942, accused of violating the Peace Preservation Law. In the preceding two years, he had been actively publishing a number of papers on Japanese social policy and the labour system under the wartime economy. Many of these appeared in popular journals like *Chūō Kōron* and *Kaizō*, which had a general readership. Writing about Japan's advanced national defence system, new labour order and social policy, Hattori had to choose his words very carefully, at a time when free speech was being severely suppressed. Nevertheless, he always managed to express his criticism of the current situation, and his sharp eye for spotting problems and his lucid

440 For a discussion of the Leipzig Agreement and its implications, see Mason 1993, pp. 168-171.

analysis make his papers still worth reading today.[441] Because he used Nazi social policy and its labour system as a yardstick for his critical analysis of the Japanese situation, his articles from this period take the form of a comparative study of Nazi Germany and Japan. His main points may be summarised as follows:

(1) Nazi Germany, already at the stage of Monopoly Capitalism, has a typically highly developed industrial structure, and, with a powerful heavy and chemical industry, has established a defence economy. Having inherited a social policy and labour system associated with the stage of Monopoly Capitalism, the Nazi government has finessed the labour system to best adapt it for the national defence economy. This system is beginning to display a new form of the "social state", distinct from the traditional social policy and labour system founded on imperialistic exploitation.

It is the production system, supported by a workforce of cooperative workers labouring on behalf of the wartime economy that particularly characterises Nazi Germany. It is this cooperative system of production that Hattori regards as the modern form of social policy: a labour system that emphasised labour and performance, suppressed profit seeking activities, and practiced developed social policy considerations. This view differs greatly from his previous understanding of the Nazi regime, which focused on the connection between the Nazi party's autocratic power and monopoly capital, and critically viewed their dismantling of the labour unions and denying workers autonomy, as well as their implementation of a totalitarian class structure according to profession. This critical analysis changed dramatically into one that embraced the Nazi regime, even approving its military aggression as the "advancement" of its new social policy and labour system.

Like Kazahaya Yasoji, Hattori regarded the Nazi regime as emerging from the highly evolved stage of capitalism, and focused on its advanced modernity. Also like Kazahaya, Hattori found some elements of the "social state" in the Nazi

441 See Hattori 1966-1976, vol. 4 and explanatory notes to vol. 2. In the postwar period, research into social policy focused particularly on Hattori Eitarō's argument with Ōkōchi Kazuo, and much has been written on this topic. Hattori's criticism of Ōkōchi began with the contemporary analysis of the wartime system. Ujihara 1966 and Nishioka's notes to Hattori's *Collected Works* (Hattori 1966-1976), and those of Nishioka in particular, state that Hattori's interpretation of Nazism at the time was based on an attitude critical to fascism. My own view on this point appears in the text. Tim W. Mason traces the principles of the Nazi labour system and the workplace community to the Weimar Republic, and emphasises continuities from the Weimar system and the modernity of Nazi ideas (Mason 1974).

labour system and social policy, which he saw as being built on the system inherited from the Weimar Republic and its social democracy. In that his view overlaps with observations of Nazism found in postwar comparative studies of Japanese and German fascism by scholars like Maruyama Masao, it can be said such studies have inherited his understanding.[442] Some modern German scholars also regard Nazi ideas about the "social state" important, in that there were certain continuities with it in postwar Western Germany. Recent research in Japan too places emphasis on the effects of rationalisation and modernisation within the wartime total mobilisation system.[443] Hattori contends that the "social state" is established when a country is moving towards the preparatory stage of a wartime economic system, in other words, shifting towards a defence economy, and so can be seen as a predecessor of current German and Japanese scholars.

Hattori also pointed out that the germs of the "social state" had already sprouted during World War I, the first total war ever fought. The Nazi system could not have come into existence had it not been for the "legacy" of the Weimar social democratic labour system, which inherited them. This observation came ever more to the fore with the weakening of his earlier criticism of the totalitarian aspects of the Nazi regime and the state suppression of workers' rights. Hattori was clearly one-sided in his later emphasis on the modern and developed aspects of the Nazi system. Nevertheless, we must take into consideration the fact that he linked his interpretation of the Nazi system closely to criticism of the contemporary labour system and social policy in Japan, despite severe suppression of the freedom of speech and thought. It is tempting to think that Hattori intentionally took such a stand in reaction to the tense political and social climate in which he worked. Certainly the tension under which he produced his studies sets them apart from the products of today's scholarship.

(2) Hattori maintained that Japan had striven to establish a defence economy based on models from the Nazi economic and labour systems, and was getting closer to the German level. Hattori shared this observation with Morito Tatsuo, who put considerable emphasis on the influence of both the German Labour Front and the Nazi idea of works community (*Betriebsgemeinschaft*) on Japan's Industrial Patriotic Association.[444] Hattori approved Japan's closer

442 Maruyama 1964, pp. 56 ff., Maruyama 1995, vol. 3, pp. 288 ff.

443 About the trend and its problematic aspects, see Kawase, 1997. In relation to the trend, see papers by Yamanouchi and M. Prinz, in Yamanouchi et al eds. 1995. See also Prinz and Zitelmann 1991.

444 Morito 1941, especially pp. 12 ff.

approach to the Nazi model in terms of labour and social policy as a move towards modernisation and rationalisation, as well as being connected with the need to expand production and mobilise and strategically allocate labour in a concentrated effort to establish a wartime economy. He thought of this as an epoch-making transformation that would help overcome traditional weaknesses and inefficiencies in the Japanese labour system and improve the labour system structurally.

(3) Hattori's approval was coupled with his critical view of Japan's backwardness in its labour system and social policy, with a lack of any social safety net in the form of a minimum or average wage. He maintained that this backwardness was closely linked with management practices in private enterprises, such as low wages, long working hours, a scramble for skilled workers, a tendency to recruit cheap labour, and overall low productivity, as well as with an aversion to, and evasion of, state control over working conditions. While "the German model of large-scale management is modern and rational", the Japanese model places an "excessive and almost exclusive emphasis on the strength of will power and discipline", while the spirit of leadership appears in the traditionalist mode of "treating the company as a family".[445]

Hattori agreed with Kazahaya that traditional and feudal elements still had a strong hold on Japan's labour system, that its social policy lacked a solid foundation, and that the underdeveloped economic system was the direct cause of the backwardness of the labour system, while "structural dependence on Anglo-American capitalism" and the unequal exchange of goods enforced by Anglo-American imperialism provided an indirect cause. Instead of seeing the relationship between social policy and imperialism only in a conflicting and negative context, Hattori focused on the fact that the social policy of western imperialist countries, including Germany, had been founded on the excess profits gained from forced unequal exchanges with colonies, quasi-colonies and late-emerging capitalist countries, and examined the backwardness of social policy in Japan in this context.[446]

(4) Hattori stressed that a wartime economic and labour system required the drafting of basic laws for labour and social policy and the strengthening of the function of the Industrial Patriotic Association, and that this could help prevent private enterprise from exploiting the workforce. He emphasised that the

445 Hattori 1966-1976, vol. 4, pp. 210 ff. and p. 247.

446 Hattori 1942d, pp. 9 ff., Hattori 1966-1976, vol. 4, chapter 3, part 4, pp. 258 ff. Hattori did not however think that Japan had never gone through its own imperialistic, developmental stage.

Industrial Patriotic Association, the core organisation of the new labour system, should expand its sphere of influence as a stronghold for workers, and advocated that control associations, the base for the New Economic Order, be deterred from unilaterally intervening in the labour system, and urged the two organisations to work in cooperation with one another. Further, state control must be imposed on private industry to stop individual capitalists from exploiting workers arbitrarily and resisting the introduction of measures to improve working conditions. The "public aspects of both labour and management" must be recognised and institutionalised, and this could only be realised through some state control over private business activities.

He believed too that Japan had to implement a social policy not only of "production" but also of "redistribution"; this latter was the form implemented in western countries that thanks to the excess profits generated by imperialism. Japan though had to seek another way, curbing the capitalistic drive for private gain and channelling the funds so generated into social policy planning within the framework of the New Economic Order and the New Labour System, forwarding them both simultaneously. He believed that the unity of "redistribution" and "production" policy was possible only through this process.[447]

(5) Hattori's standpoint was always with labour and workers. He believed that only within the framework of a wartime economy, which enables systemic economic expansion and mobilisation, could workers attain greater autonomy and their own organisation. This however necessitated setting up a structure so workers could actively "cooperate" in the wartime system. Nevertheless, he thought of a distributive and productive social policy and labour system not merely as a temporary objective for the sake of the wartime economy, but as part of the construction of a permanent foundation for a modern and rational social policy and labour system. What he envisioned was the creation of a new Japanese-style social state by means of the wartime economy, an idea shared by Ōkōchi Kazuo and Morito Tatsuo, whose views were more "concrete" and advanced than the "constructive criticism" of previous studies of the system of mobilisation for total war.

(6) As we have already seen, Japan's mobilisation system for total war was inseparable from Tennōism (the emperor system) and the ideology of *kokutai*, the national polity centred on the sole sovereignty of the emperor, while the

447 Hattori thus stressed the significance of a traditional foundation for distributive social policy, which is an implicit criticism of Ōkōchi Kazuo, who regarded social policy as part of economic and production policy.

Industrial Patriotic Association had close links with the ideas of "Kokutai no hongi" (Cardinal Principles of the National Polity), issued by the Ministry of Education in 1937, and *jigyō ikka* (enterprise as family). Hattori was adamantly opposed to Japan's traditional reliance on spirit (*seishinshugi*) and familism (*kazokushugi*). He strongly believed that Japan had to break with such traditions and switch to a modern Nazi-type system. This was regarded by the government as being critical of the national polity and the emperor system, inextricably linked with traditional Japanese spiritism and familism, Hattori was arrested in the autumn of 1942, charged with violating the Peace Preservation Law.

Naniwada Haruo

Knowledge of Nazi Germany in the prewar and wartime periods, and the idea of Japanese distinctiveness based on it, drew attention to what was similar in conditions between Germany and Japan, and what in turn was different to the liberalistic and individualistic ideas of Britain and the United States. The question of what was distinctively Japanese was usually discussed in terms of a perception of what was common between Japan and Germany. There was however another type of discourse that gave a unique value to the Japanese nation itself, based on an emperor system found nowhere else in the world. Such a viewpoint not only rejected Marxism and liberalism but also denied Hitler's Nazism as well, as something completely different in nature to what it was to be Japanese. This was the stance taken by the school of Japanist economics which tried to theorize traditional Japanese thought since ancient times as an economic doctrine. During the war it linked itself with the national power and succeeded in establishing a dominant role for itself. Naniwada Haruo, a leading exponent of this type of theory, serves as a good example for examining the comparison made between Japan and Germany, or, more exactly, the discussion that there was no comparison to be made between the two countries.

Criticism of the Nazi view of labour

In April 1942, Naniwada Haruo (1906-1991) of the Tokyo Imperial University published "A Japanese View of Labour" (*Nihonteki kinrōkan*) as the first volume of a series of books dealing with the theory of Industrial Patriotism, at the request of the Greater Japan Industrial Patriotic Association (Sanpo: *Dai Nippon sangyō hōkokukai*). Its manifesto, taking as its basis the "Cardinal Principles of the National Polity" (*Kokutai no hongi*), included the identification of industry with the national interest, serving the imperial well-being (*kōun fuyoku*), the enterprise as a family (*jigyō ikka*), functional service (*shokubun hōkō*), the prosperity of imperial Japanese industry, the importance of labour, a life of fortitude and honesty (*gōken meirō*) and nurturing national power. Naniwada included the manifesto in his introduction, criticising not only Marxist and individualistic economic thought, but also the "new thought", that is, Nazi economic ideas. He asserted that in Japan, "only a restoration of the economic doctrine of old can be permitted".[448]

Asserting the "destructive function" of liberal and Marxist economic thought, Naniwada positioned Nazism as Germany's saviour from their "baneful influence". This had been possible because the Nazi party had made the race/people (*Volk*) and the racial/people's community (*Volksgemeinschaft*) its supreme ideology. Political supremacy was achieved, with "the economy" reduced to a means to an end. "The priority of common good over self-interest" is the expression of this, he said. Thus Naniwada evaluated the Nazi placing of *Volk* over the economy positively, since it was through this that liberal and Marxist economic ideas were "subjugated". However, he criticised the Nazi economics policy as retaining an antagonistic relationship between management and labour and employing the notion of *Volk* to hold that antagonism in check from without. In this sense, Nazism had not been able to break away completely from individualism.

Naniwada was even more thoroughgoing in his concept of "race" (*minzoku*), and subsumed economics within it. The economic system, he said, takes form as the communal life of human beings and the particular communal (or ethnic) group, so that economic life is not simply a group of individuals engaging in economic activities. Rather the economy, conducted collectively by the communal group, i.e. "race", is a real existence. This means that the individual participates in economic life as a member of a "race", so that capitalists and workers are related first through the racial or communal identity they share, before they are linked through the economy. This being so, he concluded, there can essentially be no antagonistic relationship between the two groups.

The originality of the Japanese communal and national structure

According to Naniwada, what determines the foundation of the economy is the distinctive nation/community (*minzoku*)[449]. Because Japan has a different

448 Naniwada 1942, chapter 1, p. 5. For a full picture of Naniwada's economics and idea of the state, see Ikeda 1988, part 3.

449 *Minzoku* cannot be translated easily. Among the terms used, we find "culture", "ethnos", "nation-state", and "race". Japanese definitions vary, according to the scholar, from "race" to "nation". Early twentieth century discourse tended not to

communal and national structure (*minzoku kōzō*) to other countries, the way its economy works is also different. What makes Japan distinct is its national polity (*kokutai*), a consanguineous and spiritual unity centred on the emperor. By the time the Japanese had become one communal group, "a state whose structure can be seen nowhere else in any other country", had already been formed.[450] This structure was unique because all members of the community, being joined in a blood relationship, belonged to a "family state" (*kazoku kokka*), whose family head was the emperor. It was also unique at a spiritual level, because of the "the unity of the emperor and his subjects" (*kunmin ittai*), expressed through the loyalty and service of all nationals towards the emperor.

Naniwada did not regard this structure as connoting a direct relationship between the people and the state (the "ethno/racial state" under the emperor system). Rather, he viewed the Japanese people in terms of "family" (*ie*) and the connections between families, which came together to make up regional society, that is, "birth place" (*kyōdo*). All were connected in a three-dimensional relationship that Naniwada termed the "communal relationship of the three types of human relations, family, birth place and state".[451] By the expression *minzoku kōzō*, Naniwada meant a community of interacting relationships based on the farming of irrigated rice in a monsoon-type climate, which consisted of the family (not the horizontal relationship between husband, wife and child so much as a vertical communal relationship of blood ties between parent and child), the region/ birth place where families were joined by geographical ties (the natural village) and "the state as a consanguineous and spiritual unity" centring on the emperor.

---

use *minzoku* to mean "race" (in the sense of a definable ethnic group); for example, Rudolph Springer's concepts of "nation" and "state" were introduced with the terms "minzoku" and "kokka" respectively. A work of 1916(Nakamura 1916), quoted in Doak 1998, says "*Minzoku* corresponds both to the English word "nation" and the German word *Volk*. But these two words in English and German are not precisely defined". The author insisted it was a political term, not one based on physical appearance. See Doak 1998, pp. 189-191. This definition of *minzoku* as "nation" has remained influential. However the boundaries between ethnic group/race and nation remain blurred. As a compromise, and because I feel it reflects Naniwada's idea of *minzoku*, which centres on community, with a spiritual and exclusivistic dimension, I will in principle employ the term "nation/community".

450 Naniwada 1942, pp. 45 ff.

451 Naniwada 1938-1943, particularly vol. 4 (1941). This volume had reached its sixth printing within two months, and its tenth printing within five months.

Japanese economics had developed, Naniwada said, on two cornerstones in the face of invasion by foreign capital, the protection of the national wealth and cheap labour. Both of these cornerstones had been supported by "the economy of the rural village". The unfairly heavy financial burden placed on rural villages and the high rents that tenant farmers had to pay brought pressure to bear on the farm economy, resulting in the ejection of cheap labour from the farm into industry. Naniwada insisted that the tenacious and ingrained strength within the farming community to bear this burden was in truth a mark of the threefold communal structure operating within the village. It was because of the "solid family ties and local bonds" of the village and the "strong consciousness of the national polity" there that "the village had continued for seventy years to shoulder the development of modern industry in the cities while bearing a tax burden much higher than in urban centers as well as suffering from high rents."[452] Such a communal/national structure, "the eternal structure belonging to us, the Japanese race", was unique to Japan, and furthermore was the "eternal way of how things should be". Therefore, Naniwada concluded, the wartime economy cannot possibly be established simply by restructuring the existing system; rather, the economy has to be "the communal/national structure itself".

This understanding is in itself a consciousness of the "principles of national rule under the emperor system" (*tennōsei kokka no shihai genri*) and their logical interrogation. Naniwada considered the system of rule by the "emperor" to be a three-dimensional composite – not simply the relationship between the state and the people but rather that between the family state (united in blood and spirit under the emperor) and the family, with these two being further mediated by their relationship with the village community. There is much here that corresponds in terms of sociological analysis with the logic of imperial rule that the intellectual historian Fujita Shōzō developed in his 1966 study, entitled *Tennōsei kokka no shihai genri* (Principles of National Rule under the Emperor System).

It certainly seems as if Naniwada had preceded Fujita, having become aware some thirty years earlier of the concept and practice of what later Fujita would dissect sociologically as a theory of rule comprising the emperor system, the rural community and the family.[453] However, Naniwada's "communal/national structure" has nothing at all to do with "structure" or "mechanism" in socio-economic terms. In contrast to "structure" described in objective terms, it was

452 Ibid., vol. 5, p. 32.

453 Fujita though does not mention Naniwada at all in his work (Fujita 1966, Fujita 1997-1998, vol. 1). For Fujita, see Iida 2006.

simply a "spiritual" structure supporting the nation under the emperor system, related to social consciousness and ideas. In fact it even went beyond an objective spiritual structure, in that it laid out how the system was constituted and how it should perform, with the result it acted as the ideological reasoning for the maintenance and continuation of that system, as well as a means to reinforce it. In other words, Naniwada's "communal/national structure" itself formulated what Fujita called the principles of national rule under the emperor system and was an active factor in the support of that system. An ideology of national rule is clearly revealed in Naniwada's contention that it was "blood and spirit", the consanguineous and spiritual unity centred on the emperor, that demonstrated the "strength and tenacity" of the Japanese, "unlike anywhere else in the world", and that service to the emperor and the unity of sovereign and people were the most important elements in the national makeup.[454]

The logical interrogation and conceptualization of the emperor system and the theory of "communal/national structure" that was one with it, were indivisibly linked with ideology. At the same time it was a self-conscious inquiry that saw the importance of having an ideological construction to support the system of rule. All the same, Naniwada's thought contained many elements that owed to the research of other scholars, though he did not make this point clear. Not least among those elements was the work of the very Marxist scholars whom Naniwada and his group wanted to eliminate. Naniwada adapted their ideas, moulding them around his own point of view. A very important part of his work derived from the use he made of the various studies that emerged from the debate on Japanese capitalism. For example he positively evaluated the characteristics that the Marxian economist Yamada Moritarō (1897-1980) identified as defining capitalism in Japan in his 1934 work *Nihon shihonshugi bunseki* (Analysis of Japanese Capitalism): its militaristic and semi-serf-like character.[455] Naniwada saw militarism as the might to confront the invasion of foreign capital, and the semi-feudal landholding system, semi-serf-like small cultivation, high rents and low wages, which Yamada had decried, as the "tenacious strength" of farmers

---

454 Naniwada 1943, pp 134 et seq.

455 Yamada called emperor system (Tennoism) "Napoleonic", and said it was sustained by the middle class of independent farmer, and spoke of the "two-story arch", with the "patriarchal family" as the lower arch and the "Napoleonic spirit" as the upper. He pointed out the early signs of the breakup of that supporting pillar of the "Napoleonic spirit", middle class farmers who were sustained by sericulture. Yamada 1934, pp. 34 et seq., 52, 61 et seq., 135. Yamada 1983-1985, vol. 2. Naniwada made the Japanese as a whole the supporters of the idea of the communal/national structure.

who had withstood the burdens and pressures imposed upon them by Japanese economic expansion. In the end, Naniwada linked them to the spirit of service to the emperor and the ideology of state, birthplace and family. Naniwada also used works such as *Nihon nōson shakaigaku genri* (Principles of Japanese Rural Sociology, 1940) by Suzuki Eitarō (1894-1966) in his conceptualization of the family and the native place, in one place completely out of context. The concept of the "communal/national structure" was a partial recombination of specific elements of the distinctive Japanese socio-economic structure that had been elucidated by research up to that time and their reconstitution as a spiritual and conceptual framework.[456]

Nazi Similarities with the Japanese Idea of National Distinctiveness

Naniwada Haruo regarded the threefold structure of state, local community and family to be unique to the Japanese, and thought of it as eternal.[457] His ideas had a great influence on ideological and cultural policy before and during the war, beginning with the National Spiritual Mobilization Movement (1937) and the Greater Japan Industrial Patriotic Association (1938) and also functioned as the dominant thought during the time of the wartime economy. However they were considered secondary to the economic ideas that upheld the economic mechanism itself, both at the stage of the war preparedness economy and later the war economy, and were excluded from it. Thus their impact stopped with ideological and spiritual issues. Establishing systems to prepare for total war, and then to wage it, necessitated the restructuring of the existing capitalistic economic

456 For more on Naniwada, see Ōuchi 1962 (2nd printing), p. 301. Suzuki 1940, on which Naniwada depended for his description of the relationship between the family and the native place, studied the social uniformity of the rural village, and at the same time the great changes that came about as a result of trading cooperative regions, cooperative regions of economic interests, and, influenced by Charles J. Galpin, the rural-urban (rurban) community. This was then an analysis of urbanisation and social differentiation in rural villages (village industry). This was an important perspective regarding the internal breakup of the "communal/national structure", but Naniwada ignored it.

457 Yabe Teiji (1902-1967), a professor of the Tokyo Imperial University and an advisor to Konoe Fumimaro, comparing the totalitarianisms of Italy, Germany and Japan, pointed out, in terms of political science, that Japan's totalitarian system was based on a national polity of imperial (Tenno) sovereignty through a theocracy supported by the patriarchy of the people. He insisted that it was the purest model of a totalitarian system in so far as totalitarianism should aim towards the reconstruction of the community. Yabe 1943, S. 81.

mechanism. However Naniwada, who stressed the national ("*minzoku*") regulation of the economy, opposed the basis on which it was to be carried out, reacted by insisting on a strengthening of the idea of the communal/national structure, a spirit of a community founded on ethical human relations, and service to the emperor. His "spiritual" stance opposed the restructuring of the existing capitalist system, calling instead for its preservation as far as possible.

This agreed with the position taken by the business community. As we have seen, business circles had bitterly opposed planned reforms to, and restructuring of, the economic setup as proposed by the Showa Research Association in particular. As well, they had reacted negatively towards the direction being taken by the Cabinet Planning Board and reform bureaucrats in proposing controls on profit-seeking by firms through the New Economic Order. In asserting a Japanese traditionalist "Way of Economics", Naniwada was setting up a contraposition.[458] From the point of view of business circles, Naniwada's ideas must have been welcome, and so his theory of a communal/national structure did not remain simply within the realms of the ideology of the imperial state but was able to serve to bolster the idea that Japanese capitalism should dominate during a period of war.

Naniwada thus effectively rejected economists' theories of the wartime economy and dispassionate discourse on regenerating the wartime economy to expand production. His theories of "nation and the economy" and "augmenting military strength" could not however provide a system for the urgently needed economic mobilisation. His communal/national structure theory remained simply as an ideological construct within the logic of the overall wartime system; its claims contributed to the strengthening of the ideological construct "spiritually", so we can say they played a role in supporting the principles of national rule under the emperor system from the ideological point of view.[459]

Fit-for-purpose restructuring principles aimed at the establishment of a system to prepare for total war as well as a war economy were devised, as we have seen, by reform bureaucrats in the Cabinet Planning Board and other places. They were aware of the Nazi German economic order and its policy thinking and from them extracted a "logic" of structural reform in order to set up systematically a wartime economy. The theory of a national defence economy that

---

458 See Chapter 5 above.

459 After the war, Ōuchi Hyōe 1962 wrote that Naniwada's "Nation and the Economy" (Naniwada 1938-1943) and *Kokutai no hongi* (1937) together formed the basis of Japan's "ideology" and "science". This is an overestimation. We can only see in Naniwada's a straightforward discourse on the idea of Japan's distinctiveness.

they devised included such German-derived ideas as the priority of the common good over self-interest, the leader principle, government and private sector cooperation, the systematization of economic organizations, a community of common interest between management and employees, and restrictions on dividends. Their "logic" was more than simply "logic", however; it included a "spiritual" perspective. Like in Nazi Germany, a "world view" was definitely emphasised as a proviso of structural reform. The reform bureaucrats linked their "logic" to traditionalist ideas about the emperor system, and joined ideas about Japanese distinctiveness that Naniwada had stressed to their own thinking about restructuring the economy, that Naniwada had rejected. The principles of national rule under the emperor system that were incorporated into Japan's "war system" were able to reach completion through the New Economic Order. Naniwada's ideas about the national structure and Japan's distinctiveness were thus united with the very discourse that he himself had rejected, and were to act as a reinforcement of it.[460]

The distinctiveness of Japan's spiritual structure of family, local community and nation that Naniwada had described corresponded to the country's own distinctive economic and social structure. Naniwada did not analyse that structure objectively; in fact he refused to do so. Nevertheless, the Marxian Kōza-ha scholars, had already done so academically, in the course of the debate on Japanese capitalism, and scholars such as Kazahaya Yasoji, Hattori Eitarō, Ōkōchi Kazuo and Ōtsuka Hisao continued their work in this respect.

As we have seen, the extent to which they recognised Japanese distinctiveness varied among them, and this recognition was also connected with comparisons they made with Nazi Germany. Characteristic was Kazahaya, who described Japan as combining "post-Hitler" and "pre-Bismarckian" elements. Nevertheless, Japanese distinctiveness in this case is a difference premised on elements in common with Germany. Modern Nazi Germany, as the outcome of capitalistic growth, was understood as the end of that development. Compared to it, Japanese-type distinctiveness (the Japanese model) was understood to combine two different stages – post-Hitler modernity and pre-Bismarckian backwardness.

460 Fujita 1966, pp. 134 ff., 150 ff., Fujita 1998, I, pp. 166 ff., 186 ff. See also Chapter 5 above. Fujita wrote about the stance of the reform bureaucrats, but made no mention of their conception of the New Economic Order regarding the vitally important expansion of production in wartime, or the controlled economy. As a result, the position of the theory of total war in the principles of national rule under the emperor system is not clear and there is insufficient analysis of its relationship with the nation, local community and family. See the discussion in Takeyama 1982.

Here, Japanese distinctiveness was perceived as "backwardness" capable of a transition to the Nazi German situation, and so homogenous with developments in Germany. For these scholars, making comparisons between Japan and Germany was integrally related to the growth of capitalism.

Naniwada, by contrast, avoided the application of the concept of the capitalist economy to Japan, and made ethno-national characteristics (*minzokusei*) predominant regarding the economy. He regarded the ties of "communities of ethical human relations" (*jinrinteki kyōdōtai*) – that is, nation and community/family (earth and blood) – to be peculiar to Japan. His view permitted capitalistic labour relations when they were completely regulated by such ties, but it was based on an understanding essentially different to the Nazi idea that such relations could be stipulated from without according to the concept of race (*Volk*). To him, the distinctive characteristics of a people were eternal, universal and greatly desirable, and he denied any point of commonality between Japan and Germany in the idea of race/people (*minzoku*).

All the same, this idea that Naniwada so stressed, together with the concept of earth and blood and the world view derived from it with its spiritual and ethical dimension, were also the most important and distinctive features of Nazism. Naniwada's theory of the communal/national structure, which was a criticism of the inadequacy of the Nazi concept of *Volk* and an attempt to make it more thoroughgoing, actually already had a very great deal in common with the Nazi ideas which premised it. In his "Nation and Society" (*Kokka to keizai*), he mentioned that it was Friedrich von Gottl-Ottlilienfeld who had given him the idea of the communal/national structure;[461] Gottl's ideas, which placed great emphasis on the form through which human communal life might be realised, were very close to the Nazi concept of the people's community (*Volksgemeinschaft*) and acquired a place in the official Nazi economics.[462] Nazism regarded *Volk* as the people's community (*Volksgemeinschaft*) linked together in organic harmony by blood and soil (*Blut und Boden*); this *Volksgemeinschaft*, believed to have eternal unity, was given the highest value. The Nazis stressed the need to develop agriculture, and looked to the farming class as the origin of the blood ties of the German people, to protect racial purity, to increase the population and to provide the supply of food,

461 Naniwada 1938-1943, Foreword to vol. 4. Ikeda 1988, pp 64 ff. For the study of Friedrich von Gottl-Ottlilienfeld in Japan, see Ōbayashi 1971. Gottl (1868-1958) was a German economist and a leading figure in the Historical School who distinguished between knowledge-based technological progress and true technical progress in the actual social context.

462 Kruse 1988, pp. 112 ff., Woll 1988, pp. 71 ff., Janssen 2000.

emphasising that they should be strong and healthy.[463] Naniwada's communal/national structure was a Japanese-style recasting of these Gottl and Nazi ideas.

Naniwada's ideas of the relationship between the people and the community of ethical human relations, and of a blood-and-soil based communal/national structure and the Nazi concepts of *Volksgemeinschaft* and *Blut und Boden* completely overlap each other. Similarly, Naniwada's stress on the distinctiveness of the Japanese people, and the Nazi theory of Aryan racial supremacy both share an emphasis on racial superiority and the dissimilarity of other races. Moreover, Naniwada and Nazism alike made these ideas their world view, looking on them as their own unique concepts, and used them as ideological constructs to exact obedience from their people. In this sense too they share a common ground. Naniwada's communal/national structure, which so insisted that it was of a completely different nature to Nazi ideas, in fact exhibited most strongly their shared attributes. Naniwada's ideas about the relationship between the people and the community in terms of human relations in fact exhibited most strongly their shared attributes.

We have seen how Wagatsuma Sakae and Kada Tetsuji criticised characteristic features of Nazi policy, in particular *Volksgemeinschaft* (*Blut und Boden*), racism and anti-Semitism. Nanbara Shigeru, Wagatsuma's colleague in the faculty of law at the Tokyo Imperial University, was another Japanese social scientist who attacked the ideas of *Volksgemeinschaft* linked with racism as irrational. Their criticism of German National Socialism involved at the same time a criticism of the ideological emphasis on the distinctiveness of the Japanese people and on the power of religious Tennoism, not only by the government but by many academics at the universities of wartime Japan. Criticism of Nazi Germany was thus often a metaphor of the Japanese situation at the time, when direct questioning of policy was impossible due to government suppression.

During the war, Naniwada's discourse was greatly valued by the government and succeeding in establishing for itself a dominant role in the sphere of economics. By contrast, critical social scientists like Kazahaya and Hattori who criticised the situation in Japan through a comparison with Germany and were arrested in 1942, were regarded as dangerous by the government. In a situation where the freedom of study and speech was curtailed by the government, Japanese social scientists maintained and developed their analysis of the situation in Japan through comparisons with European countries and the United States, in particular, Germany.

---

463 For an excellent contemporary analysis of this policy from the standpoint of political theory, see Nanbara 1942, ch. 4. For a more recent study, see Nakamura 1990, ch, 4.

Making comparative analyses between Japan and the United States/Europe was not limited to social scientists. We have seen already that leading members of the government accepted the examination of Japanese development through such comparisons. Their acceptance and introduction of the various policies of Nazi Germany, rather than those of liberal Britain and the democratic United States, were the outcome of such comparative examination. In fact, these wartime comparative studies paved the way for the new start of the social sciences in Japan after World War II.

References

Contemporary

Akamatsu, Kaname (1937). *Sangyō tōseiron*, Tokyo: Chikura shōbo.

Akamatsu, Kaname (1942). "Kokubō keizaigaku no sōgō benshōhō". In Akamatsu Kaname, Nakayama Ichirō and Ōkuma Nobuyuki, *Kokubō keizai sōron*. Tokyo: Ganshōdō.

Akimaru, Jirō (1988). *Rōfū jiden* (privately published).

Akimaru, Jirō (1989). "Akimaru kikan no tenmatsu". In *Arisawa Hiromi no Shōwashi*, Hensan iinkai ed. *Kaisō*. Tokyo: Tōkyō daigaku shuppankai, pp. 61-68.

Allen, George Cyrill (1939). *Japanese Industry: Its recent development and present condition*. I. P. R. Inquiry Series, New York.

Arisawa, Hiromi (1931). *Karuteru, torasuto, kontserun*. Tokyo: Kaizōsha.

Arisawa, Hiromi (1937a). *Sensō to keizai*. Tokyo: Nihon hyōronsha.

Arisawa, Hiromi (1937b). *Nihon kōgyō tōseiron*. Tokyo: Yūhikaku.

Army Ordnance (1931). The Journal of the Army Ordnance Association. Pledged to public service in effecting industrial preparedness for war as our strongest guarantee of peace.

Asahi, Isoshi (1939). *The Economic Strength of Japan*. Tokyo: The Hokuseido Press.

Azuma, Mitsutoshi (1942). *Nachisu minpōgaku no seishin*. Tokyo: Iwanami shoten.

Barth, Eberhard (1939). "Der fachliche und regionale Aufbau der gewerblichen Wirtschaft", in Otto Mönckmeier ed. *Jahrbuch für nationalsozialistische Wirtschaft*. München: NSDAP.

Beckerath, Herbert von (1930). *Der moderne Industrialismus*. Jena: G. Fischer. English translation by Robinson Newcomb and Franziska Krebs. *Modern Industrial Organization: an economic interpretation*. New York/London: McGraw-Hill (1933).

Bentham, Jeremy (1789). "Manual of political economy", in John Bowring ed. *The Works of Jeremy Bentham*, vol.3 (1843,1962). New York: Russell & Russell-INC (1962).

Berkenkopf, Paul (1936). "Gewerbe und Gewerbepolitik", in H. H. Lammers and H. Pfundtner eds., *Grundlagen, Aufbau und Wirtschaftsordnung des nationalsozialistischen Staates*, vol. 3, Berlin.

Berle, Adolf A. and Means, Gardiner C (1932). *The Modern Corporation and Private Property*, first ed., New York: the Macmillan Company, 1932, rev. ed., New York, 1968. A Japanese translation (1958) by Kitajima Tadao, Tokyo: Bungadō ginkō kenkyūsha.

Bloomfield, Mayer (1919). *Management and Men. A record of new steps in industrial relations*. New York: The Century Co.

Bonn, Moritz Julius (1934, 1935). "Rationalization". In *Encyclopaedia of the Social Sciences*. New York: Macmillan.

Brady, Robert (1933 [1974]). *The Rationalization Movement in Germany: A study in the evolution of economic planning*. Berkeley: University of California Press.

Chō, Moriyoshi (1933). *Nachisu – Hittorā undō, shisō, seisaku*. Tokyo: Nihon hyōronsha. Included in Chō 1939.

Chō, Moriyoshi (1934). *Fasshoteki tōsei keizai*. Tokyo: Nihon hyōronsha.

Chō, Moriyoshi (1939). *Nachisu keizai kensetsu*. Tokyo: Nihon hyōronsha.

Cohen, Jerome B. "The Japanese economy, 1940-1945." *Far Eastern Survey*, vol. 15, no. 24 (Dec. 4, 1946), pp. 361-370.

Cole, George Douglas Howard (1921), *Guild Socialism: A plan for economic democracy*. New York: Frederick A. Stokes Company. New edition Red and Black Publishers, 2009.

Colegrove, K. (1938). "Japan as a totalitarian state." *Amerasia* (March 1938).

Contemporary Japan (1936)(1941). A Review of Japanese Affaires. Foreign Affaires Association of Japan.

Dictionary of Economics (1930-36), ed. Osaka University of Commerce. Tokyo: Iwanami shoten.

Dutt, R. Palme (1934). *Fascism and Social Revolution*. London: M. Lawrence Ltd. Japanese translation 1935.

Fahs, Charles B. (1940). *Government in Japan, Recent Trends in its Scope and Operation*. I.P.R Inquiry Series. New York: Institute of Pacific Relations.

Feder, Gottfried (1919). Das Manifest zur Brechung der Zinsknechtschaft des Geldes. ("Manifesto for Breaking the Bondage of Interest"). *Kritische Rundschau 2*. In Barbara Miller Lane and Leila J. Rupp eds., *Nazi ideology before 1933: a documentation*. Manchester University Press ND, 1978.

Feder, Gottfried (1924). *Der Deutsche Staat auf nationaler und sozialer Grundlage. Neue Wege in Staat, Finanz und Wirtschaft*. München. (12th ed. 1933).

Feder, Gottfried (1927) (146.-155. ed.1934). *Das Programm der N.S.D.A.P. und seine weltanschaulichen Grundgedanken*. München.

Fischer, Guido (1936). *Wehrwirtschaft. Ihre Grundlage und Theorien*. Leipzig: Verlag von Quelle & Meyer. Japanese translation by JMG *Junsen keizai to senji keizai* (mimeograph, October 1937). Also another by Itō Kōdō, *Kokubō keizairon*, Banrikaku, 1940.

Frederick, J. George (1932). *Readings in Economic Planning*. New York: The Business Bourse.

Fujita, Keizō (1932). "Rātenau", in *Keizaigaku Jiten*, vol. 5. Tokyo: Iwanami shoten.

Fujita, Keizō (1936). *Karuteru tōsōron*. Osaka: Kōbundō shoten.

Fukuda, Yoshiharu (1939). *Furansu keikaku keizai* (*Sekai keikaku keizai* 4). Tokyo: Kawade shobō.

Funk, Walther (1941). *Wirtschaftsordnung in neuen Europa*, Wien June 1941.

Gō-danshaku kinenkai (1943, reprinted 1988). *Danshaku Gō Seinosuke kun den*. Tokyo.

Godō, Takuo (1939). "Jikyoku to sangyōjin", in Monbushō kyōgakukyoku ed. *Kyōgaku sōsho*, vol. 5. 5th ed. May 1944.

Gotō, Kiyoshi (1934). "Nachisu no rōdō hōsei", in Sugimura et al eds., *Nachisu no hōritsu*. Tokyo: Nihon hyōronsha.

Hasegawa, Yasube (1937). *Haitō tōsei no kenkyū*, Tokyō: Chikura shobō.

Hasegawa, Yasube (1942). "Senji keizaika no haitō seigen", in *Keiei keizai no shomondai*, ed. Ueda Sadajirō hakase kinen ronbunshū hensan iinkai, Tokyo: Kagakushugi kōgyōsha.

Hashimoto, Katsuhiko (1940). A Japanese translation of T. Veblen, *Absentee Ownership and Business Enterprise in Recent Times: the Case of America* as *Amerika shihonshugi hihan*, Tokyo: Hakuyōsha.

Hattori, Eitarō (1934). "Doitsu shakai minshushugi shakai seisaku ron no hōkai katei", in Tōhoku Imperial University, the Faculty of Law and Literature ed. *Jushūnen kinen keizai ron shū*, Tokyo: Iwanami shoten.

Hattori, Eitarō (1935). "'Zentai shugi = shokugyō mibun teki' shakai seisaku riron kōsō no kadai – doitsu shakai seisaku ron shi danpen", in Tōhoku Imperial University, the Economic Society ed. *Kenkyū nenpō keizaigaku*, vol. 3.

Hattori, Eitarō (April 1941a). "Nachisu 'shakai kokka' no tenbō", in *Chūō kōron* the 56th year, spring special issue. Tokyo: Chūō kōronsha.

Hattori, Eitarō (April 1941b). "Nachisu no ōshūshinshakai-chitsujo no kōsō", in *Kaizō*, vol.23, no 7.

Hattori, Eitarō (September 1941c). "Kōdo kokubō kokka to rōdō taisei no shinro", in *Chūō kōron*, the 56th year, no 9. Tokyo: Chūō kōronsha.

Hattori, Eitarō (March 1942a). "Senji shakai seisaku to keizai = kinrō shintaisei – sanpō to tōseikai no kanren ni oite –" *Shōkō keizai*, vol.13, no. 3.

Hattori, Eitarō (June 1942b). "Senji rōdō to seisan zōkyō no kadai", in *Nihon hyōron*, vol. 17, no. 6. Tokyo: Nihon hyōronsha.

Hattori, Eitarō (1942c). "Yōroppa kōiki ken shakai seisaku no tenkai", in *Chosakushū* (1967-1976), Hokan. Tokyo: Miraisha.

Hattori, Eitarō (1942d). "Kinrō-seisanryoku kōyō no nihonteki-kadai", in *Kaizō*, vol. 24, no. 7.

Hattori, Eitarō (August 1942e). "*Daitōa kensetsu ni okeru kinrō taikei*", in *Chūō kōron*, the 57th year, no. 8, Tokyo: Chūō kōron.

Hattori, Eitarō (1967). *Chosakushū I: Doitsu shakai seisaku ron shi*, vol. 1, Tokyo: Miraisha.

Hattori, Eitarō (1966-1976). *Hattori Eitarō chosakushū*, Tokyo: Miraisha.

Heiden, Konrad (1934). *A History of National Socialism*. London: Methuen. Translated from *Geschichte des Nationalsozialismus* (1932) and *Geburt des dritten Reiches* (1934).

Helfferich, Emil (1940). "A New Economic World Order". *Contemporary Japan*, June 1940, pp. 706-713.

Helfferich, Emil (1965). "Lenkung und Leistung der deutschen Wirtschaft. Vortrag (gekürzt) vor der "Japan Economic Federation" im Industriellen Klub in Tokyo am 12. März 1940", in *Ein Leben*, vol. 5. His speech was published in *Keizai jōhō* (June 1940), as Staatsrat Emil Helfferich, Sensō tōsei to kigyō sōi – Doitsu tōsei keizai no genjō (*Keizai jōhō seikei hen*).

Helfferich, Emil (1948-1965). *Ein Leben*. vols 1-4. Hamburg: Dulk, 1948-64; vol. 5. Mettcker und Söhne, Jever 1965.

Hijikata, Seibi (1932). *Fashizumu*. Tokyo: Iwanami shoten.

Hijikata, Seibi (1933a). "Tōsei keizai to Nihon seishin". *Keizai ōrai*, vol. 8, no. 3 (March 1933).

Hijikata, Seibi (1933b). *Tōsei keizai seiji kikō. Nihon tosei Keizai zenshu*, vol. 7. Tokyo: Kaizōsha.

Hilferding, Rudolf (1910). *Das Finanzkapital. Eine Studie über die jüngste Entwicklung des Kapitalismus*, Vienna: Brand.

Hoashi, Kei (1941). *Tōseikai no riron to jissai*. Tokyo: Shinkeizaisha.

Hoche, Werner ed. (1933-1939). *Die Gesetzgebung des Kabinetts Hitler: die Gesetze in Reich und Preußen seit dem 30. Januar 1933 in systematischer Ordnung*. Berlin: F. Vahlen.

Holt, John Bradshaw (1936). *German Agricultural Policy*. Chapel Hill: University of North Caroline Press.

Hon'iden, Yoshio (1938). *Tōsei keizai no riron*, Tokyo: Nihon hyōronsha.

Hon'iden, Yoshio (1940). *Shintaiseika no keizai*. Tokyo: Nihon hyōronsha.

Hoover, Calvin (1933). *Germany Enters the Third Reich*. New York: The Macmillan Company.

Hoover, Calvin (1937). *Dictators and Democracies*. New York: The Macmillan Company.

Horitsu Jihō (1934).

Ishikawa, Hiroyoshi ed.(1990). *Yoka-goraku kenkyu kisobunken-shū*, vol. 16. Tokyo: Ōzora-sha.

Ishikawa, Kōji (1940). *Shintaisei no shidō genri*, Tokyo: Yūhikaku.

Itō, Kōdō (1940). *Kokubo keizairon*. Tokyo: Banrikaku.

Jitsugyō no nihon (January 1941). Kakushin-kanryō, shintaiseio kataru-zadankai.

Kada, Tetsuji (1932a). *Kokuminshugi to kokusaishugi*. Tokyo: Dōbunkan.

Kada, Tetsuji (1932b). *Nihon kokka shakaishugi hihan*. Tokyo: Shunjūsha.

Kada, Tetsuji (1933). "Doitsu kokumin shakaishugi no keizaikan". *Mita gakkai zasshi*, vol. 27, no. 3. Reprinted almost in its entirety in Kada 1940a.

Kada, Tetsuji (1939). *Jinshu, minzoku, sensō*. Tokyo: Keiō shobō.

Kada, Tetsuji (1940a). *Tenkanki no seiji keizai shisō*. Tokyo: Keiō shobō.

Kada, Tetsuji (1940b). *Seiji, keizai, minzoku*. Tokyo: Keiō shobō.

Kada, Tetsuji (1942a). *Sensō honshitsuron*. Tokyo: Keiō shobō.

Kada, Tetsuji (1942b). *Nihon keizai gakusha no hanashi*. Tokyo: Keiō shobō.

Kagakushugi kōgyō (June 1938).

Kaizō jikyoku ban 14 (1941). Keizai shintaisei no jittai.

Kaizō jikyoku ban 14 (1941). Kakushin kanryō shintaisei wo kataru zadankai.

Kawashima, Takeyoshi (1949). *Shoyūkenhō no riron*. Tokyo: Iwanami shoten. New edition 1987.

Kazahaya, Yasoji (1937a and 1938 (the 4th edition)). *Nihon shakai seisaku-shi*, Tokyo: Nihon hyōronsha. Reissued in two volumes in 1951, Tokyo: Aoki bunko.

Kazahaya, Yasoji (December, 1937b). "Nihon sangyō kikō to seisan-ryoku kakujū", in *Kagaku shugi kōgyō*, vol. 1, no. 7.

Kazahaya, Yasoji (1938a). "Daisan no michi", in *Rōdō no riron to seisaku*, Tokyo: Jichōsha.

Kazahaya, Yasoji (January, 1938b). "Nihon sangyō shihon no kachi kōsei no henka o tsujite mita seisanryoku kakujū", in *Kagakushugi kōgyō*, vol. 1, no. 8.

Kazahaya, Yasoji (July-October 1939a). "Nihon sangyō kikō no saihensei *(1-4)*", in *Kagaku shugi kōgyō*, vol. 3, nos. 2-5.

Kazahaya Yasoji (September 1939b). "Nihon no senji keizai shinten to shakai rōdō seisaku", in *Shin-doitsu, Shin-doitsu kokka taikei geppō, vol. 3.*

Keizaigaku jiten (1930-32). Ed. Institute of Economics, Osaka University of Commerce. Tokyo: Iwanami shoten.

Keizai jōhō, seikei-hen (March 1940).

Keizai ōrai. (May 1932).

Keizai renmei (January 1941), vol. 11, nos. 1 and 2.

Keynes, J.M. (1926). *The End of Laissez-faire*, London: Hogarth Press. In *The Collected Writings of John Maynard Keynes*, 1931, 1972. An German translation: *Das Ende des Laissez-Faire. Ideen zur Verbindung von Privat- und Gemeinwirtschaft*. München & Leipzig: Duncker & Humblot, 1926. A Japanese translation by Miyazaki Giichi (1981), *Keynes zenshū*, vol. 9, Tokyo: Tōyō keizai shinpōsha.

Kikaku (January 1938).

Kikakuin ed. (1938). *Sekai keikaku keizai,* 6 vols (vol 4, 1939). Tokyo: Kawade shobō.

Kikakuin ed. (1989). *Kokka sōdōin hō*. Facsimile edition. Tokyo: Nihon tosho sentā.

Kikuchi, Haruo (1940). *Nachisu senji keizai taisei kenkyū*. Tokyo: Tōyō shokan.

Kikuchi, Haruo (1941). *Nachisu rōmu dōin taisei kenkyū*, Tokyo: Toyō shokan.

Kimura, Masutarō (1939). "Keizai dantai no chūsūkikan mondai", in *Kagakushugi kōgyō,* vol. 2, no. 11 (April).

Kinoshita, Hanji ed. (1941). *Shintaisei jiten*. Tokyo: Asahi shinbunsha.

Kishi Nobusuke (1932). "Ōshū ni okeru sangyō gōrika no jissai ni tsuite", *Sangyō gōrika,* 4.

Kishi Nobusuke (1934). "Sangyō gōrika yori tōsei keizai e." *Sangyō gōrika,* 12.

Koana, Tsuyoshi (1938). *Doitsu kokubō keizairon*. Tokyo: Moriyama shoten.

Koana, Tsuyoshi translated and edited (1939). *Sensō keizai to shōkō kaigisho*. Tokyo: Shōkō gyōseisha.

Koana, Tsuyoshi (1940). *Nachisu no sensō keizai seisaku*. Tokyo: Jidaisha.

Kobayashi, Ryōsei ed. (1942). *Shin Doitsu seiji keizai goi*. Tokyo: Nikkō shoin.

Koellreutter (1939). "National Socialism and Japan", *Contemporary Japan* vol. VIII, No. 2, April 1939, pp. 178-188.

Kojima, Seiichi (1929). *Sangyō gōrika*. Tokyo: Chikura shobō.

Kojima, Seiichi (1930). *Kigyō tōsei-ron*. Tokyo: Chikura shobō.

Kojima Seiichi (1932). *Nihon keikaku keizairon*. Tokyo: Chikura shōbo.

Kojima, Seiichi (1939). "Keizai dantai no zenmenteki kaiso o ronzu", *Shōko keizai,* vol. 7, no. 2 (February).

Kojima, Seiichi (1940). *Nachisu tōsei keizai dokuhon*. New edition. Tokyo: Chikura shōbo.

Kojima, Seiichi (1941). *Nihon senji sangyō tōseiron*. Tokyo: Chikura shōbo.

Kokusaku kenkyūkai monjo mokuroku (1991). Ed. Tōkyō daigaku fuzoku toshokan. Tōkyō: Yūshōdō Shuppan.

Kolbe, W., H. Martzloff, F. Behrens eds. (1939). *Der Vierjahresplan. Eine Sammlung der amtlichen Bestimmungen erläutert aus der praktischen Arbeit.* Berlin-Halensee 1936.

Kunihiro, Kazuto (1939). *Tōsei keizai to karuteru, kumiai*. Tokyo: Nihon hyōronsha.

Kyōchōkai ed. (1936). *Nachisu rōdōhō*. Tokyo: Kyōchōkai.

Kyōchōkai kaiwakai (1945). *Zaidanhojin kyochokai-shi*. Tokyo.

Lederer, Emil (1922). *Grundzüge der ökonomischen Theorie*. Tübingen: J.C.B. Mohr. Translated into Japanese in 1926 by Arisawa Hiromi and Ōmori Yoshitarō as *Riron keizaigaku* (Tokyo: Meizensha).

Lederer, Emil (1925). "Konjunktur und Krisen", in *Grundriss der Sozialökonomik*, vol. 4, *Spetifische Elemente der Modernen Kapitalistischen Wirtschaft*, Part 1. Tübingen: J.C.B. Mohr, pp. 354-413. Translated into Japanese in 1939 by Tanaka Seiichi.

Lederer, Emil (1931). *Technische Fortschritt und Arbeitslosigkeit*. Tübingen: J.C.B. Mohr; Genf 1938. Translated into Japanese in 1942 by Takayama Yokichi as *Gijutsu keizairon* (Tokyo: Kagakushugi kōgyōsha).

Lee, John (1923). *Industrial Organization, Developments and Prospects*. New York: Prentice-Hall.

Lehnich, Oswald (1928). *Kartelle und Staat; unter Berücksichtigung der Gesetzbung des In-und Auslandes*. Berlin: R. Hobbing.

Liefmann, Robert (1930). *Kartelle, Konzerne und Trusts*. Stuttgart: Ernst Heinrich Moritz. 8th edition.

Ludendorff, Erich (1935). *Der totale Krieg*. München: Ludendorffs Verlag, g.m.b.h. Translated into Japanese by Mano Toshio as *Kokka sōryokusen* (Tokyo: Mikawa shobō, 1938). Translated into English as *The Nation at War* (London: Hutchinson, 1936).

Machida, Tatsujirō (1935).Kyōchōkai shakaiseisaku-gakuin gakuyukai, *Shuchō*, no. 14, June.

Machida Tatsujirō (1940). "Sangyō hōkoku undō no gensei to sangyō hōkokukai no kinō". *Tōsei keizai*, vol. 1, no. 3 (November).

Makino Sensei kanreki shukuga hōrironshū (1938). Tokyo: Yūhikaku.

Mann, F. A. (1937). "The new German company law and its background". *Journal of Comparative Legislation and International Law*, Third Series, vol. XIX, part IV.

Mansfeld, Werner ed. (1941). *Die Ordnung der nationalen Arbeit*. 12th ed. Berlin: C. Heymann.

"March of Events" (1940). *Contemporary Japan*, vol. IX, no. 12, December 1940. pp. 178-188.

Marshall, Alfred (1890). *Principles of Economics*, London: Macmillan, 2nd ed. 1891, 3rd ed. 1895, 4th ed. 1898, 5th ed. 1907, 6th ed. 1910, 8th ed. 1927. A Japanese translation by Baba Keinosuke, Tokyo: Tōyō keizai shinpōsha, 1965-1967.

Marshall, Alfred (1907). "The social possibilities of economic chivalry", *Economic Journal*, vol. 17, no. 65 (March 1907). A Japanese translation by Kanamaki Kenji in *Masharu Keizaigaku Senshū* (Selected Works of Marshall Economics), Sugimoto Eiichi ed., Tokyo: Nihon hyōronsha, 1940 (3rd ed.).

Marshall, Alfred (1919). *Industry and Trade*. London: Macmillan. 4th ed. 1924.

Masuchi, Yōjirō (1944). "Gunju gaisha no seikaku", in *Gunju gaisha*, vol. 1 of *Kōgyō keieiron shū*. Tokyo: Sankaidō.

Matsumoto, Jōji (1940), *Kabushiki gaisha hōkaisei no yōten*. Tokyo: Ganshōdō shoten.

Matsuo, M. (1935). "The control of industry in Japan." *Far Eastern Survey*, vol. 4, no. 14.

Matsuo. M. (1936). "The Japanese state as industrialist and financier." *Far Eastern Survey*, May 25, 1936, pp. 105-110.

Miki, Kiyoshi (1938). "The China affair and Japanese thought". *Contemporary Japan*, vol. VI, no. 4, March 1938, pp. 601-610.

Miki, Kiyoshi (1939). *Shin-Nihon no shisōgenri* in *Miki Kiyoshi zenshū*, vol. 17. Tokyo: Iwanami shoten.

Minemura, Teruo (1942). *Hō to tōsei keizai*. Tokyo: Tōyō shokan.

Minobe, Yōji (1938). "Kōgyō seisaku no Nihonteki tenkan". *Kagakushugi kōgyō*, vol. 2, no. 1 (June).

Minobe, Yōji (1941a). "Keizai shintaisei kanken". *Nihon hyōron* 16 (March).

Minobe, Yohji (1941b). "The principles of the new economic structure". *Contemporary Japan*, February 1941, pp. 178-188.

Minobe, Yōji (1942). *Senji keizai taisei kōwa*, Tokyo: Tachibana shoten.

Minoguchi, Tokijirō (1940). "Kōdo kokubō kokka to rōdō taisei". *Tōsei keizai*, vol. 1, no. 3 (November).

Mises, Ludwig Edler von (1929), *Die Kritik des Interventionismus. Untersuchung zur Wirtschaftspolitik und Wirtschaftsideologie der Gegenwart*. Jena: Gustav Fischer Verlag. English translation *A Critique of Interventionism*, 1976.

Mitsufuji, Masaru (1941) "Waga kabushiki gaishahō no seikaku to sono henshitsu" 1, 2, *Minshōhō zasshi*, vol. 14, nos. 5 and 6.

Miura, Tetsutarō (1939). *Shin keizai taisei no riron to shian*. Tokyo: Tōyō keizai shinpōsha.

Miyazaki, Masayoshi (1938). *Tōa renmeiron*. Tokyo: Kaizōsha.

Monbushō ed. (1937). *Kokutai no hongi*. Tokyo: Monbushō. English translation: *Kokutai no hongi: Cardinal principles of the national entity of Japan*. Cambridge, Mass: Harvard University Press, 1949.

Mori, Takeo (1933, 1939). *Senji tōsei keizairon*. Tokyo: Nihon hyōronsha.

Morito, Tatsuo (1941). *Doitsu rōdō sensen to sangyō hōkoku undō*. Tokyo: Kaizōsha.

Mowrer, Edgar Ansel (1933). *Germany Puts the Clock Back*. London: John Lane Company.

Mukai, Shikamatsu (1926). *Torihikisho no rironteki kenkyū*. Tokyo: Maruzen.

Mukai, Shikamatsu (1927). *Shōken shizyō soshiki*. Tokyo: Maruzen.

Mukai, Shikamatsu (1928). *Haikyū shizyō soshiki*. Tokyo: Maruzen.

Mukai, Shikamatsu (1929). *Keiei keizaigaku sōron*. Tokyo: Chikura shobō.

Mukai, Shikamatsu (1931). *Sangyō no gōrika*. Tokyo: Nihon hyōronsha.

Mukai, Shikamatsu (1932). *Sōgō torihikisho ron*. Tokyo: Nihon hyōronsha.

Mukai Shikamatsu (1933). *Tōsei keizai genri. Nihon tosei keizai zenshū*, vol.1. Tokyo: Kaizōsha.

Mukai, Shikamatsu (1934). *Torihikisho tōki to kabushiki kinyū*, Tokyo: Moriyama shoten.

Mukai, Shikamatsu (1934). *Shōgyō kumiai keiei ron*, Tokyo: Tōyō shuppansha.

Mukai, Shikamatsu (1937). *Gendai shōgyō gairon*, Tokyo: Ganshōdō shoten.

Mukai, Shikamatsu (1938). *Nihon shōgyō seisaku*, Tokyo: Chikura shobō.

Mukai, Shikamatsu (1943). "Keikaku keizai ka no keizai dantai". *Tōsei keizai*, vol. 6, no. 1.

Muramoto, Fukumatsu (1937). *Seisan kanri*. Tokyo: Chikura shobō.

Naimushō keihokyoku ed. (1938). *Shakai undō no jōkyō, 10*. Reprint (1971-72) Tokyo: San'ichi shobō.

Nakagawa, Yonosuke (1944). *Nachisu shakai no kihon kōzo no kenkyū*. Kyoto: Yamaguchi shoten.

Nakajima, Kumakichi (1931). "Sangyō gōrika ni okeru sandai kichō". In *Sangyō gōrika shiryō*, 2nd series. Tokyo: Tōkyō shōkō kaigisho.

Nakajima, Kumakichi (1951). *Seikai zaikai 50 nen*. Tokyo: Dai Nippon yūbenkai kōdansha.

Nakamura (Nakayama), Kyūshirō (1916). *Kyokutō no Minzoku. Gendai sōsho.* Supervision Tokutomi Iichirō, ed. Yoshino Sakuzō. Tokyo: Minyūsha.

Nakanishi, Torao (1932). "Kabushiki gaisha ni okeru shoyū to keiei no bunri", *Keiei keizai kenkyū,* 13.

Nakanishi, Torao (1968). "Keiei kōzo no henka to toppu manejimento no yakuwari", in *Gendai keieigaku no kenkyū*, eds. Nakamura Tsunejirō, Ōtsuka Hisao, Nabeshima Tatsu and Mōri Shigetaka. In *Yanagawa Noboru sensei kanreki kinen ronbunshū*, Tokyo: Nihon seisansei honbu shuppanbu.

Nakayama Ichirō zenshū (1973). 10 vols. Tokyo: Kodansha.

Nanbara, Shigeru (1942). *Kokka to shūkyō*. Tokyo: Iwanami shoten.

Naniwada, Haruo (1938-1943). *Kokka to keizai*, 5 vols. Tokyo: Nihon hyōronsha.

Naniwada, Haruo (1942). *Nihonteki kinro-kan*. Dainihon-sangyō hōkokukai. Tokyo.

Naniwada, Haruo (1943). *Senryoku zōkyo no riron*. Tokyo: Yuhikaku.

Nathan, Otto (1944). *The Nazi Economic System. Germany's mobilization for war.* Duke University Press. Reissued 1971, New York: Russell & Russell.

National Industrial Conference Board (1931). *Rationalization of German Industry*. New York: National Industrial Conference Board.

Naumann, Friedrich (1897). *National-sozialer Katechismus*. Berlin: Buchverlag der "Zeit" (Bousset & Kundt).

Naumann, Friedrich (1915). *Mitteleuropa*. Berlin. English translation: *Central Europe*, with an introduction by W.J. Ashley and translated by C.M. Meredith. London: P.S. King & Son, Limited, 1916.

Neumann, Franz (1942, 1944). *Behemoth: The Structure and Practice of National Socialism 1933-1944.* First edition 1942, Oxford: Oxford University Press; Second edition 1944, Toronto, New York etc.: Oxford University Press; Reprinted 1963, New York: Octagon Books.

Nichiman zaisei keizai kenkyūkai ed. (1937a). *Nachisu keizaihō*. Tokyo: Nihon hyōronsha.

Nichiman zaisei keizai kenkyūkai ed. (1937b). *Doitsu ni okeru gunju kōgyō no taisei*. Tokyo: Nichiman zaisei keizai kenkyūkai.

Nichiman zaisei keizai kenkyūkai (1937c). *Junsen keizai to senjikeizai.*

Nichiman zaisei keizai kenkyūkai ed. (1938). *Doitsu yonkanen keikaku hōrei shū*. Tokyo: Japanese translation of Kolbe et al., 1939.

Nichiman zaisei keizai kenkyūkai shiryō (1970). Tokyo: Nihon kindai shiryō kenkyūkai.

Nihon hyōron (March 1941).

Nihon keizai renmeikai (February 1940), *Doitsu ni okeru tōsei keizai no jitsujō.*

Nihon kōgyō kurabu chōsaka (December 1940 and the third edition, February 1941). *Hitora-seijika doitsu shihonshugi no henbō.* Tokyo: Jitsugyo no nihonsha.

Nihon kōsei kyōkai (1939). *Daiikkai Nihon kosei taikai hōkokusho.*

Nihon shihonshugi hattatsushi kōza (1932-33). Tokyo: Iwanami shoten.

Nihon tōsei keizai zenshū (1933-34). 10 vols. Tokyo: Kaizōsha.

Vol. 1, *Tōsei keizai genri* (Principles of the controlled economy), Mukai Shikamatsu (1933).

Vol. 2, *Tsūka shinyō tōsei hihan* (Criticism of currency credit control), Ryū Shintarō (1934).

Vol. 3, *Kakaku tōseiron* (On price control), Kawai Yoshinari (1933).

Vol. 4, *Tōsei keizai zaiseiron* (On the controlled economy and finances), Itō Hanya (1933).

Vol. 5, *Nihon keizai tōseiron* (On Japanese economic control), Takahashi Kamekichi (1933).

Vol. 6, *Sangyō dōin keikaku* (Planning industrial mobilization), Arisawa Hiromi (1934).

Vol. 7, *Tōsei keizai seiji kikō* (Political framework for a controlled economy), Hijikata Seibi (1933).

Vol. 8, *Nichiman tōsei keizai* (The controlled economy in Japan and Manchuria), Kojima Seiichi (1933).

Vol. 9, *Tōsei keizai hihan* (Criticism of the controlled economy), Inomata Tsunao (1934).

Vol. 10, *Tōsei keizairon sōkan* (General view of the debate over the controlled economy), Sakisaka Itsurō (1934).

Nishihara, Kan'ichi (1936). "Kabushiki gaisha ni okeru nachisu shisō" Part 1, *Hōgaku kyōkai zasshi,* vol. 54, no. 8.

Ohlin, Bertil (1938). "On the future economic organization of society", in *The World's Economic Future* (Sir Halley Stewart Lecturers, 1937). London: Allen & Unwin.

Ōkōchi, Kazuo (1979). *Kurai tanima no jiden*. Tokyo: Chūō kōronsha.

Ōkōchi, Masatoshi (1941). *Seisan dai'ichishugi*. Tokyo: Kagaku shugi kōgyōsha.

The Oriental Economist (1934)(1940). Tokyo: Tōyōkeizai shinpōsha.

Ōshima, H. T. (1942). "Japan's 'New Economic Structure'». *Pacific Affairs*, vol. 15, no. 3, pp. 261-279.

Ōsumi, Ken'ichirō (1932). "Kabushiki gaisha no kihon kannen ni kansuru Hausuman no kenkai" 1, *Hogaku ronshū*, vol. 27, no. 4.

Ōsumi Ken'ichirō (1953). *Kabushiki gaishahō hensenron* 3, Tokyo:Yūhikaku.

Ōsumi, Ken'ichirō, Yagi, Hiroshi and Ōmori, Tadao eds. (1937). *Doitsu shōhō, III Kabushikihō*, Tokyo: Yūhikaku. Reissued, 1956, Yūhikaku.

Ōtsuka, Hisao (1938). *Kabushiki gaisha hasseishi ron*, Tokyo: Yūhikaku. In *Ōtsuka Hisao chosakushū*. Tokyo: Iwanami shoten, 1969.

Ōtsuka, Hisao (1965), "Betrieb to keizai gōrishugi", in Ōtsuka Hisao ed. *Makkusu Vebā kenkyū*. Tokyo: Tokyo daigaku shuppankai. vol. 1.

Ōtsuka, Hisao (1969). *Ōtsuka Hisao chosakushū*, vol. 1. Tokyo: Iwanami shoten.

Ōtsuka, Hisao (1982). *The Spirit of Capitalism. The Max Weber thesis in an economic historical perspective*. Translated by Masaomi Kondo. Tokyo: Iwanami shoten, 1982.

Ottwalt, Ernst (1932). *Deutschland erwache! Geschichte des Nationalsozialimus*. Vienna and Leipzig: Hess.

Ōuchi, Hyōe (1937a). "Zōzei rokuoku, genzei san'oku. Sono kokuminteki igi", in *Chuokoron*, the 52th year, New year edition 1937.

Ōuchi, Hyōe (1937b). "Nachisu no shinchiho-seido wa chuōtōsei de naika", in *Chuo koron*, the 52th year, April.

Ōuchi, Hyōe (1962) (2.ed.). *Keizaigaku 50nen*. Tokyo: Tokyo daigaku shuppankai.

Passow, Richard (1930). *Kartelle*. Jena: G. Fischer.

Paul, Eden and Cedar (1921). *In Days to Come*. London: George Allen & Unwin Ldt.

Rathenau, Walther (1917). *Von kommenden Dingen*. Berlin: S. Fischer. Reissued in *Gesammelte Schriften*, vol. 3. Berlin: S. Fischer, 1925. Translated into English by E. and C. Paul as *In Days to Come*, London: G. Allen and Unwin, 1921.

Rathenau, Walther (1918). *Die neue Wirtschaft*. Berlin: S. Fischer. Reissued in *Gesammelte Schriften*, vol. 5. Berlin: S. Fischer, 1929. Translated into English as *The New Political Economy* in 1918.

Rathenau, Walther (1919). *Autonome Wirtschaft*, Jena: E. Diedrich.

Rathenau, Walther (1929). *Vom Aktienwesen. Eine geschäftliche Betrachtung*, in *Gesammelte Schriften*, vol. 5. Berlin: S. Fischer, 1929.

Reupke, Hans (1930). *Das Wirtschaftssystem des Faschismus*. Berlin: R. Hobbing.

Reupke, Hans (1931). *Der Nationalsozialismus und die Wirtschaft*. Berlin: O. Elsner.

Reuter, Fritz ed. (1930). *Handbuch der Rationalisierung*. Berlin: Spaeth & Linde.

Royama, Masamichi (1937). "Kakushin gikai no tenbo", in *Chuo koron*, the 52th year, February.

Ryū, Shintarō (1939). *Nihon keizai no saihensei* (The Reorganisation of the Japanese Economy). Tokyo: Chūō kōronsha.

Sakisaka Itsurō (1934). *Tōsei keizairon sōkan. Nihon tōsei keizai zenshū*, vol. 10. Tokyo: Kaizōsha.

Sakomizu, Hisatsune (1942). *Kinyū tōseikai no shinro*. Tokyo: Shinkeizaisha.

Sakuta Sōichi (1941). *Keizai no michi*, Tokyo: Kōbundō.

Sangyō gōrika (1930-1936). Vols. 1-20. Tokyo: Nihon shōkō kaigisho. Reprint (1999) eds. Kuroda Kenji and Sasaki Satoshi. Tokyo: Gozando shoten.

Sangyō hōkoku renmei ed. (1940). *Kakkoku no kokumin soshiki to rōdō soshiki*. Unknown: Sangyō hōkoku renmei.

Schlegelberger, Franz, et al eds. (1937). *Aktiengesetz vom 30. Januar 1937. Berlin: Vahlen.*

Schmalenbach, Eugen (1928). "Die Betriebswirtschaftslehre an der Schwelle der neuen Wirtschaftsverfassung". *Zeitschrift für handelswissenschaftliche Forschung*, 22: 241-51. Translated into Japanese by Toki Masazō and Saitō Takao, *Kaisō no jiyū keizai*, Tokyo: Moriyama shoten, 1960.

Schmalenbach, Eugen (1959). *Dynamic Accounting*. Translated by G. W. Murphy and Kenneth S. Most. London: Dee and Company.

Schmoller, Gustav (1920). *Grundriss der allgemeinen Volkswirtschaftslehre*, vol. 2. München/Leipzig.

Schumann, Frederick L. (1935). *Hitler and the Nazi Dictatorship*. London: R. Hale & Company.

Schumpeter, Elizabeth Boody, ed. (1940). *The Industrialization of Japan and Manchukuo 1930-1940. Population, raw materials and industry*. New York: The Macmillan Company.

Seligman. Edwin R. A. ed. (1934). *Encyclopaedia of the Social Sciences*, vol. 14. New York: The Macmillan Company.

Shigen. (1932)(1937). Shigenkyoku ed. 1931-1937.

Shigenkyoku ed. (1930). *Furansu kokka sodoin hoan* (Kenkyu shiryo 2, January 1930).

Shigenkyoku ed. (1933). *Beikoku sōdōin keikaku*. Tokyo: Kurita shoten.

Shigenkyoku ed. (1937). *Furansu kokka sōdōin hōan* (Kenkyu shiryo, 6-2, May 1937).

Shin doitsu kokka taikei (1939-1941).12 vols. Tokyo; Nihon hyōronsha.

Shizuta, Hitoshi (1943). *Karuteru to keizai dantai*. Tokyo: Nihon hyōronsha.

Shoko keizai (February 1938). Zadankai, keizai tōsei chūsū kikan mondai, in Tokyo shōkō kaigisho ed., *Shōko keizai*, vol. 5, no.2.

Shōwa kenkyūkai (1937). *Minkan keizai chūsū kikan shian*. Tokyo: Shōwa kenkyūkai.

Shōwa kenkyūkai (1939). *Burokku keizai ni kansuru kenkyū*. Tokyo: Seikatsusha.

Shōwa shakai keizai shiryō shūsei (1985). vol. 10. "Rikugun Akimaru kikan (sensō keizai kenkyūhan) ni kansuru ken" (June 1940). Tokyo: Daitobunka daigaku toyo kenkyūjo.

Solzbacher, Wilhelm (1933). *Walther Rathenau als Sozialphilosoph. Die Überwindung der Entseelung*. Köln: Reich und Heimat Verlag.

Sombart, Werner (1922). *Luxus und Kapitalismus*. München: Duncker & Humblot. English translation: *Luxury and capitalism*. Ann Arbor: University of Michigan Press, 1967. Japanese translation by Tanaka Kyūichi: *Shashi to shihonshugi*. Tokyo: Jiritsusha, 1925.

Sombart, Werner (1927). *Der moderne Kapitalismus*. Leipzig: Dunker and Humblot. First edition 1902, vol. 1, 3. ed. 1919. 6. ed. 1924, vol. 2, 4. ed. 1921, vol. 3, 1927-28.

Sombart, Werner (1929). *Die drei Nationalökonomien*. München: Duncker & Humblot. Japanese translation by Kojima Shōtarō: *Mittsu no keizaigaku*. Tokyo: Yūfūkan shobō, 1933.

Sombart, Werner (1932). *Die Zukunft des Kapitalismus*, Berlin/Charlottenburg 1932. A Japanese translation by Shinkawa Densuke, in *Nagasaki kōshō kenkyūkan ihō*, vol. 20, nos. 3 and 4. A summarized Japanese translation was made by Suzuki Akira in *Sekai daishisō zenshū*, 86, Tokyo: Shunjūsha, 1933.

Sombart, Werner (1932). *The Future of Capitalism*. Berlin: Buchholz & Weisswange.

Spann, Othmar (1921). *Der wahre Staat. Vorlesungen über Abbruch und Neubau der Gesellschaft*. Leipzig: Quelle & Meyer, 3rd edition 1931. Japanese translation 1934.

Spiegel, Henry William (1940). "Wehrwirtschaft: economics of the military state". *The American Economic Review*, vol. XXX, no. 4, December 1940, pp. 713-723.

Strachey, John (1933). *Menace of Fascism*. London: Victor Gollancz Ltd.

Strasser, Otto (1932). *Aufbau des deutschen Sozialismus*. Leipzig: Wolfgang Richard Lindner Verlag.

Suekawa, Hiroshi, coauthor (1942). *Kokubō keizaihō taisei*. Tokyo: Yūhikaku.

Sugimoto, Eiichi (1943). *Tōsei keizai no genri*. Tokyo: Nihon hyōronsha.

Sugimura Shōzaburō, Wagatsuma Sakae, Kimura Kameji and Gotō Kiyoshi eds. (1934). *Nachisu no hōritsu*. Tokyo: Nihon hyōronsha.

Sugimura, Kōzō (1943), *Eidan keizai no rinri*, Tokyo: Dairi shobō.

Sugiyama Kyōju kanreki shukuga ronbunshū (1942). Tokyo: Iwanami shoten.

Suzuki, Eitarō (1940). *Nihon noson-shakaigaku genri*. Tokyo: Jichōsha. Reprint (1990). Tokyo: Kuresu shuppan.

Syrup, Friedrich (1936). "Arbeitseinsatz und Arbeitsbeschaffung", in H. H. Lammers and H. Pfundtner eds. *Grundlagen, Aufbau und Wirtschaftsordnung des nationalsozialistischen Staates*, vol. 3. Berlin.

Takabatake, Michitoshi (1959-62). "Seisanryoku riron", in *Tenkō no kyōdō kenkyū*, vol. 2, ed. Shisō no kagaku kenkyūkai. Tokyo: Heibonsha.

Takamiya, Susumu (1942). *Kigyō shūchūron*. Tokyo: Yūhikaku.

Takemura, Tadao (1938). *Tōsei keizai to keiki hendō*. Tokyo: Yūhikaku.

Takemura, Tadao (1941). *Keizai shintaisei no hatten hōkō*. Tokyo: Tōkyō ginkō shūkaisho.

Tamaki, Hajime (1938). *Amerika keikaku keizai*. (*Sekai keikaku keizai* 6). Tokyo: Kawade shobō.

Tamarushima, Takeo (1986). *Meijijin no keieigaishi: aru yakuin no bibōroku*. Tokyo: Keisō shobō.

Tanaka, Kōtarō (1934). "Nachisuteki hō rinen no shisōshiteki bunseki oyobi hihan". *Chūō kōron*, the 49th year, May.

Taniguchi, Yoshihiko (1935). *Bōeki tōsei no kenkyū*. Tokyo: Yūhikaku.

Taniguchi, Yoshihiko (1940). *Shintaisei no riron*. Tokyo: Chikura shōbo.

Tawney, R. H. (1921,1922). *The Acquisitive Society*. London: G. Bell and Sons Ltd. A Japanese translation: *Kakutoku Shakai*, translated by Yamashita Shigekazu, in *Sekai Shisō Kyōyō Zenshū*, vol. 17 *Igirisu no Shakaishugi Shisō* (The Collected Works of World Ideas 17: British Socialist Ideas), Tokyo: Kawade shobō shinsha, 1963.

*Tokyo Asahi Shinbun (*1938). July 24. 1938.

Tōsei keizai (September 1940), vol. 1, no. 1, Shin seijitaisei to keizaikai.

Tschierschky, Siegfried (1930). *Kartellpolitik: eine analystische Untersuchung*. Berlin: Carl Heymanns.

Tsumagari, Kuranojō (1942). *Nihon tōsei keizai hō*. Tokyo: Nihon hyōronsha.

Ueda. Tatsunosuke (1941). "Keizai shintaisei no sekaikan". *Tōsei keizai,* vol. 2, no. 4 (April).

Ueda, Tatsunosuke (1942a). *Keizaijin, shokubunjin*. Tokyo: Risōsha.

Ueda, Tatsunosuke (1942b). "Ueda Hakase no kigyōsha shokubun-ron", in *Keiei keizai no shomondai*, ed. Ueda Sadajirō hakase kinen ronbun-shū hensan iinkai. Tokyo: Kagakushugi kōgyōsha.

Ueda, Teijiro (1913). *Kabushiki-gaisha keizairon*. Tokyo: Nihon hyōronsha.

Ueda, Teijirō (1926). "Tōnēshi cho kakutoku no shakai", in Ueda Teijirō, *Shakai kaizō to kigyō*. Tokyo: Dōbunkan.

Ueda, Teijirō (1928). *Kabushiki gaisharon*. Vol. 11 *Shakaigaku sōsho*. Tokyo: Nihon hyōronsha. 6th edition 1937.

Ueda, Teijirō (1944a). *Kabushiki-gaisha keizairon*. In *Ueda Teijirō Zenshū,* vol. 2. Tokyo: Nihon Hyōronsha. First published 1913; revised and enlarged 1921 (6th edition), 1923 (7th edition), 1924 (8th edition). Republished Tokyo: Daisan shuppan, 1975.

Ueda, Teijirō (1926,1944b). *Shakai kaizō to kigyō*. In *Ueda Teijirō Zenshū*, vol. 4. Tokyo: Dōbunkan.

Ueno, Yōichi (1929). *Sangyō nōritsuron*. Tokyo: Chikura shobō.

Uyeda, Teijiro (1938). *The Small Industries of Japan. Their growth and development* (A Report in the International Research Series of the Institute of Pacific Relations). London/ New York: Oxford University Press. (Reissued by New York/ London: Routledge, 2000.).

Veblen, T. (1923) *Absentee Ownership and Business Enterprise in Recent Times: the case of America*. London. New edition: New Brunswick/ London: Transaction Publishers, 1997, with an Introduction by Marion J. Levy, Jr. Translated into Japanese by Hashimoto Katsuhiko as *Amerika shihonshugi hihan* in 1940.

Wagatsuma, Sakae (1934a). "Nachisu minpō riron". *Hōgaku kyōkai zasshi*, vol. 52, nos. 4-5. Included in Wagatsuma et al 1934. Reprinted in Wagatsuma 1966, I.

Wagatsuma, Sakae (1934b). "Nachisu no shihō genri to sono rippō". *Hōritsu jihō*, 6, no. 3.

Wagatsuma, Sakae (1938). "Nachisu no shoyūken riron". In *Makino Sensei kanreki shukuga hōrironshū* (1938). Tokyo: Yūhikaku. Reprinted in Wagatsuma 1966, I.

Wagatsuma, Sakae (1942). "Nachisu no keiyaku riron". In *Sugiyama Kyōju kanreki shukuga ronbunshū* (1942). Tokyo: Iwanami shoten.

Wagatsuma, Sakae (1948). *Keizai saiken to tōsei rippō*. Tokyo: Yūhikaku.

Wagatsuma, Sakae (1966). *Minpō Kenkyū* I, II. Tokyo: Yūhikaku.

Wagatsuma, Sakae ed. (1956). *Sengo ni okeru minpō kaisei no keika*. Tokyo: Nihon hyōronsha.

Wagatsuma Sakae, Sugimura Shōzaburō, Kimura Kameji and Gotō Kiyoshi eds (1934). *Nachisu no hōritsu*. Tokyo: Nihon hyōronsha.

Wagatsuma Sakae Sensei tsuitō: Tokushū, Wagatsuma hōgaku no sokuseki. Special issue of *Jurisuto*, 21 June 1974.

Wakimura, Yoshitarō (1997). "Gakusha to sensō", *Nihon gakushiin kiyō*, vol. 52, no. 3 (March).

Warriner, D. (1931). *Combines and Rationalisation in Germany 1924-1928*. London: P. S. King.

Watanabe, Tetsuzō (1930). *Sangyō gōrika*. Tokyo: Nihon hyōronsha.

Webb, Sidney and Beatrice (1920). *The History of Trade Unionism* [Rev. ed. extended to 1920]. London: Longmans, Green and Co.

Webb, Sidney and Beatrice (1921). *The Consumers' Cooperative Movement*. London: Longmans, Green and Co.

Wernicke, Johannes (1907). *Kapitalismus und Mittelstandspolitik*. Jena: G. Fischer.

Wernicke, Johannes (1925). "Mittelstandbewegung", in *Handwörterbuch der Staatswissenschaften*, ed. Ludwig Elster et al., vol. 4. Jena: G. Fischer.

Wertheimer, Mildred S. (1935). *Germany under Hitler*. New York, Foreign Policy Association; Boston: World Peace Foundation.

Winter, J. M. and D. M. Joslin eds. *R.H. Tawney's Commonplace Book*. Cambridge: Cambridge University Press, 1972. Translated into Japanese by M. Hamabayashi and Y. Morimoto, titled *Aru Rekishika no Jidai Hihan*. Tokyo: Miraisha, 1975.

Withers, Hartley (1920). *The Case for Capitalism*. London: Eveleigh Nash Co. Ltd.

World Social Economic Planning (1932). Material contributed to the World Social Economic Congress, Amsterdam, August 1931. Published by the International Industrial Relations Institute, ed. M.H. Fleddérus.

Yabe, Teiji (1943). Zentai-shugi seiji, in *Nihon kokkakagaku taikei*, vol. 4. Tokyo: Jitsugyo no nihonsha.

Yamada Moritarō (1934). *Nihon shihonshugi bunseki*. Tokyo: Iwanami shoten.

Yamada, Moritarō (1983-1985). *Yamada Moritarō chosakushū*, 6vols., eds. Kobayashi Masanari et al. Tokyo: Iwanami shoten.

Secondary

Abe, Hirozumi (1975). *Nihon fashizumu kenkyū josetsu*, Tokyo: Miraisha. New edition (1995).

Akisada, Yoshikazu (1996). "Shakai kagakusha no senjika no ajia kan". In Furuya Tetsuo ed. *Kindai Nihon no Ajia ninshiki*. Tokyo: Ryokuin shobō.

Aldcroft, Derek H. (1970). *The Inter-War Economy: Britain 1919-1939*. London: Batsford.

Amdam, Rolf Petter ed. (1996). *Management Education and Competitiveness, Europe, Japan and the United States*. London: Routledge.

Andō, Yoshio (1963). *Gendai Nihon keizai-shi nyūmon*. Tokyo: Nihon hyōronsha.

Andō, Yoshio (1987). *Taiheiyō sensō no keizaishiteki kenkyū*. Tokyo: Tokyo daigaku shuppankai.

Appel, Michael (1992). *Werner Sombart: Historiker und Theoretiker des modernen Kapitalismus*. Marburg: Metropolis.

Arima, Manabu (1983). "Senji rōdō seisaku no shisō". *Shien*, 120.

Asai, Yoshio (2001). *Sengo kaikaku to minshushugi – Keizai fukkō kara kōdo seichō e*. Tokyo: Yoshikawa kōbunkan.

Barclay, David E. (1978). "A Prussian socialism? Wichard von Moellendorff and the dilemmas of economic planning in Germany, 1918-19". *Central European History,* vol. 11, no. 1, pp. 50-82.

Barkai, Avraham (1977). *Das Wirtschaftssystem des Nationalsozialismus. Der historische und ideologische Hintergrund 1933-1936.* Köln: Verlag Wissenschaft und Politik. English translation: *Nazi economics: ideology, theory, and policy.* Translated by Ruth Hadass-Vashitz. Oxford: Berg, 1990.

Barshay, Andrew E. (1988). *State and Intellectual in Imperial Japan.* Berkeley: University of California Press.

Barshay, Andrew E. (2004). *The Social Sciences on Modern Japan: the Marxian and Modernist Traditions.* Berkeley: University of California Press.

Beckmann, George M. and Genji Ōkubo (1969). *The Japanese Communist Party, 1922-1945.* Stanford: Stanford University Press.

Berger, Godon (1977). *Parties Out of Power in Japan, 1931-1941.* Princeton, N.J.: Princeton University Press.

Berger, Gordon (1983). "New order movement". *Kōdansha Encyclopedia of Japan,* vol. 5, pp. 365-66. Tokyo: Kōdansha.

Berger, Gordon (1988). "Politics and mobilization in Japan, 1931-1945". In *The Cambridge History of Japan,* vol. 6. Cambridge: Cambridge University Press.

Berghahn, V. R. (1988). "Corporatism in Germany in historical perspective", in Andrew Cox and Noel O'Sullivan eds. *The Corporate State: Corporatism and State Tradition in Western Europe*, Aldershot: Edward Elgar, pp. 104-122.

Bōeichō bōei kenshūjo senshishitsu (1967). *Rikugun gunju dōin* 1(Keikakuhen). Tokyo: Asagumo shinbunsha.

Bowen, R.H. (1971). *German Theories of the Cooperative State*, New York: Russell and Russell. Originally published 1947.

Brandt, Karl (1993). *Geschichte der deutschen Volkswirtschaftslehre*, vol. 2. Vom Historismus bis zur Neoklassik, Freiburg i. Br.: R. Haufe.

Brendon, Piers (2002). *The Dark Valley: A panorama of the 1930s.* Vintage; Reprint edition.

Brown, Roger H. (2009). "Shepherds of the people: Yasuoka Masahiro and the new bureaucrats in early showa Japan". *The Journal of Japanese Studies,* vol. 35, no. 3.

Cairncross, Alec (1978). "Keynes and the planned Economy". In *Keynes and Laissez-Faire*, ed. A. P. Thirlwall, pp. 36-58.

Carpenter, Luther P. (1973). *G. D. H. Cole : an intellectual biography*. Cambridge: Cambridge University Press.

Carroll, Berenice A. (1968). *Design for Total War: arms and economics in the Third Reich*. The Hague; Paris: Mouton.

Challener, Richard D. (1965). *The French Theory of the Nation in Arms, 1866-1939*. New York: Russel & Russell.

Chickering, Roger, Stig Förster, Bernd Greiner eds. (2005). *A World at Total War: global conflict and the politics of destruction, 1937-1945*. Washington, D.C.: German.

Chō, Yukio and Sumiya, Kazuhiko eds. (1971). *Kindai Nihon keizai shisōshi II*. Tokyo: Yūhikaku.

Cohen, Jerome B. (1949). *Japan's Economy in War and Reconstruction*. Minneapolis: University of Minnesota Press. Reprint: *Japanese Economic History 1930-1960*, vol. II, London: Routledge, 2000.

Cook, Simon (2008). "Poetry, faith and chivalry: Alfred Marshall's response to modern socialism." *History of Economics Review* (January).

Cox, Andrew and Noel O'Sullivan eds. (1988). *The Corporate State. Corporatism and the state tradition in western Europe*. Aldershot: Edward Elgar.

Daniels, Gordon and Tsuzuki Chushichi eds. (2002). *The History of Anglo-Japanese Relations 1600-2000*, vol. 5 *Social and cultural perspectives*. London: Palgrave Macmillan.

De Bary, William Theodore et al eds. (2005). *Sources of Japanese Tradition, 1600 to 2000*. New York: Columbia University Press.

De Bary, William Theodore ed. (2008). *Sources of East Asian Tradition: the modern period*. New York: Columbia University Press.

Dennis, Norman and A. H. Halsey eds. (1988). *English Ethical Socialism. Thomas More to R. H. Tawney*. Oxford: Oxford University Press.

Doak, Kevin Michael (1998). "Culture, ethnicity and the state in eary twentieth-century Japan", in Minichiello, Sharon ed. *Japan's Competing Modernities: issues in culture and democracy, 1900-1930*. Honolulu: University of Hawaii Press.

Dower, John W. (1986). *War without Mercy: race and power in the Pacific war*, New York: Pantheon Books.

Duus, Peter and Daniel I. Okamoto (1979). "Fascism and the history of pre-war Japan, The failure of a concept." *The Journal of Asian Studies*, vol. 39, no. 1

(November 1979): 65-76. Reprinted in S.S. Large ed. *Shōwa Japan, Political, Economic and Social History 1926-1989,* vol. 1, pp, 155-168.

Engwall, Lars and Vera Zamangi (1998). *Management Education in Historical Perspective.* Manchester: Manchester University Press.

Farquharson J. E. (1976). *The Plough and the Swastika. The NSDAP and agriculture in Germany 1928-45.* London/Beverly Hills: Sage.

Fitzgibbons, Athol (1988). *Keynes's Vision: A new political economy.* Oxford: Oxford University Press.

Fletcher, Wiliam Miles (1975). "Ideologies of political and economic reform and fascism in prewar Japan: Ryū Shintarō, Rōyama Masamichi, and the Shōwa Research Association". PhD dissertation, Yale University.

Fletcher, William Miles (1979). "Intellectuals and fascism in early Shōwa Japan." *The Journal of Asian Studies* 39: 1, pp. 39-63. Reprinted in S.S. Large ed. 1998.

Fletcher, William Miles (1981). "Nihon fashizumu to chishikijin". In Nihon gendaishi kenkyū ed. *Nihon fashizumu* I. Tokyo: Ōtsuki shoten.

Fletcher, William Miles, III (1982). *The Search for a New Order, Intellectuals and Fascism in Prewar Japan.* Chapel Hill: The University of North Carolina Press.

Forrester, David A. R. (1993). *Eugen Schmalenbach and German Business Economics.* New York and London: Garland Publishing Inc.

Fujimura, Michio (1981). "Kokka sōryokusen taisei to kūdetaa keikaku," in Miwa Kimitada ed. *Saikō, Taiheiyō sensō zenya.* Tokyo: Sōseiki.

Fujita, Shōzō (1966). *Tennosei kokka no shihai-genri.* Tokyo: Miraisha.

Fujita, Shōzō (1997-1998). *Fujita Shōzō chosakushu,* 10 vols. Tokyo: Misuzu shobo.

Furukawa, Takahisa (1992). *Shōwa senchūki no sōgō kokusaku kikan.* Tokyo: Yoshikawa kōbunkan.

Gao, Bai (1994). "Arisawa Hiromi and his theory for a managed economy." *Journal of Japanese Studies,* 20:1, pp. 115-153.

Gao, Bai (1997). *Economic Ideology and Japanese Industrial Policy.* Cambridge: Cambridge University Press.

Garon, Sheldon (1987). *State and Labor in Modern Japan.* Berkeley and Los Angeles: University of California Press.

Gauntlett, John Owen and Hall, Robert King (1949). *Kokutai no hongi:cardinal principles of the national entity of Japan.* Cambridge, MA: Harvard University Press.

Geiger, Rudolf (1959). *Die Entwicklungstendenzen des Kapitalismus bei Keynes, Schumpeter und Burnham*. Zürich: Polygraphischer Verlag.

Gendaishi shiryō 8 (1964). Nitchū sensō. Tokyo: Misuzu shobō, 1964.

Gonjō, Yasuo, Hirota Akira and Ōmori Hiroyoshi eds. (1996). *Nijū seiki shihon-shugi no seisei*. Tokyo: Tōkyō daigaku shuppankai.

Gordon, Andrew (1991). *Labor and Imperial Democracy in Prewar Japan*. Berkeley: University of California Press.

Gow, Ian (2004). *Military Intervention in Pre-war Japanese Politics*. London: Routledge Curzon.

Groenewegen, Peter D. (1998). *Alfred Marshall: Critical Responses*. London: Routledge.

Hadley, Eleanor M. (1989). "The diffusion of Keynesian ideas in Japan". In Peter A. Hall ed. *The Political Power of Economic Ideas: Keynesianism across nations*. Princeton: Princeton University Press.

Hara, Akira (1998). "Grains before rice". In Harrison, Mark ed. *The Economics of World War II*. Cambridge: Cambridge University Press.

Hara, Akira ed. (1995). *Nihon no senji keizai*. Tokyo: Tōkyō daigaku shuppankai.

Hara, Akira (2013). *Nihon senjikeizai kenkyū*. Tokyo: Tokyo daigaku Shuppankai.

Hara, Akira and Nakamura, Takafusa (1973). "Keizai shintaisei" In Nihon seiji gakkai ed. *Konoe shintaisei no kenkyū* [*Nenpō Seijigaku* 1972]. Tokyo: Iwanami Shoten.

Hara, Terushi ed. (1998). *Waseda-ha ekonomisuto retsuden*. Tokyo: Waseda daigaku shuppanbu.

Harootunian, Harry (2000). *Overcome by Modernity. History, culture, and community in interwar Japan*. Princeton, New Jersey: Princeton University Press.

Harrington, Lewis E. (2009). "Miki Kiyoshi and the Shōwa kenkyūkai: The failure of world history". *Positions*, vol.17, no. 1, pp. 43-72.

Harrison, Mark ed. (1998). *The Economics of World War II*. Cambridge: Cambridge University Press.

Haruyama, Hideo (1981-1982). "Wagakuni ni okeru kabushiki gaisha shihai-ron no tenkai", 1-2, *Shōkei Ronshū*, vol. 16, nos. 3-4 (1981), vol. 17, nos. 2-3 (1982).

Hatano, Sumio (1980). "Tōa chitsujo to chiseigaku". In *Nihon no 1930-nendai*, ed. Miwa Kimitada. Tokyo: Sōryūsha.

Havens, Thomas R. H. (1978). Valley of Darkness: the Japanese people and World War Two. New York: Norton.

Hayashi, Kentarō (1971). "Japan and Germany in the interwar period". In Jams William Morley ed. *Dilemmas of Growth in Prewar Japan*. Princeton: Princeton University Press.

Hayashi, Masao and Morimoto, Yoshiteru (1975). *Aru rekishika no jidai hihan*, Tokyo: Miraisha. (A Japanese translation of *R. H. Tawney's Commonplace Book*, ed. and with an introduction by J.M. Winter and D.M. Josline, Cambridge: Cambridge University Press, 1972.

Hein, Laura Elizabeth (2004). *Reasonable Men, Powerful Words: political culture and expertise in twentieth-century Japan*. Berkley: University of California Press.

Henderson, W. O. (1951). "Walther Rathenau, A pioneer of the planned economy." *The Economic History Review, New Series*, 4:1 (1951): 98-108.

Herbst, Ludolf (1982). *Der totale Krieg und die Ordnung der Wirtschaft: die Kriegswirtschaft im Spannungsfeld von Politik, Ideologie und Propaganda 1939-1945*. Stuttgart: Deutsche Verlags-Anstalt.

Hirota, Isao (1994). *Gendai Furansu no shiteki keisei*. Tokyo: Tokyo daigaku shuppankai.

Hirowatari, Seigo (1979). "Daisan teikoku ni okeru burujoa-hō no 'tenkan'". In Tokyo daigaku shakai kagaku kenkyūjo ed. *Fashisumu-ki no kokka to shakai* 5. Tokyo: Tokyo daigaku shuppankai.

Hirschmeier, Johannes and Tsunehiko Yui (1975, 1981). *The Development of Japanese Business 1600-1980*. 2nd edition. London: Allen & Unwin.

Hoepke, Klaus-Peter (1968). *Die deutsche Rechte und der italienische Faschismus*. Düsseldorf: Droste.

Hon'iden zeminaaru no kai (1971). *Daigaku no zeminaaru*. Tokyo: Chūō kōron jigyō shuppan.

Honjō, Shigeru (1982). *Emperor Hirohito and His Chief Aide-de-camp: the Honjō diary, 1933-36*. Translation by Mikiso Hane. Tokyo: University of Tokyo Press.

Honma, Shigeki (1978). "Kokka sōdōin hō to kokka sōdōin taisei." In *Shōwa no hō to hōgaku*. Tokyo: Nihon hyōronsha.

Hoshi, Takeo and Anil Kashyap (2004). *Corporate Financing and Governance in Japan: the road to the future*. Cambridge MA: MIT Press.

Hoston, Germaine A (1983). 'Tenko: Marxism and the national question.' *Polity*, vol. 16, no. 1, pp. 96–118.

Hoston, Germaine A (1984). "Marxism and National Socialism in Taishō Japan: the thought of Takabatake Motoyuki". *Journal of Asian Studies*, vol. 44, no. 1, pp. 43-64.

Hoston, Germaine A. (1986). *Marxism and the Crisis of Development in Prewar Japan*. Princeton: Princeton University Press.

Iida, Yasuzo (2006). *Sengo-seishin no kōbō*. Tokyo: Misuzu shobo.

Ikeda, Hajime (1988). Ken'i-shugi kokka no isō, Tokyo: Ronsosha.

Ikeda, Yukihiro and Mishima, Noriyuki eds. (2001). *Keiō Gijuku no keizaigaku (Fukuzawa Sensei botsugo hyakunen kinen)*. Tokyo: Keiō gijuku toshokan.

Ikeo, Aiko (1997). "Keynes and Keynesian economics in pre-WWII Japan". *Nihon bunka kenkyūjo kiyō*, 80, pp. 271-308.

International Labour Office (2000). *Japanese Economic History 1930-1960*. London: Routledge (reprint).

International Labour Office (2000). *Industrial Labour in Japan*, vol. 5 *Japanese Economic History*. London: Routledge (reprint).

Ishii, Teruhisa (1952). *Shōhō*, Tokyo: Keisō Shobō. Revised and reissued, 1959.

Ishida, Takeshi (1984). *Nihon no shakai kagaku*. Tokyo: Tokyo daigaku shuppankai.

Itō, Nozomi (1998). "Shōwa kenkyūkai ni okeru tōa kyōdōtairon no keisei". In *Kindai Nihon no Ajia-kan*, ed. Okamoto Kōji. Tokyo: Minerva shobō.

Itō, Takashi (1974). "'Kyokoku icchi' naikakuki no seikai saihensei mondai 2", *Shakai kagaku kenkyū*, vol. 25, no. 4.

Itō Takashi (1981). *Shōwa jūnen-dai shi danshō*, Tokyo: Tokyo daigaku shuppankai.

Itō, Takashi (1987). "Mōri Hideoto ron oboegaki", in *Nenpō kindai Nihon kenkyū, 9 Senji keizai*, ed. Kindai Nihon kenkyūkai. Tokyo: Yamakawa shuppansha.

Itō, Takashi (1989). "'Kokuze' to 'kokusaku', 'tōsei', 'keikaku'", in *Nihon keizaishi, 6 Nijū kōzō*, ed. Nakamura Takafusa and Odaka Kōnosuke. Tokyo: Iwanami shoten.

Itoh, Mayumi (2003). *The Hatoyama Dynasty: Japanese political leadership through the generations*. London: Palgrave Macmillan.

Janssen, Hauke (2000). *Nationalökonome und Nationalsozialismus. Die deutsche Volkswirtschaftslehre in den dreissiger Jahren*. Marburg: Metropolis-Verlag (2. überarbeitete Aufl.)

Joerges, Christian and Navraj Singh Ghaleigh eds. (2003). *Darker legacies of law in Europe: the shadow of National Socialism and fascism over Europe and its legal traditions*. Oxford: Hart Publishing.

Johnson, Chalmers A. (1978). *Japan's Public Policy Companies*. Washington D.C.: American Enterprise Institute for Public Policy Research.

Johnson, Chalmers A. (1982). *MITI and the Japanese Miracle. The growth of industrial policy, 1925-1975*. Stanford: Stanford University Press.

Kanda, Fumito (1978). "Shōwa kyōkō-ki no shakai undō", in Tokyo daigaku shakai kagaku kenkyūsho ed., *Fashizumu-ki no kokka to shakai* I. Tokyo: Tokyo daigaku shuppankai.

Kasza, Gregory J. (1993). *The State and the Mass Media in Japan, 1918-1945*. Berkeley: University of California Press.

Katō, Ryū ed. (1979). "Hon'iden Yoshio sensei nenpu", in *Hon'iden Yoshio sensei ikōshū*, Tokyo: Ningen no kagakusha.

Katō, Toshihiko (1977). "Gunbu to tōsei keizai", *Shakai kagaku kenkyū*, vol. 29, no. 1.

Katō, Toshihiko (1979). "Gunbu no keizai tōsei shisō", in Tokyo daigaku shakai kagaku kenkyūjo ed. *Fashizumu-ki no kokka to shakai* 2. Tokyo: Tokyo daigaku shuppankai.

Kawahara, Hiroshi (1978). "Senjika rōdō no shisō to seisaku". In Waseda daigaku shakai kagaku kenkyūjo ed. *Nihon no fashizumu* III. Tokyo: Waseda daigaku shuppanbu.

Kawamura, Tetsuji (1998). *Dainiji taisenki Amerika senji keizai no kenkyū*. Tokyo: Ochanomizu shobō.

Kawase, Yasufumi (1997). "Nachisu no kindaika-ronsō", in *Rikkyō keizaigaku kenkyū*, vol. 50, no.4.

Keiō gijuku daigaku hyakunenshi (1962). Tokyo: Keio gijuku daigaku shuppankai.

Keizai dantai rengokai zenshi (1962). Ed. Keizai dantai rengokai. Tokyo: Keizai dantai rengokai.

Kerde, Ortrud (1999), "The ideological background of the Japanese war economy". In Pauer, Erich ed., *Japan's War Economy*. London: Routledge.

Kindai Nihon kenkyūkai ed. (1987). *Nenpō, kindai Nihon kenkyū 9, senji keizai*. Tokyo: Yamakawa shuppansha.

Kinzley, William Dean (1991). *Industrial Harmony in Modern Japan: the invention of a tradition*. London: Routledge.

Kobayashi, Hideo (1995a). *Chōkanryō*. Tokyo: Tokuma shoten.

Kobayashi, Hideo (1995b). *"Nihon kabushiki gaisha" o tsukutta otoko, Miyazaki Masayoshi no shōgai*. Tokyo: Shōgakukan.

Kobayashi, Hideo, Okazaki Tetsuji, Yonekura Seiichirō and NHK zairyōhan eds. (1995). *"Nihon kabushiki gaisha" no Shōwashi*. Osaka: Sōgensha.

Kocka, Jürgen ed. (1979). *Kapitalismus, Klasssenstruktur und Probleme der Demokratie in Deutschland 1910-1940: ausgewählte Aufsätze von Emil Lederer*, Göttingen: Vandenhoeck und Ruprecht.

Kōketsu, Atsushi (1981). *Sōryokusen taisei kenkyū*. Tokyo: San'ichi shobō.

Kokushi daijiten (1979-1997). Vol. 3, "Kakushinsha" (Takeyama Morio). Tokyo: Yoshikawa kōbunkan.

Koot, G. M. (1987). *English Historical Economics*, 1870-1926. Cambridge: Cambridge University Press.

Krebs, Gerhard (1984). *Japans Deutschlandpolitik 1935-1941: eine Studie zur Vorgeschichte des Pazifischen Krieges*. Hamburg (Gesellschaft für Natur- und Völkerkunde Ostasiens e. V.)

Kruse, Christina (1988). *Die Volkswirtschaftslehre im Nationalsozialismus*. Freiburg i. Breisgau: Rudolf Haufe Verlag.

Kudo, Akira and Tajima Nobuo eds. (2008). *Nichidoku kankeishi, 1890-1945*, 3 vols. Tokyo: Tokyo daigaku shuppankai. Translation (partly)(2009): Kudo, Tajima, Erich Pauer eds. Japan and Germany: two latecomers to the world stage, 3 vols. Folkestone: Global Oriental.

Kurihara, Masaru (1974). "Nachisu tōkōryo no rekishi", parts 1 and 2. *Seiyō shigaku*, vol. 90, nos. 3, 4.

Kurihara, Masaru (1981). *Nachisumu taisei no seiritsu*. Tokyo: Mineruva shobō.

Large, Stephen S. (2010). *Organized Workers and Socialist Politics in Interwar Japan*. Cambridge: Cambridge University Press. First published 1981.

Large, Stephen S. ed. (1998). *Shōwa Japan: political, economic and social history, 1926-1989*, vol. 1 1926-1941. Routledge Library of Modern Japan. London: Routledge.

Larsen, Stein Ugelvik (2001). *Fascism outside Europe: the European impulse against domestic conditions in the diffusion of global fascism*. Social Science Monographs. University of Michigan.

Laux, Frank (1998). *Die Lehre vom Unternehmen an sich. Walther Rathenau und die aktienrechtliche Diskussion in der Weimarer Republik.* (Schriften zur Rechtsgeschichte, 74). Berlin: Duncker & Humblot GmbH.

Lebovics, Herman (1969). *Social Conservatism and the Middle Classes in Germany, 1914–1933.* Princeton: Princeton University Press.

Lebra, Joyce C. ed. (1975). *Japan's Greater East Asia Co-Prosperity Sphere in World War II, Selected Readings and Documents.* Kuala Lumpur: Oxford University Press.

Lehmbruch, Gerhard (2001). "The institutional embedding of market economies: the German 'model' and its impact on Japan", in Wolfgang Streeck and Kozo Yamamura eds. *The Origins of Nonliberal Capitalism. Germany and Japan in comparison*, Ithaca and London: Cornell University Press.

Lenger, Friedrich (1994). *Werner Sombart, 1863-1941. Eine Biographie.* München: Beck.

Linder, Marc (1987). *The Supreme Labor Court in Nazi Germany: a jurisprudential analysis.* Frankfurt a. M.: Klosterman.

Loth, David (1958). *Swope of G. E.: The story of Gerard Swope and General Electric in American business.* New York: Simon and Schuster.

Lüpold, Martin and Gerhard Schnyder (2009). "Horse, cow, sheep, or 'thing-in-itself'? The cognitive origins of corporate governance in Switzerland, Germany and the US, 1910s-1930s". Working Paper 383, Centre for Business Research, University of Cambridge.

Machida, Tatsujirō ed. (1965). *Kyōchōkaishi.* Tokyo: Kyōchōkai kaiwakai.

Mainichi shinbunsha ed. (1972). *Shōwa shisōshi e no shōgen.* Tokyo: Mainichi shinbunsha.

Marshall, Byron K. (1978). "Academic factionalism in Japan. The case of the Tōdai Economics Department, 1919-1939." *Modern Asian Studies,* vol. 12, no. 4, pp. 529-51.

Marshall, Byron K. (1992). *Academic Freedom and the Japanese Imperial University, 1868-1939.* Berkeley: University of California Press.

Maruyama, Masao (1964). *Gendai seiji no shisō to kōdō.* Tokyo: Miraisha.

Maruyama, Masao (1969). *Thought and Behaviour in Modern Japanese Politics.* Edited by Ivan Morris. London and New York: Oxford University Press. Expanded edition.

Maruyama, Masao (1995). *Maruyama Masao shū*, vol. 3. Tokyo: Iwanami shoten.

Masai, Akira (1996). "Nachisu shōhongaku no Nihon e no eikyō", in *Shōwa shōhōgakushi*, eds. Kurasawa Yasuichirō and Okushima Takayasu. Tokyo: Nihon hyōronsha.

Mason, Timonthy W. (1966). "Labour in the Third Reich, 1933-1939". *Past and Present,* 33.

Mason, Timonthy W. (1968). "The primacy of politics – politics and economics in National Socialist Germany". In S. J. Woolf ed. *The Nature of Fascism*. London: Wiedenfeld and Nicolson.

Mason, Timonthy W. (1974). "Zur Entstehung des Gesetzes zur Ordnung der nationalen Arbeit, vom 20. Januar 1934". In H. Mommsen, D. Petzina and B. Weisbrod eds. *Industrielles System und politische Entwicklung in der Weimarer Republik*. Düsseldorf: Droste Verlag.

Mason, Timonthy W. (1993). *Social Policy in the Third Reich. The working class and the "National Community"*. Translated by John Broadwin. Ed. Jane Caplan. Providence, RI: Berg. Translation of *Sozialpolitik im Dritten Reich: Arbeiterklasse und Volksgemeinschaft*. Opladen: Westdeutscher Verlag, 1977.

Mason, Timonthy W. and Jane Caplan eds. (1995). *Nazism, Fascism and the Working Class*. Cambridge: Cambridge University Press.

Masui, Ken'ichi (1998). "Shōwa 12-15 nen no mita keizai gakubu no senseitachi". *Kindai nihon kenkyū* 15.

Matsuo, Takayoshi (1995) ed. and comment. *Miura Tetsutarō ronsetsushū: Dainihonshugi ka shōnihonshugi ka*. Tokyo: Tōyōkeizai shinpōsha.

Matsushima, Harumi (1978). "Keizai 'kokusaku' no kōsō to sono tenkai katei". In Sakasai Takahito et al eds. *Nihon shihonshugi – tenkai to ronri*. Tokyo: Tokyo daigaku shuppankai.

Matsuura, Masataka (1995). *Nitchū sensōki ni okeru keizai to seiji*. Tokyo: Tokyo daigaku shuppankai.

Matsuura, Masataka (2002). *Zaikai no seiji keizai shi*. Tokyo: Tokyo daigaku shuppankai.

McQuaid, Kim (1977). "Competition, cartellization and the corporate ethic. General Electric's leadership during the New Deal era, 1933-1940". *American Journal of Economics and Sociology,* vol. 36, no.4 (September 1977), pp. 417-428.

Michaelides, Panayotis G. and John G. Milios (2009). "Joseph Schumpeter and the German Historical School." *Cambridge Journal of Economics,* 33, pp. 495–516.

Michalka, Wolfgang (2010). “From war economy to new economy: World War I and the conservative debate about the ‘other’ modernity in Germany”. In Bernd- Rüdiger Hüppauff ed. *War, Violence and the Modern Condition*. Berlin: de Gruyter. Reprint. pp. 77-98.

Mikuriya, Takashi (1996). *Seisaku no sōgō to kenryoku*. Tokyo: Tōkyō daigaku shuppankai.

Mimura, Janis (1998). “Technocratic visions of empire: technology bureaucrats and the ‘New Order’ for science-technology”, in Harald Fuess ed. *The Japanese Empire in East Asia and its Postwar Legacy*. München: Indicium: pp. 97–118.

Mimura, Janis (2011). *Planning for Empire: Reform bureaucrats and the Japanese wartime state*. Studies of the Weatherhead East Asian Institute, Columbia University. Ithaca, NY: Cornell University Press.

Mitani, Taichirō (1997). *Kindai nihon no sensō to seiji*, Tokyo: Iwanami shoten.

Mitchell, Richard H. (1976). *Thought Control in Preward Japan*. Ithaca, N.Y.: Cornell University Press.

Miwa, Yasushi (1988). *Nihon fashizumu to rōdō undō*. Tokyo: Azekura shobō.

Miyajima, Hideaki (1984). “Sangyō gōrika to jūyō sangyō tōseihō”, in *Nenpō kindai Nihon kenkyū 6, Seitō naikaku no seiritsu to hōkai*, ed. Kindai Nihon Kenkyūkai. Tokyo: Yamakawa shuppansha.

Miyajima, Hideaki (1988). “1930 nendai Nihon ni okeru dokusen seisaku shisō”, in *Nihon kindaika no shisō to tenkai*, ed. Sakasai Takahito kyōju kanreku kinenkai. Tokyo: Bunken shuppan.

Miyajima, Hideaki (1993). “Senji keizaika no jiyūshugi keizairon to tōsei keizairon”. *Shiriizu Niho kingendaishi 3, Gendai shakai e no tenkei*. Tokyo: Iwanami shoten.

Miyajima, Hideaki (2004). *Sangyō seisaku to kigyō tōsei no keizaishi*. Tokyo: Yūhikaku.

Miyake, Masaki (1975), *Nichidokui sangoku dōmei no kenkyū*. Tokyo: Nansōsha.

Miyake, Masaki (1996). *Nichidoku seiji gaikōshi kenkyū*. Tokyo: Kawade shobō shinsha.

Miyake, Masaki ed. (1999). *Berlin, Wien, Tokyo*. Tokyo: Ronsōsha.

Miyata, Mitsuo (1991). *Nachi doitsu no seishin-kozō*. Tokyo: Iwanami shoten.

Mizuno, Hiromi (2008). *Science for the Empire: scientific nationalism in modern Japan*. Stanford: Stanford University Press.

Moriya, Fumio (1982). *Nihon shihon shugi bunseki no kyoshōtachi*. Tokyo: Shiraishi shoten.

Morris-Suzuki, Tessa (1989). *A History of Japanese Economic Thought*. London: Routledge.

Mühlberger, Detlef (2003). *The Social Bases of Nazism, 1919-1933*. Cambridge: Cambridge University Press.

Nagao, Ryūichi (1982). "Teikoku kenpō to kokka sōdōin hō". In *Nenpō kindai Nihon kenkyū 4. Taiheiyō sensō*. Tokyo: Yamakawa shuppansha.

Nagashima, Osamu (1986). *Nihon senji tekkō tōsei seiritsushi*. Kyoto: Hōritsu bunkasha.

Nakamura, Mikio (1990). *Nachi-tō no shisō to undō*. Nagoya: Nagoya daigaku shuppankai.

Nakamura, Takafusa (1971). *Economic Growth in Prewar Japan*. Translated by Robert A. Feldman. New Haven and London: Yale University Press.

Nakamura, Takafusa (1974). "Ryu Shintaro to tosei keizai", *Rekishi to jinbutsu* (April 1974): 66-74.

Nakamura Takafusa (1987). "'Junsenji' kara 'senji' keizai taisei e no ikō", in *Nenpō kindai Nihon kenkyū* 9. Tokyo: Yamakawa shuppansha.

Nakamura, Takafusa (1988). "Depression, recovery, and war, 1920-1945." In *The Cambridge History of Japan*, vol. 6. Cambridge: Cambridge University Press. Reprinted in *Shōwa Japan. Political, economic and social history, 1926-1989*, vol. 1, ed. Stephen S. Large.

Nakamura, Takafusa (1989). "Gaisetsu 1937-54nen", in *Nihon keizaishi 7, "Keikakuka" to "minshuka"*, ed. Nakamura Takafusa. Tokyo: Iwanami shoten.

Nakamura, Takafusa (1994). *Lectures on Modern Japanese Economic History, 1926-1994*. Tokyo: LTCB International Library Foundation.

Nakamura, Takafusa (1998). *A History of Shōwa Japan*. Translated by Edwin Whenmouth. Tokyo: University of Tokyo Press.

Nakamura, Takafusa and Hara, Akira (1970). Kaidai. *Nichiman zaisei keizai kenkyukaishiryō*.

Nakamura, Takafusa and Hara, Akira (1973). "Keizai shintaisei", in *Konoe shintaisei no kenkyū* (*Nenpō seijigaku* 1972), ed. Nihon seiji gakkai. Tokyo: Iwanami shoten.

Nakamura, Tadafusa and Kōnosuke Odaka (2003). *Economic History of Japan, 1914-1955: A dual structure*. Oxford: Oxford University Press.

Nakanishi Yō (1979). *Nihon ni okeru "shakai seisaku", "rōdō mondai" kenkyū*, Tokyo: Tokyo daigaku shuppankai.

Newman, Philip C. (1948). "Key German cartels under the Nazi regime". *The quarterly Journal of Economics*, vol. 62, no. 4 (Aug., 1948), pp. 576-595.

Nishinarita, Yutaka (1988). *Kindai Nihon rōshi kankeishi no kenkyū*. Tokyo: Tokyo daigaku shuppankai.

Nishioka, Yukiyasu (1976). Kaidai. *Hattori Eitarō chosakushū*, Hokan. Tokyo: Miraisha.

Nishizawa, Tamotsu (1995). "Ueda Teijirō no keizai shisō", in Sugihara Shirō ed. *Kindai Nihon to Igirisu shisō*. Tokyo: Nihon keizai hyōronsha.

Nishizawa, Tamotsu (1996). "Business studies and management education in Japan's economic development – An institutional perspective". In Amdam, Rolv Petter ed. *Management Education and Competitiveness, Europe, Japan and the United States*. London: Routledge, pp. 96-110.

Nishizawa, Tamotsu (2001). "Brentano, Marshall, and Tokuzo Fukuda: The reception and transformation of the German Historical School in Japan". In Shionoya, Y. ed. *The German Historical School: the historical and ethical approach to economics*. London: Routledge, 2001, pp. 155-172.

Nishizawa, Tamotsu (2002). "New liberalism and welfare economics: British influences and Japanese intellectuals between the wars – Fukuda Tokuzo and Ueda Teijiro". In Gordon Daniels and Chushichi Tsuzuki eds. *The History of Anglo-Japanese Relations, 1600-2000,* vol. 5, *Social and cultural perspectives*. London: Palgrave Macmillan, pp. 209-219.

Noakes, Jeremy (1980). *Government, Party, and People in Nazi Germany*. Exeter: University of Exeter Press.

Nofuji Tadashi (1973). "Erunsuto Appe no keiei seisaku to Varutā Rātenau no keiei seisaku", *Shōgaku ronshū,* vol. 20, no. 2.

Nolte, Ernst (1967). "Vierzig Jahre Theorien über den Faschismus", in *Theorien über den Faschismus*. Köln/ Berlin: Kiepenheuer & Witsch.

Notar, E. J. (1985). "Japan's wartime labor policy: a search for method". *Journal of Asian Studies,* vol. 44, no. 2, pp. 311-328.

Ōbayashi, Shinji (1971). "Keizai-tetsugaku·hohoron", in Chō and Sumiya eds. 1971.

Okada Tomoyoshi (1987). "Jiyū hōnin shugi to kabushiki gaisha", in *Keizaiteki jiyūshugi*. Tokyo: Tokyo daigaku shuppankai.

Okazaki, Tetsuji (1987). "Senji keikakukeizai to kakaku tōsei", *Nenpō kindai Nihon kenkyū*, vol. 9 *Senji keizai*. Tokyo: Yamakawa shuppansha.

Okazaki, Tetsuji (1991). "Senji keikaku keizai to kigyō", in *Gendai Nihon shakai 4, rekishiteki zentei*, ed. Tōkyō daigaku shakai kagaku kenkyūjo, Tokyo: Tokyo daigaku shuppankai.

Okazaki, Tetsuji (1997). "The wartime institutional reforms and transformation of the economic system". In Junji Banno ed. *The Political Economy of Japanese Society*, vol. 1: *The state or the market?* Oxford & New York: Oxford University Press.

Okazaki Tetsuji and Okuno Masahiro eds. (1993). *Gendai Nihon keizai shisutemu no genryū*. Tokyo: Nihon keizai shinbunsha.

Okazaki, Tetsuji, Masahiro Okuno-Fujiwara eds. (1999). *The Japanese Economic System and its Historical Origins*. Translated by Susan Herbert. Oxford: Oxford University Press.

Okazaki Tetsuji, Sugayama Shinji, Nishizawa Tamotsu and Yonekura Seiichiro eds. (1996). *Sengo Nihon keizai to keizai dōyūkai*. Tokyo: Iwanami shoten.

Okushima, Takayasu (1996). "Shōwa 13nen shōhō kaisei", in *Shōwa Shōhōgakushi*, eds. Kurasawa Yasuichirō and Okushima Takayasu. Tokyo: Nihon hyōronsha.

Ono, Harumi (1996), *Tekunokurāto no sekai to nachizumu*. Kyoto: Minerva shobō.

Onoda, Yoshio (1971). "Marsharu no kishidō ni tsuite". *Bunka kiyō*, 5.

Pauer, Erich ed.(1999). *Japan's War Economy*. London: Routledge.

Peattie, Mark R. (1975). *Ishiwara Kanji and Japan's Confrontation with the West*. Princeton, N. J.: Princeton University Press.

Petzina, Dieter (1968). *Autarkiepolitik im Dritten Reich: der nationalsozialistische Vierjahresplan*. Stuttgart: Deutsche Verlagsanstalt.

Pogge von Strandmann, Hartmut ed. (1985). *Walter Rathenau, Industrialist, Banker, Intellectual and Politician. Notes and diaries 1907-1922*. Oxford: Clarendon Press.

Prinz, Michael and Rainer Zitelmann eds. (1991). *Nationalsozialismus und Modernisierung*. Darmstadt: Wissenschaftliche Buchgesellschaft.

Prinz, Michael, Yasushi Yamanouchi, J. Victor Koschmann and Narita Ryūichi eds. (1995). *Sōryokusen to gendaika*. Tokyo: Kashiwa shobō.

Reich, Simon (1990). *The Fruits of Fascism: postwar prosperity in historical perspective*. Ithaca, N.Y.: Cornell University Press.

Rice, Richard (1979). "Economic mobilization in wartime Japan: business, bureaucracy, and military in conflict", *Journal of Asian Studies*, vol.38, no.4 (August 1979: 689-706.

Rimlinger, G. V. (1989). "Labour and the state on the continent, 1800-1939." In *The Cambridge Economic History of Europe VIII. The industrial economies: The development of economic and social policies*. Cambridge: Cambridge University Press.

Saguchi, Kazurō (1991). *Nihon ni okeru sangyō minshushugi no zentei: rōshi kondan seido kara sangyō hōkokukai e*. Tokyo: Tokyo daigaku shuppankai.

Saitō, Ken (1987). *Shinkō konzerun riken no kenkyū*, Tokyo: Jichōsha.

Sakai, Saburō (1979). *Shōwa kenkyūkai*. Tokyo: TBS Buritanika.

Sakai, Saburō (1992). *Shōwa kenkyūkai*. Tokyo: Chūō kōronsha.

Sasaki, Satoshi (1998). *Kagakuteki kanrihō no nihonteki tenkai*. Tokyo: Yūhikaku.

Sawamura, Hiroshi (1988). *A History of the National Recreation Association of Japan: 1938-1952*. Ann Arbor, Mich.: UMI.

Schweitzer, Arthur (1964). *Big Business in the Third Reich*. Bloomington: Indiana University Press.

Shibagaki, Kazuo (1979). "Keizai shintaisei to tōseikai", in Tokyo daigaku shakai kagaku kenkyūjo ed. *Fashizūmu ki no kokka to shakai*, vol. 2, *Senji nihon keizai*. Tokyo: Tōkyō daigaku shuppankai.

Shibata, Yoshio (1992). "Senji gaisha keiri tōsei taisei no tenkai", *Shakai keizaishi gaku*, vol. 58, no. 3.

Shillony, Ben-Ami (1973). *Revolt in Japan: the young officers and the February 26, 1936 incident*. Princeton, N.J: Princeton UP.

Shionoya, Yuichi ed. (2001). *The German Historical School. The historical and ethical approach to economics*. London and New York: Routledge.

Shirakizawa, Asahiko (1999). *Daikyōkōki no Nihon no tsūshō mondai*. Tokyo: Ochanomizu shobō.

Shiryō Nihon-gendaishi (1980-). Tokyo: Ōtsuki shoten.

Shisō (1997). Special issue, *1930 nendai no Nihon shisō*, no. 882.

Shisō no kagaku kenkyūkai ed. (1959-62). *Kyōdō kenkyū, tenkō*, 3vols. Tokyo: Heibonsha.

Shokoseisakushi (1964). Vol. 11, ed. Tsūshō sangyō shō.

Shōwa dōjinkai ed. (1968). *Shōwa kenkyūkai*, Tokyo: Keizai ōraisha.

Sims, Richard (2001). *Japanese Political History since the Meiji Renovation*. London: C. Hurst and Co.

Smith, R. Elberton, ed. (1959). *The Army and Economic Mobilization. The United States army in World War II, the War Department*. Washington, D.C.: Office of the Chief of Military History, Department of the Army.

Sohn, Yul (2005). *Japanese Industrial Governance: protectionism and the licensing state*. London: Routledge.

Sommer, Theo (1962). *Deutschland und Japan zwischen den Mächten 1935-1940*. Tübingen: Mohr. Translated into Japanese as *Nachisu Doitsu to gunkoku Nihon* by Kanemori Shigenari. Tokyo: Jiji tsūshinsha, 1964.

Spang, Christian W. and Wippich, Rolf-Harald eds. (2006). *Japanese-German Relations, 1895-1945: war, diplomacy and public opinion*. London: Routledge.

Steeck, Wolfgang and Kozo Yamamura eds. (2005). *The Origins of Nonliberal Capitalism: Germany and Japan in comparison*. Ithaca, N.Y.: Cornell University Press.

Stegewerns, Dick (2003). *Nationalism and Internationalism in Imperial Japan: autonomy, Asian brotherhood, or world citizenship?* London: Routledge.

Sugayama, Shinji, Okazaki Tetsuji, Nishizawa Tamotsu and Yonekura Seiichi eds. (1996). *Sengo Nihon keizai to keizai dōyūkai*. Tokyo: Iwanami shoten.

Sugihara, Shirō (1992). *Nihon no keizaigakushi*. Suita: Kansei daigaku shuppanbu.

Sugihara, Shirō and Toshihiro Tanaka eds. (1998). *Economic Thought and Modernization in Japan*. Cheltenham, UK: Edward Elgar.

Sugiyama, Mitsunobu (2001). *Sengo Nihon no 'shimin shakai'*. Tokyo: Misuzu shobō.

Sunaga, Noritake (2004). "Shōkō kaigisho no kikō kaikaku to shōkō keizai kai no katsudō", in Yanagisawa Asobu and Kimura Kenji eds, *Senjika ajia no Nihon keizai dantai*. Tokyo: Nihon keizai hyōronsha.

Sutton, Antony C. (1975). *Wall Street and FDR*. New York: Arlington House Publishers.

Suzaki, Shin'ichi (1997). "Sōryokusen rikai o megutte". *Nenpō, Nihon gendaishi* 3 (Sōryokusen, fashizumu to gendaishi). Tokyo; Gendai shiryō shuppan.

Suzuki, Asao (1998). "Daitōa kyōeiken no shisō". In Okamoto Kōji ed. *Kindai Nihon no Ajia kan*. Kyoto: Mineruva shobō.

Suzuki, Yoshinori (1983). *Kabushiki gaisha no keizai gakusetsu*, Tokyo: Shinhyōron.

Suzuki Yuzuru (2005). "The adaptation of western management ideologies: the revised capitalism of Keizai Doyukai in postwar Japan." *International Journal of Japanese Sociology*, vol. 14, no. 1 (November 2005): 70-83.

Swope, Gerald (1931). *The Swope Plan: details, criticisms, analysis*. New York: The Business Bourse.

Tajima, Nobuo (1992). *Nachizumu gaikō to "Manshūkoku"*. Tokyo: Chikura shobō.

Takabatake, Michitoshi (1960). Seisanryoku riron – Ōkochi Kazuo · Kazahaya Yasoji, in Shiso no kagaku kenyūkai ed. *Kyōdō kenkyū, tenkō*, vol. 2. Tokyo: Heibon-sha.

Takahashi, Hikohiro (2001). *Senkanki nihon no shakai kenkyū sentā*. Tokyo: Kashiwa shobō.

Takahashi, Hisashi (1980). "Tōa kyōdōtai ron – Rōyama Masamichi, Ozaki Hotsumi, Kada Tetsuji no baai". In *Nihon no 1930-nendai*. ed. Miwa Kimitada. Tokyo: Sōryūsha.

Takeda, Haruhito (1993). "Jūkagakukōgyōka to keizai seisaku", in *Shiriizu Nihon kingendaishi 3, Gendai shakai e no tenkei*. Tokyo: Iwanami shoten.

Takeda, Haruhito (1999). *Nihonjin no keizai kannen*. Tokyo: Iwanami shoten.

Takeyama, Morio (1982). "Nihon fashizumu no bunkashiteki haikei", in Asanuma Kazunori et al eds. *Hikaku fashizumu no kenkyū*. Tokyo: Seibundō.

Tansman, Alan ed. (2009). *The Culture of Japanese Fascism*. Durham, NC: Duke University Press.

Taylor, James and Warren Shaw eds. (1997). *The Penguin Dictionary of the Third Reich*. London: Penguin Books.

Teranishi, Jūrō (1994). *Emergence of Loan Syndication in Wartime Japan: an investigation into the historical origin of the main bank system*. Economic Development Institute of the World Bank.

Teranishi, Jūrō (2005). *Evolution of the Economic System in Japan*. Cheltenham UK: Edward Elgar Publishing.

Terrill, Ross (1973). *R. H. Tawney and His Times. Socialism as fellowship*. Cambridge, Mass.: Harvard University Press.

Thirlwall, A. P. ed. (1978). *Keynes and Laissez-faire: The third Keynes seminar held at the University of Kent at Canterbury, 1976*. London: Macmillan.

Tipton, Elise K. (1997). *Society and the State in Interwar Japan*. London: Routledge.

Totsuka, Hideo (1971). "Shakai seisaku-ron no hensen", in Chō Yukio and Sumiya Kazuhiko eds. 1971.

Townsend, Susan C. (2009). *Miki Kiyoshi 1897-1945, Japan's itinerant philosopher*. Leiden: Brill.

Tsūshō sangyōshō ed. (1961-1985). *Shōkō seisakushi*. Tokyo: Shōkō Seisakushi Kankōkai.

Tsutsui, William M. (1998). *Manufacturing Ideology: scientific management in twentieth-century Japan*. Princeton: Princeton University Press.

Tsuzuki, Chūshichi (2000). *The Pursuit of Power in Modern Japan, 1825-1995*. Oxford: Oxford University Press.

Turner, Henry Ashby, Jr. (1985). *German Big Business and the Rise of Hitler*. New York/ Oxford: Oxford University Press.

Ujihara, Shōjirō (1966). Kaidai. *Hattori Eitarō chosakushū*, vol. 5. Tokyo: Miraisha.

Umeda, Toshihide, Takahashi Hikohiro and Yokozeki Itaru (2004). *Kyōchōkai no kenkyū*. Tokyo: Kashiwa shobō.

Vagts, Detlev F. (1966). "Reforming the 'modern' corporation: perspectives from the German". *Harvard Law Review*, 80. pp. 23-89.

Verdinger, Hans and Kawamoto Ichirō (1969). *Doitsu to Nihon no kaisha-hō*. Tokyo: Shōji hōmu kenkyūkai.

Vieler, Eric H. (1999). *The Ideological Roots of German National Socialism*. New York, etc.: Peter Lang.

Vincent, C. Paul ed. (1997). *A Historical Dictionary of Germany's Weimar Republic, 1918-1933*. Westport, Conn.: Greenwood Press.

Von Münch, Ingo and Uwe Broderson (1982). *Gesetze des NS-Staates: Dokumente eines Unrechtssystems*. Paderborn: Ferdinand Schöningh.

Wagner, Peter (1991). *Social Sciences and Mdern States: national experiences and theoretical crossroads*. Cambridge: Cambridge University Press.

Wakimura (1997). "Gakusha to sensō". *Nihon gakushiin kiyō*, vol. 52, no. 3.

Walters, William and Haahr, Jens Henrik (2005). *Governing Europe: discourse, governmentality and European integration*. London: Routledge.

Weiss, Hermann (1993). "Ideologie der Freizeit im Dritten Reich. Die NS-Gemeinschaft 'Kraft durch Freude'. *Archiv für Sozialgeschichte*, 33.

Woll, Helmut (1988). *Die Wirtschaftslehre des deutschen Faschismus*. München: R. Oldenbourg Verlag.

Yagi, K. (1997). "Economic reform plans in the Japanese wartime economy. The case of Shintaro Ryu and Kei Shibata". In Aiko Ikeo ed. *Economic Development in Twentieth Century East Asia: the international context*. London: Routledge, 1997.

Yagi Kiichirō (1999). *Kindai Nihon no shakai keizaigaku*. Tokyo: Chikuma shobō.

Yamaguchi, Toshiaki (1979). "Kokka sōdōin kenkyū josetsu – daiichiji sekai taisen kara shigenkyoku no seiritsu made". *Kokka gakkai zasshi*, vol. 92, nos. 3-4.

Yamaguchi, Yasushi (1976). *Gendai Fashizumu no shochōryū*, Tokyo: Yūhikaku.

Yamanouchi, Yasushi (1993)." Senjiki no isan to sono ryōgisei", in *Shakai kagaku no hōhō III. Nihon shakai kagaku no shisō*. Tokyo: Iwanami shoten.

Yamanouchi, Yasushi (1996). *Sisutemu shakai no gendaiteki isō*. Tokyo: Iwanami shoten.

Yamanouchi, Yasushi (1999). *Nihon no shakai kagaku to Veebaa taiken*. Tokyo: Chikuma shobō.

Yamanouchi, Yasushi, J. Victor Koschmann, Narita Ryūichi eds (1995). *Sōryokusen to gendaika*. Tokyo: Kashiwa shobō.

Yamanouchi, Yasushi, J. Victor Koschmann and Narita Ryūichi eds (1998). *Total War and Modernization*. Ithaca, N.Y.: Cornell University Press.

Yamazaki, Bunji (1970). "Fisshā no pātnāshafutoron". In Kaidō Susumu and Yoshida Kazuo eds. *Doitsu keiei gakusetsu shi*. Kyoto: Mineruva shobō.

Yamazaki, Shirō (1987). "Seisanryoku kakujū keikaku no tenkai katei", in *Nenpō kindai Nihon kenkyū 9, Senji keizai*, ed. Kindai Nihon kenkyūkai. Tokyo: Yamakawa shuppansha.

Yamazaki, Shirō (2002). "Seisanryoku kakujū keikaku shiryō", in Hara Akira and Yamazaki Shirō, *Senji keizai sōdōin kankei shiryōshū*. Tokyo: Gendai shiryō shuppan.

Yamazaki, Shiro (2011), *Senjikeizai sōdointaisei no kenkyū*. Tokyo: Nihonkeizai hyoron-sha.

Yanagisawa, Osamu (2001). "The impact of German economic thought on Japanese economists before World War II". In Shionoya, ed. *The German*

Historical School. The historical and ethical approach to economics. London and New York: Routledge.

Yanagisawa, Osamu (2002). "'Gemeinnutz geht vor Eigennutz' im Streit um die Neue Wirtschaftsordnung in Japan in der kritischen Zeit". In Rainer Gömmel and Markus A. Denzel eds. *Weltwirtschaft und Wirtschaftsordnung (Festschrift für Jürgen Schneider zum 65. Geburtstag)*. Stuttgart: Steiner.

Yanagisawa, Osamu (2008a). "Nachisu seisaku shisō to keizai shintaisei - nihon keizaikai no juyō", in Kudō Akira and Tajima Nobuo eds. *Nichidoku kankeishi 1890-1945*, vol. 3. Tokyo: Tokyo daigaku shuppan kai.

Yanagisawa, Osamu (2008b). *Senzen senji nihon no keizai shisō to nachizumu*. Tokyo: Iwanami shoten.

Yanagisawa, Osamu (2012a). "Der Einfluss der deutschen nationalsozialistischen Wirtschaftsideen auf die neue ökonomische Ordnung Japans vor dem Zweiten Wektkrieg", in Heinz D. Kurz ed., *Studien zur Entwicklung der ökonomischen Theorie XXVII. (Schriften des Vereins für Socialpolitik)*, vol. 115/XXVII. Berlin: Duncker & Humblot.

Yanagisawa, Osamu (2012b). "Die nationalsozialistische Wirtschaftsorganisation als Modell für die japanische Neue Wirtschaftsordnung für den totalen Krieg", in Karl Hardach ed. *Internationale Studien zur Geschichte von Wirtschaft und Gesellschaft*. Frankfurt a. M. et al: Peter Lang.

Yanagisawa, Osamu (2013). *Nachisu-doitsu to shihonshugi: Nihon no moderue*. Tokyo: Nihonkeizai hyōronsha.

Yasuda, Hiroshi (1991). "Kanryō to rōdōsha mondai - Sangyō hōkokukai taiseiron". In Tokyo daigaku shakai kagaku kenkyūjo ed. *Gendai Nihon shakai* 4, *Rekishiteki zentei*. Tokyo: Tokyo daigaku shuppankai.

Yonetani, Masafumi (1997). "Senjiki Nihon no shakai shisō". *Shisō*, no. 882.

Yoshida, Kazuo (1976). *Doitsu gōrikaundōron*. Kyoto: Minerva shobō.

Yoshii, Hiroshi (1987). *Nichidokui sangoku dōmei to nichibei kankei*. Tokyo: Nansōsha.

Yoshimi, Yoshiaki (1977). "Senzen ni okeru 'nihon fashizumu' kan no hensen - 1931 - 1937", in *Rekishigaku kenkyū*, 451.

Young, Louise (1998). *Japan's Total Empire. Manchuria and the culture of wartime imperialism*. Berkeley/Los Angeles/London: University of California Press.

Young, Robert J. (1978). *In Command of France: French foreign policy and military planning, 1933-1940*. Cambridge: Havard University Press.

Yui, Masaomi (1978). "Gunbu to kokumin tōgō", in Tokyo daigaku shakai kagaku kenkyūjo ed., *Fashizumu-ki no kokka to shakai* I. Tokyo: Tokyo daigaku shuppankai.

Yusa, Michiko (1998). "Philosophy and inflation. Miki Kiyoshi in Weimar Germany, 1922-1924". *Monumenta Nipponica,* vol. 53, no. 1, pp. 45-71

Index of Names

Z